Praise for *A Liberation Theology of the Brain*

A Liberation Theology of the Brain offers no less than a new worldview, based on science, history, and theology. Yet, lofty as that sounds, Dr. Santos-Rolón presents it with a down-to-earth, conversational tone that is a delight to read and makes it easy to see the relevance to our everyday lives.

—Martha J. Farah, director, Center for Neuroscience & Society, University of Pennsylvania

This rare book comes from my dear colleague, friend, and companion, with whom I had the privilege of serving in our first-call congregation. A gifted theologian, brilliant neuroscientist, dedicated pastor, and compassionate advocate, he embodies a truly unique combination of talents. With remarkable depth and clarity, he articulates how God's power not only confronts systems of injustice in the world but also dismantles the oppressive structures within us, liberating both our minds and our hearts. Bold and prophetic, this book is essential reading for anyone interested in the intersection of faith, science, and liberation. It offers a compelling invitation to engage with the future God is shaping both within us and in the world around us.

—Amsalu T. Geleta, lead pastor, Christ Lutheran Church, Baltimore

This book is a pioneering work that brings together neuroscience and theology with a decolonial perspective. Its relevance transcends all contexts, making it undeniably significant. The author offers systematic, intellectually sound, embodied, and scientifically anchored wisdom—a rare combination that few thinkers can achieve.

—Antje Jackelén, archbishop emerita, Church of Sweden

For those of us who work in academia and other areas of life with issues of science, theology, and decoloniality, this book is a map to guide us on the incessant journey for integral spirituality. It opens paths to that search and meaningful relationship with the Mystery we are passionate about and that liberates us.

—Agustina Luvis-Nuñez, academic and student affairs dean, Seminario Evangélico de Puerto Rico

A new advance on the frontier of postcolonial liberation theology! Taking direction from discoveries in brain science, Carmelo Santos-Rolón walks us step-by-step through religious experience toward other-centering, reintegrating the self, and authentic transformation. A great stride forward!

—Ted Peters, coeditor of *Theology and Science*

In this dynamic read, Santos-Rolon invites us to hold in curiosity and tension the paradox that can exist at the intersection of science and religion. He invites us to listen carefully to the rich lessons this paradox can yield toward greater self-literacy, the gift of true liberation, and the healing it informs. It is a must read if one is interested in excellence and a commitment to deeper understanding of the body-mind-brain connection!

—Bridget Pigue, ThD, Emery University Hospital Midtown Director of Operations, Emory Spiritual Health

Thinking beyond the presumed dichotomy between science and religion, *A Liberation Theology of the Brain* is an invitation to dialogue. Drawing from works of cognitive science and neurology, it offers us a lucid exploration of what science and theology can teach each other about transformation to heal the wounds of the world. Rich and engaging, this book is a valuable contribution to liberation and decolonial theologies.

—Mayra Rivera, Andrew W. Mellon Professor of Religion and Latinx Studies, Harvard University

Few Puerto Rican theologians have published in this area of research. In this sense Carmelo Santos-Rolón's contribution is a fresh and unusual introduction to this area of study. His strong academic background in the area of science and insightful understanding of Christian theology makes his book a valuable introduction to this field . His valuable reflection in considering this field also lies in the clarity and inviting nature of his approach. His use of short stories to engage the reader in a complex analysis of the complicated, challenging, but fruitful nature of the dialogue among neuroscience, Christian theology, and decolonial approaches to knowledge is not just exciting, but also enlightening. This first effort in socializing to a broader audience his splendid experience in research, shrewd reflection, and ministerial practice promises a productive contribution in the years to come.

—José David Rodríguez, Augustana Heritage Chair of Global Mission and World Christianity, and professor emeritus of systematic theology, Lutheran School of Theology at Chicago

This wonderful book leads us into the neuroscience of emotions, opening up the apostle Paul's invitation to "be transformed by the renewing of the mind." Weaving together the best of brain science with liberation theology and sacraments, Santos-Rolón shows how the power of God's Spirit can liberate us for healing wounds of colonization and slavery. The mind is a storyteller, a creator of worlds. This book will transform your mind. It is a joy to read.

—Barbara Rossing , author of *The Rapture Exposed: The Message of Hope in the Book of Revelation*

A Liberation Theology of the Brain is a brave new work in the theology of nature—in this case, of one of nature's most complex systems, the human brain, and its place in human persons and communities. As the book notes, most everything one wants to write, especially about the brain, takes easily to paper or digital media. Knowing what is trustworthy is another matter entirely and is anything but easy. Dr. Carmelo

Santos-Rolón offers a novel theological contribution that is an invitation to authentic interdisciplinary dialogue for students and scholars about how to understand the deep implications that studying the human brain has for theology about human persons and communities. He reveals how relying on one's intuitive sense of the reality of human brains, minds, persons, and communities is a sure way to be stuck in error and to miss the glories of realities that resist preconceptions of both scientists and theologians. His book is a bit iconoclastic and asks us to embrace liberation from these confusions and errors. He has given us a readable, accessible, and intelligible way to begin that journey.

—Michael Spezio, associate professor of psychology,
data science, and neuroscience, Scripps College

A LIBERATION THEOLOGY OF THE BRAIN

A LIBERATION THEOLOGY OF THE BRAIN

NEUROSCIENCE, THEOLOGY, AND DECOLONIZING EMOTIONS

CARMELO SANTOS-ROLÓN

FORTRESS PRESS
Minneapolis

A LIBERATION THEOLOGY OF THE BRAIN
Neuroscience, Theology, and Decolonizing Emotions

30 29 28 27 26 25 3 4 5 6 7 8 9

Library of Congress Cataloging-in-Publication Data

Names: Santos-Rolón, Carmelo, author.
Title: A liberation theology of the brain : neuroscience, theology, and decolonizing emotions / Carmelo Santos Rolón.
Description: Minneapolis : Fortress Press, [2025] | Includes bibliographical references and index.
Identifiers: LCCN 2024049727 (print) | LCCN 2024049728 (ebook) | ISBN 9781506496504 (print) | ISBN 9781506496511 (ebook)
Subjects: LCSH: Liberation theology. | Neurosciences--Religious aspects--Christianity.
Classification: LCC BT83.57 .S26 2025 (print) | LCC BT83.57 (ebook) | DDC 230/.0464--dc23/eng/20250108
LC record available at https://lccn.loc.gov/2024049727
LC ebook record available at https://lccn.loc.gov/2024049728

Cover design: Kristin Miller
Cover image: compilation of stock illustrations from Getty Images

Print ISBN: 978-1-5064-9650-4
eBook ISBN: 978-1-5064-9651-1

To my children, Pablo and Ella; to my life partner and best friend, Jennifer; and to my sisters and parents. You are my inspiration, my joy, and my hope.

And to all those who have given me the great honor of being their pastor, especially the people of San Marcos/St Mark's to whom I said I had to go write a book. Ten years later, here it is: this is the book I had to write.

I prophesied as God commanded me, and the breath came into them, and they lived.

—Ezekiel 37:10

CONTENTS

Part III
The Power of God's Otherwise

ACKNOWLEDGMENTS

This book is dedicated to my children, Pablo and Ella—"always a listening ear"—and to my wife and best friend, Jennifer. You have accompanied me through the very long journey of dreaming this book into being; thank you for the encouragement when the writing was tough and for the joy you have brought to this task. And Jennifer's insights from her coaching practice, with a strong emphasis on somatics (in the lineage of the Strozzi Institute) have been very enriching. I am also grateful to my parents and sisters for their unconditional love and support: you, too, helped make this possible.

The book is also dedicated to all those who have given me the honor of being their pastor. It was by walking with them and sharing in their joys and sorrows that I learned to listen to the living word that is theology, a word that liberates, decolonizes, and gives abundant life even in the midst of suffering and death. Thank you, San Marcos/St Mark's, Hope, Trinidad, Sagrada Familia, and Angelica, for teaching me how to be a pastor. It is a holy and sacred thing to observe over the years how the living word of God in the power of the Holy Spirit really touches lives and brings healing and empowerment to individuals and communities. I am also deeply grateful to the church where I grew up, Iglesia Luterana Divino Salvador in Cataño, Puerto Rico, the spiritual womb where my spirit was formed and my passion for theology was ignited and shaped. Their lives of prayer and staunch faith and love showed me what following Christ is all about, and my pastor, Carmelo Nieves, taught me to be a theologian in *arroz con habichuelas* (rice and beans—that is, in the language of the everyday people). A word of gratitude is also due to the great Puerto Rican artist "Pichilo" Nieves Montañez, for patiently listening to my ideas and providing us with the initial sketches for the art on the cover of this book; we did not end up using his original drawings, but they helped me visualize what I wanted to communicate with the cover: a brain is never a brain alone but always as part of a body and in relationship to other bodies and brains. The image is of a person contemplating their own brain from within it. I am grateful to the graphic designers at Fortress, especially Kristin Miller, for capturing that idea and turning it into the beautiful image on the cover of the book. A word of gratitude is also due to the *Journal of Lutheran Ethics* for granting me permission to use a portion of my article "Exploring the Role of Unconscious Bias in the Immigration Debate and the Transformative Power of the Church" (December 13, 2013, https://www.elca.org/JLE/Articles/27).

Thank you to my editor extraordinaire, Laura Gifford, for believing in me and in this project and for asking the provocative question, "Is there a book there?" Thank you for your accompaniment as a midwife of sorts. The labor lasted much longer than I had anticipated; you provided me with the perfect balance between patience and gentle prodding.

In writing this book, I have acquired a deep sense of respect and gratitude for other writers, who risk being misunderstood by putting in print their insights and ideas. I have tried to give credit to all those whose work I have used directly in creating this book: the brilliant storytelling of Anthony de Mello; the profound insights of Thích Nhât Hanh (a Vietnamese Buddhist monk whose teachings have helped me be a better Christian); the powerful preaching of that modern-day prophet, Cornel West; and the delicate portrayal of the complexities of religious experiences in Mark Salzman's novel, *Lying Awake*. In addition, the many talks and interviews (made available on YouTube) of the phenomenal Spanish neuroscientist Nazareth Castellanos, who years before it was accepted and even at the risk of her reputation in the scientific community, was already championing the intricate interdependence of the brain and the body, especially the heart, the lungs, and the gut, and the importance of understanding them in their larger spiritual and cultural milieu. I have learned much from the indefatigable work of physician Gabor Maté on holistic medicine and the role of the toxic culture in which we are immersed in the diagnosis of physical and mental disease. I am grateful to my friend and Latina philosopher Mariana Alessandri for conversations over the years about Kierkegaard, Anzaldúa, Unamuno, and the importance of not conflating having negative emotions with somehow being broken. I recommend her book, *Night Vision: Seeing Ourselves Through Dark Moods* (Princeton University Press, 2023). Thank you to Archana Pathak for being an occasional writing partner and sharing with me her tricks for getting unstuck. And thank you to Ralph Piper for teaching me to believe and trust in my own voice. There have been so many others to whom I am grateful for their contributions to my own thinking—there have been so many over the years that it is impossible to remember them all, and I must apologize if I have inadvertently left anyone out.

I am also grateful to neuroscientists Michael Spezio and Robert Glassman for guiding my initial incursions into the fascinating world of cognitive science and affective and decision-making neuroscience during my PhD studies. They always insisted that I go beyond popular books in neuroscience and make sure to study and understand the actual scientific papers published in peer-reviewed journals. Given the general audience I wish to reach with this book, I have referenced many popular books, but in doing the research, I have followed their advice and immersed myself in the scientific literature as much as possible, and barely survived! There is such a richness and complexity of perspectives and internal debates in the world of modern neuroscience that for the nonspecialist, it can be overwhelming and dizzying. I hope I have done justice to the science while making it available to a larger audience. I am also very grateful to the University of Pennsylvania's Center for Neuroscience & Society; its director, Dr. Martha Farah; and their fabulous faculty for creating the neuroscience boot camp, which allowed me to immerse myself in the world of neuroscience and gain a better understanding of its various methodologies, instrumentations, applications, and philosophical assumptions. This program helped me learn the language of neuroscience so that I could have the conversation that this book is.

I am also very grateful to all the churches, universities, seminaries, and retreat centers that have invited me over the years to teach about the intersection of theology, ministry, and brain science. Among many others, I want to acknowledge the Philosophy Department of the University of Texas Rio Grande Valley in Brownsville; the Luther Academy in the Rockies (Wartburg Seminary); El Seminario Evangélico de Puerto Rico (Centro luterano de formación teológica José David Rodríguez Rivera); the Luther Symposium on Spirituality at Gettysburg (now United) Seminary; First Call Theological Education of Region 1 of the Evangelical Lutheran Church in America (ELCA); Calumet Retreat Center in Freedom, Massachusetts; Hope Lutheran Church in

College Park, Maryland; and Christ Church in Baltimore, Maryland. In addition to my own pastoral work, conversations with deacons, bishops, chaplains, pastors, and activists (especially those of CASA and VOICE) have helped sharpened these ideas and make them more practical for social justice.

A word of gratitude is also owed to Georgetown University's School of Theology and Religious Studies, especially to Dr. Terry Reynolds and Dr. Theresa Sanders, for believing in me and giving me the opportunity to design and teach the course God & the Brain. Over the years, the questions, ideas, and challenges from students and colleagues were invaluable. You all forced me to go deeper and wider in my thinking.

I must also thank all my teachers from over the years for teaching me the craft and beauty of doing theology, especially a theology that is not afraid to get its hands dirty, a theology not for angels but for real human beings in the midst of the complexities of being human—for example, the legacies of coloniality, racism, sexism, classism, homophobia, transphobia, xenophobia, and so many injustices. But also, the realities of dreams and aspirations, of hopes, and of daring activism to make the world a better place, to participate in God's great enterprise of *creatio continua*, continuously creating life out of the nothingness of death, meaning out of pain and suffering, and purpose out of the senselessness that sometimes life appears to have.

There are too many to name them all here, but I want to thank at least some of those teachers who had a deep influence in my thinking: José David Rodríguez Sr., my first theology teacher and the one who taught me that when properly understood, there is no difference between Lutheran theology and liberation theology. José David Rodríguez Jr., who made me feel that the Lutheran School of Theology at Chicago (LSTC) was truly my home and who taught me the importance of confessing the faith in the vernacular. Antje Jackelén, who not only oversaw my PhD dissertation but also taught me the rigors of serious interdisciplinary dialogue. Phil Hefner, who introduced me to the fascinating world of the dialogue between religion and science. Vítor Westhelle, who insisted that we look outside the frame, and listen to the voices there, in order to understand what is inside of it. Dwight Hopkins, Robert "Bob" Cathey, and Guillermo Hansen, among others, who introduced me to the wide range of modern and contemporary theological methodologies and modeled the discipline of the careful reading of theological texts in their proper contexts. Barbara Rossing, David Rhodes, Ed Krentz, Ralph Klein, and Ted and Barbara Hiebert, who taught me the art and science of finding the word of God in the Scriptures through careful use of ancient languages, scientific tools of textual interpretation, and prayerful exegesis. Kathy Billman and Thanda Gnobo, who taught me to translate theology into pastoral work. Linda Thomas, who introduced me to the wide range of liberation theologies beyond the Latin American and US Latinx context. Dr. Richard Perry, who taught me that activism and theology go together.

To the mentors and teachers of the Hispanic Summer Program and the Hispanic Theological Initiative (HTI), who taught me to do theology *latinamente*: thank you, Joanne Rodríguez, for your encouragement over the years and your magnificent leadership of the HTI; thank you, Luis Rivera Rodríguez and Wentzel van Huyssteen, for serving as my mentors, thank you, Luis Rivera Pagán, for introducing me, many years ago, to the work of Walter Mignolo and the world of decoloniality. Thank you, Justo González, for teaching me the importance of history in the theological task and to read history in a noninnocent way. Thank you, Jeannette Rodríguez, who through her teaching at the Hispanic Summer Program, helped me understand what patriarchy is and to commit myself to do my part in confronting it and dismantling it. And thank you, Ulrike "Uli" Guthrie, writing coach and editor who taught us HTI fellows the art of writing academically and to believe in our voice. Finally, my apologies to those whom I have not named; thank you to all of you who in one way or another helped me conceive this book. I have been blessed with great teachers, mentors, coaches, and friends over the years. I hope that I have done justice in this book to what you taught me.

Finally, I must say something about the title of this book, *A Liberation Theology of the Brain*. At first, I resisted that title. Liberation theology is not simply a school of thought, it is a long tradition of faithful people who, in obedience to the gospel, lived their lives in solidarity with and in defense of the poor and the oppressed, even to the point of martyrdom. They embodied the message of the gospel by assuming for themselves the fate of the people they had been called to serve. In their preaching, praxis, and theologizing, they unveiled structures of oppression in such ways that great physical, institutional, and reputational violence was unleashed against them,. Many were killed, tortured, exiled, fired, defrocked, and accused of being criminals, communists, or even terrorists. They endured all that in the name of Christ, out of genuine love for the people they served, and in obedience to the faith.

How dare I then use that name? I acquiesced to using it in the end because I wish to honor them with my work, and I hope that in some way, what I have written here has been inspired by their work and sacrifice. Perhaps it can also help introduce new generations to their magnificent work. In any case, I pray that by the grace of God, this book will be a "liberation theology," not in title only but also in spirit and impact. May this book be an instrument for liberation and healing. That is my prayer. Amén.

Introduction

The Joy of Science and Theology and the Promise of a Decolonial Liberation Theology of the Brain

BEFORE BECOMING A pastor and a theologian, I was originally trained as a chemist. Organic chemistry and, more specifically, the synthesis of organometallic compounds was what I loved most. I liked to figure out how molecules are assembled, but also, and especially, I liked mixing things. Sometimes the results of mixing molecules can be new materials, new medicines, and even new insights into how nature works. At other times, it just blows up in your face.

I remember once walking into the lab and seeing one grad student carefully pouring one compound into another while another student stood behind him, nervously pointing a fire extinguisher at him and his concoction. Fortunately, they didn't end up having to use the extinguisher that day. (We worked with materials that were highly sensitive to moisture in the air.) One of my dear professors, Dr. Ingrid Montes, always reminded us: when it comes to chemistry, the paper will take whatever you write on it, but even if it looks perfect on paper, it is in the lab where you will find out whether it works or whether it will blow up and make a mess.

I am no longer a practicing chemist. But old habits die hard. I no longer mix dangerous chemicals, except maybe when I try to cook, but I now like to try to mix ideas, methodologies, and perspectives, like mixing science and religion or neuroscience, theology, and decolonial studies. Sometimes, it doesn't work. But on other occasions, it works beautifully, resulting in new ways of looking at life, at nature, at each other, at ourselves, and even at God.

Science and Religion Need Each Other

My experience has been that many people are hungry for opportunities to explore how science and religion can complement each other rather than compete against each other. My experience has also been that religion and science are two of the most powerful motivators for human action. Therefore, if we want to have a real chance at addressing some of the major challenges facing us today, we would improve our odds of effecting real change by viewing religion and science as part of the solution rather than ignoring or vilifying one or the other.

Religion and science do not need to be seen as enemies or as incompatible. Unfortunately, there are some religious traditions that refuse to even consider the possibility that science might be a gift from heaven to help us discover God's wonders in creation and to help us find effective ways to participate in God's work of bringing healing and peace to the world that God so dearly loves. Similarly, it is frustrating to witness how many brilliant scientists use their platforms to ridicule religious faith and mock that which they often clearly have not taken the time to understand.

It is true that religion and science have good reasons to be suspicious of each other. Religion has a long history of being used as an excuse to silence new ideas (like Galileo's), to bolster oppressive systems (like slavery and patriarchy), and even to justify horrendous violence (like genocide). And science as an institution has had its share of guilt and complicity in, for example, turning God's sacred creation, deserving of respect, into a mere collection of spiritless and valueless objects and processes to be probed, experimented on, cut apart, and exploited (via technological innovation), thrown away as trash to satisfy the needs and unquenchable greed of a relatively small segment of humanity rather than truly being at the service of the common good. Science has also bolstered ways of thinking that have resulted in the suffering of many human beings who do not conform to the model of the ideal, healthy, (hu)man created by modern Western science.

The truth is that both science and religion are done by humans. Even if one claims access to natural, objective facts and the other to divine revelation, it is humans who are responsible for interpreting that revelation—and even deciding what counts as revelation and what doesn't. It is fallible humans who have to decide what facts are relevant, how to collect them, how to analyze them, and what theory, model, or method to use, vis-à-vis those preferred by other research groups or institutions. Therefore, if both science and religion are done by humans, we should not be surprised that they, as institutions, also bear the marks of human finitude, fallibility, and sin. That simply means that we need an attitude of openness for honest criticism and different perspectives. By definition, we cannot see our blind spots. The only way to see our blind spots is by either moving so that we can look at something from a different perspective or inviting others located in a different place to share what we are missing.

Therefore, it seems that not only are science and religion compatible with each other, but they also actually need each other. Religion—or more accurately, theology, which is a function of religion—can open dimensions of reality that science knows nothing about. And science can illuminate aspects of reality that would otherwise escape the theological gaze.

A Call for Dialogue

There are various ways in which theology and science could relate to each other. I already mentioned the first way, which is conflict. A second way in which science and religion could relate, and I am following here the typology developed by Ian Barbour in his now classic book *Religion and Science: Historical and Contemporary Issues,*[1] is simply being independent from each other. That is, the subject matter and methodologies of science and theology are so different that they don't conflict with each other simply because they are not dealing with the same realities. According to this perspective, science has to do with natural phenomena and theology has to do with the supernatural, which is beyond the purview of science and includes things like the salvation of souls and the reality of God according to God's revelation. When I was a science undergraduate student, this is the model that I encountered the most, among both students and professors. They simply kept those two dimensions of their lives hermetically sealed from each other. That, however, cannot last long, because science does touch upon matters that are dear to theology, such as the origins of the world and the nature of the human soul (especially in neuroscience).

Another possible way for science and religion to relate is by integration. This is the fourth option in Barbour's typology. The idea is that for science and theology to be helpful, they must aim for an understanding of reality that is all-encompassing. Even though there are things that

---

1. Ian G. Barbour, *Religion and Science: Historical and Contemporary Issues, A Revised and Expanded Edition of Religion in an Age of Science* (HarperSanFrancisco, 1997).

theology addresses that are beyond the scope of science, and vice versa, at some point they need to be brought together in order to construct a coherent view of reality. In my opinion, one difficulty with this laudable and necessary goal is that it risks devolving into a conflict between competing possible explanations for similar phenomena. For example, are religious experiences to be understood as the product of brain chemistry and neurology alone, which can be explained without the need to invoke the intervention of God or any other spiritual agents, or are they to be understood as the result of divine inspiration or some kind of spiritual activity? If we rush too quickly to integration, we might miss something important in the process. That is why, even though Barbour and most religion and science scholars that I have had the honor of learning from espouse integration as the goal, I prefer to dwell a little longer on Barbour's third option: dialogue.

Dialogue as a method for relating science and theology is based on the premise that before we can do anything else, we need to understand each other. Science and theology might be using similar words to describe the world and what they study, but every now and then, it becomes clear that those same words mean very different things when they are uttered by scientists than when they are uttered by theologians. What is the mind? What is the body? What is God? What is creation? Moreover, what is the point of studying and understanding the mind, the body, God, and creation? What assumptions from each discipline must be understood to make sense of the results, methods, and even what counts as data and evidence? And can we hold different truths, sometimes contradictory to each other but nonetheless obviously true in their own right, before quickly feeling the need to keep one and discard the other? What can we learn, or how can we grow, if we learn to hold the tension of paradox for a little while and listen attentively to the lesson that is there for us? Can we apply that same habit to other realms of our life beyond the practice of science and theology, such as our interactions with people with religions, political persuasions, ethnic origins, sexual orientations, gender identities, or economic classes different from our own?

This book is an invitation to a dialogue between theology and neuroscience from a decolonial perspective. The dialogue between theology and neuroscience, and the cognitive sciences in general, has already been going on for over half a century. A lot of exciting work has been done in the neuroscience of religious experience and the cognitive science of religion and on the theological implications of that work. The particular interest of this book is to bring some of that work to the project of healing the colonial wounds that we all carry collectively and individually on our minds and brains and, as we shall soon see, our bodies. That is the conversation I wish to invite you to.

Why Decoloniality?

At first it might seem to some that to speak of colonialism and decoloniality is anachronistic. The truth is, however, that even today there continue to be countries, territories, and peoples subjected to colonial relations, even if they are called by different names. Moreover, even those who are not directly members of those territories, countries, or peoples are nonetheless affected by the dynamics of coloniality. How come? Because the present bears the marks of its past. I wish I could remember who said this, because I would like to give her credit, but a conference speaker made this point by reminding us that when we go to see a physician, they always ask us about our family history. Is there a history of diabetes or hypertension or cancer or depression in your family? We cannot heal the present by ignoring the past. As Harvard decolonial theologian Mayra Rivera puts it, our present bodies are haunted by our colonial pasts.[2]

The past shapes the present. For that reason, we need to examine how the wounding happened in the first place in order to understand the wounds that afflict our society today. The good news is that because the past is connected to the present, it is possible to touch and heal the past by healing the present. In the process, we might also be able to heal the future because it is also only from the present that we are able

2. She borrows the image of haunting, specters, and ghosts from the postcolonial theorist Gayatri Chakravorty Spivak and the deconstructionist Jacques Derrida, as well as from Latin American literature and the embodied experiences of Latinas in the US and in her native Puerto Rico. See her essays "Ghostly Encounters: Spirits, Memory, and the Holy Ghost," in *Planetary Loves: Spivak, Postcoloniality, and Theology*, ed. Stephen D. Moore and Mayra Rivera (Fordham University Press, 2011), 118–35; "Thinking Bodies: The Spirit of a Latina Incarnational Imagination," in *Decolonizing Epistemologies: Latina/o Theology and Philosophy*, ed. Ada María Isasi-Díaz and Eduardo Mendieta (Fordham University Press, 2012), 207–25; and her book *The Touch of Transcendence: A Postcolonial Theology of God* (Westminster John Knox Press, 2007).

to touch the future. The past might shape the present, but the present does not have to be a prisoner of that past. However, as therapists and spiritual directors know very well, when we refuse to acknowledge or even examine the past, we become prisoners of it and, to use Rivera's image again, are constantly haunted by its ghosts.

Decoloniality is about examining how the colonial past of modernity, which includes much more than just the United States (from where I am writing this book), has shaped the present in which we live. It includes how to resist and, whenever possible, dismantle those institutions, practices, and systems that continue to subjugate a significant segment of humanity and creation for the benefit of the privileged few.

Everybody knows, even if they choose to ignore it, that the tremendous wealth and power of the wealthiest and most powerful nations today has been built on the forced labor of enslaved human beings and on land taken illegally and immorally by violence, force, and/or deceit. Coloniality was (and is) about taking possession of lands, extracting their wealth, and establishing international markets to increase that wealth. In order to do that successfully, you need a lot of land, a lot of hands to do the work, and security to protect the lands from their original inhabitants, the rightful owners trying to take them back, to protect them from people who refuse to be enslaved or to work for indecent salaries, and to protect the products and the wealth from those who might want to steal or reclaim them.[3] In other words, for the colonial project to work, a scaffolding of institutions, systems, practices, and laws needed to be created and put in place.[4] That scaffolding included institutions like transnational commercial companies (the East India Company, for example), colonial governments, militias, police bodies, legal systems, and eventually, even constitutions. It is important to keep in mind that the purpose of that institutional scaffolding was not to look after the well-being of all the people—"We the People"—but specifically and intentionally to ensure the smooth operation of the colonial

3. I use quotation marks because the original inhabitants didn't think of the land as something that could be owned, as if it were private property.

4. I develop this idea in my essay "Lutheran Theological Resources to Confront White Supremacy," in *Confronting Racism and White Supremacy in the US: Theological Perspectives for the Twenty-First Century*, eds. Michael R. Fisher Jr. et al. (Friendship Press, 2024).

project and the interests of those financing it. Even when there were people with good intentions who sincerely wanted to seek the well-being of their colonial subjects or slaves, the fact remains that this was not the main point or driving force of the colonial project. And even when refugees from European countries came to the "new world," not to seek wealth but simply to escape religious persecution and poverty in their own lands, their ability to find asylum was a function of the colonial project, which both benefited them and benefited from them. That is the family history of the modern world in which you and I live, and to say so is not to disparage anything that we might hold dear but to understand it in its proper context. We don't bring up the family history to shame but to heal.

Now, in addition to the colonial project's institutional scaffolding, something else was needed. It is simply not possible for anyone to commit the kind of sustained and systemic violence and oppression necessary to maintain the colonial project without first (in their minds) stripping the victims of their God-given dignity and *imago dei* (image of God)—and, by the way, profoundly wounding their own in the process. For millions of precious human beings from the African continent to be bought and sold like cattle, transported overseas (with many of them dying in the process and simply tossed overboard), and then forced to work under inhumane conditions generation after generation for centuries requires a special kind of collective hardening of the heart. Similarly, in order to force indigenous populations to obedience and to terrorize them with the kind of violence they were subjected to, it is first necessary to convince yourself that they are something other than human. Hence the need for the creation of cognitive-affective categories in which to place those who need to be subjected and abused, categories that I do not wish to reinforce by putting them in print.

Why Theology and Neuroscience?

I believe the cognitive sciences and recent developments in the neuroscience of emotions can help us understand how that categorization of the "other" took (and takes) place, forming one of the invisible foundations upon which the entire colonial project was built. Those cognitive-affective categories haunt us today like specters from our colonial past. Decolonial activist/thinker Catherine E. Walsh explains the task at hand in a way that highlights the interconnectedness of different systems of oppression and the need to understand them in connection with each other.[5] In the book *On Decoloniality*, she explains that:

> decoloniality denotes ways of thinking, knowing, being, and doing that began with, but also precede, the colonial enterprise and invasion. It implies the recognition and undoing of the hierarchical structures of race, gender, heteropatriarchy, and class that continue to control life, knowledge, spirituality, and thought, structures that are clearly intertwined with and constitutive of global capitalism and Western modernity. Moreover, it is indicative of the ongoing nature of struggles, constructions, and creations that continue to work within coloniality's margins and fissures to affirm that which coloniality has attempted to negate.[6]

Religion and theology had and continue to have an important role in the colonial project, that of buttressing those hierarchical structures mentioned by Walsh, by which humans were divided and labeled in order to justify their exploitation and marginalization and, at times, even attempts at their extermination. Theology and religion endowed those hierarchical structures and the anthropological categorizations supporting them with a feeling of realness or naturalness and even of moral necessity. They baptized them as willed by God, the Creator, and therefore as a mere fact of nature and of the natural development of history. As we shall see, religion, with its rituals, practices, symbols, and narratives, has the power to do that. But from a theological perspective, that is to distort and misuse what was originally intended as a blessing. Nonetheless, precisely because religion has such power, it can also be part of the solution. When used properly, the elements of religion—such as sacred words, sacraments, rituals, practices, community, and so on—can be means by which God's Spirit brings about healing and decolonizes us from the inside out.

---

5. Decolonial theorists emphasize the inseparable interconnectedness of theory and praxis and of thinking and feeling; to honor that commitment, I will refer to them as "activists/thinkers."

6. Walter D. Mignolo and Catherine E. Walsh, *On Decoloniality: Concepts, Analytics, Praxis* (Duke University Press, 2018), 17.

Hence, the purpose of this book is to open a space for conversations about how theology, religion, neuroscience, cognitive science, and decolonial thinking and living might orient us in our collective journey of colonial healing. Hopefully, the result of mixing such different disciplines and methodologies will be different than when I tried to mix dangerous chemicals in the lab. The proof will not be on the paper but in the "lab" of lived praxis and decolonial spirituality that this work wishes to help inspire.

Overview

This book, or conversation, is organized in three main parts:

Part I: The Creativity of the Mind-Body-Brain
Part II: The Mystery of Transcendence
Part III: The Power of an Otherwise

The first part, chapters 1–3, is an exploration of how the mind and brain works, with particular attention to how beliefs about God, other people, ourselves, and even reality in general are formed and what happens in the brain and nervous system when people have experiences of a religious kind. The first chapter looks at the mind from the perspective of the cognitive sciences of religion and the manifold cognitive devices operating beneath our consciousness that make our conscious experience possible. In the second chapter, we go on a tour of different regions, circuits, and systems in the brain and hear stories about how major discoveries were made. We will learn the tremendous contributions of the body to how the brain works. The body, the brain, and the mind belong together. Chapter 3 concludes the first part of the book with an exploration of what might be happening in people's minds/brains/bodies when they have religious experiences and how those experiences can transform the scaffolding of biases and prejudices that centuries of coloniality, racism, and heterosexism have programmed into our embodied brains and minds.

In the second part, on the mystery of transcendence, we journey to the other side of the horizons of science to explore what lies outside the frame of science's gaze. There, in chapters 4–6, we examine the nonscientific factors that go into doing science and learn about the importance of having more than one lens to view reality. One important principle of decoloniality is the acknowledgment and lifting of ancestral ways of knowing and being that have been subjugated. Those "subjugated knowledges" have important contributions to make to the modern world.[7] After going beyond science, we then explore those experiences that take us to the limits of our minds, of our experience of the world, and even of our own selves. Experiences like death, suffering, awe, and mystical ecstasy convey to us that there is a richness to reality, a depth or a transcendence within, that invites us to expand the way we perceive and experience life, each other, and reality itself. In chapter 6, the last of this part of the conversation, we review the different names that different religious and philosophical traditions have given to that mystery.

In the final part of the book, on the power of the otherwise, we focus the conversation on the role of words in general and of the Word in particular, speaking from a theological perspective, in shaping how we experience and even perceive reality, including the reality of each other, of God, of ourselves, and of what is possible and desirable. In order to appreciate the role of language and the Word in shaping our experience of reality, we first need to examine the role of the emotions in human experience. Thus, in chapter 7, we look at how emotions are shaped from deep within the body and how it is words that give them their final shape. I propose that our cognitive-affective systems function like a sort of generative grammar that gives moral and ontological weight and texture to our perceptual reality. Those generative affective grammars bear the marks of the historical cultural milieus in which we have been raised, and therefore bear the marks of coloniality, and its twin siblings of racism and (hetero)patriarchy. In chapters 8 and 9, I make the argument that from a theological perspective, those generative affective grammars can be transformed through the action of the sacred word, with the power of the divine Spirit. In chapter 8, we dive into an exploration of how the Word (i.e., word of God or living word) is capable of bringing about such powerful changes, and in chapter 9, we explore what liberation theologies and decolonial thinking/praxis can

---

7. Vítor Westhelle, "Scientific Sight and Embodied Knowledges: Social Circumstances in Science and Theology," *Modern Theology* 11, no. 3 (July 1995): 341–61; and Otto Maduro, "An(other) Invitation to Epistemological Humility: Notes Toward a Self-Critical Approach to Counter-Knowledges," in Isasi-Díaz and Mendieta, eds. *Decolonizing Epistemologies: Latino/a Theology and Philosophy* (Fordham University Press), 87–103.

offer us for this task of dismantling the colonial hierarchies of oppression and exorcising its specters that haunt us. I propose a hermeneutics of suspicion for neuroscience and a theopoetics of the mind-body-brain. Finally, in chapter 10, we look at hope and its generative power to bring God's promised future into the present. It is through hope that we are able to recognize that a different world is possible, an "otherwise" to the systems of injustice that we have inherited. And it is hope that inspires us to plant the seeds of that tomorrow today.

I hope you will join the conversation and the holy task of working for the healing of the wounds that we all carry in one way or another. I was invited into this conversation many years ago when I went from chemistry to seminary. After completing my bachelor of science at the University of Puerto Rico, I went to the Lutheran School of Theology at Chicago, where I received my master of divinity, master of theology, and PhD. It was there that, thanks to the work of the Zygon Center for Religion and Science, I learned the alchemy of mixing science and theology for the purpose of the divine work of healing and liberation. It was also there where my dissertation advisor and now the bishop emerita of the Church of Sweden, the Rev. Dr. Antje Jackelén, insisted that in order to have a dialogue, I needed real dialogue partners and not just books. And so, because my dissertation was on the dialogue between neuroscience, the cognitive sciences, and the theology of the Holy Spirit, I reached out to the now late Dr. Robert Glassman, psychology professor at Lake Forest College and to Dr. Michael Spezio, at the time jointly working at Caltech and Scripps College. They guided me in my journey into the world of neuroscience and cognitive science. That world is so complex and fascinating that I am still wandering within its labyrinthian paths.

I also had the privilege of receiving further training at the University of Pennsylvania Neuroscience Bootcamp from Dr. Martha Farah, director of the Center for Neuroscience & Society, and the amazing faculty at the program. Then I had the great honor of joining Georgetown University's Theology and Religious Studies faculty, where I taught while also serving as a local pastor until I accepted a call to serve in the office of the presiding bishop of the Lutheran Church, ELCA. At Georgetown I had the opportunity to design and teach a course that I called God & the Brain. I was also able to teach other courses, such as The Problem of God and Latinx Theology & Ethics. The conversations with students and faculty there were tremendously enriching, and their questions pushed me to go deeper into the research and to clarify my own ideas. I owe a great debt of gratitude to all of them.

I also owe a debt of gratitude to the amazing grassroots activists and everyday people with whom I got to serve in my ownactivism/thinking, especially the people of CASA, CASA in Action, and Virginians Organized for Interreligious Community Engagement (VOICE). From them I learned the power of crossing boundaries, listening deeply to each other, and daring to believe that "*Sí se puede*" ("Yes, it is possible") and that the very act of believing that an otherwise was possible actually makes it possible.

Finally, there are the people to whom this book is dedicated, all those who have given me the honor of calling me "pastor," especially the members of San Marcos/St Mark's in Springfield, Virginia; of Hope in Annandale, Virginia; of Angelica in LA, and of Trinidad and Sagrada Familia in Chicago. They taught me to be a pastor and a theologian. As my own pastor, Rev. Carmelo Nieves, used to ask me about my theological thoughts, "How would you say that in *arroz con habichuelas*, in rice and beans?" The people of the churches I have served taught me how to do theology in "rice and beans," a theology that does not serve to feed my ego but to feed the people with the life-giving Word. More than ten years ago, I left San Marcos/St Mark's with the intention to write this book. Here it is! It took me a decade, but I did it. I hope I have done justice to what all the people listed above, and so many more, have taught me over the years. I hope you will join the conversation.

Part I

The Creativity of the Mind-Body-Brain

CHAPTER ONE

The Mind

Creator of Worlds

> Do not be conformed to this age, but be transformed by the renewing of the mind, so that you may discern what is the will of God—what is good and acceptable and perfect.
>
> —Romans 12:2

THE MIND IS a storyteller, a creator of worlds, not a mere mirror or camera reflecting back reality exactly as it is. Using information collected by the senses, and combining it with memories, feelings, and expectations, the mind weaves into being the universe that constitutes our reality. That does not mean that there is no objective reality out there. It simply means that our minds are part of that reality, we are part of that reality, and the only access we have to that reality is through our embodied minds.

A recurrent theme across religious traditions is the susceptibility of the mind to deception and the need for the mind to be liberated or renewed. In a similar way, liberation and decolonial theologies seek to unveil the ways in which our minds and, consequently, our perception of reality have been distorted by the processes of colonization that have given shape to the world in which we live today. We have inherited a world that bears the marks, or even the open wounds, not only of the project of colonization but also of a long history of slavery; of the exploitation of the labor of immigrants from all over the world, from Ireland and China to Latin America and the Caribbean; of the oppression of women's bodies and labor; of the immoral appropriation of land from the nations and tribes that were the original inhabitants of these lands; and of processes of physical and cultural genocide. That reality, painful to acknowledge, continues to shape our present world by way of things such as institutional practices, laws, inequitable distribution of resources, perduring habits, and implicit biases that too often end up having deadly consequences on vulnerable members of our society.[1] Eventually, such aberrations of the way things should be become normalized in our minds. They begin to be perceived as reality and therefore as inevitable rather than as a distortion of reality, a corruption of the way God, the Creator, intends things to be, "what is good and acceptable and perfect" (Romans 12:2).

The renewing of the mind in the context of the distortions of historical systems of oppression requires a conversion, a turning around to perceive reality from a different perspective. It requires a willingness to open oneself to the experiences of others, especially the experiences of those being crushed by "reality," and the experience of having dreams and visions of an alternative reality that is life-giving and wholesome. As the prophet Isaiah (43:19) put it: "I am about to do a new thing; now it springs forth; do you not perceive it?"

To understand how that process of the renewal of the mind might take place, and how we can contribute to such renewal and consequent transformation of ourselves and of reality, it will be helpful to explore how the mind creates the reality that we perceive. For that purpose, we turn to the sciences of the mind in this chapter and then to the sciences of the brain in the next.[2] We shall see later that mind and brain are but two aspects of one reality; therefore, one cannot be properly understood without the other. Furthermore, we shall also see that the mind/brain is "embodied, embedded, and enactive."[3] The mind/brain is a part of

---

1. See, for example, Nikole Hannah-Jones et al., eds., *The 1619 Project: A New Origin Story* (One World, 2021); Laura E. Gómez, *Inventing Latinos: A New Story of American Racism* (New Press, 2020); Ibram X. Kendi and Jason Reynolds, *Stamped: Racism, Antiracism, and You* (Little, Brown & Co., 2020); Michelle Alexander, *The New Jim Crow: Mass Incarceration in the Age of Colorblindness* (New Press, 2012); and Vine Deloria Jr., *Custer Died for Your Sins: An Indian Manifesto* (University of Oklahoma Press, [1969] 1988).

2. Often the terms *neuroscience* and *cognitive science* are used as umbrella terms that cover all the different approaches to the study of the brain and the mind. However, to be precise, cognitive science is the study of the cognitive functions of the brain and neuroscience refers to the study of the physical brain and its processes; increasingly, there is significant overlap between the two, even to the point of the development of new fields, such as cognitive neuroscience. To avoid confusion, I distinguish between the mind and the brain and the sciences that focus on one or the other.

3. Francisco J. Varela et al., *The Embodied Mind: Cognitive Science and Human Experience* (MIT Press, 1995), especially chapter 8, "Enaction: Embodied Cognition," 147–84.

the body, existing within networks of other embodied minds/brains (people), and for the purpose of acting in certain ways, needed for surviving and thriving. Let's keep that in mind as we turn now to a brief exploration of the scientific study of the mind from the perspective of cognitive science.

The Mind as a Computer

A breakthrough in the scientific study of the mind happened in the 1950s as a result of advances in what today we refer to as computer science.[4] The idea was simple but powerful: What if the mind works like a computer? That was the beginning of the cognitive revolution in the study of the mind. From that point on, there has been a symbiotic and reciprocal relationship between developments in computer science and developments in cognitive science. Computer programs are engineered to learn the way minds learn, and by observing how computer programs function, cognitive scientists acquire new insights on how minds work. Such reciprocity has reached a new climax in the now pervasive presence of machine learning and artificial intelligence technologies.

The basic idea in cognitive science is that the mind consists of *representations* of reality and operations performed on those representations that yield results in the form of perceptions, beliefs, behaviors, and emotional states. An understanding of the important role of affect in cognition took a while to be fully appreciated within cognitive science, but as we shall see in the next two chapters, it is now clear that emotions, feelings, and affect are essential to the proper functioning of the mind and are inseparable from it.[5]

A representation is the way elements of reality are encoded in the mind. When someone sees a tree, for instance, the actual tree is not present in their mind, but rather what appears within the field of conscious experience is a representation of the tree. The same is true of the experience of hearing a bird chirping or any other input

---

4. This overview of cognitive science is based mostly on Paul Thagard, *Mind: Introduction to Cognitive Science*, 2nd ed (MIT Press, 2005).

5. Alain Berthoz, *Emotion & Reason: The Cognitive Neuroscience of Decision Making*, trans. Giselle Weisse (Oxford University Press, 2003), especially chapter 6, "Deliberating with One's Body: Me and My Second Self," 109–33.

information we receive through our senses. What we perceive is not the thing itself but rather the result of how the mind has encoded and processed that information. That means that perception itself is interpretation. Cognitive scientists have identified various processes and algorithms (the equivalent of code in computer programs) operating without our conscious awareness that are responsible for the interpretation that happens even before we become aware of what is going on and that results in the way we perceive and experience reality. I propose to think of those algorithms and processes as resulting in what I will call, borrowing language from Noam Chomsky[6] and George Lindbeck,[7] generative affective-cognitive grammars of experience, or simply, affective grammars. But first, let's explore the various components of the mind's architecture, according to cognitive science, and how they operate.

The Architectonics of Cognition

7 ± 2

What does it mean to refer to structures in the mind that shape beliefs? One of the earliest findings that gave researchers a hint that the mind has an internal structure was the finding that working memory has limits, but those limits can be tricked if information is *chunked* in certain ways.[8] In 1956 cognitive scientist George Miller famously argued that there is a limit to the number of items that humans can hold in their working memory at any given time.[9] That number, now famous in popular culture, is seven plus or minus two. That does not mean that one can remember no more than seven numbers at once. What it means,

6. Noam Chomsky, *Language and Mind*, 3rd ed. (Cambridge University Press, 2006), especially his definition of generative grammar, 149–50.

7. George A. Lindbeck, *The Nature of Doctrine: Religion and Theology in a Postliberal Age* (Westminster John Knox Press, 1984), especially his discussion on the grammar-like regulative role of doctrine, 18–19 and 79–84.

8. Thagard, *Mind*, 6, 48–50.

9. For the original paper, see George A. Miller, "The Magical Number Seven, Plus Minus Two: Some Limits on Our Capacity for Processing Information," *Psychological Review* 63 (1956): 81–97.

rather, is that in order to be able to hold larger amounts of information in mind, one can organize the information into chunks—that is, meaningful clusters of information in which each cluster counts as one item. An example of this is memorizing phone numbers. The first three numbers count as one because it is the area code; similarly, one can group numbers into a meaningful category, which will reduce the amount of memory space it occupies.

The Structure of Beliefs

In the same way that there are slots, so to speak, for memory items, there are also different kinds of slots into which the mind organizes the information it receives.[10] The nature of those slots and the kinds of operations carried out on the information they contain is the subject of ongoing research and debate among cognitive scientists. In fact, even a quick review of the various models, methodologies, and theories within cognitive science can be overwhelming.[11] Nonetheless, there are some very basic generalities that can be affirmed about the structure of the mind. The understanding outlined in this chapter is derived mostly from the application of cognitive science to the study of religion,[12] but a fundamental claim of cognitive science is that the cognitive structures that underlie religious beliefs are not different from those underlying all other kinds of beliefs.[13] Let us, then, further examine those cognitive structures and dynamics in broad lines.

We must begin with the idea espoused by the French philosopher and mathematician René Descartes: contrary to material things, which

---

10. For an easy-to-follow explanation of these mental templates, see Justin L. Barrett, *Why Would Anyone Believe in God?* Cognitive Science of Religion Series (Altamira Press, 2004), especially chapter 1, "What Does It Mean to 'Believe'?," 1–19; for a more technical discussion see Thagard, *Mind*, 3–22.

11. See, for example, Robert J. Stanton, ed., *Contemporary Debates in Cognitive Science* (Blackwell, 2006); and Carl Senior et al., eds., *Methods in Mind* (MIT Press, 2006).

12. Ilkka Pyysiänen and Veikko Anttonen, *Current Approaches in the Cognitive Science of Religion* (Continuum, 2002); Pascal Boyer, *Religion Explained: The Evolutionary Origins of Religious Thought* (Basic Books, 2001); Barrett, *Why Would Anyone Believe in God?*

13. Boyer, *Religion Explained*, 93–135.

are extended in space and can be divided into parts, the mind is a substance, a kind of thing that subsists in and of itself and which is one, indivisible, and nonphysical.[14] Contrary to Descartes' perspective, cognitive science postulates that the mind is not one simple thing or substance but actually a complex set of processes carried out by the *wetware* of the brain and the nervous system (this is analogous to the hardware on which computer programs or software run). Importantly, most of those processes take place beneath the threshold of consciousness, which means that we are not aware that they are happening.[15] This is similar to, but different from, the psychoanalytic insight that there is an unconscious level in the mind shaping our thoughts and actions. Cognitive science, being an interdisciplinary field, borrows many concepts from evolutionary psychology, especially the idea that the human mind is the result of a long process of evolution and adaptations. Through that journey of evolution, the mind developed different strategies to address specific challenges and opportunities that it encountered. The human mind is an accumulation and adaptation of those cognitive programs. This way of understanding the mind has been called the Swiss-knife model,[16] "the mind as a workshop,"[17] or even a "team of rivals."[18]

The main idea is that the mind does not operate as a single processing unit but as a collection of processes. Those processes sometimes work in tandem, with the results of one being passed to the others for further processing in what is called a feed-forward network.[19] Other processes are loops where the processed information is then sent back to

---

14. René Descartes, *Meditations on First Philosophy*, 3rd ed. (Hackett, 1993), 17–24.

15. Barrett, *Why Would Anyone Believe in God?*, 2.

16. The main idea, as used in the cognitive science of religion, comes from John Tooby and Leda Cosmides, "The Psychological Foundations of Culture," in *The Adapted Mind: Evolutionary Psychology and the Generation of Culture*, ed. Jerome H. Barkow et al. (Oxford University Press, 1992), 163–228.

17. Barrett, *Why Would Anyone Believe in God?*, 3–6.

18. David Eagleman, "The Brain Is a Team of Rivals," in *Incognito: The Secret Lives of the Brain* (Pantheon, 2011), 101–50.

19. Gregory R. Peterson offers a helpful explanation of this process in the section "The Mind as an Information Processor" in *Minding God: Theology and the Cognitive Sciences* (Fortress Press, 2003), 36–41; see also Thagard, *Mind*, 113–17.

previous cognitive slots for further processing.[20] And sometimes there are processes that are in tension with each other, sometimes producing bizarre results, as we shall see below when discussing the phenomena of illusions. There is also redundancy built into our cognitive system so that if one process is compromised, a parallel one can take over. In chapter 3, when discussing the neuroscience of religious experiences and especially the model proposed by the neuroscientist Patrick McNamara, we will see that this division of labor in the mind, combined with the way our genes and neurons operate, results in a fragmentation of the self that religious experiences can help overcome.[21] But I am getting ahead of myself. Let us return to our exploration of how the cognitive devices of the mind operate to form beliefs that, as mentioned above, are experienced not simply as ideas but as perceptions of how things actually are "out there."

Upon detecting something, the mind immediately proceeds to place it in an ontological category;[22] that is, it places it in the best available slot. For example, is this thing that I am perceiving an object or an agent, an artifact (like a tool) or an animal? That first layer of slots is meant to determine what kind of thing this is. Depending on what category the object of perception (or, more accurately, its representation) fits into, a series of other slots then open up. These slots have already been populated with information or assumptions that allow us to know something about the reality we are encountering, even if this is the first time we have encountered this specific object, being, or circumstance.[23] An analogy that I find helpful is that of hyperlinks. When you click on them, a new window opens with new data.

For example, if something is categorized as an animal, then the mind immediately issues assumptions about it, like that it can die, that it

20. These loops are often organized hierarchically. See Malcom Jeeves and Warren Brown, *Neuroscience, Psychology, and Religion: Illusions, Delusions, and Realities about Human Nature*, Templeton Science and Religion Series (Templeton Press, 2009), especially the section on "A Nested Hierarchy of Action Loops," 42–43.

21. Patrick McNamara, *The Neuroscience of Religious Experience* (Cambridge University Press, 2009).

22. Barrett, *Why Would Anyone Believe in God?*, 4–5.

23. For this and the following discussion, see Boyer, *Religion Explained*, 40–45; and Barrett, *Why Would Anyone Believe in God?*, Table 1.1 "Mental Tools," 5.

can reproduce, that it has to eat, and that it experiences needs and wants and can act based on those needs and wants. If, however, the thing we have before us is categorized by the mind as an object, then our cognitive apparatus immediately tells us that it cannot feel, that it cannot think or move on its own, and that it cannot reproduce or experience wants or needs. In that way, the mind is constantly producing beliefs about the reality we encounter. Those beliefs are more than just opinions; they take the form of perceptions and intuitions and of convictions and knowledge. We will see in chapter 7, when discussing the relationship between emotion and language, that when those concepts become paired with emotions, the reality they point to assumes an ontological weight that makes them appear as undeniably real, regardless of the facts, because they can even become constitutive of the facts.[24] This will be important in understanding the creation and perpetuation of the racial, ethnic, heterosexist, etc. scaffolding of coloniality. But let us now return to our general discussion of the internal operations of the mind according to cognitive science.

According to this perspective, then, beliefs are our assumptions, conscious and unconscious, about reality. In a circuitous way, beliefs about reality are generated by the internal operations of the mind; those beliefs, in turn, structure the way reality is experienced, and the experiences of reality then influence those cognitive processes and structures through which reality is represented in the mind. From the perspective of cognitive science, the same cognitive apparatus that allows people to perceive things such as rocks, trees, and animals also generates our beliefs in other areas, such as religion, politics, race, and gender.[25] Furthermore, why some beliefs seem more believable than others can also be explained by the operations of the cognitive machinery of the mind; what it cannot answer is whether any given belief is actually true or false, accurate or misleading.[26] For that, other approaches are needed, as we shall see in the second part of this book.

---

24. Lisa Feldman Barrett, "Emotion as Social Reality," in *How Emotions Are Made: The Secret Life of the Brain* (Mariner, 2018), 128–51.

25. Justin Barrett, "How We Conceive of Humans," in *Cognitive Science, Religion, and Theology: From Human Minds to Divine Minds*. Templeton Science and Religion Series (Templeton Press, 2011), 73–95.

26. Barrett, *Cognitive Science, Religion, and Theology*, 146–69.

Let us take a closer look at the structure and dynamics of the cognitive devices that generate and support our beliefs.

Reflective and Nonreflective Beliefs

In his book *Why Would Anyone Believe in God?* cognitive scientist Justin Barrett, an expert in developmental cognitive psychology and a pioneer in the field of the cognitive science of religion, explains that there are two basic types of beliefs: reflective and nonreflective beliefs.[27] Reflective beliefs are ideas and conclusions we hold as the result of conscious processes of reflection, thought, and analysis. Nonreflective beliefs, on the other hand, serve as the cognitive foundation upon which reflective beliefs are built. Nonreflective beliefs are intuitive, fast, and mostly unconscious (but are not to be confused with the Freudian or Jungian unconscious).[28]

Depending on the specific domain they're addressing, nonreflective beliefs are sometimes referred to by terms such as *folk physics*, *folk psychology*, or *folk ontology*.[29] The main idea is that we carry in our minds inherent assumptions about the types of things we encounter in the world and what we can expect of them in terms of their qualities and behaviors. Those expectations that are automatically elicited in turn trigger behavioral scripts that orient how we interact with the reality, object, person, etc. that we have before us. When students walk into a classroom for the first time and choose a chair to sit on, they don't typically first examine the chair to see if it is solid enough to hold their weight. Without thinking about it, the student simply sits on the chair.

When we encounter something, it gets picked up by our perceptual system through the senses and a representation of it is formed in the mind. Immediately, as part of that process, the mind automatically decides what kind of reality this is. For example, is it a living creature,

---

27. This is akin to Daniel Kahneman's distinction between fast/instinctive and slow/deliberative thinking in his book *Thinking, Fast and Slow* (Farrar, Straus and Giroux, 2011).

28. For a brief overview of the psychoanalytic approach to the study of the mind, see the coda at the end of this chapter.

29. See, for example, Dan Sperber and Lawrence Hirschfeld, "The Cognitive Foundations of Cultural Stability and Diversity," *Trends in Cognitive Sciences* 8, no. 1 (2004): 40–46.

an animal, a human-made artifact, a natural object, or a person? With that initial categorization, which is intuitive and automatic, comes a series of nonreflective beliefs. If it is a living creature, then it has a body, it dies, it needs to eat in order to survive, it produces offspring that are similar to itself, and so on. Value judgments are also issued: this animal is dangerous, this animal is cute, this animal is delicious, this animal is of no interest to me, etc.

The Agency Detector

Another interesting feature of the mind is that it has a bias for attributing intentional agency to ambiguous phenomena. Barrett refers to the cognitive system that senses or attributes agency as the "agency detection device." In the case of humans, this device is overtly sensitive or hyperactive; thus, he names it the hypersensitive agency detection device (HADD).[30] If you are in a room by yourself and suddenly hear a noise behind you and glimpse movement, your mind automatically assumes that the noise and movement were caused by an agent. If a cup falls from a desk, our first instinct is to assume that someone made that happen. According to evolutionary psychologists, the reason for this bias for agency over attribution in our nonreflective belief systems is that it provided our ancestors with a survival advantage. They lived surrounded by predators and other dangers lurking behind rocks, bushes, or trees. Having an automatic system that would make them respond immediately to sudden noises or movement would allow them to evade attacks from, for example, snakes, scorpions, and other predators. Similarly, in the context of hunting, that hypersensitivity for agency would allow them to perceive the signs that there was game nearby, thus allowing them to bring dinner to their communities.

The Mind Reader

At the same time that the HADD allows us to intuit the presence of an agent, a second cognitive device also kicks in—namely, the *theory of mind (ToM)*.[31] This system issues intuitive assumptions about the

30. Barrett, *Why Would Anyone Believe in God?*, 32–44.

31. Barrett, *Why Would Anyone Believe in God?*, 4–5.

intentions of the potential agent(s) detected by the HADD: Is it about to attack us, or is it getting ready to run away? Did it detect our presence? ToM is a mind reader. When we interact with others, it is the ToM that allows us to guess their intentions. Why are they smiling? Why did they put their hand on my shoulder? Why did that butterfly just come to my window? Why did my car swerve left rather than right, thus avoiding that accident? The ToM assumes a sort of mind at work in the actions of the agent that the HADD has detected. We try to read the intentions underlying the actions or effects we have just perceived and that our HADD has categorized as caused by an agent. This is, in turn, connected with behavioral scripts that will get activated and will drive how we respond to the situation at hand. Remember that these are nonreflective beliefs, so they are fast and intuitive, and often result in people acting before having had a chance to think about how they (re) act or even why they are reacting at all, much less whether their actions are adequate and appropriate.

Social Regulators

In addition to examining cognitive devices that make intuitive inferences about things and events, cognitive scientists also hypothesize the presence of cognitive devices that regulate social interactions.[32] Such social regulators will categorize agents in a hierarchy of power relative to us. Therefore, some agents will be viewed as superior to us while others will be viewed as inferior and yet others as equals. When someone who is categorized highly in the cognitive device for social regulation comes into our presence, the corresponding behavioral scripts that will immediately drive us to feel internal pressure to show them due deference—such as by standing up, bowing, shaking their hand, smiling, or ceding them our chair—are set in motion.

Memorability

I mentioned above that nonreflective beliefs serve as the foundation for reflective beliefs. One interesting feature of the human mind hypothesized by cognitive scientists is that if a minimal number of nonreflective beliefs get violated, then an idea or experience will become more

32. Barrett, *Why Would Anyone Believe in God?*, 5–6.

memorable than it would be otherwise.[33] However, if too many nonreflective beliefs are violated, then the idea or experience simply becomes nonsense or impossible to believe.

Witnessing a person walking through a wall without breaking it would be highly memorable. Our nonreflective belief about walls is that other solid objects cannot go through them. So, a person walking through a wall would catch our attention because it is counterintuitive, and it would be believable because it does not violate too many of the other nonreflective beliefs used in our perception of the situation. Similarly, the idea of ghosts or spirits is believable and highly memorable because all it requires is the removal of the body from the equation. Once you remove the body, all the nonreflective beliefs about bodies can be paused, so the person can float in the air, walk through walls, be invincible, and so on.

There can also be instances when properties from one kind of reality are transferred to another. That was, for instance, the genius of Walt Disney: he transferred a humanlike person into Mickey Mouse. Apparently, you can do it with as random a thing as a sponge (SpongeBob SquarePants) and it still works! According to the cognitive science of religion, religious experiences are believable and memorable partly because they are minimally counterintuitive. Just because an experience is minimally counterintuitive does not necessarily mean that it is not real or that it is nothing but an illusion, a delusion, or a misfiring of our cognitive neural apparatus. It simply tells us why certain beliefs are more memorable than others. But it is helpful to know that the mind has a penchant for certain types of beliefs and that they will "stick" whether they are true or not.[34]

Elements That Reinforce Beliefs

On top of the internal structure of beliefs, there are also external factors that reinforce beliefs.

---

33. Barrett, *Why Would Anyone Believe in God?*, 22–26.

34. The idea of "epidemiology" of beliefs has been elaborated on by Dan Sperber. See, for example, his chapter "The Epidemiology of Beliefs" in *The Social Psychological Study of Widespread Beliefs*, ed. C. Fraser and G. Gaskell (Oxford Science Publications and Clarendon Press, 1990), 25–44.

Cognitive Dissonance Reduction

One such factor is called cognitive dissonance reduction.[35] When there is a discrepancy between our beliefs and our actions, pressure builds up in our cognitive systems. Eventually, that pressure becomes unbearable, and we end up either aligning our actions with our beliefs or changing our beliefs to coincide with our actions. Interestingly, cognitive scientists have found that it is most often our beliefs that get changed in order to become aligned with our actions or circumstances. This has tremendous implications for spirituality and for the project of cognitive and affective liberation. Changing our beliefs is not enough; we must also change our actions and circumstances. If we act in ways that contradict our beliefs and values (or our faith), our mind will eventually believe our behaviors more than the beliefs we claim to have. Thus, it is important to have spaces and opportunities where we can rehearse the behaviors and lifestyles that we want to see reflected in our beliefs and in the larger society. Perhaps the idea of "fake it till you make it" is not such a bad idea after all. From the perspective of faith and theology, then, we must examine the liturgies of the church, the rituals, the prayers, the art decorating our worship spaces, the way we arrange ourselves collectively during our prayer services, and so on and ask ourselves what beliefs those practices reflect and reinforce. Then we must ask ourselves what changes need to be implemented in order to align those practices with the values of the gospel that we wish to embody.

Inoculation Effects

Inoculation effects are another factor in the reinforcement of beliefs.[36] They refer to the experience of facing hostility directed at one's beliefs so that one must give a defense of said beliefs. When one can do so successfully, the beliefs become more ingrained in us and acquire an aura of truth. This is combined with the opposite experience—namely, awareness that there are many other people who hold similar beliefs to ours. That gives us a sense of security so that even if some aspects of our beliefs seem impossible to understand, contradict our common sense, or go against the grain of accepted scientific explanations of reality, at least we can rely on the conviction that so many people cannot be

35. Barrett, *Why Would Anyone Believe in God?*, 62–63.

36. Barrett, *Why Would Anyone Believe in God?*, 63–64.

wrong. Moreover, we can also trust that among so many people, there surely are some who can understand and explain what we can't. These factors operate on all beliefs, from faith in eternal life to faith in the fact that other people we encounter have minds and feelings like we do or that scientific theories like the theory of evolution or the Big Bang are certainly true even if we are not familiar with the details of the evidence supporting such beliefs.

Ritual Actions

Rituals also contribute to the strengthening of beliefs.[37] We already saw the role that rituals play in cognitive dissonance reduction. They also play a function as a generative matrix for religious and existential meanings and for group identity formation.[38] Rituals are embedded in rich symbols, narratives, and sometimes, myths. Through the rituals of their community, participants can access the generational wisdom of that community to help them discern how to navigate specific challenges and opportunities. Through ritual, that wisdom also gets encoded in the participant's cognitive apparatus. Our focus here is on religious rituals; however, it must be kept in mind that according to the cognitive science approach, rituals can also be specific to other domains, such as becoming a member of a gang, of a political movement, of a particular sports culture, or of a social grouping. The same cognitive systems and dynamics are at work in those different settings to reinforce the particular beliefs that define that group. The rituals themselves might differ, but the cognitive dynamics underlying them are the same, at least from a cognitive science perspective.[39]

Anthropologist and cognitive scientist Harvey Whitehouse distinguishes between two general types of rituals: one-off rituals and frequent

---

37. Barrett, *Why Would Anyone Believe in God?*, 70–73.

38. Harvey Whitehouse, "Implicit and Explicit Knowledge in the Domain of Ritual," in Pyysiänen and Anttonen, *Current Approaches in the Cognitive Science of Religion*, 133–52.

39. E. Thomas Lawson and Robert N. McCauley, "The Cognitive Representation of Religious Ritual Form: A Theory of Participants' Competence with Religious Ritual Systems," in Pyysiänen and Anttonen, *Current Approaches in the Cognitive Science of Religion*, 153–76.

rituals.[40] One-off rituals tend to be very emotionally intense, sometimes putting participants at great risk and inflicting pain, both physical and psychic. They are often initiation rites, whereby people are welcomed into a special community or into a special role within their community. The ritual does not happen in isolation, however. It is preceded by a long period of apprenticeship or preparation, whereby the person who will be undergoing the ritual acquires a sort of symbolic grammar[41] that will allow them to interpret the experiences that will accompany the ritual.[42] Thus, even years and decades after undergoing the ritual, its memory will continue to produce symbolic material that will help the person navigate different situations in life. Additionally, the fact that the ritual often involves risk and intense pain, or at least discomfort, to the person functions as a way to seal the participant's loyalty to the ritual community. To the community, it shows that this person is loyal enough to undergo that ordeal for them, and to the person going through the ritual, it activates cognitive dissonance reduction, so that their beliefs and loyalty eventually align with those of the group. These effects do not only belong to religious communities, but they are also at work in any group, whether in sports teams, gangs, fraternities, sororities, professional guilds, or secular associations. And the rituals do not have to be formalized in the ways we tend to think of rituals.

The second type of rituals are of the frequent kind.[43] According to cognitive scientists, these types of rituals lend themselves to external interpretations; the people who perform them do not often know exactly what they mean or why they are doing them, but an external authority figure provides the meaning for them. Mastery in the ritual then allows for the ritual to function as a way of ingraining those beliefs

---

40. Whitehouse, "Implicit and Explicit Knowledge," 133–52. He builds his proposal on the model of memory consolidation by A. Karmiloff-Smith, *Beyond Modularity: A Developmental Perspective on Cognitive Science* (MIT Press, 1992).

41. This is my term, but he refers to a process of exegesis to interpret both the ritual and life events based on the ritual. See Whitehouse, "Implicit and Explicit Knowledge," 147.

42. Whitehouse, "Implicit and Explicit Knowledge," 144–47.

43. Whitehouse, "Implicit and Explicit Knowledge," 135; see also, Barrett, *Why Would Anyone Believe in God?*, 69–70.

in the participant's mind (and body) as well as reinforcing the behavioral codes associated with such beliefs.

Implications

Illusion Versus Reality

Sometimes those unconscious cognitive systems can result in bizarre mistakes and illusions, a fact skillfully used by magicians and illusionists.

During a recent trip to New York City, I had the opportunity to visit the Museum of Illusions. It is an eerie experience to witness how our senses can be tricked into perceiving things differently than the way we think they actually are. A person can seem incredibly tall or very short depending on where they stand inside a carefully designed box. Because of the angles inside the box, if a person inside of it is closer or farther away from a viewer outside of the box, the viewer's mind interprets it not as closer or farther, but rather as taller or shorter. Painters use this proclivity of the mind, which translates contrasts in lines, angles, shades, and hues into three-dimensional space, to open up a sense of depth and relief on what is otherwise a flat surface. A student once told me that while she was on vacation with a friend, they came across an artist who was using colored chalk to paint the image of a precipice on the sidewalk. Even though the friend had seen the artist create the drawing, she felt too scared to walk on top of it because she had the strong sense that she would fall off the cliff. The friend's mind was not just perceiving what was on the sidewalk; her mind was actually interpreting it as it was perceiving it.

In that same museum, there are drawings of spiral lines. Even though the lines are static, they suddenly begin to "move" in a dizzying, spiraling motion when the viewer fixes their gaze on a particular spot. Of course, the actual lines on the wall are not moving at all, but the observer actually sees them moving. Descartes was right: perception can be deceiving. But then, is the way we perceive reality ever an accurate reflection of the way things are in reality, or is it interpretations all the way down? The key word here is *reflection* because, as mentioned above, what becomes available to our minds when we perceive reality is not the reality itself but a representation of that reality. Our experience of reality is the experience of the images used by our minds to represent reality.

When I taught God & the Brain, I would give my students an exercise called the Stroop test to illustrate the way mental representations work.[44] It consists of a screen with words written in different colors. The words themselves are the names of colors, such as red, blue, or orange. Sometimes the color and the word coincide, but most of the time they do not. Students are asked to read the words out loud as fast as they can and then to say the color of the word instead of reading the word. The exercise always ends in laughter. Reading the word seems to be easier than identifying the color. It is a strange but funny experience wanting to say one thing (the color of the word) but hearing yourself and your classmates say something else instead (the word itself). The exercise helps us notice the way that different cognitive programs are running in parallel at the same time. One is trying to determine the color while the other one is trying to read the word. This illustrates that the way the cognitive devices in the mind are arranged is not in serial order but rather is often in parallel, even if information from one system frequently gets conveyed to other systems, including processes of feedback loops.

Another exercise that I would give God & the Brain students was to show them pictures of faces: two pictures per slide. The two faces were identical except that one was upside down. In addition to that, in both pictures the mouth and other features of the face would be altered so that they were upside down in relation to the rest of the face. I would then ask the students if there was something odd with either of the pictures. They would immediately point out that the mouth was upside down in the normal one. They would not immediately detect that the same was true of the upside-down picture! The reason is that the brain uses a few points of reference on the picture to anticipate what it is viewing and then issues a prediction. That prediction takes the form of a mental image, which is what we perceive.

Something similar happens with the perception of intentional behavior. In the 1940s, psychologists Fritz Heider and Marianne Simmel devised an experiment where students would view a video of a few geometric figures moving around.[45] There is a big rectangle, two

---

44. You can take the Stroop test at https://youtu.be/gjesfzWozo4?si=9smu2ojW5g6LFSx3.

45. F. Heider and M. Simmel, "An Experimental Study of Apparent Behavior," *American Journal of Psychology* 57 (1944): 243–49, cited in Barrett, *Why Would Anyone Believe in God?*, 44, n. 4.

triangles, and one circle. The triangles and circle approach the rectangle, which then opens or closes, with the result that a shape that was outside sometimes ends up inside. The shapes would also come close to each other or move far away from each other at different speeds. The result is the perception that one of the triangles is bullying the circle and the other triangle comes to the rescue, trapping the bully triangle inside the rectangle. At least, that is one of the stories that the mind tells itself to make sense of what it is seeing. Interestingly, however, what it sees is simultaneously shaped by the story that it is telling itself. It seems that just as the mind's perception of depth and movement is the result of a process of unconscious interpretation, so is the attribution of agency and intention to certain kinds of actions and circumstances.

Sometimes the cognitive structures and dynamics through which our minds perceive reality can result in bizarre illusions that can often be funny and even fun. But at other times, the illusions generated by those systems can have more serious results.

Implicit Bias

When we encounter a person, our cognitive devices immediately begin to process that encounter. A representation of the person is immediately and unconsciously produced in the mind. That image provokes an unconscious search for categories in the mind and for the implicit beliefs about that category (the folk knowledge referred to above) with its accompanying behavioral scripts. This all happens instantaneously. The HADD detects an agent (someone who acts based on intentions and purposes), the ToM tries to intuit its intentions, and our behavioral scripts trigger possible appropriate actions. Before our reflective, slow, deliberative beliefs come online, allowing us to determine if the judgments of our nonreflective belief systems were accurate, we might find ourselves acting.

Thus, when we turn and see a face, we might jump and gasp only to immediately realize that it is our friend standing right next to us. Under other circumstances, it might be that our nonreflective beliefs have been inundated by negative associations of certain types of faces, skin colors, or types of dress with danger (for example, a Black phenotype, Arab accent, or turban). When faced with a person who fits those characteristics, our behavioral scripts for fight or flight might be automatically activated, sometimes resulting in tragic, horrible consequences. A Black child playing with a water gun gets shot down by the police; desperate migrants seeking asylum are left to die and rot in the desert because they are viewed as invaders, potential criminals, or an infection; trans youth are humiliated, attacked, and disfigured; Indigenous girls and boys are disappeared or murdered with little to no accountability. The illusions generated by the colonized mind are deadly.

This is not just speculation. Cognitive scientists have devised experimental methods to measure the way implicit bias operates despite our best intentions. In an article in the *Journal of Lutheran Ethics* titled "Exploring the Role of Unconscious Bias in the Immigration Debate and the Transformative Power of the Church,"[46] I summarize how these experiments are carried out in the following way:

> An important example of one such indirect measurement of implicit bias is the Implicit Association Test (IAT). Originally developed by Anthony G. Greenwald and colleagues,[47] and later adapted and revised by others, this approach is based on how the human mind implicitly categorizes information in a way such that images and concepts that are considered to be similar are automatically coupled together and are therefore easy to associate. Greenwald uses the example of the implicit association between male faces with male names and female faces with female names. In the test each image or concept is paired up with a behavioral response. You are instructed to say "hello" whenever you see a male face or a male name, and to say "good-bye" whenever you see a female face or a female name. The names and the faces are selected to be unambiguous. Then the procedure changes slightly. The instruction now is to continue to say "hello" when male images are flashed

46. Carmelo Santos, "Exploring the Role of Unconscious Bias in the Immigration Debate and the Transformative Power of the Church," *Journal of Lutheran Ethics* (December 13, 2013), https://www.elca.org/JLE/Articles/27.

47. A. G. Greenwald et al., "Measuring Individual Differences in Social Cognition: The Implicit Association Test," *Journal of Personality and Social Psychology* 74 (1998): 1464–80.

on the screen, but to say good-bye, instead of "hello," when male names appear. Likewise, when female faces appear the response should be "good-bye" but when female names appear the correct response should be "hello." The result is a significant decrease in the reaction time.

The test becomes more interesting when images are paired up with words that have emotional connotations. Consider the following variation of the test. Words appear on a computer screen, one at a time. If the word is the name of a flower, you click a key with your right index finger. If the word names something pleasant, also click with the right index finger. Alternatively, if the word that appears names something unpleasant, you are instructed to click with the left index finger on a different key; if the word is the name of an insect, also click with the left index finger. For the second phase of the experiment the two latter terms are switched. Now you are supposed to click with the right index finger for words that name flowers or unpleasant things. Click with the left index finger if the word names an insect or a pleasant thing. The reaction speed decreases considerably when unpleasant words are associated with flowers, and pleasant words with insects. Greenwald describes his own reaction after he performed the test: "When I experienced the slowing I found to my surprise that I could not overcome it—repeating the task did not make me faster. If I tried to go faster, I just started making errors when I was trying to give the same response to flower names and unpleasant words. This was a mind-opener."[48] Responses become slower because participants have to override the intuitive subconscious associations that already exist in the participants' minds among concepts or images. Therefore, the test offers an indirect way to determine what images or concepts participants intuitively associate with positive meanings on the

48. A. G. Greenwald and B. A. Nosek, "Attitudinal Dissociation: What Does It Mean?" in *Attitudes: Insights from the New Implicit Measures*, ed. R. E. Petty et al. (Erlbaum, 2008), 65–82, cited in G. Beatie, *Our Racist Heart? An Exploration of Unconscious Prejudice in Our Everyday Life* (Routledge, 2013), 139–40.

> one hand, and what images or concepts participants intuitively associate with negative meanings, on the other.
>
> Tests like the IAT allow researchers to compare peoples' reported attitudes about race, ethnicity, class, gender, etc., vis-à-vis their implicit attitudes.[49] In those types of experiments participants are asked to rate their relative attitudes towards their own group and towards a different group (e.g., White versus Black).[50] . . . Then they go through a series of tasks similar to those described above. But instead of insects or flowers this time, what is flashed are faces and words with positive meanings or negative meanings. You may take the test online at: https://implicit.harvard.edu/implicit/.

Sadly, those implicit biases, or cognitive illusions, also infect the minds of peoples and groups against whom they are deployed. This is part of the perniciousness and pervasiveness of systems of marginalization and minoritization. Once I had a conversation with a young man from an African country. We were discussing the history of colonialism in our respective countries. At the end of the conversation, my friend said, "The problem we have is that after we were able to get rid of the colonizers, we learned that they had left mini colonizers behind. Before they colonized us; now we colonize ourselves." In the words of that fierce critic of colonialism Frantz Fanon, by way of Homi Bhabha, the cognitive distortions effected in the colonized individual by the white supremacist project of colonialism create a situation where the former "desires not merely to be in the place of the white man but compulsively seeks to look back and down on himself from that position."[51]

The illusions generated by the cognitive systems of the mind are not accidental. If our minds are like computers, then racism, sexism, xenophobia, transphobia, homophobia, ableism, and any other ideologies and

---

49. R. H. Fazio et al., "Variability in Automatic Activation as an Unobtrusive Measure of Racial Attitudes: A Bona Fide Pipeline?," *Journal of Personality and Social Psychology* 69 (1995): 1013–27.

50. Beatie revised and expanded the IAT to measure implicit bias based on ethnicity as well as on race; for a description of his method, see Beatie, *Our Racist Heart?*, 151–63.

51. Homi Bhabha, *The Location of Culture* (Routledge, 1994), 86.

implicit biases that disfigure our mental representation of those who are supposed to bear our heavenly Creator's image can be thought of as viruses in the cognitive systems of the mind (and, as we shall see shortly, of the body as well). Such illusion-generating cognitive viruses are the way in which the coloniality of power became encoded in our minds.

Liberation, then, requires the transformation of our reality through the renewal of our minds. That involves a process of decolonizing not only our beliefs and biases but also, at a deeper level, a renewal of the very cognitive apparatus that weaves our perceptual world into existence. That renewal, as I argue in the following chapters, requires a process of decolonizing emotions; that is, the transformation has to be of our holistic embodied selves. It is my contention that theological language, incarnated in practices, narratives, sacraments, symbols, and relationships, has the power to do that.

Renewing Our Minds

My proposal, explored in this book from the perspective of the Christian faith, is that many of our religious symbols, rituals, narratives and practices have the power to renew our minds when engaged in ways that are faithful to the spirit of Jesus and the prophetic tradition that he was a part of. These items can bring about a transformation that includes the liberation of the brain through the decolonization of the cognitive and, as I argue in the following chapters, affective process that has been wounded by the contexts of coloniality, patriarchy, white supremacy, and other systems of exclusion, exploitation, and marginalization.

From the perspective of what we have gleaned about the functioning of the mind from cognitive science, it is important to lift up the need to "debug" the cognitive devices operating underneath our conscious mind. One way to do so is by fostering a critical and inquisitive mind and a spirituality of curiosity about those who are different from us, especially those whom we have been taught to mistrust, to fear, and even to hate. There is no substitute for actually daring to meet the other and to enter into relationships with each other, especially those with whom we find it difficult to do so. Otherwise, instead of actually knowing each other, what we think we know is simply the mental representation of others, with their accompanying intuitive characteristics generated not by reality but rather by the biases passed on and accumulated from generation to generation. Later in the book, I will argue for the importance of language in the process of debugging or decolonizing our minds, but here I want to dwell on the importance of human encounters for such transformation.

Churches, synagogues, masjids, gurdwaras, and other places of worship that are places of encounter with the holy Other can also become spaces for encounters with our human others. In reality, both from the perspective of faith and from the perspective of science, there is no "other"; we are all related, but we have become alienated from each other in such ways that we have forgotten the fundamental insight that, together, we constitute one body and that we are therefore members of each other. What happens to one affects all the others whether we know it or not, and what benefits the whole must also be for the benefit of the individual members. Opportunities to meet each other, to listen to each other's stories, and to become acquainted with each other's dreams, yearnings, joys, and sorrows is a powerful way to shatter the illusions generated by the colonized mind. Additionally, literature and art can be a powerful way to enter the world of the other in transformative ways, such as through the work of literary geniuses Tony Morrison,[52] Gloria Anzaldúa,[53] Edwidge Dandicat,[54] Ocean Vuong,[55] and many others.

Through rituals, religious spaces can become opportunities for rehearsing different, more wholesome ways of relating to each other. As we saw above, rituals have the power to reshape our beliefs. Rituals such as kissing or embracing (as some churches do during the passing of the peace), especially when they are done with people whom we know are different from us or have ideological differences from us, can begin to transform the unconscious predispositions that we might have against them. Other rituals become embodied forms of becoming aware that a different world (a different way of relating to each other) is possible. A powerful practice that can be done alone or in the company of others and is helpful in transforming once-implicit biases and instinctive reactions to others is the practice of contemplation. For instance, in his book *Teachings on Love*, the Vietnamese Buddhist monk Thích Nhât

52. Toni Morrison, *Beloved* (Vintage International, 1987).

53. Gloria Anzaldúa, *Borderlands/La Frontera: The New Mestiza*, 3rd ed. (Aunt Lute Books, 2007).

54. Edwidge Danticat, *Breath, Eyes, Memory* (Vintage Contemporary, 1994).

55. Ocean Vuong, *On Earth We're Briefly Gorgeous* (Penguin, 2019).

Hanh offers several examples of concrete contemplation exercises where we can practice extending compassion to those who have hurt us or to those whom we have hurt and learn how to change the frame through which we perceive those whom we have learned to mistrust or hate.[56]

From the perspective of those who live under the enduring effects of external and internalized forces such as coloniality, racism, heteropatriarchy, and other historical forms of oppression and marginalization, it is important to sharpen the critical edge of our minds and not be afraid to constantly ask why. How did things come to be this way? Could they be otherwise? Why not? It is also helpful to remind ourselves of the difference between the representation of us in the collective imaginary of our society displayed in movies, political discourses, and people's "innocent" jokes (i.e., microaggressions) and the way things actually are.[57] I am not the caricature that this society, under the influence of collective and individual sin, presents of me. You are not the caricature that they say you are! Who we are is a mystery, not static but in a constant process of becoming, of being renewed and constantly enriched, of shortcomings and mistakes but also of learnings from those shortcomings and mistakes.

We are the children of generations that came before us and that managed to somehow beat the odds and pass their lives on to us. We must seek with curiosity the story of who we are and where we came from. Often, that story is not written in books but in oral traditions, in songs and dances, in legends and myths, in heirlooms and family lore, and in practices and particular ways of saying and doing things. Somehow those traditions live on and are available to us if we know whom to ask and if we have the patience to receive them, unlearning what we thought we knew and learning how to learn anew. We must feed those elements to our minds, to the cognitive devices that create the perceptual worlds in which we live, including, as we shall see shortly, even the bodies we inhabit. Those "subjugated knowledges" and traditions, that ancestral wisdom, has the power to renew our minds and transform our reality in liberating and healing ways.

56. Thích Nhất Hanh, *Teachings on Love* (Parallax Press, 2007).

57. The word *imaginary* here and throughout the book refers loosely to Jacques Lacan's concept of the mental contents used to construct a person's self-identity. We will briefly explore the work of Lacan in the coda of this chapter.

Ultimately, from a perspective of faith, the renewal of our minds and the transformation of our reality is a gift from the divine Spirit. In chapter 4, we will explore how it might be that the divine Spirit brings about that change from the bottom up, from our bodies all the way to our brains and minds, from our guts to our cerebral cortex, and from there to the reality we live in. But for now, we can simply say that God's Spirit operates by incarnated means, and so it is by receiving those concrete means that we open ourselves to the stirring action of the Spirit that brings about renewal and transformation. Those means are not ethereal or abstruse; they are simple, mundane, and earthly. They are stories, symbols, food, rituals, and experiences that, to use a phrase from my own Lutheran tradition, when they are imbued with the promises of God become the means of God's action in the world—in, on, under, within, and through them.

In order to understand how those wonder-full things take place, we must first turn our attention to the locus where they happen; that is, we must now examine how the embodied brain and the nervous system operate.

Conclusion

In this chapter, we have seen that the mind seems to have an internal structure and that it is possible to decipher that structure. We learned that the mind consists of many processes operating like computer programs acting on mental representations of reality and that most of this happens below the threshold of conscious awareness. We also learned that those processes do not operate in a lineal series but more in parallel, even if the information generated by one process can then be fed into another cognitive system. The result is that there is sometimes division within our minds and between our beliefs and actions.

We saw how cognitions consist of beliefs that are of two kinds: reflective and nonreflective. We explored how nonreflective beliefs support reflective ones and how they are shaped by internal dynamics (like the memorability of minimally counterintuitive beliefs) and external influences (like the effects of rituals on beliefs). Finally, we emphasized throughout the chapter that the same cognitive processes underlying religious beliefs are responsible for all beliefs in general and that by beliefs, cognitive scientists refer to knowledge, whether that knowledge is true or not.

The reason we have spent time exploring the structure of the mind according to cognitive science is because it is with our minds that we make sense of both religious experiences and the world in general. It is with the mind that we read the significance of the sacred in religious symbols and rituals, and it is with the mind that we make sense of our relations to other people and to reality. Therefore, it is important to understand as much as possible which of the attributes that we perceive about God, ourselves, others, social structures and dynamics, and the world in general come from the realities themselves and which features might be more the result of the systems through which we perceive, know, and experience them. In the end, it is not possible to disentangle the mind from that which the mind perceives, but it is helpful to be aware of the structures and systems shaping our perceptions and knowledge and the dynamics that shape them. In the end, all knowledge is provisional and tentative and should always be open to revision when more adequate alternatives emerge.

Coda

Other Approaches to the Study of the Mind

Even though the focus of this book is on the implications of cognitive and affective neuroscience for a liberation and decolonial theology, it is important to acknowledge the significant contributions that other approaches to the study of the mind have made, to psychology, to theology, and to decolonial studies. It is impossible to do justice to each of these approaches in this limited space, but let's explore them in general strokes.

Introspection

Perhaps the oldest approach to studying the mind is via introspection. We all have a mind; therefore, if we want to study the mind, where better to start than by turning our mind upon itself and comparing it to how we observe the minds of others functioning? For example, Plato wrote that his teacher, Socrates, examined in-depth the processes by which the mind seems capable of acquiring knowledge. He did so by employing thought experiments and dialectical dialogues to examine different issues from various perspectives. In a classic example, he observed how a servant who was not formally trained in mathematics was nevertheless able to acquire new knowledge in the subject by simply following a thought process guided by his interlocutor. The servant was able to "recollect" mathematical facts that he had not previously known.

This led Socrates to conclude that since the newly acquired mathematical knowledge was not derived from observing external things but exclusively through mental reasoning, it must be that the mind had somehow actually had access to those ideas but had forgotten them. This was the genesis of the famous thesis, unfolded by Plato, that there is a realm of pure ideas and, furthermore, that the human mind corresponds to an immortal soul that prior to becoming enfleshed in a human body, communes with the pure ideas in that realm. Therefore, the process of learning is actually a process of remembering, and the process of teaching is a kind of cognitive midwifing, what Plato, following Socrates, called maieutic.

Plato's disciple, Aristotle, took a very different approach and came to the conclusion that the ideas do not actually exist in a realm separate from the material one but rather are inherent to the things themselves. Therefore, it is by studying the things in themselves and the relationships among them that we are able to acquire right ideas. In that way, Aristotle's ideas were a precursor to science based on observation, whereas Plato's became the precursor of the rationalist tradition, which viewed knowledge derived from pure reasoning as more trustworthy than knowledge acquired through empirical observation. Socrates, Plato, and Aristotle had a profound influence on the way Christian theology has come to understand the human mind and person in general.

Augustine of Hippo used Plato's psychology and epistemology, as well as Neoplatonism, to develop his theological anthropology, whereas Thomas Aquinas did the same with the thought of Aristotle. The Danish philosopher and theologian Søren Kierkegaard went back to Socrates as one of his main sources of inspiration. From Augustine we get a deep appreciation for mystical intuition as a source of knowledge; from Aquinas we get an emphasis on the importance of observation and rigorous reasoning as an avenue to trustworthy knowledge; and from Kierkegaard we get the importance of considering one's perspective and the dynamics of existence as key to understanding how the mind works.

René Descartes was another foundational thinker in the Western tradition who made use of the introspective approach. He reflected on how the knowledge we acquire through the senses can be deceiving (like the exhibits at the Museum of Illusion, mentioned above). He set out on an intellectual quest for a rock-solid foundation upon which we could build true, accurate knowledge. After a long and meticulous process of introspective reasoning, Descartes arrived at his famous conclusion: "I think, therefore I am" (*cogito, ergo sum*). He believed that was the most fundamental idea because it was undeniable, and thus all knowledge had to be built on that foundation for it to be secure. He also came to the realization that when we observe reality, there seem to be two different kinds of things: the things that are being observed and the things doing the observing. The things being observed seemed to him to be characterized by the fact that they are extended in space and can be divided into parts. Thus, he called them *res extensa* (extended stuff or substance). He characterized the thing doing the observing—that is, the mind—as not being divisible and not being extended in space. He simply called it *res cogitans* (thinking stuff or substance). To Descartes, then, we owe the dividing of reality into material stuff (including the human body and brain) on the one hand and nonmaterial minds on the other. And even though he postulated that the *res cogitans*, the soul, lived in the brain (in the pineal gland), his legacy has been a dualism that divorced the body from its mind and the mind from its body. In theology, this idea had the effect of devaluing issues related to the body and to material reality while overvaluing matters of the supposedly disembodied mind/soul.

Another influential Western thinker in the Western introspective tradition, whom we already met above, is Søren Kierkegaard. Working at the intersection of theology, philosophy, and literature, he dove deep into existential questions of the human experience. What was unique about his approach is that he explored those questions from different personality types and perspectives. He actually assumed different personalities through the use of pseudonyms, while he also wrote things under his own name. For instance, he explored how reality is experienced from the perspective of three different stages of human development: the aesthetic (sensual), the ethical (duty), and the religious (faith). Philosophers in the existentialist tradition, like Jean-Paul Sartre, Albert Camus, and Martin Heidegger, received from Kierkegaard the idea that instead of thinking of the human being in terms of a stable essence that can be identified and characterized, humans are in the process of becoming whatever they will be as they exist. As Kierkegaard comically put it in the title of one of his writings: "From the Papers of One Still

Living."[58] Authentic existence is what distinguishes humans as such and what makes it impossible to produce an all-encompassing theory capable of predicting human behavior and decision-making. Therefore, lived experience is the arena where introspective insights get tested. The closest he came to describing the structure of the human mind or person was to say that humans are a synthesis of the finite and the infinite; that is, we experience ourselves as finite creatures who are capable of embracing the infinite.

Those are only a few examples of the influence of the introspective approach to studying the human mind in the Western tradition. In Eastern traditions, that approach has been more prominent, especially in fields such as Buddhist psychology. A shortcoming of the introspective approach is that the human mind is notoriously fickle, again as demonstrated by the Museum of Illusions, and a lot of the mental processes that lead to our actions are often hidden from introspection. In a very real way, we are a mystery to ourselves. Nonetheless, as neuroscientist Antonio Damasio puts it, "Introspection has its limits, but it has no rival, let alone a substitute. It provides the only direct window into the phenomena we wish to understand."[59]

It has been argued that a lot of the European continental philosophical tradition has in fact been an introspection projected onto historical processes or an abstract spiritual force shaping society.[60] The introspective approach has been tremendously important for theology as well, particularly for mystical theology and Protestant liberal theology, where inner experience served as an entry point to the experience of the divine.

The challenge of the introspective approach both in theology and in philosophy is how to distinguish between the machinations of the human imagination and the realities one is trying to understand. As we saw above, the cognitive science of religion might offer a helpful

---

58. Søren Kierkegaard, "From the Papers of One Still Living," in *The Essential Kierkegaard*, ed. H. Hong and E. Hong (Princeton University Press, [1838] 2000), 13–19.

59. Antonio Damasio, *Feeling and Knowing: Making Minds Conscious* (Vintage, 2021), 8.

60. See Robert C. Solomon, *Continental Philosophy since 1750: The Rise and Fall of the Self*, History of Western Philosophy vol. 7 (Oxford University Press, 1988), 4–5.

theoretical framework to address that challenge, which in theology is connected to the question of idolatry—that is, of elevating things that are not God (including, as Ludwig Feuerbach demonstrated, projections of one's self) to divine status. Notwithstanding those issues, the introspective approach continues to be irreplaceable in theology, philosophy, and the scientific study of the mind.

Behaviorism

A rival approach to introspection is behaviorism. During the first half of the twentieth century, behaviorism was the dominant approach to the scientific study of the mind or, more precisely, of behavior. If introspection sought to explore the mind by going deep within it, behaviorists assumed that what happens inside the mind is not available for scientific examination because it is too subjective and mysterious. Searching for a more scientific approach, behaviorists decided to focus on that which they believed could be observed directly and meticulously measured: they focused on behaviors. The behaviorist approach consisted of finding associations between input information and output behavior.

Though Ivan Pavlov was not a strict behaviorist, his work, particularly his experiments that led to the theory of classical conditioning, were a precursor to behaviorism. He set up an experiment where dogs were fed right after being exposed to a signal, like the ringing of a bell or the flashing of a light. He observed that the dogs would begin salivating when they heard the bell or saw the light, in expectation of the meal. Interestingly, after a while, the dogs would salivate after the signal even if they were not given any food. The dogs were conditioned to respond to an external input with a specific behavior. Later, behaviorists took that to mean that behavior is a function of the environment.

Thus, in the behaviorist approach, the internal life of the mind was not only seen as irrelevant for the study of human and animal behavior, but also, by extension, it was perceived as extraneous to the forces that truly shaped the human person. A critique of the original behaviorist approach is that it did not account for the dimension of thought in human behavior and therefore undervalued the aspects of agency and subjectivity in human decision-making. Nonetheless, as we shall see in chapter 2, the clever experimental designs of the behaviorists eventually opened the door for finding ways to observe thought processes indirectly by measuring physiological or behavioral responses correlated to such thought processes. Additionally, the rigorous examination of environmental factors with behavioral responses has led to important insights and therapies to aid people dealing with trauma and post-traumatic stress disorder. Today, cognitive behavioral therapy, which combines elements of behaviorism and cognitive psychology, is one of the most effective approaches to addressing a wide range of mental health issues.

Furthermore, behaviorism's search for statistically significant correlations between input information and output responses (whether behavioral or physiological) paved the way for studying spiritual phenomena and practices such as mystical experiences, altered states of consciousness, meditation, prayer, and many others by measuring corresponding physiological markers in practitioners. The challenge of those approaches lies in ascertaining causation rather than simple correlation. Another challenge is to tease apart the overwhelming complexity that goes into human behavior, cognition, and decision-making, particularly when it involves religious beliefs, practices, and spiritual experiences. We will explore how researchers are navigating those opportunities and challenges in chapter 3 when we deal with neurotheology and the neuroscience of religious experience.

Psychoanalysis

Another approach to the study of the human mind that was also prevalent during the first half of the twentieth century and continues to have its faithful followers today, though in modified form, is the psychoanalysis pioneered by the Austrian psychiatrist Sigmund Freud and later developed by analysts and intellectuals such as Carl Jung, Jacques Lacan, Erich Fromm, Anna Freud, Melanie Klein, Juliet Mitchell, Jacqueline Rose, and Julia Kristeva. If the introspective approach focused almost exclusively on thought and behaviorism on behaviors, psychoanalysis focused on the unconscious aspects of both thought and behavior, especially as they related to people's emotional experience. Freud, based on his clinical observations, zeroed in on the idea that the real causes of a lot of human behaviors and ideations are actually beyond our control and are hidden from our conscious awareness. To use an analogy, if our mind is like a house, a lot of what goes on in the house is happening in the basement, in the unconscious, where we cannot see it.

According to this school of thought, many of these unconscious processes are the result of experiences with strong emotional import, which primarily happen during the formative years of our infancy and childhood. The forces of the unconscious are shaped by our biological drives, urges, and desires (what Freud called the id); by our societal norms (internalized as the superego); and especially by the influences of our parental and other significant relationships and experiences in early childhood. Those forces are hidden from our conscious, self-aware self (the ego) and manifest themselves indirectly as bizarre behaviors, strange dreams, slips of the tongue, and other neuroses. There is a never-ending struggle between our conscious self and the desires and fears of the powerful unconscious dimension of our personality, which are in the unconscious because they have been repressed. This repression occurs because the desires and fears are deemed unacceptable by the internalized rules of society, morality, or religion that structure our idea of who we are supposed to be and how we are supposed to behave.

The dynamics that shape our unconscious drives begin in early childhood. Think, for example, of a baby's desire for the mother's breast or milk. How the mother responds to that need/desire will be an important factor for the way in which that child will relate to others, even as an adult. Similarly, the child's yearning for the mother's love (Freud actually spoke of the incestuous desire of the child for the parent, but later psychoanalytic schools have moved away from Freud's hyperfocus on that aspect) and the experience of the child observing how the father is the recipient of that love make the child jealous of the father (according to Freud's patriarchal, heteronormative worldview), leading to secret fantasies of eliminating him as a way of removing the only obstacle to acquiring the object of desire.[61] Freud made use of the Greek myth of Oedipus to illustrate this dynamic; hence the name "Oedipus complex." The father's position in the family and in society represents the object of desire and is symbolized by the phallus. The phallus is not necessarily the biological penis but the power associated with the paterfamilias in Western civilization.

---

61. As a side note, Freud's daughter Anna Freud was also a brilliant psychologist and dedicated her life to understanding the healthy mental and emotional development of girls and young women. Lisa Damour's *Untangled: Guiding Teenage Girls Through the Seven Transitions into Adulthood* (Ballantine, 2017) is partly inspired by Anna Freud.

The father figure, however, also represents a force of repression for the child, not only because it is the father who has what the unconscious desires, but also because it is the figure of the father who keeps the child from gaining access to the object of their desires. Thus, Lacan speaks of the "no of the father," which has a play of significations in French and also sounds like "the name of the father" (*le nom du père*). It is the "no" of the father—that is, the law of the father—that sets the boundaries between the child (and, eventually, the adult that the child will become) and the object of their secret desire. The father is feared, resented, and desired at the same time.

In addition to the formative influences of parental relations in the child's psyche, psychoanalysis also considered the way powerful emotional experiences later in life shaped human behavior and thought patterns. Those experiences that are too threatening, shameful, confusing, or overwhelming become pressed down (that is, repressed) to the dark basement of the human unconscious. However, they are so powerful that from within the unconscious, they influence behaviors, emotional responses, and thoughts. Those unconscious forces can be accessed only obliquely. It is through dreams, "Freudian slips" of the tongue (when we accidentally say something very different from what we meant to say that yet seems revealing of our true but repressed desires), and other indirect ways (such as the Rorschach inkblot test and techniques designed to elicit spontaneous, uncensored storytelling) that psychoanalysts can identify and analyze the unconscious forces driving the problematic behaviors or oppressive thought patterns. The psychoanalyst, then, together with the patient, attempts to decipher the intrinsic code operative in the deployment of those signs by the unconscious, similar to trying to figure out the grammar of an unknown language. That way, the secret drives are brought to light and, ideally, lose their grip on the patient because now the patient has become aware of the real reason for their neurotic behaviors, compulsions, or thought patterns and can channel them in healthier and more constructive ways.

Psychoanalysis has gone beyond the study of individual minds and is now also applied to study societal dynamics in general. This approach has been particularly fruitful in analyzing the collective unconscious forces active in our culture, driving sexism, racism, xenophobia, homophobia, transphobia, ableism, and classism as well as in analyzing regimes of systemic oppression like patriarchy, white supremacy, and colonialism. By wedding psychoanalytic techniques and insights with literary theory, social analyses such as Marxism and cultural anthropology have, with various degrees of success, been able to interpret the ways that cultural productions like novels, songs, plays, movies, jokes, language in general, and even monuments, museums, religious texts and practices, architecture, and city design, display traces of the hidden forces that structure oppressive systems of exclusion and hierarchical orderings of society. Thus, psychoanalysis has become a very powerful tool in the work of feminist, postcolonial, decolonial, and queer thinkers,[62] as well as in the work of liberation theologians.

However, one big shortcoming of the psychoanalytic approach is that it depends too much on the subjectivity of the analyst. Like the introspective approach, it lacks an objective way to validate its interpretations. Nonetheless, it has proven to be a powerful lens into the hidden forces shaping the human mind and behavior, and in theology it has provided a helpful grammar to translate the dimensions of faith, spirituality, and religion in the human experience into alternative but complementary language beyond the specialized terminology and inside language of any given religious group.[63]

---

62. See Jan Campbell, *Arguing with the Phallus: Feminist, Queer, and Postcolonial Theory. A Psychoanalytic Contribution* (Zed Books, 2000).

63. An example is the way Paul Tillich applied the categories of what he called depth psychology to theological loci; see, for example, his *Dynamics of Faith* (Perennial Classics, 1957).

CHAPTER TWO

The Brain

Temple of the Body

> For it was you who formed my inward parts;
> you knit me together in my mother's womb.
> I praise you, for I am fearfully and wonderfully made.
> Wonderful are your works;
> that I know very well.
>
> —Psalms 149:13-14

Introduction

Searching for the Mind

Where Mind Happens

Brains

THE UNDERSTANDING THAT the brain is the organ of the mind is of recent vintage. It was only after scientists realized that there was a causal link between damage to the brain and the impairment of mental functions that it became obvious that mind and brain were connected. That was further confirmed thanks to the development of technologies that allowed for the selective and precise activation or inhibition of particular regions (or neural networks) of the brain in order to examine how mental and behavioral functions were affected by such manipulations. Those technologies included surgically cutting specific regions, using special drugs to disrupt functioning, applying electrical or magnetic pulses to the regions of interest, or more recently, knocking out or switching genes involved in the functioning of particular neural networks and then observing what effects those interventions had in the cognitive and behavioral responses of the organism being studied (from worms and mice to monkeys and humans).[1] The evidence for the central role of the brain in mental functioning is overwhelming. There is also increasing evidence, however, that to speak of the brain in isolation of the body and of its environments is a distortion of reality.[2]

Hearts and Guts

Prior to the consensus that the brain is where the mind happens, the heart and the cardiovascular system in general was seen as another option.[3] In the Hebrew and Christian Scriptures, it is the heart that is mostly associated with the mind, but the kidneys, the gut, and perhaps the throat are also associated with functions of the mind. Contrary to contemporary usage, the heart is associated with thinking and deliberative decision-making, whereas the viscera (the kidneys and the gut) are linked with the emotional or affective dimensions of the mind. Nonetheless, in biblical thought in general and especially in the Hebrew Scriptures, the mind is not conceived as a separate entity in and of itself but rather as a function of the entire person,[4] and the person is always a member of a community, a *corpus* that is as important to their personhood as the other body. The famous tension between the flesh and the spirit, articulated so powerfully by Paul in his letter to the Romans,[5] is

1. Elisabeth A. Murray and Mark G. Baxter, "Cognitive Neuroscience and Nonhuman Primates: Lesion Studies," in Senior et al., *Methods in Mind*, 43–68.

2. For a beautiful and rigorously scientific reflection on the dependence of the brain and the mind on the body and its environment, see Antonio Damasio, *Looking for Spinoza: Joy, Sorrow, and the Feeling Brain* (Mariner Books, 2003), especially chapter 5, "Body, Brain, and Mind," 183–220; in Spanish, see Nazareth Castellanos, *Neurociencia del cuerpo: Cómo el organismo esculpe el cerebro* (Barcelona: Editorial Kairós, 2022).

3. Malcolm Jeeves and Warren S. Brown summarize the debate between the encephalic and the cardiovascular theories in "From Soul to Mind: A Brief History," *Neuroscience, Psychology, and Religion*, 24–30.

4. Allen C. Myers, ed., "Mind," in *The Eerdmans Bible Dictionary* (Eerdmans, 1987), 720–21.

5. "For those who live according to the flesh set their minds on the things of the flesh, but those who live according to the Spirit set their minds on the things of the Spirit. To set the mind on the flesh is death, but to set the mind on the Spirit is life

not a fight between two parts of the human being but rather a tension between two possible orientations of the entire embodied person.[6] As noted above, contemporary neuroscience is also embracing the idea that the mind or the functions of the mind do not live in any one particular organ or segment of the human brain or body but rather that they are enabled by the working together of many networks throughout the brain and the human body and distributed among their physical, natural, and cultural environments.

Lessons from Phrenology

Mapping the Mind on the Head

The idea underlying phrenology was that the bumps on the head corresponded to areas of the brain that were more prominent in some people than in others. And, most importantly, each spot on the brain corresponded to a specific mental ability or function or to an aspect of the personality. Therefore, by examining the bumps on someone's head, it was possible to assess the qualities of their mind. The way that brain scans are used today in the popular media is worryingly similar to phrenology. The problem with phrenology, as it turns out, is that it did not account for the flexibility (plasticity) and dynamism of the human brain and the role of the body and the environment in shaping it.

---

and peace. For this reason the mind that is set on the flesh is hostile to God; it does not submit to God's law—indeed, it cannot, and those who are in the flesh cannot please God" (Rom 8:5–8).

6. For explorations of different biblical views of the human person, including the embodied brain, informed by the sciences of the mind and brain, see, for example, Nancey Murphy, *Bodies and Souls, or Spirited Bodies?* Current Issues in Theology (Cambridge University Press, 2006), especially chapter 1, "Do Christians Need souls? Theological and Biblical Perspectives on Human Nature," 1–37. See also Joel B. Green, ed., *What About the Soul? Neuroscience and Christian Anthropology* (Abingdon Press, 2004); and in Spanish, Giacomo Canobbio, *Sobre el alma: Más allá de mente y cerebro* (Salamna, España: Ediciones Sígueme, 2010); Pius-Ramón Tragán, ed., *Neurociencias y espíritu: ¿Abiertos a una vida eterna?* (Navarra, España: Verbo Divino, 2012); and Carmelo Santos, *Estudiando la Biblia desde una perspectiva de neurociencia: cuatro estudios bíblicos*, http://www.esperanza.us/wp-content/uploads/2021/09/Estudiando-la-Biblia-desde-una-perspectiva-de-neurociencia-cuatro-estudios-bíblicos.pdf.

Phrenology was also flawed from a scientific perspective because it relied on only observations and speculation but did not have a rigorous process for testing its speculations (experimentation) or a means for them to be falsified, which is fundamental for the development of reliable scientific knowledge.[7] Phrenology was also deeply problematic and dangerous because it was used as a weapon in the arsenal of the racist (including anti-Semitic), sexist, and ableist colonial project to try to give scientific grounding to untrue notions of the natural or innate inferiority and defectiveness of certain types of humans versus others.[8] White European heterosexual males of means were the model and archetype against which all others were measured.[9]

Dangers of the Ideal Brain

That danger is still present in contemporary uses of neuroscience. Is there a male brain versus a female brain? Is there such a thing as a gay brain or a straight brain, a nonbinary brain or a trans brain? A normal brain versus an autistic brain? Is there a Black, Latinx, Asian, Middle Eastern, or Native American brain? Is there a desirable brain type that psychiatric, psychological, therapeutic, pedagogical, penal, or religious interventions ought to seek to replicate, to use as a model for molding other (defective? underdeveloped?) brains? Of course, there are genuine forces that can do real damage to the human person and distort our brains, inhibiting them from functioning properly, but one must be vigilant of what biases and stereotypes (historical, cultural, disciplinary, and individual) get smuggled into our ways of assessing brain and mental health.

---

7. This is the assessment of Jeeves and Brown in *Neuroscience, Psychology, and Religion*, 30–36.

8. See, for example, the analysis of Susan Branson in "Phrenology and the Science of Race in Antebellum America," *Early American Studies* 15, no. 1 (Winter 2017): 164–93. However, in Stephen Jay Gould makes a distinction between "craniology," which he believed to be racist, and phrenology, which he defended as anti-racist because of the flexibility the multiplicity of spots on the head provided for diversity. "With such a view," he explains, "no number could possibly express general human worth. " (*The Mismeasure of Man* [W. W. Norton, 1996], 22). Unfortunately, I think history contradicts him on that point.

9. See Walter D. Mignolo, "The Invention of the *Human* and the Three Pillars of the Colonial Matrix of Power: Racism, Sexism, Nature," in Mignolo and Walsh, *On Decoloniality*, 153–76.

We must bear in mind that the brain, too, is a creation of the mind, which is not to say that the brain is not real but that the reality we encounter when we deal with brains is the mental representation of the brain that we have received from the functioning of our cognitive apparatuses under the influence of our schooling, cultural formation, and many other factors. Good science is aware of its own limits and that its models are only, at best, partial and provisional approximations of the reality (or a fragment of the reality) it seeks to understand.

Mesmerizing Pictures

When I attended the Neuroscience Boot Camp at the University of Pennsylvania, one of the professors, a renowned expert in the diagnosis and treatment of Alzheimer's disease, related the following story. He had been one of a small number of clinicians who had helped map Alzheimer's disease onto brain scans. In other words, the clinicians would assess (diagnose) patients with the condition and then radiologists would take scans of their brains and compare them to scans of people who had not been diagnosed with Alzheimer's disease. Certain similarities emerged. For example, the scans of several of the patients diagnosed with the condition exhibited common patterns of decreased activity in certain regions. However, not all people with similar brain scans presented with the symptoms of the disease. Likewise, there were patients who did present with the symptoms but did not have the pattern of the other patients on their brain scans. The interesting thing was that the professor diagnosed a patient with Alzheimer's disease after the project was over and the diagnosis was rejected by the insurance company. The reason they offered, said the professor with a tone of irony in his voice, was that the clinical assessment did not include a scan. He exclaimed that the only way the insurers would know those scans correspond to someone who might have the disease is because clinicians told them so, but now they believe the scan more than the clinician! When we look at a brain scan, or even at an actual brain, we might think that we are looking at an objective reality, but we are actually viewing a representation of that reality, as we saw in the previous chapter. The fascination with the brain and with the pretty images that neuroscientists can produce of the brain and its functions risks a myopic focus that distorts the reality by reducing it to one of its fragments.[10] The brain is important, but I have never seen a brain able to operate apart from its body and its proper environment, which includes other brains, other bodies, and their environments.

Where Brains Happen

Therefore, as we begin to explore the brain's anatomy and physiology (in very general strokes) it is important to be mindful of the following: when thinking about brains, we must think in the plural even when we speak in the singular; otherwise, we risk distorting that which we seek to understand. Brains need each other to function properly, just as bodies need each other to survive and thrive. How could a newborn survive without the care of others? How could our brains learn language without others to teach us? The poet John Donne put it beautifully: "No man is an island, entire of itself; every man is a piece of a continent, a part of the main."[11] The same is true of both the brain and the body: no brain is an island unto itself. A brain is but a piece of the continent that is the body, which incorporates vast networks of nerve extensions from and to the brain plus rivers and estuaries of neurotransmitters, hormones, enzymes, and much more.

And the continent of the body itself belongs to a planet that includes other continents of human bodies and brains plus our fellow nonhuman creatures, including animals, plants, fungi, minerals, and so on. In other words, brains do not exist alone. They are part of bodies that need certain kinds of environments (physical, material, social, cultural, and spiritual) in order to survive and thrive. When I speak of the brain in this chapter and in this book, I shall always be referring to the brain as distributed throughout the body by way of the nervous system, in relationship with the other organs and systems of the body, embedded in particular environments and networks of relationships, and immersed in worlds of meaning and purpose.[12]

---

10. For an analysis on how brain images are constructed, see Joseph Dumit, *Picturing Personhood: Brain Scans and Biomedical Identity* (Princeton University Press, 2004); and in Spanish, see Marino Pérez Álvarez, "El magnetismo de las neuroimágenes: Moda, mito e ideología," *Papeles del Psicólogo* 32, no. 2 (2011): 98–112, https://www.papelesdelpsicologo.es/pdf/1946.pdf.

11. John Donne, "Expostulation," *Devotions upon Emergent Occasions* (University of Michigan Press, [1624] 1959), no. 16, 108–9.

12. In doing so, I am following the lead of Varela et al., *The Embodied Mind*.

Furthermore, brains are created and creators at the same time. They are created because they are the result of the processes of nature that gave rise to them. From the perspective of faith, those natural processes participate in God's awesome work of creation.[13] Brains are also creators because, as we saw in the previous chapter, they create the perceptual worlds that we inhabit. Moreover, in creating those worlds, the brain also creates itself![14] As we shall see below, the brain operates by way of connections between neurons (supported by other types of cells called glial, or "white matter," plus rivers of neurochemicals, such as neurotransmitters, hormones, enzymes, DNA, and RNA), and every time we have a new experience, a new thought, or a new perception, neurons form or strengthen connections and networks of connections in the brain and across the embodied nervous system.

As our brains (co)create themselves and the perceptual worlds we inhabit, we also participate in the creation of the external worlds we share with others.[15] Through imagination, action, technology, collaboration, politics, activism, and so on, we give shape to the actual worlds

---

13. It is possible to understand the process of creation as both the free, intentional act of a loving God, creator of all that is, and as the result of natural processes as described by scientists. For examples of different ways of articulating that healthy and creative tension between science and theology, see John F. Haught, *Making Sense of Evolution: Darwin, God, and the Drama of Life* (Westminster John Knox Press, 2010); Karl E. Peters, *Dancing with the Sacred: Evolution, Ecology, and God* (Trinity Press International, 2002); Langdon Gilkey, *Nature, Reality, and the Sacred: The Nexus of Science and Religion*, Theology and the Sciences (Fortress Press, 1993); Alejandro García-Rivera, *The Garden of God: A Theological Cosmology*, Theology and the Sciences (Fortress Press, 2009); Celia Deane-Drummond, *Creation Through Wisdom: Theology & the New Biology* (T&T Clark, 2000); Catherine Keller, *Face of the Deep: A Theology of Becoming* (Routledge, 2003).

14. The brain is not alone in its ability to co-create itself, as it turns out that autopoiesis, as Chilean biologist Humberto Maturana called it, is a common feature in the biological world. See Humberto R. Maturana and Francisco J. Varela, *The Tree of Knowledge: The Biological Roots of Human Understanding*, trans. Robert Paolucci (Shambhala Publications, 1992). The original Spanish version is *El árbol del conocimiento: Las bases biológicas del entendimiento humano* (Santiago, Chile: Lumen, editorial universatria, 2004).

15. This idea that humans are active participants in sculpting their own brains goes back to the Spanish biologist and artist Santiago Ramón y Cajal, to whom we owe knowing what neurons look like and how they are connected to each other. See Michael Gazzaniga et al., *Cognitive Neuroscience: The Biology of the Mind*, 4th ed. (W.W. Norton, 2014), 8–9; and in Spanish, see Nazareth Castellanos, "El cerebro de

we live in. Those worlds, in turn, will influence the formation of our brains and the brains of the future generations. Thus, one of my teachers, theologian Phil Hefner, often spoke of human beings as "created co-creators."[16] Given the fact that our brains are created co-creators, the processes of liberation must include freedom not only from the external conditions that imprison us, our communities, and our planet but also from the internal processes by which the brain forges the cognitive and emotional chains that imprison us from within, which then has tangible effects on the material world in which we live.

The reality that our brains weave for us can be of a world opened to change and new possibilities or of a world that is static and unchangeable. In one world, oppression, misery, and injustice are just the way things are, and the only way of coping with it is stoic acceptance. Then nothing changes, and our nonreflective belief that there is nothing that can be done to change things becomes confirmed. In the alternative possibility, we feel in our guts and heart that acceptance of a world of misery, oppression, and injustice cannot possibly be the only option, and we dare to dream of a different reality and weave, together with other dreamers, visions of a different world. Shared dreams collectively become visions and visions become goals, which inspire actions, tentative experiments, and then projects. Some of these projects will crystalize in new possibilities, changing the landscape of what is real and what is possible and making a way where there previously seemed to be none:

> I am about to do a new thing;
> now it springs forth; do you not perceive it?
> I will make a way in the wilderness
> and rivers in the desert.
> (Isa 43:19)[17]

Don Santiago," en *El espejo del cerebro*, séptima edición (Madrid: La huerta grande, 2022), 17–37.

16. Philip Hefner, *The Human Factor: Evolution, Culture, and Religion* (Fortress Press, 1993), especially chapter 2, "A Theology of the Created Co-Creator," 23–51; see also his book *Technology and Human Becoming* (Fortress Press, 2003).

17. See also Isa 65:17–18a.

The vision is not of a heaven far removed from this material world. The promise is not for souls apart from their bodies. The divine vision is of a radical transformation of this world, which includes our bodies, bodies that are the temple of the divine Spirit, bodies that are gently embraced by the fine fibers of the nervous system, bodies that almost mystically find their abode in the temple of the brain so that rather than experiencing disparate members, we experience ourselves and our bodies as one. Let's explore how this biological magic happens.

An Overview of the Human Brain and Its Study

At first glance, the brain does not look like much. It is a small, wrinkled piece of gelatinous flesh that does not seem to do much. No wonder Aristotle thought its only purpose was to refrigerate the blood![18] But upon closer inspection, it becomes clear how breathtakingly complex and beautiful the brain actually is. It took the professional rivalry between an Italian biologist and a Spanish artist-scientist in the late 1800s to early 1900s to bring the magnificent miniature forest that is the brain to the fore.

The story of this discovery is fascinating. The Italian biologist Camillo Golgi invented a chemical method of staining brain cells with a silver compound that turned individual neurons black, making them easier to examine under a light microscope. However, when viewed under a light microscope, brain tissue appears to be a tangled mess of fibers.[19] In fact, the way neurons look under the microscope is so unique compared to other biological tissues that it took scientists some time to realize that the brain, too, is made of cells. Brain tissue looks like a very dense forest. Golgi's method allowed for individual trees, or neurons, to be distinguished from their neighbors. There remained, however, a conundrum. How are the individual trees in the brain forest connected

---

18. Jeeves and Brown, *Neuroscience, Psychology, and Religion*, 25.

19. The overview of brain structures and functions presented here and used throughout the book is my own integration and interpretation of various sources, principally Gazzaniga et al., *Cognitive Neuroscience*; Antonio Damasio, *Descartes' Error: Emotion, Reason, and the Human Brain* (Quill, 2000) and *The Feeling of What Happens: Body and Emotion in the Making of Consciousness* (Harcourt, 1999); Castellanos, *Neurociencia del Cuerpo*; and the other sources cited throughout.

to each other? Golgi defended the position that neurons are physically connected to each other. His rival, Santiago Ramón y Cajal, defended the position that there is actually a tiny gap separating one neuron from the next. Cajal was right. The irony is that it was thanks to Golgi's method that he was able to prove it. That and the fact that he was an innate artist with a love of drawing. With a lot of patience, an endless supply of cow brains made available by his friend the local butcher, a simple light microscope, and his pad and pencil, the Iberian gave us the first images of what the trees of the neuronal forest look like. In 1906 Golgi and Cajal shared the Nobel Prize for their work on elucidating the structure of the nervous system.

Neurons, Axons, and Dendrites

The tiny gaps connecting neurons, discovered by Cajal (and Golgi), are known as synapses, or synapsis in the singular. The main body of the neuron, called the soma (from the Greek word for body), is like the trunk of the tree from where many extensions branch out, like the limbs of a tree. Those branches are called dendrites, and they are the sensors that receive the signals sent by other neurons. On the opposite side of the neuron's soma is a long extension called the axon. It is through the axon that the neuron sends information to other neurons, which is then received by their corresponding dendrites. Those signals travel through the neurons' axons and dendrites in the form of an electrical charge until they reach the synaptic gap. At that point, the axon releases a neurochemical molecule that is transported across the synaptic gap by another kind of molecule until it is delivered to the receiving dendrite. When the right amount of the required neurochemical has reached the receiving dendrite, its neuron begins to build up voltage until it spikes and the signal travels across its body and out the axon, reaching out to the next neuron and so on. However, the signals sent from one neuron to another can be excitatory, thus activating that neuron or network of neurons, or inhibitory, thus stopping or slowing down the activity of the receiving neuron or network of neurons. This fact is going to be important to remember in the next chapter when we explore what might be happening in the brain when people undergo mystical experiences.

The long fibers of axons and dendrites have segments wrapped in a material called myelin, which functions as an electrical insulator so that the electrochemical pulse won't leak out as it travels up the dendrite and down the axon. There are openings that allow for the sodium and potassium pumps that power the process to charge. In any case, an interesting fact is that in the developing brain of teenagers, the networks of neurons associated with prudence and impulse control are not fully myelinated, but those responsible for emotional, passionate responses are fully developed. The result is that parents and caregivers are in for a fun ride as they care for their beloved teens. But perhaps that is also why, throughout history, youth have always been powerful agents of change who throw themselves passionately, body and soul, into social and religious causes. Joan of Arc, Greta Thunberg, Malala Yousafzai, Mary of Nazareth, and Miriam (Aaron and Moses's sister) come to mind, despite the great differences among them and their historical circumstances.

Neurons, axons, dendrites, synapses, myelin sheaths, potassium/sodium pumps, neurotransmitters, and neurotransporters are not the only important elements of the brain. Even though going into detail is beyond the scope of the present work, it is important to at least become aware of other details regarding the brain. In addition to neurons, there are other kinds of cells throughout the brain, like those that produce the myelin sheathes. Initially, neuroscientists believed that the role of these glial cells was merely to provide insulation and scaffolding for neurons and occasionally clean up the waste left behind by the synaptic transport process. Recently, however, it has becoming increasingly clear that they play a more active role in the function of the brain and might be involved in processes of healing and regeneration. Research in this area is ongoing and fascinating.

Two Hemispheres, One Mind

One of the most obvious features of the human brain is that it is divided into two hemispheres.[20] For the most part, the structures of one hemisphere resemble those of the other hemisphere. But there are subtle differences in function, which are still being investigated. In the processing of language, for example, the dominant hemisphere (usually the left) focuses on the semantics and syntax of language. The right hemisphere,

---

20. The outline presented here is based mostly on my interpretation of Joseph LeDoux, *The Emotional Brain: The Mysterious Underpinnings of Emotional Life* (Simon & Schuster, 1996), 13–15, 32–33.

in turn, seems to focus more on tone, prosody, the emotional undertones of language, and the general categories to which words and phrases belong. If we were to receive words in only our nondominant hemisphere (the right one for the vast majority of people), we would most likely be unable to consciously see or hear the word, according to our conscious experience, but we would be able to guess what general category it might belong to, and we might even react to the word in ways that are emotionally appropriate.

The two hemispheres of the brain are connected by a thick layer of nerve fibers (axons and dendrites) called the *corpus callosum*. As soon as information arrives at a neural structure in one hemisphere of the brain, it sends that information to its counterpart in the other hemisphere. There is a lot of redundancy built into the processes of the brain, so if one part fails, another one might be able to take over. Unfortunately, there are also undesirable things that can get communicated from one hemisphere to another, such as the neural electrical discharges that cause epileptic seizures. In order to keep those neural electrical storms of seizures from spreading, after testing the procedure on non-human animals, neurosurgeons and patients decided that it was safe and worth the risk to cut through the thicket of nerve fibers of the corpus callosum connecting the two hemispheres. The procedure worked, but there were surprising side effects.

Neuroscientists Roger Sperry and Michael Gazzaniga conducted several experiments on these patients to assess how having a "split-brain" affected their perception and other cognitive processes. When images of composite objects, like a group of fruits (bananas, apples, etc.) arranged in the shape of a face, were shown to only the dominant hemisphere, the patients were able to see the fruits but not the face! When the image was shown to only the nondominant (i.e., right) hemisphere, only the face was perceived, and the fruits could not be identified.

Another interesting result was that when patients were shown images or words that required actions or that were designed to elicit an emotional response (like showing the face of a well-known hideous mass murderer), they would claim that they didn't see anything if the image was presented to only the non-dominant side. However, they would either proceed to carry out the instruction that had been presented to their non-dominant hemisphere or would respond emotionally—for instance, by suddenly getting angry at the researchers, even though they didn't consciously perceive the prompt. When asked to explain their behaviors, they always proceeded to offer believable but false explanations. For instance, "I waved because I thought I saw someone that I knew [not because the image instructed me to wave]." Or "I am angry at you because of the stupid questions you ask [not because you showed me a picture of Adolf Hitler]." This led Gazzaniga to postulate that we have a narrator function in the brain, driven mostly by the prefrontal cortex (especially on the left hemisphere), which is constantly monitoring our actions and issuing plausible explanations of our behavior in the form of stories that we tell ourselves. We are thus reminded, once again, of the representational nature of our experience of reality and the creative role of the mind/brain in weaving into being the reality we live in.

Division of Labor in the Brain

The way the brain weaves our reality into being relies on the division of labor among many different networks in the brain and throughout the body. The division of labor in the brain should not be confused with the type of modularity espoused by the phrenologists. Rather, it is more accurate to think of it as nodes in large networks that are embedded within and are part of larger networks and so on. Within that system, there is redundancy. That is why, for instance, a young child who suffers damage to brain regions involved in the production or understanding of language can have other networks in their brain take on similar functions. Due to the evolutionary process by which the different systems and functions of the brain became set in place, there is a certain level of parallel functioning among some regions, as we explained in the previous chapter when dealing with the cognitive devices of the mind. Just as the parallel functioning of cognitive devices could result in bizarre illusions, the nature of the neural networks that support our conscious experience of reality can also sometimes result in strange experiences.

For instance, sometimes the neural circuits responsible for processing different kinds of sensorial perception do not become properly separated during the natural process of brain maturation, which includes the elimination of neural connections in the infant brain (the technical term is *neural* or *synaptic pruning*). That process is guided by genetics but also by the type of environment and stimulus available to the child. For example, the circuits that process colors and those that process sound may remain connected, resulting in the perception of sound in color! Similarly, some people are able to perceive certain shapes (like a number) in a certain color or to taste sounds. That phenomenon is called synesthesia.[21] It is believed that many artists are synesthetes, which allows them to perceive the world in ways that are different from the rest of us, and some would say that it allows them to access an aesthetic richness in reality that the rest of us can come to know only through their artistic representations. In any case, the point is that the brain operates through the interconnection of large webs of interconnected networks containing circuits and nodes dedicated to specific functions as part of a process of extended processing. The brain is neither an aggregate of independent neural modules nor a single master processing organ; it is something in between.

Correlating Structure and Function

How can scientists know what functions specific regions of the human brain are involved in? The oldest technique used to probe the relation between activity in regions of the brain and behavior is the study of brain lesions.[22] We already encountered this approach above when discussing patients who needed to have the corpus callosum connecting the two hemispheres surgically severed in order to stop epileptic seizures from spreading and causing greater damage to the brain. Disconnecting the two hemispheres resulted in peculiar ways of perceiving and interpreting reality, which allowed neuroscientists to attribute particular processes and functions to one hemisphere or the other.

Lesions

Prior to surgeons' and scientists' ability to conduct surgical modifications in the living human brain, they had to rely on observing the effects that strokes or accidental brain injuries had on patients' physical and mental functioning. Perhaps the most famous example of this approach was the case of the French physician Paul Broca, who postulated the existence of a specific brain region located on the left side of the head,

---

21. V. S. Ramachandran, *A Brief Tour of Human Consciousness* (Pi, 2004), 18–21.

22. Gazzaniga et al., *Cognitive Neuroscience*, 83–85; Murray and Baxter, "Lesion Studies," in Senior et al., *Methods in Mind*, 43–68.

slightly above the ear and toward the front (this is near the back of what is now called the frontal lobe).[23] Broca's proposal was supported by the postmortem examination of the brain of a man who had suddenly lost the ability to produce meaningful language, either spoken or written. This is now called Broca's aphasia. Later, another region of the brain was identified as being responsible for the ability to understand language. This time the proposal was brought forth by the German anatomist Carl Wernicke.[24]

That region, now known as Wernicke's area, is located on the left side of the head as well but toward the back, in the temporal lobe, on a crest-shaped area referred to as the superior temporal gyrus and near the fissure that separates the temporal lobe from the parietal lobe. An important caveat is that while those language areas, Broca's and Wernicke's, are on the left-brain hemisphere for 95 percent of the population, they are actually located on whichever is the dominant hemisphere, depending in part, for example, on whether people are left- or right-handed.

Another famous instance of this approach is patient H. M.,[25] who lost a region of the brain deep inside the temporal lobes (the region next to the temples, slightly over the ears) called the hippocampus (or hippocampi in the plural). Tragically, with the loss of the hippocampi this patient also lost the ability to form new memories and was condemned to living in the eternal past. Thanks to research conducted on this patient and others with similar circumstances, it is now clear that the hippocampi are essential to the encoding and decoding of memories.

A Note on Justice

It is unfortunate that so much of our present knowledge of brain function came as the result of the misfortune of those with injured brains. Maybe one way of thinking about it is that through their sacrifice, many others have been able to find healing and succor. That does not eliminate the pain and suffering of the original patients, but it brings important knowledge from tragedy. It is a very different thing, however, when that

---

23. Duane P. Schultz and Sydney Ellen Schultz, *A History of Modern Psychology*, 6th ed., (Harcourt Brace, 1996), 51.

24. Gazzaniga et al., *Cognitive Neuroscience*, 473.

25. Gazzaniga et al., *Cognitive Neuroscience*, 379–80.

pain and suffering did not come as the result of accidents or diseases but rather because of societal systems that put the bodies of people racialized or categorized in certain ways at the disposal of others deemed normal by that society. This was the case in situations such as Nazi Germany and the experiments conducted by the US on Black Afro-descendant Americans in the infamous Tuskegee syphilis trials,[26] as well as the surgical interventions (e.g., mass sterilization) and experimentation conducted on the bodies of Native American and Caribbean women.[27] The scientific community still must come to terms with that reality and find ways to repair the damage done, which endures in different ways in those communities.

Scans, Electricity, and Magnetism

Now back to our original question: How are neuroscientists able to figure out what goes on in the brain? And how can they even measure brain activity and find relationships of correlation and even causality between neural functioning and physical or mental actions and behaviors? The last hundred years have seen an explosion in technologies capable of measuring different aspects of brain function and the association between brain physiology and physical, mental, or emotional behavior.[28] As I write these lines, we are celebrating the centennial of the first recording of the brain's electrical activity via an electroencephalogram (EEG). Incidentally, the EEG was invented by the German psychiatrist Hans Berger almost accidentally; what he was actually interested in was the possibility that telepathy might happen through electromagnetic waves.[29] It turns out that telepathy might not be real, but this investigation resulted in the invention of a powerful tool for investigating the brain.

---

26. See Elizabeth Nix, "Tuskegee Experiment: The Infamous Syphilis Study," History, May 16, 2017, https://www.history.com/news/the-infamous-40-year-tuskegee-study, and https://www.cdc.gov/tuskegee/about/timeline.html?CDC_AAref_Val=https://www.cdc.gov/tuskegee/timeline.htm.

27. Ñapa, "Eugenics and Reproductive Coercion in Puerto Rico," Center for Latin American & Caribbean Studies, April 28, 2002, https://uwm.edu/clacs/eugenics-and-reproductive-coercion-in-puerto-rico/.

28. For an overview, see Senior et al, *Methods in Mind.*

29. Gazzaniga et al., *Cognitive Neuroscience*, 14–15.

EEG relies on the fact that the flow of electricity in the brain generates electromagnetic waves in close proximity to that area.[30] Depending on the rate of neuron firing, the waves will oscillate at different speeds, from gamma being the fastest (greater than forty-five cycles per second, called hertz) to delta waves, produced in deep sleep, between 0.2 and 2 hertz being the slowest.[31] The most common waves while we are awake and paying attention to something are alpha waves, between eight and twelve hertz. Both alpha and theta waves are associated with meditative states. The theta waves are correlated to alertness of internal cognitive and affective processes. It is possible to detect what type of brain waves are being generated by different general areas of the brain. This is done by placing a web of wave detectors on specific spots on the scalp. This also allows scientists to assess what general regions of the brain might be involved with particular tasks. An advantage of EEG is that it is noninvasive (although it can be a bit messy because of the substance used to fix the electrodes to the scalp), but its spatial resolution is poor compared to other methods. In the last decades, scientists have begun to experiment with combining EEG with other instruments, such as scanning. This can be challenging due in part to the magnitude of the magnetic fields generated by scanning machines and their potential interference with EEG measurements.

EEG works because of the electrochemical nature of how neurons communicate with each other, described above. Another technique that capitalizes on the electrochemical dynamics of brain activity is transcranial magnetic stimulation (TMS).[32] Ever since Michael Faraday's experiments and James Clerk Maxwell's equations, we know that electricity and magnetism belong together. A current (flow of electrons) will generate an equivalent magnetic field perpendicular to the flow of electricity, and a magnetic field can generate the flow of an electrical current. TMS consists of an array of small magnets placed on different spots around the head, which when activated, alter the normal flow of electrochemical pulses by which networks of neurons communicate

30. Gina Rippon, "Electroencephalography," in Senior et al., *Methods in Mind*, 237–62.

31. Castellanos, "La gran orquesta," in *Neurociencia del cuerpo*, 22–32.

32. Lauren Stewart and Vincent Walsh, "Transcranial Magnetic Stimulation in Human Cognition," in Senior et al., *Methods in Mind*, 1–26.

with each other. Neural networks can thus become temporarily activated or deactivated by focusing the magnetic field on them. That way, neuroscientists can imitate the effects of brain lesions in particular regions of the brain and examine the effects produced by inhibiting or exciting different areas.

An intriguing application of this technique by the Canadian neuroscientist Michael Persinger—which we will explore in more detail in the next chapter, on the neuroscience of religious experiences—is to stimulate regions of the brain known to be involved in religious experiences. By retrofitting a motorcycle helmet with the TMS magnets on its inside and creating conditions of sensorial deprivation for those undergoing the procedure, Persinger claims that his "God-helmet" is capable of inducing religious experiences.[33] The results have been mixed and difficult to reproduce by other laboratories.[34] These results are not surprising because, as should become increasingly obvious throughout this book, religious experiences require much more than just the activation of a cluster of neurons in the brain. In addition to the mediation of specific brain circuits, which we will explore in the next chapter, religious experiences require the contributions of the body and of linguistic-symbolic interpretive matrices that make it possible for the experiences to assume stable meanings and meaningful expressions.

There are many more methods for studying the brain, but the last set of technologies that we will examine in this chapter for correlating physical or mental activity with brain activity are scanning technologies. Scanning or imaging techniques, such as functional magnetic resonance imaging (fMRI), positron emission tomography (PET), and single-photon emission computed tomography (SPECT) scans,[35] work by constructing images of segments of the brain and highlighting changes in structure or activity in specific regions of interest. On top of an image of the general structures of the patient's brain, generated through a computed tomography (CT) scan, other images are

---

33. Barbara Bradley Hagerty, *Fingerprints of God: The Search for the Science of Spirituality* (Riverhead Books, 2009), 134–42.

34. For an analysis and assessment of Persinger's research, see Anne L. C. Runehov, *Sacred or Neural? The Potential of Neuroscience to Explain Religious Experience* (Vandenhoeck & Ruprecht, 2007), 67–136.

35. Gazzaniga et al., *Cognitive Neuroscience*, 91–95, 104–10.

superimposed in scales of black and white or of colors. Those scales represent the higher (dark) or lower density (white) of a given brain structure or an increase (red) or decrease (green) in the activity of a brain region. An increase of activity in a neural circuit is associated with an increase in hemoglobin-rich blood flow in the same area. By tagging the hemoglobin with a radioactive isotope, or simply measuring the natural emissions of the molecules involved, it is possible to measure whether a given region of the brain has had an increase in blood flow or a decrease. Through a complicated process of computer-powered statistical and spatial analysis, a gradient of pixels is generated and superimposed on the corresponding region of the CT-scan generated image. By taking a scan of the brain during a control task and then taking another image while the patient performs the experimental task (for example, praying, meditating, looking at facial expressions, or reading a story), it is then possible to compare the brain at rest with the brain in connection to the task or input of interest. Often, various images are averaged together so that the images that are reported in the end do not correspond to any single person's brain but to the average of those examined.[36]

I have taken the time to go into so much detail regarding how brain scan images are produced to make the point that they are not photographs of the brain. They are—here is that word again!—representations of what is going on in a given area of the brain under very specific conditions.

Now let's explore some concrete structures in the brain that are key to the way the embodied mind weaves our perceptual and experiential reality into being.

A Tour of Some Key Brain Structures

Let's take a look at some of the brain structures most relevant for the purposes of this book,[37] beginning with the four lobes into which the

---

36. For a detailed explanation of how fMRI works, see Peter A. Bandettini, "Functional Magnetic Resonance Imaging," in Senior et al., *Methods in Mind*, 193–235.

37. For an accessible introduction to the brain, see Rita Carter, *Mapping the Mind* (University of California Press, 1999); Ramachandran, *A Brief Tour of Human Consciousness*; and Eagleman, *Incognito*. For a more technical treatment, see Gazzaniga et al., *Cognitive Neuroscience*. What follows is based in part on those texts.

outer cortex of the brain is divided. They are, from the back of the head to the front, as follows:

The Cerebral Cortex

- The occipital lobes

 This is the area of the brain at the back of our heads. It is fitting that we begin our exploration of the brain cortex at the back because that is the way that information flows in the brain. The sensorial organs, like the eyes and the ears, transform the input they receive from the external world into electrochemical pulses that travel down the neuronal highway, by way of the thalamus in the center of the brain, all the way to the occipital lobes at the back.

 From there, according to a hypothesis known as the two-stream model,[38] the information will be processed and sent back to the front via two streams. One will flow on the top of the brain (dorsal stream) and the other one via the sides and belly of the brain (the ventral stream). The dorsal stream allows us to place that which is being perceived into a three-dimensional matrix in space and to figure out how to relate to it in terms of its physical use or purpose. The processing that happens on the ventral stream allows us to determine what kind of thing we are perceiving. This is similar to the model of cognitive categorization that we encountered in chapter 1, where one system designates the category to which the perceived thing belongs and then other cognitive processes intuit what attributes we can assume that it has, while yet other cognitive devices produce a kind of script for what to do with it or how to relate with it.

 In any case, all this happens only after the information has left the occipital lobes. What takes place on the actual occipital lobes is that perceptual information is analyzed for shapes, angles, colors, and other basic geometric and physical features. For example, kittens that have been raised

38. Gregory Hickok, "A Primer on Brain Organization," in *The Myth of Mirror Neurons* (W. W. Norton, 2014), 243–48.

in environments where they never had the opportunity to see vertical lines become selectively blind to vertical lines because the neurons dedicated to detecting and analyzing that feature of visual information did not mature.[39] Trauma to the back of the head can result in blindness, and focal injuries in the occipital lobes can result in selective blindness. It should not be surprising that this region of the brain exhibits an increase in activation when people engage in contemplative practices, such as contemplating a religious icon. But it might be surprising to learn that even in the absence of a physical image, just by recalling it in the mind's eye, that region also sees an increase in activation.[40]

- The parietal lobes

  This is where the body lives in the brain! Or at least one of the places. Using the careful application of electrical pulses directly to regions on the brain's surface during an open brain procedure, Montreal neuroscientist Wilder Penfield was able to map the body on the brain.[41] When the electrode touched a particular spot, the result would be felt in a specific part of the body. In the end, he discovered that on the cerebral cortex, there are two strips of neural tissue placed like two tiaras, one next to the other, on the head. One of them is on the parietal cortex and the other one is right in front of it, in the frontal cortex. These are now called the somatosensory cortex.[42] While the strip on the frontal lobes is responsible for sending instructions to the organs of the body, the one on the parietal lobe is responsible for receiving information from the body.

---

39. G. G. Blasdel et al., "A Physiological and Behavioural Study in Cats of the Effect of Early Visual Experience with Contours of a Single Orientation," *Journal of Physiology* 265, no. 3 (1977): 615–36.

40. See "Vision" in Gazzaniga et al., *Cognitive Neuroscience*, 184–97.

41. Wilder Penfield and Edwin Boldrey, "Somatic Motor and Sensory Representation in the Cerebral Cortex of Man as Studied by Electrical Stimulation," *Brain: A Journal of Neurology* 60 (1937): 389–443.

42. Gazzaniga et al., *Cognitive Neuroscience*, 330.

Different parts of the body have different amounts of neural tissue dedicated to them on the somatosensory cortex, and this correlates to how sensitive different parts of the body are.[43] There is an important function of this region and will become extremely important later on when discussing the neuroscience of mystical experiences. In coordination with other nearby regions of the brain, this part is involved in creating the representation of the body that we experience as our own. In other words, this is where our bodies are created as we perceive and experience them. This is the temple where our bodies communicate with us. Later, I will propose that the body is, in turn, the temple from where the divine Spirit brings about the transformation of our brains, the renewal of our minds, and the decolonization of our emotions, which in turn orients the necessary decolonial praxis for the construction of a more just and wholesome reality.

- The temporal lobes

  We already met the temporal lobes above when discussing language and the misfortunes of Broca's and Wernicke's patients, although Broca's area is more on the frontal lobe than the temporal lobe. Nonetheless, the temporal lobes play an important role in the processing of language,[44] especially in remembering verbal information and in detecting the emotional import of linguistic expressions. Deep within the temporal lobes lies an extremely important structure called the hippocampus. This structure is involved in memory and attention processes, but we will examine it below, when exploring the limbic system.

  An interesting part of the temporal lobe, called the fusiform gyri (or gyrus in the singular), seems to be dedicated to processing faces.[45] This is the neuronal circuit that powers the upside-down face illusions discussed in chapter 1. It is also involved in higher-level processing of visual information as part

43. Ramachandran, *A Brief Tour of Human Consciousness*, Figure 1.5, 12.

44. Gazzaniga et al., *Cognitive Neuroscience*, 471–80.

45. Gazzaniga et al., *Cognitive Neuroscience*, 222, 249–53.

of the ventral stream mentioned above. It could be said that the temporal lobes add cognitive depth and affective texture to our perceptions. As we will discuss in the next chapter, neurologists have found that there is a link between temporal lobe epilepsy and religious experiences. This is not surprising given the role of this part of the brain in intuitively attributing meaning to perceptions.[46]

- The frontal and prefrontal lobes

  The frontal lobe, as the name indicates, is located at the front of the head, right above the eyes. The prefrontal cortex is the frontmost section of the frontal lobe. The prefrontal cortex is the region of the brain responsible for the most sophisticated aspects of the human mind. This region appears to have primary responsibility for carrying out executive functions, such as monitoring, analyzing, reasoning, and making decisions.[47] However, as we will see shortly, without proper input from other regions of the brain, and without the contributions of the body, the prefrontal cortex cannot function properly.

  The left or dominant prefrontal cortex is where Gazzaniga placed the function of *the interpreter*, as we learned when exploring the cases of patients with split brains.[48] This also seems to be the locus where intentional action is initiated in the brain. Thus, it is not surprising that as we shall see in the next chapter, when neuroscientists studied the brains of monks and nuns during meditation, they saw a significant increase in activation in that region, corresponding to the willful focusing of attention during meditation and contemplative prayer.

  As we shall see below, when we make the decision to act, a neural representation of the desired end-state forms in the prefrontal cortex, and then once the action has been carried out, that image is compared with the new state of affairs resulting

---

46. See the discussion on the role of temporal lobe areas involved in happiness in Gazzaniga et al., *Cognitive Neuroscience*, 461.

47. Gazzaniga et al., *Cognitive Neuroscience*, 508–20.

48. See Gazzaniga et al., *Cognitive Neuroscience*, 620–21, and LeDoux, *The Emotional Brain*, 13–15 and 29–34.

from our action.[49] If there is a good-enough match between the two, then the action is deemed successful and we move on. If there is a mismatch, then we try again, make a new comparison, and so on. This process, which we will explore below in more detail, does not only apply to external affairs. It also applies to the formation of our very sense of self, the perceptual and affective story we tell ourselves about who we are. As we will see in the next chapter, religious experiences—mediated by religious language, rituals, symbols, and narratives—play a decisive role in the process of embodied subject-formation and therefore are also key in the process of decolonizing our embodied minds.

The work done by the frontal cortices would be incomplete without the contributions of a group of brain structures buried deep within the brain, traditionally known as the limbic system.

The Limbic System

Deep underneath the cerebral cortex, below the corpus callosum, toward the center of the brain, and on top of the brain stem where the spinal cord becomes the brain lie a set of brain nuclei responsible for, among other things, the emotional dimensions of our experience of reality. Some of these structures were originally labeled as the limbic system, from the Latin root *limbus*, which means "on the edge," because some of them were on the inner (medial) edge of the brain where the two hemispheres face each other.

Sometimes authors refer to these structures of the brain as the mammalian (or paleomammalian) brain and to the deeper structures in the brain stem as the reptilian brain. They call them reptilian because of their role in maintaining the basic processes of life and their presence in the brains of reptiles. This nomenclature, originally proposed by the neuroscientist Paul MacLean, was taken up in family systems theory and other popular applications of neuroscience.[50] The idea is that when

---

49. See "Goal Oriented Behavior," in Gazzaniga et al., *Cognitive Neuroscience*, 511–55.

50. See R. L. Reep, "Comparative Neurobiology: History," *Encyclopedia of Neuroscience* (Academic Press 2009), 1211–20, https://doi.org/10.1016/B978-008045046-9.00951-7.

we are in the grip of the reptilian brain, we are acting based on only our most animalistic survival instinct (eat, defend against potential predators, reproduce with a proper mate, and so on). When we are in the grip of the (paleo)mammalian brain, we are being guided mostly by our emotions and gregariousness, as opposed to when we are under the guidance of our neomammalian brain and the neocortex's, but especially the frontal cortex's, executive functions. This is when we are able to rein in our behavior and go from being reactive to being responsive. In fact, one of the first books attempting to do theology using neuroscience as a main source relied heavily on this model, seeing in it traces of the Trinitarian character of God's activity in the world according to Christian theology.[51]

A problem with the triune brain model, despite its heuristic power, is that it occludes the new ways in which the old structures might operate in the human brain.[52] After all, as we cautioned above, even though each structure plays a key role in the functioning of the brain, the parts are better understood not as isolated modules but as nodes in large networks and loops. Thus, we must be careful when drawing conclusions about the human brain based on results drawn from animal models. There seems to be a lot of overlap but also some important differences. Such

---

51. They conclude: "Because we view the human mind as a prime connection between humanity and the universe of which it is a part, we ourselves regard the brain as both metaphor and analogue. When the brain is driven by fear and anxiety, its state suggests 'increasing entropy.' The 'center does not hold'; brain functions are not optimally integrated. Except in situations where fight-or-flight is truly appropriate, such a brain is unlikely to promote the well-being of its owner or its neighbors. In contrast, when the brain is integrating and complexifying, it seems to echo the complexifying course of the emerging universe. The brain may then be seen as a metaphor of an emerging God—even though it is not God. Thus we have developed a way to move from examination of the working brain to identification of clues to God's ways of being God." James B. Ashbrook and Carol Rausch Albright, *The Humanizing Brain: Where Religion and Neuroscience Meet* (Pilgrim Press, 1997), 163. Their emphasis on the brain's work of integrating and complexifying (i.e., humanizing) resonates with me and is akin to the emphasis in liberation theologies on wholeness and flourishing. Their explanations of how the brain works is very thorough and helpful; their theological positivism, however, is where I cannot follow them.

52. See Patrick R. Steffen et al., "The Brain Is Adaptive Not Triune: How the Brain Responds to Threat, Challenge, and Change," *Frontiers in Psychiatry* (April 1, 2022), https://doi.org/10.3389%2Ffpsyt.2022.802606.

models are helpful,[53] but we cannot simply assume that because the brain functions in a certain way in a mouse, rat, cat, or monkey it therefore functions exactly the same way in humans. Animal models are but one piece of the puzzle; they are an important and helpful piece, but they do not constitute the totality of the puzzle.

Keeping that in mind, let us now turn our attention to key structures in the limbic system and adjacent areas.

- The amygdala

  Immediately above the brain stem are two almond-shaped structures called the amygdalae (or amygdala in the singular).[54] This is the brain structure most often linked with intensely emotional experiences, especially ones involving negatively valanced emotions such as fear. It seems to be responsible for quickly detecting salient information in the environment and in the body that is important for survival. For example, it detects when we are facing imminent danger or when an important opportunity appears before us. It sends a jolt of emotion through the body and redirects attention in the direction of the threat or opportunity. Scientists have observed that when animals, such as monkeys, do not have a functioning amygdala, they do not display their normal reactions of fear when facing threats, such as snakes. Likewise, artificial stimulation of their amygdala often results in aggressive behaviors. The amygdala works closely with the hypothalamus, the hippocampus, and the cingulate cortex. Some have referred to the amygdala as the *watchdog* of the brain.[55] It has direct neural connections to our sensorial apparatus, circumventing other structures involved in conscious, cognitive processes. It shapes perception and memory.

53. A case in point is the discovery of mirror neurons in monkeys—that is, neurons in the motor cortex of monkeys that become active when they engage in activities such as grabbing and eating a banana but also become activated when they see other monkeys carrying out those same actions. For a critique of the extrapolation of mirror neurons from monkeys to humans, see Hickok, *The Myth of Mirror Neurons*.

54. What follows is based on LeDoux, *The Emotional Brain*, 157–65.

55. Andrew Newberg et al., *Why God Won't Go Away: Brain Science and the Biology of Belief* (Ballantine, 2001), 44–45.

- The hypothalamus

  In front of the amygdala, resting on top of the pituitary glands, is a structure called the hypothalamus.[56] It monitors and regulates the autonomic nervous system, such as the fight-or-flight response. When rats in a laboratory are given the choice between eating or pulling a level that will send pleasurable electrical signals to their hypothalamus, they tend to prefer pulling the level even to the point of dying of starvation. The hypothalamus helps translate brain events into body states and helps translate body states into embodied affective experience.

- The thalamus

  Above the hypothalamus is a large egg-shaped structure called the thalamus. It has been called "the Grand Central Station of the brain" because most of the information that flows into the brain by way of our senses goes directly to the thalamus, which then decides where in the brain that particular type of information needs to go.[57] It has been proposed that there are two general routes for neural information from the senses to flow:[58] one is sent by the thalamus to cortical areas where conscious experience emerges, and the other route, which is much faster, goes directly to the amygdala and hypothalamus, bypassing momentarily conscious experience and triggering emotional and behavioral responses aimed at averting any possible threats or ceasing time-sensitive opportunities.

- The hippocampus

  Moving now farther away from the bottom and middle of the brain to the lobes on the sides, known as the temporal lobes, we find a structure buried deep within them, shaped in the form of a seahorse, and therefore called the hippocampus (or hippocampi in the plural). This structure, which works in tandem with the others mentioned above, plays an important

---

56. LeDoux, *The Emotional Brain*, 79–85.

57. Gazzaniga et al., *Cognitive Neuroscience*, 45–46.

58. Le Doux, *The Emotional Brain*, 163–65.

role in memory and attention.[59] It receives input from the amygdala, creating a curious effect referred to as *amygdala hijack*.[60]

The amygdala can send instructions for the hippocampus to block any information that is not relevant to whatever the amygdala has detected is existentially urgent at the moment. This allows us to avoid distractions and focus on the immediate threat or opportunity before us. However, it also means that when we are in the heat of a disagreement with someone, experiencing emotions like anger, fear, or anxiety, the amygdala sends instructions to the hippocampus to allow only memories that are relevant to (and thus confirm) what we are feeling at the moment. Consequently, at that moment when we or our interlocutor are in the grip of intense emotion, our/their recollection of events is not as accurate as we/they might think.[61] Our moods and emotions have a deep effect on the way we remember (and misremember) things and even on the way we experience and live things in the first place.[62]

A recent intriguing finding is that the ability of neurons in the hippocampus to repair and reproduce themselves is linked with the health of the microbiome in our guts (which, incidentally, coincides with that of our gums).[63] Thus, our diet also has a profound impact on the way we experience, feel,

---

59. Gazzaniga et al., *Cognitive Neuroscience*, 65.

60. Amygdala hijack or emotional hijack refers to the sequestration of memory by the amygdala so that only information relevant to the situation at hand and that confirms one's emotional state is available to one's conscious mind. For a discussion on how the amygdala modulates attention, learning, and memory, see Gazzaniga et al., *Cognitive Neuroscience*, 444–47.

61. According to LeDoux, "these are self-perpetuating vicious cycles of emotional reactivity. Arousal [of the amygdala] locks you into whatever emotional state you are in when arousal occurs, unless something else occurs that is significant enough and arousing enough to shift the focus of arousal" (*The Emotional Brain*, 290).

62. Damasio, *The Feeling of What Happens*.

63. See, for example, John F. Cryan and Timothy G. Dinan, "Mind Altering Microorganisms: The Impact of the Gut Microbiota on Brain and Behavior," *Nature Review Neuroscience* 13, no. 10 (October 2012): 701–12; and E. Sherwin et al., "Microbiota and the Social Brain, *Science* 366, no. 6465 (November 1, 2019):eaar2016,

and remember the world. In another set of experiments, it was found that silence also aids in the neurogenesis of hippocampal neurons.[64]

- The insula

  Hidden deep within the juncture where the temporal, parietal, and frontal lobes meet is the insula. This structure seems to be responsible for making our experiences ours.[65] In other words, it links our embodied, cognitive, and affective experiences with the sense of "I" so that what happened to my body happened to me, and the experience of intentionally moving my limbs or performing any other action is the experience of me carrying out such actions. Fascinatingly, this structure communicates directly with the heart, not the poetic, figurative heart but the actual heart that pumps blood. The heart sends signals to the brain, helping to regulate its function and mark its rhythms![66] In my opinion, this area is one of the most fascinating structures of the brain, but because of its anatomical inaccessibility, it is also one of the most difficult ones to study.

- The cingulate cortex

  Mediating between the cortical lobes and the structures in the midbrain, such as the amygdala, the hypothalamus, and

---

doi: 10.1126/science.aar2016, PMID: 31672864; in Spanish, see Castellanos, "El intestino," in *Neurociencia del cuerpo*, 87–121.

64. Imke Kirste et al., "Is Silence Golden? Effects of Auditory Stimuli and Their absence on Adult Hippocampal Neurogenesis," *Brain Structure and Function* 220, no. 2 (2015): 1221–28.

65. Damasio has suggested that the insula, together with other cortices, "in the right hemisphere holds the most integrated representation of the current internal state of the organism at the level of the cerebral hemispheres, along with representations of the invariant design of the musculoskeletal frame" (*The Feeling of What Happens*, 156). Damasio proposes that such integrated representation of the internal states constitutes the foundation of our sense of embodied self-hood, which then serves as a self-reference for all our experiences (e.g., that feeling of pain is happening to me, that visual perception is mine, etc.); he calls it the "proto-self."

66. Castellanos, "El corazón," in *Neurociencia del cuerpo*, 159–202.

the thalamus, is a belt-like cluster of neurons called the cingulate cortex.[67] It receives the unconscious experience generated in the subcortical regions (and the body) and transmits them to the frontal cortex. In the process, it transforms them from unconscious to conscious experience. This is one of the regions that neuroscientists have found to get the most benefits from prayer and meditation.[68] With a regular practice of meditation, contemplative prayer, or mindfulness, it becomes thicker and more able to detect and regulate emotions and habitual behaviors.[69]

- The basal ganglia

  There is a collection of nuclei, known as the basal ganglia, located between the cingulate cortex and the other structures of the limbic system explored above. These clusters of neural circuits were originally known to be associated with movement and muscle control, but it is now becoming increasingly clear that they also play an important role in linking behaviors with risks and rewards. The basal ganglia seems to be partly responsible for the feeling of satisfaction that accompanies the successful completion of a task. It is therefore also involved in the formation of addictive behaviors and compulsions.[70]

There are many more structures that are important for the brain's functioning. We have focused only on those that will be important later on when we try to understand the neurophysiological processes through which spiritual transformation and affective decolonization might take place. For that purpose, there is also another element of brain functioning that we need to mention here: neurotransmitters.[71]

---

67. Gazzaniga et al., *Cognitive Neuroscience*, 428–29.

68. Castellanos, *El espejo del cerebro*, 45–53.

69. See, for example, Yi-Yuan Tang et al., "Short-Term Meditation Increases Blood Flow in Anterior Cingulate Cortex and Insula," *Frontiers in Psychology* 6 (February 25, 2015): 212, https://doi.org/10.3389/fpsyg.2015.00212.

70. Gazzaniga et al., *Cognitive Neuroscience*, 47–49, 510.

71. Gazzaniga et al., *Cognitive Neuroscience*, 33–35.

The Chemistry of the Brain

It was explained above that for neurons to communicate with each other, they need a special kind of molecule to carry the electrochemical pulse from one axon to its corresponding dendrite. These molecules are called neurotransmitters. There are dozens of different kinds of neurochemicals at work in the brain (and throughout the body). Some of the better-known ones are discussed below:

Oxytocin

Made in the hypothalamus, and secreted during sex and childbirth, this hormone is linked with feelings of romantic love and filial bonds.[72] For instance, oxytocin has been found to be partly responsible for the prairie vole's monogamous mating behavior.[73] Some people refer to oxytocin as the love hormone (it is both a neurotransmitter and a hormone, which begins to give us a hint of the overlap between the functions of the brain-nervous system and the body-immune system). If it has not been done already, it would be interesting to measure the levels of oxytocin during religious practices such as contemplative prayer—which, for example, focuses on the love of Christ or on the compassion of Buddha—or even just while reading sacred stories that illustrate compassion. It would also be interesting to study the long-term effects of such practices and experiences on the levels of oxytocin and other hormones.

Endorphins

Another example of hormones that are also neurotransmitters are the endorphins.[74] They, too, are produced in the hypothalamus and released

---

72. For a general overview, see Carter, *Mapping the Mind*, 76; for an example of experiments on the influence of this hormone in social behaviors in nonhuman animals, see H. K. Caldwell and H. E. Albers, "Oxytocin, Vasopressin, and the Motivational Forces That Drive Social Behaviors," *Current Topics in Behavioral Neuroscience* 27 (2016): 51–103.

73. For an overview of this research and its implications for understanding human bonding behavior, see Steven Phelps et al., "Monogamous Prairie Voles Reveal the Neurobiology of Love," *Scientific American* (February 1, 2023), https://www.scientificamerican.com/article/monogamous-prairie-voles-reveal-the-neurobiology-of-love/.

74. Carter, *Mapping the Mind*, 29 and 68–69.

by its neighbor the pituitary gland and by the hypothalamus. This fact is going to become important in the next chapter when we examine the contributions of the body to religious experience. Endorphins are often referred to as a *feel-happy* hormone; their activity is associated with feelings of pleasure and a general sensation of well-being, such as what some people experience after exercising, while eating chocolate, and during sexual intercourse. Additionally, endorphins help relieve pain, as they are natural opiates (in fact, morphine works by mimicking endorphins in the brain).

Adrenaline

Also known as epinephrine, adrenaline is produced by the adrenal glands (near the kidneys; remember the biblical insight, referred to in the previous chapter, that some functions of the mind were carried out by the kidneys and the gut). Adrenaline is released in response to stressful situations, thus triggering the fight-or-flight response and its associated activation of the sympathetic nervous system in the body (to be explored below).[75] An intriguing project would be to measure the levels of adrenaline/epinephrine in the blood of practitioners engaging in rituals of Santeria or Candomblé, traditional African religions imported and adapted to the Caribbean and the Americas, where prayer is done through drumming and intense dancing while summoning the attention of deceased ancestors and other spirits. We shall see in the next chapter how such rituals might trigger mystical experiences of absolute union with all living beings and with the Creator.

Cortisol

This hormone-neurotransmitter is closely associated with chronic stress and the damage that it produces on mental health and on the body's systems.[76] Medical studies investigating the effects of meditation and mindfulness practices on the body have shown that they can help lower the levels of cortisol in the blood. More recently, cortisol has been implicated in the biological mechanisms by which the effects of stress and

---

75. Gazzaniga et al., *Cognitive Neuroscience* , 38–39.

76. Gazzaniga et al., *Cognitive Neuroscience*, 415.

trauma are passed down from one generation to the next.[77] Thus, as we engage in strategies to address the transgenerational traumas of coloniality, racism, heterosexism, and other ills, further studies into this hormone and its associated nervous, immunological, and genetic systems will be key to finding healing and a path toward wholesomeness.

Dopamine

Together with serotonin, dopamine is a key player in the model for the neuroscience of religious experiences that we will be exploring in the next chapter. Dopamine is part of the reward system in the brain. An increase in dopamine happens when we form a goal or a desire in our minds and feel close to achieving it.[78] In a healthy brain, an increase in dopamine will accompany the formation of the intention to act (that is, the desire to change something from state A to state B), and by activating the relevant brain circuits between the prefrontal and limbic cortices by way of the basal ganglia and the cingulate cortex, it generates the feelings that are the drive for actually acting on one's intentions.

When things go wrong, however, this process can also result in habit-inducing behaviors and addictions.[79] In order to understand why this is the case, it might be helpful to keep in mind that it is not the satisfaction of the desire, or the accomplishment of the goal, that is associated with an increase of dopamine in the brain but rather its promise. To borrow a metaphor from hunting, it is not the catch but the hunt that triggers this pleasure-inducing neurochemical, and the riskier the behavior, the greater the pleasure accompanying the desired reward. That is so because the way the brain functions is by constantly issuing comparisons and contrasts. Thus, risk amplifies the distance between the current state of affairs and the desired one, augmenting the tension generated by the desire. The problem is that the brain is too efficient, so the next time that one engages in the risky behavior with potentially high reward, the brain will need more stimulation in

---

77. See, for example, Gabor Maté, "Mutiny on the Body: The Mystery of the Rebellious Immune System," in *The Myth of Normal: Trauma, Illness & Healing in a Toxic Culture* (Avery, 2022), 68–84.

78. Gazzaniga et al., *Cognitive Neuroscience*, 526–30.

79. Carter, *Mapping the Mind*, 68–69.

order to generate the same sensation of pleasure experienced before. The behavior will have to be much riskier, the stakes of the bet much higher, and the odds more dangerous. Too much dopamine in the brain can result in euphoria, difficulty controlling one's impulses, and in extreme cases, hallucinations and psychotic episodes. Too little dopamine in the brain can result in low motivation to act and the inability to engage in necessary behaviors for a healthy daily life.

Serotonin

There is an inverse relationship between serotonin and dopamine. When the levels of dopamine reach a certain level, serotonin kicks in and brings the levels of dopamine down.[80] If dopamine is associated with the experience of desire, serotonin is connected to the experience of satiation. They are both feelings of pleasure but of a different kind. An increase in serotonin activates circuits in the brain that indicate to us that the goal has been reached, the desire has been satisfied, our purposeful actions have succeeded, and we can now move on to something else. Lower levels of serotonin give us the sensation that the outcome of our action is somewhat askew or not quite right. So, we must try it again and again and again. Alternatively, higher than normal levels of serotonin could result in the sensation that everything is perfectly fine even when it is not. Like dopamine, high levels of serotonin can also result in hallucinations and psychotic episodes. Healthy levels of serotonin allow our brains to feel a general sense of well-being and an appropriate feeling of satisfaction with the way things are, which is one of the potential contributions of religious worldviews/practices, as we shall see later on.

One last thing must be highlighted about serotonin. While dopamine is synthesized near the base of the brain, most serotonin (about 95 percent) is produced in the gut, where fascinatingly, our microbiome and the rhythms of the gut's palpitations modulate the moods of our brain.[81] No wonder the gut has been called the second brain! This leads us, then, to ponder the contribution of the body to the brain. If the brain

---

80. See, McNamara, *The Neuroscience of Religious Experience*, 139–41, and LeDoux, *The Emotional Brain*, 288–91.

81. Castellanos, *Neurociencia del cuerpo*, 108–111.

is the temple of the body, then the body is the workshop of the brain. Brain and body constitute each other.

The Brain in the Body

Where does the brain end and the body begin? Or, conversely, where does the body end and the brain begin? One cannot exist without the other; to use language from Trinitarian theology, in a strangely perichoretic dance,[82] the brain and the body coinhabit. Buddhists would say that they co-are (interbeing).[83]

The Nervous System

Down through the brain stem and the spinal cord, the brain enters the body and branches out, its delicate fingers of thin nerve fibers gently touching every organ and system in our embodied being, from the soles of our feet and the arteries in our heart to the skin and muscles in our face. Thus, the brain feels the body and senses how we are affected by the realities we encounter (physical or mental) and how our bodies are responding to them, even before our conscious minds become aware of what is going on. In the words of Antonio Damasio, one of the chief architects of the contemporary understanding of the neuroscience of emotions, of the self, and of decision-making,

> the nervous system literally "touches" the organism's interior, everywhere in that interior, and it is "touched" in return. Moreover, there is an intense cooperation between body parts and neural elements. Body and nervous system remain interactive partners rather than separate "model" and "depiction." What is ultimately imaged is neither purely neural nor purely bodily. It emerges from a dialogue, from a dynamic give-and-take between body chemistry and the bioelectrical activity of neurons.[84]

---

82. *Perichoresis* is a theological term that designates the relationship among the three persons of the Trinity that is God, whereby one person is able to fully indwell in the other person.

83. Nhât Hanh, "Interbeing," in *Understanding Our Mind* (Parallax, 2006), 210–12.

84. Damasio, *Feeling & Knowing: Making Minds Conscious* (Pantheon, 2021), 74–75.

It is for this reason that, as we shall see in the next chapter, it is not possible to restrict the work of the divine Spirit in the human person to an isolated part, whether the brain, the soul, or the mind. The locus of the Spirit's work of healing and transformation is the body-mind-brain complex. As in the beginning when the Spirit hovered over the primordial depths and summons forth from within it a new reality, so it is that by hovering throughout our embodied beings (and communities), the divine Spirit summons forth new life—healing and transformation—from within us. We will explore this further in later chapters; for now, let us return to our guided contemplation of God's amazing artwork knitted in our bodies with interwoven threads of nerves, flesh, and spirit.

The Central Nervous System

The nervous system is physically divided into two parts.[85] The first part is the bundle of nerve fibers traveling up and down the spine all the way up to the brain stem. This part, called the central nervous system, is responsible for sending neural messages back and forth between the brain and the rest of the body, although it must be noted that not all the processing happens in the brain; some of it takes place in neural nodes throughout the spine, such as the coordination of reflexes.

The Peripheral Nervous System

The other part of the nervous system is the peripheral nervous system. It consists of the webs of nerve fibers extending from the central nervous system to the peripheral boundaries of the body (the skin, which incidentally is the largest organ in the body) and everything in between. The peripheral nervous system innervates organs such as the kidneys (which have the cortisol and adrenaline-producing adrenal glands right on top of them), the heart (which, as we explain below, has a function in the regulation of conscious awareness), and the intestines (which have their own internal complex system of neurons called the enteric nervous system). The enteric system plays an important role in the regulation of moods and the generation of different hues of emotional experience. The peripheral nervous system also connects with muscle tissue, allowing for the control of motor responses through contraction or relaxation. The subset of the peripheral nervous system dedicated to voluntary processes (like intentionally moving a limb) is called the somatic nervous system.

85. Gazzaniga et al., *Cognitive Neuroscience*, 37–39.

But the part that is of most interest to us for the purposes of exploring religious experience and affective decolonization is the part dedicated to automatic or autonomous processes, which is called the autonomic nervous system.

The autonomic subbranch of the peripheral nervous system has two distinct functions on behalf of the organism: action and recovery. When the circumstances require the organism to engage in action, either to confront a threat (by fighting, fleeing, or playing dead) or to pursue an opportunity (like securing food or a mate), the sympathetic branch of the autonomic nervous system gets activated and sets in motion a cascade of physiological events that facilitate swift action. The heart beats faster, making fuel (glucose-rich blood) readily available for the body to perform the action it needs to do. The pupils become dilated, allowing for more light and therefore more information about the environment to get to the relevant circuits in the brain. The generation and consumption of energy by the body during the sympathetic response also results in an increase in sweat on the skin, which is a way for scientists to measure autonomic responses. A famous application of this is the polygraph. The sympathetic response also corresponds to an increase in neurotransmitters and hormones such as epinephrine/adrenaline, norepinephrine (which is made from dopamine), acetylcholine (which regulates heart rate and blood flow), and cortisol (which helps break down glucose to release its energy and helps to reduce inflammation in tissues as a result of the stress corresponding to the activation of the sympathetic response). Cognitively, the sympathetic response allows for the mind to hyperfocus (filtering out unnecessary or irrelevant information) on the stimuli relevant to the threat or opportunity at hand. Additionally, processes in the body that are not immediately necessary to engage in action are paused or slowed down in order to make more energy available to the relevant organs.

The other subbranch of the autonomic nervous system, working in tandem with the sympathetic, is the parasympathetic branch. After the organism has engaged in action, it needs to replenish the resources that were spent and to allow for the body and mind to recover. The effects of this system are felt when we take a warm bath, sip a cup of delicious hot tea or coffee on our favorite couch, listen to relaxing music after successfully completing an intense task, contemplate a breathtaking sunrise or sunset, enjoy the company of those whom we love and who love us, or finish making love with our partner. That last example is not gratuitous; in the next chapter, we will see that there is a link between the experience of sexual intercourse and the way some mystics describe their experience of union with Christ. In any case, the parasympathetic response corresponds to an increase in serotonin in the gut and brain, calming the enteric nervous system and resulting in an experience of relaxation and satiation. The parasympathetic response allows the body's processes to return to homeostasis, absorbing the nutrients it needs, cleansing its organs from that which is not necessary, and allowing the mind's attention to soften and relax, thereby making possible the activation of a neural network called the default mode network, which allows us to daydream, arrive at intuitive insights, and discover relevant patterns.

Both systems, the sympathetic and parasympathetic, are involved in religious experiences and rituals. Depending on the nature of the religious practice, one or the other will become activated. However, an interesting feature of these two systems, according to neurotheologian Andrew Newberg (whom we will meet in the next chapter) is that when one of those two subbranches of the autonomic nervous system becomes intensely active, it can lead to the parallel activation of its counterpart, resulting in what he terms a *spillover effect*.[86] That simultaneous activation of the sympathetic and parasympathetic response would result in the strange experience of being totally relaxed and fiercely alert at the same time. That characteristic of religious experiences would endow them with a lingering feeling of realness and specialness. However, as we will see below, it is not only religious experiences that are marked by bodily processes as significant. In fact, it seems that for any experience to become significant for us, it needs to be marked as such by processes mediated by a rich interplay of body, mind, and brain.

Emotions

The following case studies illustrate the role that the body and the emotions play in shaping the way we experience reality, including the reality of our own embodied selves.

---

86. Eugene d'Aquili and Andrew Newberg, *The Mystical Mind: Probing the Biology of Religious Experience* (Fortress Press, 1999), 23–28.

Case Studies

Remembering with Our Bodies

The first case highlights something intriguing that happened to a patient of the nineteenth-century Swiss psychologist Édouard Claparède.[87] The patient had a brain injury that had left her with the inability to form new memories. She would forget anything new that happened after about five minutes. Claparède or his assistant would introduce themselves to the patient, walk out of the room, come back after more than five minutes had passed, and ask the patient whether she remembered them. The patient would, invariably, not be able to recognize them. The next time, the psychologist hid a tack between his fingers before meeting the patient. After asking the patient if she knew who he was and the patient responding that she had no idea, the psychologist would shake hands with her, as he had been doing during previous visits; this time, however, it resulted in her hand getting pricked by the tack. The psychologist then left the room, returning after a prolonged period and asking the patient if she knew who he was. When she said that she didn't know, he extended his hand to shake hers. Her body automatically moved back, and she refused to shake hands with the psychologist. When asked why, she said she didn't know but she didn't want to. Even though her (conscious) brain could not remember, her body seemed to have formed a memory of the previous encounter and had marked this person and gesture (shaking hands) as dangerous.

Feeling What Is Real

The second case comes from neurologist V. S. Ramachandran. In his book *A Brief Tour of Human Consciousness: From Impostor Poodles to Purple Numbers*, he relates similar stories of bizarre dislocations between reality and the way it is perceived and felt. One of his patients claimed that his mother was an impostor.[88] When he talked to her on the phone, he could recognize her, but when he saw her he could not, even though he admitted she looked exactly like his mother. According to

---

87. LeDoux, *The Emotional Brain*, 180–82.

88. Ramachandran, *A Brief Tour of Human Consciousness*, 7–9.

Ramachandran, the patient's injury had caused a disruption in the flow of neural information between the regions in the temporal lobe that are involved in the processing of faces and the limbic regions responsible for the emotional valuation of that information. Without emotion, there is no recognition. In order to know reality, we must also be able to feel it.[89]

(Mis)Recognizing Our Own Bodies

The third case is a tragic yet humorous incident, related by the famous neurologist and writer Oliver Sacks. In his book *The Man Who Mistook His Wife for a Hat and Other Clinical Tales,* he tells the story of a patient he had when he was a neurology resident.[90] The patient had been in a serious accident and had endured some level of brain damage. The patient was asleep in the intensive care unit and Dr. Sacks was at the nurses' station. Suddenly, the staff heard a loud thump and a groan coming from the patient's room. When they rushed there to see what had happened, they found the patient on the floor. He said that a morbid nurse had played a trick on him, putting a severed leg from the morgue on his bed, so he grabbed it and threw it on the floor. Except it was his own leg. Sacks surmised that because the region of the brain that was injured was involved in emotional processes, the brain's ability to feel and therefore recognize the leg as its own was compromised. Even the experience of our own bodies is a perceptual story woven into our nervous system. Today, we know of conditions such as body dysmorphia and the way they trick people into misperceiving how their bodies actually are. From a decolonial perspective, one must ask what the effects of centuries of relentless misrepresentations of our bodies and of our embodied selves have been on the ways we experience our own bodies and each other's and hence on the way we treat our own bodies and each other's.

Phineas Gage's Brain

The fourth and last case study is the unfortunate story of Phineas Gage, probably the most retold incident in psychology and neuroscience

89. This is the central premise of Damasio's *The Feeling of What Happens.*

90. Oliver Sacks, "The Man Who Fell Out of Bed," in *The Man Who Mistook His Wife for a Hat and Other Clinical Tales* (Vintage, [1970] 2021), 66–69.

textbooks. Gage was a foreperson for a railroad company.[91] On the day of his accident, he was placing gunpowder in a hole that had been drilled into a rock (blasting the rock would make way for the railroad construction). He got distracted and forgot to cover the gunpowder with sawdust before tapping on it with a metal rod to make it more compact. The tapping produced a spark that triggered an explosion, shooting the metal rod in the direction of his head. It pierced his face through his left cheekbone and went through his brain, exiting through the top of his head. What was dumbfounding about his accident was that Gage did not die or even lose consciousness when it happened, but his personality suffered profound changes as a consequence. Incidentally, this happened in 1848, the same year that 55 percent of Mexico's territory was annexed to the US as what is today California, Nevada, Utah, New Mexico, Colorado, parts of Oklahoma, Kansas, Wyoming, and most of Arizona.[92] This fact may seem irrelevant to the neuroscience covered in this chapter, but is very relevant to the decolonial perspective and commitment from which this book is written, as is the role of the construction of railroads, such as the one Gage was involved in, in the western expansion of the US as part of the American manifest destiny doctrine. This doctrine resulted in the expropriation of Native lands and the importation and exploitation of foreign laborers, especially from Latin America and Asia, who were later denied proper American citizenship.[93] For now, however, let's go back to Gage's brain lesion and its huge implications for our understanding of the interplay between emotions and reason, body and brain, which is necessary for the proper functioning of the human mind.

At the time of Gage's accident, neuroscience was still in its early infancy, if that. For instance, it would be another thirteen years before Paul Broca would identify the region on the left lateral frontal cortex responsible for language production, and another twenty-six years before Wernicke would find the area responsible for language interpretation on

---

91. Damasio, *Descartes' Error*, 3–19.

92. Treaty of Guadalupe Hidalgo (1848), National Archives, https://www.archives.gov/milestone-documents/treaty-of-guadalupe-hidalgo.

93. Laura E. Gómez, "We Are Here Because You Were There," in *Inventing Latinos*, 19–61.

the left temporal area (more precisely, on the temporal gyrus of the dominant hemisphere). Therefore, the exact nature of Gage's brain lesion remained unknown until relatively recently, when Antonio Damasio; his wife, Hanna Damasio; and others were able to reconstruct them using sophisticated scanning and computerized models of Gage's skull.[94] They concluded that "the damage compromised prefrontal cortices in the ventral [i.e., underbelly section] and inner surfaces of both hemispheres while preserving the lateral, or external, aspects of the prefrontal cortices."[95]

That means that in Gage's brain, the lines of neural communication between the limbic structures (emotional processing) and the frontal and prefrontal lobe (conscious processing and deliberative decision-making) were compromised. This resulted in deficits in his self-control and decision-making faculties. Antonio Damasio explains that this is consistent with what he has observed over the years in patients with damage to similar brain regions. People with lesions to those brain regions can reason and carry out normal daily functions but, depending on the specifics of their conditions, have a hard time weighing the relative value of different options and therefore have a hard time deciding among various possible actions. Others exhibit deficits in social intelligence and moral valuations.[96] Damasio's conclusion, which has by now become so accepted that repeating it seems trite, is that reasoning and emotion belong together, especially when it comes to decision-making and action.

Models of Embodied Reasoning and Decision-Making

The Somatic Marker Hypothesis

Damasio has elaborated a model, known as the somatic marker hypothesis (SMH), to explain how emotions help guide our decision-making. In his first book, *Descartes' Error: Emotion, Reason, and the Human Brain*, he summarizes SMH in the following way:

---

94. Damasio, *Descartes' Error*, 20–33.

95. Damasio, *Descartes' Error*, 32.

96. Damasio, *Descartes' Error*, 169.

> In short, *somatic markers are a special instance of feelings generated from secondary emotions.* Those emotions and feelings *have been connected, by learning, to predicted future outcomes of certain scenarios.* When a negative somatic marker is juxtaposed to a particular future outcome the combination functions as an alarm bell. When a positive somatic marker is juxtaposed instead, it becomes a beacon of incentive.[97]

Notice that in this model, emotions are distinguished from feelings. Emotions, according to Damasio, are unconscious physiological states that arise in response to specific (perceived) circumstances; feelings, on the other hand, are embodied interpretations of those emotions. In his most recent book, *Feeling & Knowing: Making Minds Conscious*, he explains that emotions are "collections of co-occurring and involuntary internal actions (for example, smooth muscle contractions, changes in heart rate, breathing, hormonal secretions, facial expressions, posture) triggered by perceptual events."[98] Feeling, on the other hand, as he explains in *The Feeling of What Happens*,

> consists of having mental images arising from the neural patterns which represent the changes in body and brain that make up an emotion. But knowing that we have that feeling, "feeling" that feeling, occurs only *after* we build the second-order representation necessary for core consciousness. . . . they are representations of the relationship between the organism and the object (which in this case is an emotion), and the causal effect of that object on the organism.[99]

It is through the orchestration of emotions, feeling, and reasoning that we can understand reality and find meaningful and successful ways to navigate it and transform it. Let us examine how that orchestration might take place.

---

97. Damasio, *Descartes' Error*, 174. Italics in the original.

98. Damasio, *Feeling & Knowing*, 78.

99. Damasio, *The Feeling of What Happens*, 280. Italics in the original.

Action Loops and Simulations

In their book, *Neuroscience, Psychology, and Religion*, psychologists Malcolm Jeeves and Warren S. Brown, explain how the human mind goes about making decisions: "It is not so much that we stop-and-calculate and then act, but rather we are constantly acting (in some form) and making adjustments to actions based on feedback."[100] This process takes place through other processes that, as we saw in the previous chapter when exploring the computational processes underlying cognition, are arranged as "a nested hierarchy of action loops." They loop between the cognitive analytical processes in the cortical areas, especially the prefrontal and frontal lobes, and embodied simulations of actions that include the nervous system. In Jeeves and Brown's own words:

> The nervous system is, in its simplest form, an action loop. The basic task for the nervous system of all organisms is to adjust its ongoing motor activity based on sensory consequences. The nervous system modulates actions in the world by using sensory systems to monitor action outcomes, and, on the basis of this feedback, making adjustments to ongoing action. This process results in the constant cycling of an action-feedback-evaluation-action loop.

That process does not only include actual action but also, as mentioned above, simulated (imagined) action. The authors explain:

> We can trigger activity in our cortical sensory system to elicit images and sensory memories by our prefrontal cortex activating off-line parts of our cortical-sensory apparatus, or we can simulate potential actions, including speech acts, by off-line interactions between the frontal cortex and our cortical-motor system.

100. Jeeves and Brown, *Neuroscience, Psychology, and Religion*, 41.

> All of this allows human beings to think, imagine, and problem-solve "in the head" [*sic*][101] by internally simulating relevant actions (including inner speech acts).[102]

Integration of Cognition and Emotion

Neuroscientists of emotions Michael Spezio and Ralph Adolphs help us gain more granularity in our understanding of how these embodied processes of decision-making might take place. Combining Damasio's SMH with cognitive appraisal models of emotional valuation, they propose an integrated approach for emotional processing and decision-making that I find to be particularly helpful for the type of decolonial liberation theology of the brain that I am trying to develop here. According to their proposed model,

> emotional processing begins as the outcome of initial low-level evaluative processing in terms of autonormative outcomes, resulting in the activation of a set of autonomic and sensorimotor processes in the body such as heart rate, SCR [skin conductance response], pupillary dilation, changes in skeletal muscle tone, and the representations in the brain that mediate these activations. This way of categorizing emotional processing corresponds to the "body loop" and "as if loop" categories in SMH. . . . Emotional responses then go on to be used in two ways. First, they influence downstream processing in the domains of selective attention, memory encoding and retrieval, associative learning, action planning, thought, and so on. . . . Second, and equally important, they are recurrent with respect to evaluative processing functions, influencing them even as these same functions process new information coming in owing to the changes in selective attention, and so on.[103]

---

101. This does not just happen "in the head" but, as we have already seen, in the body, which includes the head but is much more than just that.

102. Jeeves and Brown, *Neuroscience, Psychology, and Religion*, 43–44.

103. Michael L. Spezio and Ralph Adolphs, "Emotional Processing and Political Judgment: Toward Integrating Political Psychology and Decision Neuroscience," in

This means that "the evaluative processing and emotional processing functions form bidirectionally coupled, iterative loops that are extended in time."[104] Furthermore, "constructs such as emotional 'states' arise from integrating throughout the evaluative-emotional downstream system. Moods arise from long-lasting activation of emotional processes, and mood disorders could be due in part to the failure of proper evaluative-emotional recurrent integration."[105] Later in the book, I will use the work of affective neuroscientist Lisa Feldman Barrett to propose that those processes that generate emotions and transmute them into the conscious feelings that guide our actions and, as we shall see shortly, even our perceptions of reality are profoundly shaped in humans by words—that is, by language and by the symbolic milieu in which the human spirit exists.

A Note on the Contributions of the Viscera to the Brain

In her book *Neurociencia del cuerpo: Cómo el organismo esculpe el cerebro* [*The Neuroscience of the Body: How the Organism Sculpts the Brain*], neuroscientist Nazareth Castellanos, an expert in the interactions between the brain and the body, offers a summary of the evidence that points to the fact that the influence of the body in the functioning of the brain is not limited to the area of emotions and feelings. It also influences perception directly. Furthermore, the rhythms (contractions and expansions) of organs like the heart, the lungs, and the gut set the rhythms of the brain's conscious perception of reality. We are all familiar with the experience of having our heartbeats, our breathing, or even our digestive system's rhythms become altered by certain experiences such as apprehension or excitement. But it turns out that the relationship also flows in the opposite direction. For instance, the state of our organs, including the microbiome in our guts, the rhythms of our breathing, and the frequency of our heartbeats, all exert a direct influence in the

The Affect Effect: Dynamics of Emotion in Political Thinking and Behavior, ed. Russell Neuman et al. (University of Chicago Press, 2007), 83–84.

104. Spezio and Adolphs, "Emotional Processing and Political Judgment," 84.

105. Spezio and Adolphs, "Emotional Processing and Political Judgment," 84.

functioning of our brains, including our attention and perception of reality.

Castellanos refers, for example, to the research led by Catherine Tallon-Baudry, who found that the brain is able to perceive an image only when the brain is responding to the information from the heart. In her experiments, according to Castellanos,

> her team registered the electromagnetic dynamic of the brain of a group of people while they were paying attention to images appearing on a screen. They were circles, which with faster or slower speed, appeared and disappeared from the screen. The people were supposed to push a button whenever they would become aware of having seen one of the circles. . . . The cardiac function was measured simultaneously with brain activity. To the surprise of the investigators, the hearts' beats had the capacity to generate a response in the brain. [It was a heart evoked response—HER—in the brain] . . . If the HER is high, that is, when the brain is responding to the heart, the experimental subjects were able to perceive the visual stimuli on the screen. If the HER is low, and therefore the brain is not responding to the heart, the object is not perceived.[106]

Furthermore, "the two main regions of the brain involved in this process were the Right Posterior Parietal cortex and the prefrontal ventromedial cortex."[107] Castellanos explains that those two regions are not directly involved in visual perception, but (as we saw in Damasio's explanation above) for the conscious experience of perception to happen, it is necessary to have a sense of self integrated to that perception, which is what those regions of the brain help with. We shall see in the next chapter that the formation of the sense of self mediated by those and other structures in the brain and the nervous system is not only important in the conscious perception of objects but also of spiritual or religious experience.

Castellanos further explains, referring to a different study, that "when the heart contracts and blood flows into the body (systole) our

---

106. Castellanos, *Neurociencia del cuerpo*, 179–80.

107. Castellanos, *Neurociencia del cuerpo*, 180.

eyes search for the most relevant information in the world that is being observed. Those eye movements may seem random but they represent the competition of information for our attention. When the heart expands and becomes full (diastole) we are soaked in the information that we have chosen as relevant."[108] Thus, the heart opens the brain to the conscious experience of perception.

The heart is not the only organ involved in orchestrating some functions of the brain. It turns out that our ability to learn successfully is connected to proper breathing.[109] There is an area in the brain, the posterior medial region (which we encountered above in Damasio's proposal), that needs to become deactivated for us to be able to focus our attention and learn properly. When we breathe properly, that region gets deactivated and learning happens effectively. Incidentally, that region is causally connected to the default mode network, a network that is active when our minds are not focusing on anything in particular and naturally engaging in daydreaming. Furthermore, it has been found that for long-term learning to take place, the hippocampus needs to be functioning with slow rhythmic waves (that is, the frequency of firing for its neurons needs to be that of gamma waves). It so happens that slow breathing fits the bill! So just as the palpitations of our heart mark the rhythms of our awareness, the rhythm of our breathing regulates our capacity for learning and remembering.

Finally, the gut plays an important role in the development, health, and functioning of the brain. The microbes in the intestines (and in our gums) have been associated with a protein called brain-derived neurotrophic factor (BDNF), which exerts a direct influence in the development of brain tissue. Castellanos refers to this molecule as the fertilizer that induces the generation of neuronal connections, especially of the hippocampus and the amygdala.[110] In animal models, the lack of BDNF resulted in deficits of memory, motivation, learning, and mood. Experiments in humans, particularly those with mood disorders, have found that consuming probiotics that contribute to the health of the gut's microbiome resulted in an increase in the mood and sense of

108. Castellanos, *Neurociencia del cuerpo*, 181–82.

109. Castellanos, *Neurociencia del cuerpo*, 140–41.

110. Castellanos, *Neurociencia del cuerpo*, 109.

well-being of the participants.[111] The gut also regulates the stress response by modulating the activity of the hypothalamic-pituitary-adrenal (HPA) axis. The healthier the gut, the stronger its ability to regulate negative emotional responses such as stress and anxiety.[112] Additionally, the peristaltic contractions and expansions of the intestines provide the brain with yet another, slower, mechanism to mark the rhythms of its functions. The gut is also important because it is where energy is generated for action, and so in the body's encounter with reality, the need for action is first instantiated in the gut. From there, we feel and then think the world of our perceptual experience into being.

Our conscious experience of reality is our experience of how our bodies are affected and respond to the ways reality "touches" our bodies or, more accurately, our embodied-spirited selves.

Conclusion

There is so much more that could be said about the ways the body and the brain are interconnected, even to the point of constituting each other. We have the brains we have because of the bodies we are (and the environments, events, and relationships through which our bodies and brains have been shaped); we have the bodies we have, and the environments and relationships we inhabit (and experience them the way we do), because of the brains we have. We are capable of relating to each other in meaningful ways because we are able, through the interplay of brain, mind, and body, to enter into the experiential world of others (even if only up to a point) and feel what they feel, see what they see, and hear what they hear. It is not despite our bodies and emotions that we are able to know the world but precisely because of and through our embodied minds or, better yet, our "spirited bodies," as theologian and philosopher Nancey Murphy says.[113]

What we experience as real, as possible, as inevitable, or as desirable is mediated by those processes of embodied-affective-cognitive valuations. That includes our perception of social dynamics and our place

111. Castellanos, *Neurociencia del cuerpo*, 113.

112. Castellanos, *Neurociencia del cuerpo*, 114–115.

113. Murphy, *Bodies and Souls, or Spirited Bodies?*

within them. It is through those processes that we not only endow certain social, economic, political, and spiritual configurations as simply *real*, or *the way things are*, but also sometimes even as *the way things ought to be*, even in the face of injustice, exploitation, and oppression. Thus, understanding those processes of affective-cognitive valuations is important for a project of decolonial liberation. If our experiences are always mediated by our brains and bodies, then it is not surprising that experiences of God, of the sacred, or of the holy are also embodied experiences. The transformations that religious experiences are able to produce are also embodied. It is "with, in, and under" the body (to use the expression from the eucharistic liturgy) that the divine Spirit decolonizes our emotions and liberates our brains. In the next chapter, we begin to explore how that happens.

CHAPTER THREE

Transformation

Divine Experiences in the Body-Mind-Brain

"My beloved is mine, and I am his."

—Song of Songs 2:16

Introduction

God's Action in, with and under the Embodied Brain

MY THESIS IS that through the action of the divine Spirit in, with, and under our bodies-minds-brains, we are set free from the deadly illusions that have been engraved in our embodied minds by centuries of coloniality, racism, heterosexism, and other evils, liberating us for effective collective and individual action to forge a reality more akin to the divine vision of abundant life and the flourishing of humanity side by side with the rest of God's creation. This process is necessarily proleptic in character and imperfect,[1] but it serves to orient our aspirations and actions and to evaluate them.

To that end, we turn our attention now to examining what might be happening in the brain and body when people have religious experiences or, as other researchers prefer to call them, experiences deemed religious.[2] The research in this area is controversial, but its findings, though preliminary and in need of further investigations, are very suggestive and worth exploring. With that caveat, let us examine what

1. *Proleptic* is a theological term that refers to influence of the expected future on the present. See "prolepsis," in Donald K. McKim, ed., *Westminster Dictionary of Theological Terms* (Westminster John Knox Press, 1996), 223.

2. That wording is a correction of the perspective offered by Ann Taves in her book *Religious Experience Reconsidered: A Building-Block Approach to the Study of Religion and Other Special Things* (Princeton University Press, 2009).

scientists have been able to elucidate about the neuroscience of religious experience. First, however, what do we mean by religious experience?

What Are Religious Experiences?

Functional Definitions

There is no single definition of religious experience. In fact, different disciplines have different definitions depending on the parameters of that discipline and on what it is interested in investigating. In sociology and anthropology, we encounter definitions that are very functional, because those disciplines are more interested in how religion functions and affects particular aspects of a society. They are not interested, as theologians or philosophers might be, in the intrinsic meanings of the content of religious beliefs deployed to explain religious experiences. In psychology, the emphasis has been on the ways religious ideations and practices are related to mental health, seeing religious experience as a symptom of neuroses or as a coping mechanism (Freud), as delusion (Richard Dawkins), or as an expression of deeper aspects of the human psyche (Jung). In cognitive science, the approach has been to focus on the question of the cognitive origins and templates of religious beliefs as a subcategory of beliefs in general but usually without exploring the referents of such beliefs.

Reductionism

In neuroscience, the approach has been to isolate a particular element of religious experiences (like mystical union, glossolalia [speaking in tongues], or compassion) or a specific practice (like meditation, prayer, or mindfulness) and then search for significant correlations between them and measurable neurophysiological functions. Another strategy is to propose models, such as the ones we will be exploring in this chapter, that explain the underlying neural activity accompanying religious phenomena but then reduce the phenomena itself to nothing but those biological processes, thus dismissing other interpretations and the spiritual dimensions of reality that those experiences point to.

Practically speaking, it is necessary for science to engage in reductionism; that is, it must study only that which its methods, models, and instruments are capable of studying. However, it is important to remember, as we shall emphasize in chapter 4, that the limits of our methods, models, or instruments do not denote the limits of reality itself. It is also important to remember that expertise in one particular aspect of a phenomenon, such as the neurological substrates of religious experience, does not automatically invest the researcher with the competency to speak authoritatively about other aspects of the phenomenon, such as its theological or philosophical dimensions.

That does not mean that scientists are not allowed to do theology or philosophy but that to do so, they must take care to acquire the necessary competencies in those areas. The same applies to theologians or philosophers wishing to engage in dialogue with the sciences. Theology is not science, and science is not theology; one cannot and should not be reduced to the other. I have tried to keep a clear distinction in this book between the science and the theology. The reader will be the judge of whether I have succeeded or not.

Religion and Religious Experience as Colonial Distortions

Regardless of the methodology used to study religious phenomena, the fact that the concepts of religion and religious experiences themselves are contested must be kept in mind. There are solid historical grounds for skepticism, because the concept of religion itself seems to have a colonial pedigree. The European Christian nations that engaged in the process of colonialism brought with them very particular notions (cognitive frames!) of what a religion is vis-à-vis other dimensions, such as politics or medicine, and imposed them on the cultures they encountered and colonized. Their practices make a category of religion and religious experience more of a projection than an objective phenomenon. Research in anthropology, history, and postcolonial studies has shed light on the fact that in many cultures, religious beliefs and practices were not clearly divided from other areas such as what we would today call medicine, science, or politics.

To single out a particular constellation of behaviors and experiences from a culture that does not make such separation and call them religious is to distort, or even artificially create, the reality one is trying to study. In other words, because the academic disciplines used to investigate religious phenomena emerged from within cultures that were deeply shaped by Christianity (or, more accurately, Christendom), the categories, intellectual tools, and the assumptions they make are a reflection of their own Christian world and not neutral or objective in relation to other, radically different cultures. Finally, other thinkers have followed Ann Taves's proposal—namely, that rather than speaking of religious experience, we should speak of experiences deemed religious, and rather than study the experiences in themselves, as if they were sui generis, researchers interested in religion should instead focus on the mental processes by which experiences are deemed religious.[3] All that is illustrative of the dizzying difficulty of offering a simple, broadly accepted definition of what religious experiences are and of what it is that people who study religious experiences are in fact studying.

An Open Inductive Approach

Rather than trying to choose from among those definitions or trying to devise my own definition of religious experience, I will leave the question open and proceed inductively, acknowledging elements of truth and limitations in all the approaches outlined above. Furthermore, an important feature of liberation and decolonial theologies is a radical acceptance of the particularity of one's own social location and the ways such location enables, limits, and shapes all knowledge, including the methodologies, assumptions, conclusions, and the criteria employed to reach knowledge—even scientific knowledge.

That does not mean that "anything goes," just that everything is conditioned by its particularities; therefore, in order to understand things properly, one must take those particularities into account as well. When a community is in power, it has the advantage that its own particularities are so omnipresent that they become invisible to that community, giving the appearance that its perspective is neither particular nor conditioned but universally applicable: "the way things are." That view is reflected in the belief that we have knowledge, while they [i.e., others] have opinions; we have science, while they have magical thinking; we have faith, while they have superstition. In chapter 4, we will go deeper into the ways that nonscientific factors influence scientific knowledge. This does not mean that scientific knowledge is not valid

3. Taves, *Religious Experience Reconsidered.*

but simply that it is circumscribed and contextual even in its universal extrapolations and applications. Good science knows that and accounts for it in its methods.

To recap, in this book we enter the phenomena of religious experiences from the perspective of curiosity and critical openness, without a forced a priori definition. Furthermore, this is an "interested" exploration (not neutral) because it is being done as part of a larger project—that is, the project of liberation and decolonization for the well-being of the human family (especially the poor, the oppressed, and the marginalized) and the flourishing of the rest of nature. It is also done from a theological perspective that engages scientific data as a potential source for theological reflection. As theologian Paul Tillich articulated, a difference between doing theology and scientifically studying religion is that the theologian stands in a position of intentional, even if critical, commitment to the faith.

Searching for Traces of Religious Experiences in the Brain

Epilepsy

Since ancient times, people have seen a connection between epileptic seizures and religious experience. That is not surprising since the characteristic feature of epileptic seizures is precisely the experience of being overpowered by a force alien to one's own self and yet operating from within one's own body. For that reason, epilepsy was called the sacred disease and its effects were attributed to either divine or demonic action. Over the centuries, with advances in fields such as anatomy, physiology, and medical science, it became possible to locate the origin of this disease in the brain. In the previous chapter, we learned that the brain operates via the flow of electrical pulses traveling from neuron to neuron and from one brain region to another and that when that flow of electricity in the brain gets out of control, it grows in intensity and spreads throughout as a storm wreaking havoc on the brains and lives of the patients. Sometimes this results in grand mal seizures, where the entire body is thrown on the ground, shaking violently. When the epileptic seizure happens in the temporal lobe (*temporal lobe epilepsy—TLE*), it can induce subjective experiences of a religious kind.

In his book *The Neuroscience of Religious Experience*, Patrick McNamara explains that "an epileptic seizure results when an abnormal and excessive synchronization of firing of brain neurons spreads across brain regions."[4] He explains that TLE seizures tend to have their origin deep within the temporal lobe, including the hippocampus, and even deeper into the limbic structures, especially the amygdala. During TLE, the "hypersynchronized and hypercharged neurons in the amygdala have the effect of chronically overstimulating the structure."[5] During the TLE episode, the amygdala sends excitatory signals to the structures on the cortex and inhibitory ones to the hypothalamus. Since the role of the amygdala is to detect events of emotional significance and tag them for the organism to act on them, one of the aspects of the experience resulting from TLE is the sense, at the cortical level, of a "greater number and frequencies of significant emotional events." It is not surprising, then, that the clinical record is replete of case studies where people undergoing TLE seizures reported having experiences of religious significance.

One thing I find intriguing in the above description of the neurology of TLE-induced religious experiences is the role of the hypothalamus.[6] If the hypothalamus connects the brain to the body, how would inhibiting it affect the subjective experience? Would it be felt as a disembodied experience? Could that be a contributing factor to the devaluation of the body that we find in certain strands of religiosity and mysticism? Furthermore, if it is true that we need a sense of our embodied self (e.g., Damasio's *proto-self*)[7] as a reference point for our experiences of reality, what would it mean to have an experience without that reference point? These questions are beyond the scope of this book and need empirical and experimental investigation. What can be said about it here is that the devaluation of the body has had tragic consequences throughout history. It has resulted in the neglect of the bodily

4. McNamara, *The Neuroscience of Religious Experience*, 91.

5. McNamara, *The Neuroscience of Religious Experience*, 91.

6. We will see below that in other kinds of religious experience, the hypothalamus does play an important role: rather than getting inhibited by the amygdala, it gets hyperactivated to the point of triggering intense responses in the parasympathetic and sympathetic nervous systems.

7. Damasio, *The Feeling of What Happens*, 25–26.

dimensions and needs of people and sometimes even in the practice of punishing the body for the sake of purifying the soul. It has also been used to bolster unjust hierarchies of the colonial, patriarchal, and racist kinds, whereby those peoples categorized as closer to the body (e.g., women, people of Black and Indigenous background, and people with disabilities) are assumed to be inferior to those close to spirit (in this case, understood as mind or a sort of universal reason). That served as a justification for having white men of means (and their nations) on top of the social, political, and economic hierarchy, since they were seen as closer to reason and more able to keep in check the unruly impulses of the body. This book is written from a different perspective: one in the same spirit, if not in total agreement, with proposals such as Mayra Rivera's relational transcendence in the face and touch of the other[8] and Nancey Murphy's nonreductive physicalism.[9] Bodies matter!

Going back to McNamara's proposal, what we have here, in the case of TLE seizures resulting in experiences deemed religious by those who undergo them, is an instance of religious experience as a naturally occurring phenomena. That raises the question for McNamara whether there might be a *religious circuit* in the brain, and if so, why would nature, through the processes of evolution and natural selection, endow humans with such a circuit?

A Religious Circuit in the Brain?

After reviewing the evidence, and contrary to the perspective of other neuroscientists,[10] McNamara gives an affirmative answer to the question of whether there is a religious circuit in the brain.[11] McNamara

8. Rivera, *The Touch of Transcendence.*

9. Murphy, *Bodies and Souls, or Spirited Bodies?*

10. Mario Beauregard and Denyse O'Leary argue that religious experience is the purview of the entire brain, not of a particular neural network. Beauregard is in fact one of the few neuroscientists who defends the idea of the soul as a distinct part of the human person and that the brain therefore functions not to create the experience but simply to transmit it. See *The Spiritual Brain: A Neuroscientist's Case for the Existence of the Soul* (HarperOne, 2007).

11. Before McNamara, the neuroscientist Rawn Joseph made a similar argument, identifying the limbic system as a sort of "transmitter to God." See his article "The Limbic System and the Soul: Evolution and the Neuroanatomy of Religious

surmises that "the literature on TLE-related religiosity gives us an initial clue as to the brain circuits that normally handle religious material—namely, the right-sided temporal and prefrontal networks as it is these networks that attach religious concepts to the impulses originating in the amygdala."[12] More specifically, and in technical terms, he surmises that "the most important regions of the brain for studies of religious expression appear to be a circuit linking up the orbital[13] and dorsomedial[14] prefrontal cortex, the ascending serotoninergic systems,[15] the mesocortical DA system,[16] the amygdala/hippocampus, and the right anterior[17] lobes." In addition to those regions, there are also neurotransmitters and genes involved in the process. They are, most prominently but not exclusively, dopamine and serotonin, as well as the COMT, 5-HT2A, and VMAT2 genes plus "a polymorphism[18] on the dopamine receptor gene, DRD4."[19] We won't go into that level of detail in this book, but I offer it for those who might want to go deeper into the neurology and neurochemistry of religious experience. What matters to McNamara is that these systems seem to overlap with those involved in the creation of our sense of self. But I am getting ahead of myself. The question that concerns us now is, What are those experiences like?

Experience," *Zygon: Journal of Religion and Science* 36, no. 1 (March 2001): 105–36; and his book *The Transmitter to God: The Limbic System, the Soul, and Spirituality* (University Press California, 2001).

12. McNamara, *The Neuroscience of Religious Experience*, 93.

13. This refers to the area of the prefrontal cortex immediately above the orbits of the eyes.

14. This refers to the interior wall of the prefrontal cortex where one lobe faces the other.

15. A serotonin pathway.

16. A dopamine pathway.

17. Anterior means "toward the front."

18. A *gene polymorphism* refers to the presence of a slight variation of a particular gene in a population; the idea that there can be different versions of the same gene will be a part of McNamara's proposal, discussed below, on why the self is divided and how religious experience helps with its integration.

19. McNamara, *The Neuroscience of Religious Experience*, 143.

In the novel *Lying Awake*, author Mark Salzman explores this connection between TLE and spiritual experience. The main character of Salzman's novel is Helen, a Carmelite nun whose suggestive religious name is Sister John of the Cross. She has profound religious experiences of the mystical kind where she finds herself enveloped by God's love and light in a way that is beyond any possible doubt. Salzman's prose describing the experience is beautiful, almost mystical:

> Pure awareness stripped her of everything. She became an ember carried upward by the heat of an invisible flame. Higher and higher she rose, away from all she knew. Powerless to save herself, she drifted up toward infinity until the vacuum sucked the feeble light out of her.
>
> A darkness so pure it glistened, then out of that darkness,
>
> nova.
>
> More luminous than any sun, transcending visibility, the flare consumed everything, it lit up all of existence. In this radiance she could see forever, and everywhere she looked, she saw God's love. As soon as she could move again, she opened her notebook and began writing.[20]

Even though this is a work of fiction, the description of the experience resonates with the mystical literature. In the novel, the main character uses her experiences to write beautiful poetry that inspires many. There is a problem, however. The mystical experiences of Sister John of the Cross are accompanied by terrible migraines. When they become unbearable, her mother superior instructs her to see a neurologist. After some tests, it is determined that she has a meningioma in her temporal lobe, which is causing occasional epileptic seizures and is probably responsible for her symptoms of seeing light, feeling her body dissolve into the light, and experiencing intense love and hypergraphia. Given the severeness of her migraines, she agrees to surgery to remove

20. Mark Salzman, *Lying Awake* (Knopf, 2001), 5–6.

the meningioma. Once the tumor is removed, the mystical experiences are gone as well.

Was the tumor making her neural networks create fake perceptions with no basis in reality, or was it a sort of happy accident making it possible for her temporal lobes to function as a sort of "transmitter to God" in the way, for example, that a genetic mutation allows us to see color and not just perceive reality in black and white?[21] We will come back to these questions later; right now, let's continue our exploration of the links between neural activity and religious experiences.

Inducing Artificial Religious Experiences

If there is a correlation between neural activity in the temporal lobes and religious experience, would it then be possible to provoke religious experiences by stimulating the relevant neural networks? Several tools for testing this hypothesis are available to neuroscientists. One of them, introduced earlier in this book, is transcranial magnetic timulation (TMS).[22] It consists of arrays of coils that produce magnetic fields that can be focused on specific areas of the brain through the scalp. The magnetic field interacts with the electrical fields, which allow neurons to communicate with each other. Using this tool, neuroscientists can temporarily increase or decrease activity in particular parts of the brain, even artificially creating temporary brain lesions.

As was mentioned previously, the Canadian neuroscientist Michael Persinger has adapted this technique to test whether religious experiences can be induced by stimulating the relevant parts of the brain.[23] His device, fitted into a helmet, is referred to as "the God helmet." His

---

21. Joseph, *The Transmitter to God.*

22. See Lauren Stewart and Vincent Walsh, "Transcranial Magnetic Stimulation in Human Cognition," in Senior et al., *Methods in Mind*, 1–26.

23. Michael A. Persinger, "Religious and Mystical Experiences as Artifacts of Temporal Lobe Function: A General Hypothesis," *Perceptual and Motor Skills*, 57, no. 3 part 2 (1983): 1255–62; and Michael A. Persinger and Katherine Makarec, "The Feeling of a Presence and Verbal Meaningfulness in Context of Temporal Lobe Function: Factor Analytic Verification of the Muses?," *Brain and Cognition* 20, no. 2 (1992): 217–26.

experiments, which involve sensorial deprivation while the God helmet sends magnetic waves to the temporal lobes, have had mixed results. Some have reported actual religious experiences; others describe feeling a presence, like a shadow, next to them; and yet others report just feeling strange.[24] Science journalist Barbara Bradley Hagerty underwent the God-helmet experiment. She recalls her experience thus:

> "I am utterly relaxed," I said in a thick, gravelly voice. "I feel as if I'm dissolving into the chair. It's not that I don't have boundaries, but the boundaries include the chair." Pause. "I am communing with a chair." "Great."
>
> For the reminder of the session, I felt blackness cresting over itself like roiling waves. I briefly saw a woman's face, but even in that suggestible moment, I knew these were creations of an imagination trying too hard, and certainly not the presence of a Sentient Being. Mercifully, the sessions ended a few moments later.[25]

Persinger's results have been difficult to replicate by other scientists.[26] One critique raised against his conclusions is that rather than attributing the religious dimension of the experience to the activation of the temporal lobe, it could be simply the result of normal processes of interpretation due in part to suggestibility. However, as we saw in the previous chapter, it is difficult to tease out what is a purely cognitive process of interpretation versus an embodied feeling of what is happening.[27]

---

24. Hagerty, *Fingerprints of God*, 133–48.

25. Hagerty, *Fingerprints of God*, 140.

26. P. Granqvist et al., "Sensed Presence and Mystical Experiences Are Predicted by Suggestibility, Not by the Application of Transcranial Weak Complex Magnetic Fields," *Neuroscience Letters* 379, no. 1 (2005): 1–6.

27. For a philosophical and theological assessment of Persinger's research, and others discussed below, see Runehov, *Sacred or Neural?*, 67–136.

Brain Scans of Religious Experience

In the late 1990s, a group of researchers designed a series of brain scan experiments[28] to assess what is going on in the brain when people undergo a certain type of mystical experience[29]—that is, when they have the mystical experience of becoming one with God, the universe, or reality. They coined the term *Absolute Unitary Being* to refer to the experience in a way that could encompass a wide variety of religious and naturalistic perspectives.[30] Working out of the University of Pennsylvania, psychiatrist and anthropologist Eugene d'Aquili partnered with brain radiologist Andrew Newberg and others. They recruited a group of Buddhist monks and Franciscan nuns, known for their vast experience in prayer and meditation, to scan their brains while they were having a religious experience. These studies were controversial, and the results need to be analyzed critically,[31] but they provide very intriguing leads for theological reflection.

The experiment consisted of inviting the monk or nun into a quiet room where they would pray or meditate the way they normally do. Meanwhile, they had an IV line connected to them, ready to inject them with a radioactive marker designed to accumulate in different regions of the brain depending on how active such regions were. An increase in a certain brain region would cause an increase in blood flow to that region, and a decrease in a particular brain region would result

---

28. The experiments were based on the neuropsychological model of religious and mystical states proposed by the psychiatrist and anthropologist Eugene d'Aquili and his colleague Andrew Newberg, an expert in internal medicine and radiology. See their paper "Religious and Mystical States: A Neuropsychological Model," *Zygon* 28, no. 2 (June 1993): 177–200), and their book *The Mystical Mind.*

29. Andrew B. Newberg et al., "The Measurement of Cerebral Blood Flow During the Complex Cognitive Task of Meditation Using HMPAO-SPECT Imaging," *Journal of Nuclear Medicine* 38 (1997): 95; and A. Newberg et al., "The Neurophysiological Correlates of Meditation: Implications for Neuroimaging," *Journal of the Indian Academy of Clinical Medicine* 3 (1998): 13–18. A nontechnical presentation of the research and the authors' scientific, philosophical, and theological conclusions can be found in Newberg et al., *Why God Won't Go Away.*

30. Newberg et al., *Why God Won't Go Away*, 160–62.

31. Runehov, *Sacred or Neural?*, 137–200.

in less blood flowing into that area.[32] The experimental subjects also had a string attached to one of their fingers so that when they felt that they had reached the peak of their prayer or meditation experience, they could indicate it to the researchers by pulling the string, and the flow of the marker would begin lodging throughout the brain in different proportions depending, again, on what areas were more active and which less active. They would then be taken to a PET scan machine, which would use the radiation emanating from the marker to create an image of the brain with different colors to indicate which regions were more active (intensely red) and which were less active (blues and greens). This method (PET scans) is different from fMRIs in that it does not measure the activity "live" as it is happening; rather, it takes a "snapshot" of what the brain was like in the past, the state of the brain at the moment when the marker was injected.[33] Afterward, the monks and nuns were interviewed for a phenomenological description of their religious experiences.

A Neurotheological Model of Religious Experience

The results obtained from the neuroimaging studies mentioned above were intriguing, even if their interpretation continues to be a matter of debate.[34] Newberg and colleagues found that there was an increase of activity in the prefrontal cortex and, perhaps most importantly, a very significant decrease of activity in the section of the superior parietal lobes, an area dedicated to creating the boundaries of the body and its orientation in space.[35] The increase of activity in the prefrontal cortex is consistent with meditation and prayer practices, which begin with the intention to focus one's attention on the prayer, breath, or whatever is

32. For an explanation of the use of measurements of oxygenated blood in brain-scanning techniques, such as PET, see Gazzaniga et al., *Cognitive Neuroscience*, 105.

33. Gazzaniga et al., *Cognitive Neuroscience*, 105–7.

34. Michael L. Spezio, "Engaging d'Aquili and Newberg's *The Mystical Mind: Understanding Biology in Religious Experience*: The Biogenetic Structuralist Approach of Eugene d'Aquili and Andrew Newberg," *Zygon* 36, no. 3 (September 2001): 477–84.

35. Newberg et al., *Why God Won't Go Away*, 2–10.

the object of one's focus during meditation and prayer.[36] And the sharp decrease in activity in the parietal lobes corresponds to the experience, reported by the experimental subjects, of mystical union, whether with God or the universe.[37]

Focusing Attention

In their book *The Mystical Mind: Probing the Biology of Religious Experience*, d'Aquili and Newberg proposed the following model to predict the chain of events happening in the brain and the nervous system that lead to religious experience of the mystical union type.[38] The process begins with the intention to meditate or pray, which is undergirded by the prefrontal cortex, beginning with the right hemisphere (although, as we saw in the previous chapter, there is constant communication between the two hemispheres of the brain). The intention to meditate or pray involves focusing one's attention, which means filtering out any neural input not relevant to the task at hand. That means that the right prefrontal cortex sends signals to the hippocampus, which in tandem with the thalamus, then blocks the flow of irrelevant signals.[39]

Softening of the Body in the Brain

The result is that the neural networks in the brain responsible for creating the perceptual experience of the body are still active (they are always active in normal and healthy brains) but with a dwindling flow of neural input from the senses. In the right hemisphere, those neural structures, which are located on the superior part of the parietal lobe, are responsible for creating the sense of space in which the body moves and acts. The equivalent structure in the left hemisphere, Newberg and colleagues explain, is involved in creating the sense of self and the boundaries between the environment and our embodied self. This structure—namely, the superior parietal lobe (which they dub the

36. Newberg et al., *Why God Won't Go Away*, 1–2.

37. Newberg et al., *Why God Won't Go Away*, 86–87.

38. See Figure 6.1 in d'Aquili and Newberg, *The Mystical Mind*, 111.

39. See "The Neurobiology of Mystical Experience," in Newberg et al., *Why God Won't Go Away*, 113–22.

OAA)[40]—uses the information it receives from the senses and memory to weave the (perceptual) world into being. When the inflow of information is inhibited to this area, it continues to do its work but with the limited information it is now receiving.[41]

Union with the Sacred

Imagine that you are practicing meditation or contemplative prayer. You choose an image to focus on, say, God's unfathomable love, the crucifixion, or simply the person of Jesus Christ. Now, because of the filtering effect of the hippocampus and the prefrontal cortex, the only information the superior parietal lobe has to work with is that which is the object of your contemplation. That is all the structure has to work with to weave into being the (perceptual) world that you inhabit plus the body in which you inhabit it.[42] That means that you experience the world vanishing as an illusion and the only thing that remains is whatever you chose as the object of your contemplation.[43] For Christian mystics, the world has disappeared at that moment and only Christ remains: Christ is the spatial matrix in which one now moves, lives, and has their being.

The process of being absorbed into a sacred figure begins in the right hemisphere, where the perceptual representations of the physical space inhabited by the body are generated, but as we saw in chapter 2, the two hemispheres work in tandem, so the left hemisphere's OAA also begins to deafferent. This results in the experience of the boundaries of the self softening until, as we shall see below, they eventually disappear altogether, so that our sense of bounded self is extinguished and we become totally absorbed into the sacred reality we were contemplating. If this is Christ, then in our perceptual-experiential world we die to ourselves and Christ becomes all in all. As the apostle Paul put it, "It is no longer I who live, but it is Christ who lives in me" (Gal 2:20).

40. See Figure 2.1 in Newberg et al., *Why God Won't Go Away*, 19.

41. According to this interpretation, even though that brain structure cannot receive incoming neural inputs, it can nonetheless send out its own outputs to other regions of the brain.

42. D'Aquili and Newberg, *The Mystical Mind*, 41–42.

43. Newberg et al., *Why God Won't Go Away*, 122–27.

Amygdala Activation

As we begin to experience the dissolution of the boundaries of the spatial world, namely the "I-it" or "I-them" distinctions, and as the boundaries of the embodied self begin to feel softer and disappear, the amygdala takes notice that something strange is happening. Additionally, given the intention to focus our attention, communicated to the amygdala from the frontal lobes, the amygdala sends signals to the hippocampus to block out all irrelevant information (neural pulses from the senses, memory, and so on). That adds energy to its inhibitory effects, further filtering out extraneous information and intensifying the experience of mystical union.

Hypothalamus and Nervous System Activation

The hypothalamus, which connects the brain to the body and the body to the brain via the nervous system and modulates the autonomic responses, will eventually trigger the sympathetic or parasympathetic response of the autonomic nervous system.[44] The one that gets activated first depends on the nature of the practice (e.g., relaxing seated meditation versus moving one's body rhythmically to the beat of drums). The intervention of the amygdala-hypothalamus-(para)sympathetic nervous system adds to the experience the dimension of feeling, such as, perhaps, a feeling of eeriness or even a sense of dread but also of bliss and pleasure. That chain of events is iterative, building power and increasing in intensity as the cycle repeats itself until the outcome is the total deafferentation of the right OAA, resulting in the experience that the object of contemplation (e.g., Christ) has now become the world.

The right hemisphere of the brain initiates the process, but almost immediately, the corresponding structures in the left hemisphere join in the sacred neural dance. The chain of events reflects those in the right, except that the OAA in the left hemisphere has a different function than its counterpart in the right. The left OAA has the function of creating the sense of the self and its boundaries. Therefore, when it becomes deafferented, this results in the experience of the embodied self dissolving into the world, like a drop of water falling into an ocean of water. The subjective experience is that of the person's embodied

44. Newberg et al., *Why God Won't Go Away*, 77–123.

self dissolving into the reality that the right hemisphere had created—for instance, becoming one with Christ or being absorbed into God's unfathomable love.

Paradoxical Feelings

Remember, from the previous chapter, the important role played by the body and the emotions in the way we experience the world. This is also true about mystical experiences: they are embodied experiences! This is, according to Newberg and colleagues, thanks to the participation of the nervous system via the autonomic response. With the buildup of intensity (and years of training), the sympathetic response becomes so energetic that it leads to the hypothalamus triggering the (adjacent) nerves responsible for the parasympathetic response. This *spillover effect* results in a simultaneous sympathetic and parasympathetic response, which is instantiated at the emotional level as the paradoxical experience of being utterly relaxed and fiercely alert at the same time, of feeling dread and tranquility at once.[45] Furthermore, we saw in the previous chapter that one of the roles of the body in the way we experience reality is to tag it emotionally and assign it with value (recall Damasio's somatic marker hypothesis and Spezio and Adolph's integrated cognitive affective model). Thus, the intense autonomic responses that accompany religious experiences of the kind studied by Newberg and d'Aquili tag the reality being experienced as not only real but also of an order higher than normal reality itself. The result is that the memory of such experience is accompanied with the feeling that what was experienced had a quality of being unquestionably real—that is, more real than real—plus an aura of sacredness.

Those affective dimensions underlying religious experiences of the kind described above can be amplified by adding elements that would strengthen the amygdala's involvement, such as special smells (like incense, sage, or sweetgrass), unusual postures (like the way Sufi dervishes hold one hand facing up and the other facing down while they swirl in unison), musical rhythms, and objects with high emotional content (such as the relics of saints). At the highest level of the religious experience, the brain gets tired of selectively filtering out information and it ends up blocking out all information, so that now even Christ,

45. Newberg et al., *Why God Won't Go Away*, 40–42.

God, the Buddha, or whatever object we were focusing on during prayer or meditation disappears into a background of a nothingness that is all there is, a reality (nothingness) beyond images, language, or cognitive categories. How do we make sense of such an experience? How do we describe it to others? How do we explain it to ourselves?!

Making Sense of What Is Experienced

In chapter 1, we learned that beliefs are formed in the mind through the operations of various cognitive devices and processes. It is through the action of those cognitive processes that the mind then tries to make sense of the experience.[46] Using a different nomenclature, Newberg and colleagues refer to these cognitive processes and systems as "cognitive operators." They mention the following operators as playing a role in making sense of religious experience:[47]

- the holistic operator: integrates the parts into a larger whole
- the reductionist operator: carves out the part from the whole
- the abstractive operator: creates general categories and fits what it perceives into them
- the quantitative operator: "permits the abstraction of quantity from the perception of various elements"[48]
- the causal operator: generates assumptions of cause-and-effect relationships
- the binary operator: divides the world into opposites
- the existential operator: endows perceived reality with its sense of realness
- the emotional value operator: marks reality with affective values

Through the functioning of these operators, working in tandem with our memory and language systems, the brain interprets itself to

46. For an overview on models of religious cognition, see Kelly Bulkeley, *The Wondering Brain: Thinking About Religion with and Beyond Cognitive Neuroscience* (Routledge, 2005); and James A. Van Slyke, *The Cognitive Science of Religion* (Ashgate, 2011).

47. Newberg et al., *Why God Won't Go Away*, 46–53.

48. Newberg et al., *Why God Won't Go Away*, 49.

itself (as we shall explore in more detail in chapter 6), weaving a coherent narrative to make sense of what has been experienced. This is in part why experiences cannot be reduced to simply the firing of particular brain networks.[49] I suspect, as mentioned above, that this is why religious experiences are difficult to replicate, as in the case of Persinger's God-helmet experiments.

Interpretation through language and whatever symbolic-narrative hermeneutic templates one has received from one's formative communities are not peripheral to the experience but constitutive of the experience itself, as well as the context, circumstances, and environment where the experience takes place (physical, social, and imaginative).[50] Newberg and colleagues, for example, refer to Joseph Campbell's work on the role of myths in the ways we explain reality to ourselves in meaningful ways.[51] Philosophers and theologians have also been lifting up for some time now the centrality of language and myth not only in religious and mystical experience but also in our experience of reality in general,[52] especially when the experience of reality overflows our normal categories and pushes us outside the limits of our understanding. That can happen because of tragedy, new situations that are simply beyond our comprehension, or ecstatic experiences where reality seems saturated with something that transcends it.[53]

By now it should be clear that the interpretation of any experience is not a post-facto addition but is actually constitutive of the experience itself as well as of its remembrance (re/member/ance); that is, every time the experiences are remembered, they are reassembled together anew with potential new elements and perspectives. That is what makes healing from trauma, including the transgenerational trauma of ills like coloniality, racism, and heterosexism, possible. Furthermore, I believe

---

49. Runehov, "Experiencing and Explaining," in *Sacred or Neural?*, 27–47.

50. See, for example, the model proposed by Raimon Panikkar, "Constituents of the Experience," in *The Experience of God: Icons of the Mystery* (Fortress Press, 2006), 25.

51. Newberg et al., *Why God Won't Go Away*, 55.

52. See, for example, Chomsky, *Language and Mind*; Lindbeck, *The Nature of Doctrine*; and Sue Patterson, *Realist Christian Theology in a Postmodern Age* (Cambridge University Press, 1999).

53. I am borrowing this term from Jean-Luc Marion, "The Saturated Phenomenon," in *The Visible and the Revealed* (Fordham University Press, 2008).

that through the careful use of adequate theological symbols, narratives, and rituals that tap into the types of religious experiences explored here, a sort of embodied affective-cognitive grammar of faith is gradually acquired. This grammar could allow us to dispel the internalized illusions generated by the colonial matrix of power and its other accompanying systems of exclusion and oppression and, through the decolonization of the affective and cognitive imaginary, begin to envision and enact alternative ways of being together as a society.

Religious Experience as a Creation Matrix for the Self

Why the Natural Selection of a Religious Circuit in the Brain?

One question that scientists ask themselves is, why would the evolutionary process select for a system in the brain one with the potential to generate religious experiences? According to evolutionary thinking, traits are selected for because they increase the ability of a species to survive in its environment and to pass on its genes to the next generation. It is not, incidentally, about the survival of the strongest but rather of the fittest (that is, of those species who have a good fit with their particular environments). In the case of the human brain systems that undergird religious experiences, d'Aquili and Newberg speculate that such brain systems were not selected for directly because of their religious function but rather because of their original role in mating and their secondary effects in the rearing of children.

It so happens that, according to Newberg and d'Aquili, the same neural circuits that are involved in religious experiences of the mystical union type are also the brain structures involved in the experience of orgasm during sexual intercourse. The activation of those circuits during coitus creates a sense of union between the mating partners. The experience during orgasm is one of losing one's self and blending with the other, becoming one. No wonder Genesis speaks of "becoming one flesh."[54] In any case, going back to their evolutionary explanation of the religious abilities of the human brain, d'Aquili and Newberg explain that given the vulnerability of human babies, especially in a

54. Gen 2:24.

prehistoric environment, infants have a better chance of survival if they have more than just their mother looking after them. Hence, thanks to the mystical union experience that sexual intercourse can be—with the mediation of the autonomic nervous system and the limbic and frontal cortical structures, facilitated by the intervention of hormones and neurotransmitters such as oxytocin (love), dopamine (pleasure), and serotonin (satiation)—it could result in long-lasting bonds of affection forged between the partners and, by extension, with the children. It was for that reason, according to Darwinian logic, that the ability to have experiences of mystical union became a feature of the human brain. Even if most humans don't have extraordinary experiences of ecstatic mystical union, the fact remains that to some degree, they have the neural machinery necessary to have such experiences.

Applications of the Brain's Religious Circuit to Society

Once the brain had in place the neural apparatus necessary for unitive experiences, such experiences didn't have to be confined to the realm of sex, procreation, and child-rearing. Think, for example, of the human capacity to stand and walk on two legs as opposed to four. At the time of this writing, the Olympic Games are happening, and the range of ways in which humans have been able to make use of this ability—from gymnastics to running to tae kwon do—is astounding. Similarly, the naturalistic reasons why neural, cognitive, and affective abilities emerged in the human body does not mean that they are strictly limited to those functions for which they evolved. Thus, Newberg and colleagues explain, the same neural dynamics that made possible the feeling of mystical union with one's mate also made it possible for members of the same family, tribe, or community to experience a deep sense of union vis-à-vis other groups.[55]

Initiation rites and rituals performed before going to war against other groups or before going out together into the wilderness to search or hunt for food trigger the chain of events described above, allowing the members of the family, tribe, community, or nation to experience a sort of mystical union with their group.[56] That union allows them to

55. Newberg et al., *Why God Won't Go Away*, 125–27.

56. Newberg et al., *Why God Won't Go Away*, 80–85.

work better as a unit and, when necessary, to sacrifice for each other. That sense of union could be intensified by the use of a common totemic animal or symbol, which would represent the collective identity of the group, and the rituals could include elements increasing the risks and emotional intensity experienced, thus, as we saw above, adding energy to the amygdala-hypothalamus-body axis.

The resulting experience is one of total identification (and loyalty) with one's family, tribe, or group. We will later explore how that process of collective identity formation through quasi-religious mystical experiences is one of the mechanisms by which the harmful structures and practices of coloniality, racism, heterosexism, classism, and ableism are buttressed and how, thanks to those same processes, they can be dismantled. But first, we must go deeper into exploring the religious dimensions of those experiences.

Application of the Brain's Religious Circuit to Religious Experience

Once that neural system is in place, it can also be used for transcendental purposes. Just as the system makes it possible for romantic partners to experience a sense of radical unity between them, and just as it makes it possible for groups to feel a sense of collective union, similarly, that same system makes it possible for people to experience a sense of unity with nature, with other sentient beings, with the universe as a whole, and with the divine in the many expressions in which it makes itself available to us. As mentioned before, just because an experience is the result of the activity of brain and cognitive mechanisms does not necessarily mean that the experience does not correspond to something real. In chapters 5 and 6, we will explore the theological logic that goes into exploring the mystery that these experiences seem to point to. For now, from a purely scientific (and therefore theologically agnostic) perspective, the question remains not just why nature would endow humans with brain circuitry capable of religious experiences, but why religious experiences seem to be favored, considering how widespread religiosity is across the planet.

Religious Experience as Key to Integration into a Unified Self

Now we can return to McNamara's proposal. His model is that the brain circuits underlying religious experiences are also the brain circuits involved in the formation of the self. Based on his analysis of the literature of studies on the psychology and neurology of religious phenomena, McNamara proposes that through a process that he calls *decentering*, religious experiences allow for the integration of fragmented selves into strong, unified selves.

Recall how in chapter 1 we learned that according to cognitive science, the mind is not one thing but a collection of many things, like a Swiss Army knife. And remember how we discussed that the collection of cognitive devices that constitutes the mind do not work in serial but in parallel, which means that they can sometimes be at odds with each other, as the Stroop test humorously illustrates. In chapter 2, we learned that the same is true about the physical brain—namely, that it consists of many structures, chemicals, and neural networks forming circuits, networks of circuits, and loops of nodes dedicated to particular functions and tasks. We further learned that different kinds of information are processed in the brain in different regions and little by little become integrated with other information until they are woven into a perceptual story that we tell ourselves mostly by the agency of our frontal lobes, which also determine how to act accordingly. All these circuits and systems need to be brought together to work in tandem toward a unified experience. The fact that our perception of reality is as unified and coherent as it is is a miracle!

The inner fragmented nature of the self, from a cognitive and neuroscience perspective, is even deeper than our cognitive devices and neural networks; it goes as deep as our genes. That is so because our genes come in pairs (called alleles); we receive one from our biological mother and the other one from our biological father.[57] Sometimes the two versions of a gene for a particular trait or behavior can be at odds with each other due to slight mutations in their sequences, leading to a conflict happening deep within our embodied selves. The way that genes become translated into actual traits, behaviors, or medical conditions is very complex and beyond the scope of this book.[58] Just because someone has a gene that has been correlated with a certain condition, like addiction or cancer, it does not immediately mean that the person

57. McNamara, *The Neuroscience of Religious Experience*, 34–37.

58. For a study on the genetics of religious experience, see Dean Hamer, *The God Gene: How Faith Is Hardwired into Our Genes* (Doubleday, 2004).

will develop that condition. The point here is simply to illustrate the depth to which our selves are divided and the monumental task that it is to achieve a sense of unity within one's self.

Religious experiences, argues McNamara, bring those fragments together into increasing harmony and place them under the intentional control of the executive functions of the frontal cortex. How? Through decentering. The process begins with a sense of dissatisfaction toward aspects of one's self, accompanied by negative affect and, sometimes, internal dialogue. Then there is a search in one's memory for an alternative, ideal self.[59] That can be a sacred figure, like Jesus Christ, a saint, or even a secular leader whom one reveres. Meanwhile, one's sense of self becomes temporarily suspended: "The current Self is decoupled from its control over executive resources of the individual and placed in a suppositional logical space . . . [while] a search for a possible Self that will solve the conflict or problem is launched."[60] Once an ideal model for a new self has been identified, the next step is to surrender one's old self to that sacred figure, leader, or ideal self. That takes our cognitive and affective processes offline,[61] allowing for some connections to become undone and new ones to be formed, a process of repair and renewal. The next step is a binding of ourselves to the new ideal self. According to McNamara, when this process goes well, it results in "a deep integration of personality and resolution of very deep and otherwise insoluble internal conflicts."[62]

This also translates to a greater ability to cooperate with others for the sake of commonly established goals and to seek the well-being of others, even at great costs to the self but without surrendering a healthy sense of autonomy. Even when we feel that our old self has died and that our new self is inextricably bound to the self of a religious figure, such as God, Christ, the Holy Spirit, the Buddha, Krishna, or even impersonal (or suprapersonal) spiritual forces such as the Tao or the Wisdom, the

---

59. McNamara's proposal uses the identity formation cognitive architecture model of S. Nichols and S. Stitch, "A Cognitive Theory of Pretense," *Cognition* 74, no. 2 (2000): 115–47; see also *The Neuroscience of Religious Experience*, Figures 3.1 and 3.2, 48–49.

60. McNamara, *The Neuroscience of Religious Experience*, 50.

61. See, above, Newberg and d'Aquili's model for mystical union through contemplation.

62. McNamara, *The Neuroscience of Religious Experience*, 55.

experience is one where the self is infinitely expanded and we become more authentically ourselves.

In sum, McNamara's theory is that:

> religion uses the decentering process to help transform the Self and to resolve internal conflict. The process is ongoing, involving constant growth and ever greater internal freedom and external cooperation. The executive Self is more than just a psychological and cultural construct that heals inner divisions and allows for greater social cooperation: it is also a highly sophisticated and very delicate system that is capable of handling greater computational and information-processing demands than any comparable system based on divided consciousness.[63]

That is the result when things go right. Sometimes, however, they go wrong. McNamara points out at least two ways in which the process of religious-guided decentering can go wrong.[64] One is when we choose an unworthy character as our model self. This is what happens when we fall under the influence of cult leaders, egomaniacal political leaders, toxic ideologies, and other similar situations. Because one has surrendered control of the self to them, one's self ends up being diminished rather than enlarged and strengthened. In theological terms, this is equivalent to the effects of idolatry, giving that which belongs only to God (namely, absolute trust and loyalty) to that which is not God.

From a liberation theology and decolonial perspective, this can illuminate the process by which people fall victim to dehumanizing ideologies even when they diminish one's own self. By surrendering one's self to an idolatrous idea of nation, race, political party, or ideological project that is built on the exploitation, oppression, and exclusion of some groups for the benefit of others, one is granting that ideology, national identity, or racial construction the power to shape one's very sense of self. The allure can sometimes be strong, even for those who belong to groups on the losing end, because by acquiescing and collaborating with

---

63. McNamara, *The Neuroscience of Religious Experience*, 258.

64. See "Risky Effects of Decentering," in McNamara, *The Neuroscience of Religious Experience*, 57–58.

the idolatrous system, one is rewarded with partial privileges vis-à-vis those who won't collaborate or won't acknowledge the legitimacy of the system, including the affective reward of feeling close to that model identity (the ideal self that is lifted up as a model by coloniality and other systems of oppression) that is the idol.[65]

A second way in which the process of religious-guided decentering can go wrong, according to McNamara, is when we fail to emerge from the surrendering of the self into our own renewed, liberated self. The result, which he compares with the biblical notion of the demonic or diabolic, is a further splintering of the sense of self.[66] Discussing the particular case of religious transformations through experiences of spirit possession (another pathway to the decentering mechanism), he explains that "for decentering to be complete, the autobiographical memories associated with identity 1 must be integrated into identity 2. If the integration has not yet been accomplished or has been incomplete, then consciousness is aware of two [or more] identities that are nevertheless the same as they share the same set of autobiographical memories."[67] That results in an internal conflict between two disparate identities.

From a decolonial and liberation theologies perspective, the arrested decentering process that results in the coexistence of various fragmented identities is reminiscent of phenomena such as W. E. B. Du Bois's *Double Consciousness*,[68] Frantz Fanon's, *Black Skins, White Masks*,[69] Gloria Anzaldúa's, *Border Identity*,[70] and Chela Sandoval's *Oppositional Consciousness*.[71] They are insightful models that describe the ways by

---

65. Vítor Westhelle, "Idols and Demons: On Discerning the Spirits," *Dialog: A Journal of Theology* 41, no. 1 (Spring 2002): 9–15.

66. Westhelle, "Idols and Demons,"11–12.

67. McNamara, *The Neuroscience of Religious Experience*, 189.

68. W. E. B. Du Bois, *The Souls of Black Folk* (Dover Publications, [1903] 1994).

69. Frantz Fanon, *Black Skins, White Masks* (Grove Press, [1952] 2008).

70. Gloria Anzaldúa, *Borderlands/La Frontera*.

71. Chela Sandoval, "US Third World Feminism: The Theory and Method of Oppositional Consciousness in the Postmodern World," in *Feminist Postcolonial Theory: A Reader*, ed. Reina Lewis and Sara Mills (Edinburgh University Press, 2003), 75–100.

which people living under conditions of minoritization develop various identities (whether they want to or not) that are necessary to survive the system and navigate within the demands of the dominant culture and its socioeconomic and legal structures. The problem with those tactics of hybrid identities is that even when they might work, they come at a terrible cost to the mental health of those thus fragmented and a constant sense of betrayal to one's own self: one ends up feeling like a foreigner in one's own body.

Notwithstanding those cases when things can go wrong, authentic, healthy religious experiences, led by the truly holy, have the power to set us free from the idolatrous forces that conspire to keep us in situations of dependency and from the fragmenting demonic powers of racist, heterosexist, colonial, classist, and ableist ideologies that suffocate our spirit. In the language of Christian theology, Jesus Christ represents (there is that word again) the archetype of who we have been created to be, but this is not a static model, set once and for all. Rather, it is a dynamic image, in constant process of becoming and growing, for as we become united to Christ we do not abandon our selves but rather die to false identities, including those imposed on us by sinful systems, to reemerge as fully ourselves, a self that is at once individual and communal, free and at the loving service of others, under the constant life-giving influence of the divine.

Conclusion

In this chapter, we have examined what happens in the brain and the nervous system when people are having religious experiences. We also explored what happens to the brain, the nervous system, and the self after religious experiences. We saw that there are specific brain structures and processes that clearly underlie religious experiences and that they can be triggered in many different ways, from the God-helmet (TMS) to ritual practices. The scientific study of these phenomena is still in its infancy, and much of what we think we now know will have to be discarded or radically revised with future research. But the glimpse that neuroscience has so far given us of the sacred dance that takes place in our synapses and allows us to experience the sacredness of the world and its radical spiritual unity is awesome, in the deepest sense of that word, and very provocative.

One of the reasons religious experiences of the mystical union type are important for a decolonial liberation theology of the brain is the power of these experiences to melt away the rigid boundaries forged by five hundred years of colonial, racist, and heterosexist categorizations of humans into distinct slots in the hierarchical edifice of our world. As we saw, these experiences include the dismantling of the boundaries that separate us from the rest of the world and of those divisions that have been programmed in our minds to divide, categorize, and evaluate reality. Mystics tend to get in trouble with their home religious institutions because they come to experience how artificial those divisions and categories are. They come to experience, deep in their bodies (yes, even in their guts and hearts, in their nervous system and in their limbic system), the true, inherent, sacred unity of all of God's beautiful creation. In that world, there is no room for exclusion, exploitation, or marginalization. Thus, through their writings, many mystics offer a glimpse of that possible alternative world where the open wounds of our world are healed and the unity of humanity, in all its rich diversity—including religious diversity—is celebrated. That does not mean that the mystics themselves were perfect, or able to fully live out this vision, but they were able to get a glimpse of it, and through their poetry, their testimonies, and their praxis, they offer us an opportunity to taste it as well. That includes, a taste of the divine, which is not too far from the reality experienced in the radical unity of all.

Through the mediation of the concatenation of cortical, limbic, autonomic, affective, and cognitive events of the kind described in this chapter, the reality of God is made known but not in the same way that we might know our multiplication tables or the way we know about facts and historical events. We come to know God, the ineffable reality that name points to, the way the couple in Solomon's beautiful poem, Song of Songs, know each other: in the delicious, ecstatic and very embodied embrace of love fulfilled. Love that makes us one flesh with each other. Love that, according to the Christian witness, moved God to become one flesh with us, incarnated in the womb of a young maiden from an unimportant colonial little town in Palestine for the redemption of all (that is, for our collective and individual healing and flourishing).

True, most people have never had and will never have a mystical experience of the kind experienced by Julian of Norwich or San Juan de la Cruz. But as we learned above, we all have mini mystical experiences all the time because we all have the neural circuitry for them, and it is not hard to trigger, to some degree. We get a glimpse of those experiences when we are in our own embrace of love with our partner, when we are immersed in an activity that we love, or when we are with a group of people closer to us than anyone else and feel our togetherness in a way that is more real than real. Could those be like miniature icons of the larger reality that religious experience can open up for us? Can they be like small signposts along the journey for the world that God dreams for us—the same dream caught by the prophets and mystics of yesterday, today, and tomorrow? Can we learn from them how to organize our worship life, our devotional practices, and our religious institutions to foster those types of experiences through which divisiveness melts away and the divisions and categories through which we hurt and exclude each other are dismantled?

Up to this point in the book, we have relied heavily on science as a trustworthy guide to understand our mind, brain, and body and our embodied experiences of both mundane and divine reality. A word of caution is in order, however. We must bear in mind that science is neither omniscient nor infallible (neither is religion nor theology). Science, when at its best, is actually very precise and limited in its scope. That is, in fact, what allows it to be such a powerful way to understand and explain reality. Nonetheless, science is a human activity, and as such, it is not exempt from the limitations of our minds and the systemic distortions of the systems of coloniality, racism, heterosexism, and so on in which we live. We already got a glimpse of that when discussing the role that phrenology played in reinforcing racist notions that helped support the colonial project in all its brutality. Thus, we must not simply trust science as if it were revealed truth coming straight from heaven. In order to make good use of science (and in order to do good science), we must be aware of the nonscientific factors that influence the production of scientific models, theories, and assumptions, and we must get used to living in the tension between trusting science and examining it through the lenses of a healthy and reasonable hermeneutic of suspicion. With that in mind we now turn, in the next chapter, to an exploration of the limits of science—or, to put it metaphorically, to what lies beyond the frame of the lens that is science.

Part II

The Mystery of Transcendence

CHAPTER FOUR

Frames

Beyond the Limits of Science

"Where were you when I laid the foundation of the earth?
Tell me, if you have understanding."

—Job 38:4

Introduction

Beyond Science

Science as a Blessing

THE EXPLANATORY POWER of science can be mesmerizing, as we have seen in our tour of the fascinating forest that is the human nervous system and its brain, with their flowing rivers of hormones and neurochemicals and eddies of emotions and cognitions. To be sure, science is a blessing from God, given to us from the beginning—a dormant seed planted in the fertile soil of reason, curiosity, imagination, and collaboration, all of which are marks of the image and likeness of our Creator in us (Gen 1:27 and Ps 8:5).

When I was a graduate student working on my dissertation on the intersections between the theology of the Holy Spirit and the cognitive sciences of religion, Andrew Newberg came to my school to give a conference on his work on neurotheology. Afterward, I was offered the opportunity to take him out for dinner and conversation. Chatting over a plate of delicious Chicago pizza, we talked about his work and its theological implications. Musing about what God might think about his peering into the brains of mystics, nuns, and monks while they have religious experiences, he shared the following analogy. He said,

> I like to think that it is like if I gave my daughter a sophisticated remote-control car, and when I arrive home I see that she has dismantled it and there are pieces of it everywhere. Before getting mad at her, I ask her why she did that. Then she tells me that she was curious about how it works. Would I be upset with her? No, I think I would feel very proud of her. So, I like to think that God would be proud of us for wanting to take a closer look at this wonderful gift that is the brain to learn how it works.[1]

I love Newberg's analogy. I imagine God smiling, like a proud parent or grandparent, when Santiago Ramón y Cajal drew for humanity the first pictures of neurons' dendrites, somas, and axons in all their splendor, when Rosalind Franklin took an X-ray picture of the helical shape of the DNA molecule, or even when Galileo was inspired to aim his telescope at the firmament and discovered that our planet was not the center of the universe. What an awesome gift God has given us: the ability to know God's creation, and the responsibility to care for it (Gen 2:15).

Science, Too, Bears the Marks of Sin

But the divine gift that is science becomes corrupted when we confuse our limited understanding with God's omniscient knowledge and when we usurp and misuse the gift, intended for the well-being of all, for the benefit of only a few or for our own selfish interests (Gen 11:1–9). Then what was meant to be a resource for abundant life and the wholesome flourishing of all creation becomes instead a tool for exploitation, division, and violent domination. That corruption of science as a divine gift occurred almost simultaneously with its birth as an institution, which not coincidentally, happened at the same time as the beginning of the European colonial project. The following quote personifying science from Francis Bacon, considered one of the pioneers of modern science, exemplifies the germ of this corruption: "I am come in very truth leading you to Nature with all her children to bind her to your services and make her your

1. Personal communication with author, October 2006.

slave."[2] The gift meant to benefit all was usurped by a powerful few and used as an instrument to exploit and enslave the nonhuman segment of God's sacred creation.

Writing not from a theological but from a decolonial perspective, Walter Mignolo explains that even the concept of nature itself (that is, the collective mental representation of nature), from its very origins, was an invention of the colonial project:

> *Nature* doesn't exist, or it exists as an ontological fiction—what there is is the relentless generation and the regeneration of life in the solar system from which processes emerged a species of living/languaging organisms. A limited sector of these creatures were able to define themselves as human and impose their self-referential description as standard for all living organisms of the same species.[3]

Therefore, it is no coincidence that the emergence of modern science occurred only shortly after the miscalled "discovery" of lands and peoples by European merchant explorers. We must remember that those expeditions were driven from the beginning by the economic interests of the European aristocracy (first, Iberian, but later also British, French, Germanic, and Scandinavian) and their wealthy financiers.[4] And this happened against the backdrop of fierce economic, political, military, and religious competition from the Ottoman Empire and the desire for easy access to Chinese and Indian spices and other goods.[5] So the ensuing enterprise of the extraction of massive amounts of mineral, biological, and epistemic wealth from the so called new world, shortly followed by the similar exploitation of African, Asian, and Australian lands and their peoples and facilitated by the de jure and de facto enslavement and sacrificing of millions of human lives, was the

---

2. Quoted in Margareth Wertheim, *Pythagoras' Trousers: God, Physics, and the Gender Wars* (W. W. Norton, 1997), 154.

3. Mignolo, "The Invention of the *Human*," 158–59. Italics in the original.

4. Carlos Fuentes, *The Buried Mirror: Reflections on Spain and the New World* (Mariner Books, 1999).

5. Enrique Dussel, "The Real Motives for the Conquest," *Concilium* (1990): 30–46, https://enriquedussel.com/txt/Textos_Articulos/214.1990_ingl.pdf.

condition of possibility for the blossoming of Western civilizations' Enlightenment, with its Renaissance[6] and science.[7]

How could science, including the sciences of the brain and mind, not bear the marks—the wounds—of such origins? Especially when science was recruited as a moral and juridical tool to justify the colonial project by proving "objectively" the anthropological, biological, and cognitive inferiority of the "indios" and later of the "blacks" and any other human that did not conform to the model[8] erected, no longer in the image and likeness of God but rather in the image and likeness of white, male, heterosexual, nonpeasant Europeans and their descendants.[9] Needless to say, even God and Jesus were forced into that model. It is not that European, white, heterosexual males are not made in the image and likeness of God—of course they are, like us all. Rather, it is that what was simply one particular expression of being human was used to displace all other expressions of the *imago dei*. The result was the dehumanizing of millions of God's beautiful children: their abuse, exploitation, humiliation, minoritization, and in many cases, extermination. And science was complicit in that process, as complicit as was religion, the church, and theology.

Redeeming Science

Science, including the sciences of the mind and brain, is thus both a divine gift, which continues to generate an abundance of blessings for many, and a human invention marred by sin, producing unspeakable harm on "nature with all her children."

In this chapter, I attempt to go beyond the horizons of modern science and examine what lies outside the boundaries and then turn around and look back at science from within its margins. I argue for the need to incorporate a robust hermeneutic of suspicion into the scientific

---

6. Walter Mignolo, *The Darker Side of the Renaissance: Literacy, Territoriality, & Colonization* (University of Michigan Press, 1998).

7. See "Counterhistories," in *The Postcolonial Science and Technology Studies Reader*, ed. Sandra Harding (Duke University Press, 2011), 33–150.

8. Gould, *The Mismeasure of Man.*

9. George M. Frederickson, *Racism: A Short History* (Princeton University Press, 2002).

endeavor and to accept that in addition to the knowledge produced by modern science, there are also other kinds of knowledge that are generated by other means. An open dialogue between science and those other forms of knowing and being would be beneficial for all.

Science's Frame

What does it mean to speak of the margins and horizons of science? The work of the late Brazilian postcolonial theologian Vítor Westhelle is helpful here.[10] In thinking about the interconnections between coloniality, theology, and science, he focused on the processes by which reality is represented in those fields. In his book *Eschatology and Space: The Lost Dimension in Theology Past and Present*, he explains that "representation is presence displaced from its fluid reality into a hardened portrayal and stable mold, or else it is transferred to a proxy who stands for the context."[11] Both in science and in theology, we are dealing with representations of reality through theories, hypotheses, data, experiments, and so on. Such representations give us access to the reality they represent but are not the totality of that reality.

An analogy might be helpful. A photograph could be thought of as a faithful representation of a scene when compared to, say, a painting or a verbal description of the same reality. Isn't that also the goal of science—namely, to provide an accurate rendition of the way things are in reality without any contamination from the opinions, prejudices, or subjectivity of the observer? But what about the frame? The photographer has to decide where to focus the lens and, consequently, what will be left out of the picture. Sometimes, what is left out of the picture is meaningless and would add nothing to the image. But other times, what is left out has the power to give a whole new meaning to what was photographed. There can be no picture without a frame. The very conditions of possibility for the picture constitute its limitations: the setting, the angle, the distance, the light conditions, the type of lens, the background, and so on. None of that is a problem. The problem arises

10. This chapter is inspired by Westhelle's "Scientific Sight and Embodied Knowledges," 341–61.

11. Vítor Westhelle, *Eschatology and Space: The Lost Dimension in Theology Past and Present* (Palgrave Macmillan, 2012), 92.

when we either forget the frame or try to hide it. Thus, Westhelle asks: "What is hidden from vision when science brings something to sight?"[12] Without keeping the frame in mind, the picture takes the place of the reality from which it was taken, the reality that was framed, a reality that obviously transcends the frame. The part is mistaken for the whole, and the observer's perspective is mistaken for the only possible truth.

Science, too, has frames; that is what is meant by the margins and horizons of science. Some of those frames are intentional. They constitute the strict parameters of what is being studied: the variables, the controls, and other factors. Without those parameters, scientific explanations would not be possible. Thus, when a chemist describes the properties of a compound, it is important to make visible the frame: At what temperature? Under what pressure? In what solvent? Or, in the case of neuroscience, there has to be a clear delimitation of the behavior being studied, under what conditions, and what exact regions of the brain the "lenses" of the scans are focused on. Without a clear frame, the results obtained would be too fussy to be helpful and would lend themselves to too many possible explanations and speculation. Thus, when Newberg and colleagues scanned the brains of monks, they did not produce a "picture of God," or even an image of the brain under the effects of God, but simply a computerized reconstruction of the relative metabolism of a certain compound in specific regions of the brain while the subject was engaged in a task of focusing their attention on an object or image of religious significance.

The light of science shines bright and has been able to illuminate many aspects of reality and of the human mind that had so far been shrouded in deep darkness. But that same power brings with it a strong temptation. An ancient story sheds light on that temptation.[13] Nasrudin was on all fours, looking for something he had lost. A friend offered to help and joined him in the search. After a long time of looking without any success, the friend asked Nasrudin, "Where exactly did you lose this thing?" To which he replied, "Over there, on the other side of the hill." Perplexed, the friend asked, "Why, then, are you looking for it over here?" "Because the light is brighter here," replied Nasrudin. The

12. Westhelle, "Scientific Sight and Embodied Knowledges," 343.

13. The version presented here is based on Anthony de Mello, "Searching in the Wrong Place," in *The Song of the Bird* (Image Books, 1984), 27.

light of science and technology is bright indeed, and it is illuminating many important questions regarding the nature of reality, illnesses, and mental processes. But there are strong incentives for forgetting the frame and looking for what we seek where it is not, where it has never been, and where it will never be. In the case of the neurosciences, the temptation is to reduce everything to neural activity as if the body, environment, culture, and subjective experience were not also essential to understanding human experience. Spanish thinkers have coined the term *cerebrocentrismo* (brain-centrism) to describe that increasing tendency both in the sciences of the mind and in popular culture to reduce everything to the operations of the brain.[14] As it should be clear by now, the brain is essential but not sufficient.

The temptation is to be so dazzled by the explanatory power of science that one would then believe that there is nothing beyond the boundaries of science or that science has no boundaries, no limits. This can be seen in the neuroscientific and genetic study of the human person. The idea of person, in the sense of a mind (even if fully embodied) with consciousness and some degree of freedom and agency, baffles many scientists because their theoretical framework does not allow for such a thing. It can only "see" elements such as molecules, genes, neurons, circuits, and organisms. But in the case of the human person, as in many other phenomena encountered in nature, the whole is much more than the sum of the parts. As humans, we have the advantage that we can experience that reality from within in a way that we cannot do with anything else in nature. That experience that we have of ourselves includes the capacity for transcendence.

The Danish philosopher Søren Kierkegaard claimed that human beings are a synthesis of the finite and the infinite.[15] We are finite beings with infinite aspirations. Humans, by nature, have the drive to reach beyond themselves toward others: other people, other worlds, other times, other realities, other possibilities, and even other versions of

14. Marino Pérez Álvarez, "The Magnetism of Neuroimaging: Fashion, Myth and Ideology," *Papeles del Psicólogo* 32, no. 2 (2011): 98–112.

15. "The self is a relation that relates itself to itself . . . A human being is a synthesis of the infinite and the finite, of the temporal and the eternal, of freedom and necessity . . . Considered this way, a human being is still not a self." Søren Kierkegaard, *The Sickness unto Death: A Christian Psychological Exposition for Upbuilding and Awakening* (Princeton University Press, [1849] 1980), xi.

ourselves. This human dimension of self-transcendence, which is a basic constitutive element of the spiritual dimension of the human person, can be seen in many expressions. There is, for instance, the ability to go beyond the limits of our own self and look back upon ourselves, turning our very selves into objects of our own gaze and curiosity and inquiry. There also is the capacity to transcend the physical boundaries of our physical selves to imaginatively enter into the experiential world of others through the marvelous power of empathy, sympathy, compassion, mercy, and pity, as well as of schadenfreude. And then there is curiosity and imagination, which allowed Newton to dare to try to "read the mind of the Creator" and made it possible for Einstein to ride on a train of light, thus gaining the insight that $E = mc^2$ and that time and space are relative.

Outside the Frame

Science has a lot to teach us about the social and adaptive functions of such things as imagination, empathy, and experiences of transcendence. It also has a lot to say about its biological substrates and the effects that such things have on the experiences of the human body and on the structure of the human mind. It is important that scientists continue studying those dimensions of the human experience to the extent of their capacities. But it is also important to realize that the frames of the scientific gaze—its theoretical parameters, its experimental limitations, and its ontological assumptions—delimit the types of questions and answers that science has the competence to address. As Westhelle explains, "What cannot be classified, genetically ordered, and eventually placed in a calculable matrix falls outside the picture, in the strict sense of the term. And the reverse is also true: whatever is must fit into an accepted pattern, in which it is ordered, classified, and measured."[16]

There are phenomena that are essential to the human experience that science qua science is not able to even detect. A case in point is the person in the human being. To be able to deal with the person, science, particularly the biological sciences, first needs to deny its existence and reduce it to what science is competent in dealing with: organic matter, brain circuitry, and so on. Those things must be explored, but to say that

16. Westhelle, "Scientific Sight and Embodied Knowledges," 345.

is the entirety of the human being because the view of science cannot go any further (in part due to its own historical conditioning and prejudices, as we shall see shortly) is shortsighted. It also risks sacrificing something of infinite value in the human experience.

One does not have to espouse a dualistic view of reality to appreciate that the human experience consists of much more than just our material physicality. We are our bodies, but we are also much more than just a collection of molecules, tissue, and organs. Perhaps the problem is that to begin with, we have a rather shallow notion of matter[17] and a too-ethereal view of what spirit is.[18] In the human person, matter and spirit name two aspects of the same reality. They are distinguishable but inseparable. Even the Christian notion of life after death includes an element of physicality, as can be seen in Paul's comment that when the time comes, we will not be found "naked" (that is, without a body), but rather, just as we now have the body as a house where we live, God will have prepared a building for us (2 Cor 5:4). The point is that the promise of life after death does not consist of life in the form of a disembodied soul (i.e., a ghost) but rather a more sublime and blissful form of embodiment, which is a fulfillment, not an abolishment, of our bodiliness. Paul refers to this eschatological fulfillment as a spiritual body (1 Cor 15:44).

Regardless of whether one accepts the idea of life after death in principle, to simply accuse all those who believe in it of dualism is inaccurate. It is also interesting to see how, while dualism is loudly decried in the sciences, scientists themselves continue to operate as if the minds doing science are not themselves bound and radically limited by the same physicality and materiality of the subjects they study. Furthermore, as I have been reminded by interlocutors in the past, the dualistic idea that one day they might be free of the body that causes them so much anguish comes as good news for those whose bodies are a cause of constant pain and suffering, a powerful way to reclaim their agency and power within their disability. My body might be suffering, but my spirit is intact! Be that as it may, we need both categories—body

17. For an example of a notion of matter with spiritual depth, see Pierre Teilhard de Chardin, "The Heart of Matter," in *The Heart of Matter* (Harcourt, [1968] 1978), 15–79.

18. For an alternative, embodied notion of spirit, see Rivera, "Ghostly Encounters," 118–35.

and spirit—to be true to the experience of what it is like to be human. This needn't require us to embrace the type of dualism inaugurated by Descartes, which has been so devastating for the way we relate to the rest of nature, to each other, and to our own bodies.

The Social Location of Science

We have explored above how reality overflows the limits of science and of any intellectual attempt to comprehend it. This truth in no way denies science's explanatory power and the many blessings that science and technology have brought to humanity, from treatments for hitherto uncurable conditions to amazing ways to communicate across the planet. It is important to note, however, that science is done by human beings and not by angels. In other words, just as humans are marked by fallibility and sin, so is the science and technology produced by humans. At its best, the scientific method provides correctives for this. They come in the form of peer reviews; strict requirements that results be tested by other scientists, including attempts at reproducing the original data and trying to falsify the original conclusions by providing alternative, more parsimonious explanations; and keeping all explanations in science as provisional and open to new explanations in the future. Despite that, science is not perfect and scientists cannot fully detach themselves from their prejudices, idiosyncrasies, belief systems, socioeconomic pressures, the historical and cultural milieus in which they operate and which have shaped them and the institutions that have formed them.

At a Georgetown University conference on the cognition of belief, one of the presenters pointed out the contrast between the slow pace at which good science must move, requiring sometimes longitudinal studies as well as enough time for hypotheses to be tested and conclusions to be replicated, and the urgent demands for breakthroughs so that they can be applied to new medical treatments or the production of new drugs—plus the insatiable thirst of the popular press for immediate results and headlines that are catchy and provocative. He quipped: "If I could wish for one thing it would be for the popular press to leave us alone for at least ten years, so that we can carry on our research unencumbered by such pressures."[19] He also lamented the

19. "Symposium 1: Cognitive Insights into Mechanisms of Belief," Washington, DC: Georgetown University, June 2, 2017.

ways the university promotion system creates tremendous pressure to publish regularly ("publish or perish"), sometimes leading to publishing incomplete results, conducting experiments in haste, or in some extreme but unfortunately not uncommon cases, "massaging" the data to fit the desired conclusions.[20]

When at its worst, research in cognitive neuroscience can be reminiscent of that ancient Japanese story of the master archer who departed his hometown to seek other master archers. He arrived at a village where everywhere he looked he saw a bull's-eye drawn on walls and trees with arrows in the dead center. He kept asking the locals where he could meet such a skilled archer, but they kept repeating that the person he sought was not a master archer but a fool. Finally, they explained that the secret to the archer's success was to shoot first and draw the bull's-eye later. This is a strong temptation to those with access to scanning technology, for example, who can scan the brain during different tasks and only later draw the "bull's-eye" conclusion of what regions were involved in given activities. This practice was illustrated comically by a group of neuroscientists who decided to throw a dead salmon into a brain scanner and were actually able to detect some interesting brain signals, from the dead salmon's brain![21] Fortunately, neuroscientists have been diligent in designing stricter protocols and parameters to guide their research.[22]

There is an important difference between association, correlation, and causation. Two events can be loosely associated without there being a strong correlation among them. A correlation is a statistical measurement of how closely two events are connected to each other. When scientists say that two events have a strong correlation (like, for example, a region of the brain "firing" while a part of the body moves), they mean that statistically, the chances of both happening at the same time without a connection between the two is very low. Yet that does

20. I analyze this in more detail in my essay "*Eutonia*: The Cross (In)Between Science and Theology," in *Embracing the Ivory Tower and Stained Glass Windows: A Festschrift in Honor of Archbishop Antje Jackelén*, ed. Jennifer Baldwin (Springer, 2016), 131–46.

21. Alexis Madrigal, "Scanning Dead Salmon in fMRI Machine Highlights Risk of Red Herrings," *Wired* (September 18, 2009), https://www.wired.com/2009/09/fmrisalmon/.

22. What follows is based on Jospeh W. Kable, "The Cognitive Neuroscience Toolkit for the Neuroeconomist: A Functional Overview," *Journal of Neuroscience, Psychology, and Economics* 4, no. 2 (2011): 63–84.

not necessarily mean that one event (neural firing) is *causing* the other (movement of the body). A common example to make this point is disconnecting a television from its power source and observing how the image disappears. There is a strong correlation between the two events, but it would be wrong to conclude that the image comes to the screen by way of the power cord. The power source is necessary for the image to appear on the screen, but it is not a sufficient cause for it. There is sophisticated math that allows scientists to tease apart different correlations and parse which ones stand in a relation of causation to the phenomenon they are investigating. But even that is not enough. Another important step is to investigate whether the effect we are studying can happen without the purported cause. If we can eliminate activity from a region of the brain and yet the part of the body that we are investigating still moves, then it can be ascertained that such brain region is not necessary for the effect we are studying.

Thus, to establish a relationship of causality, it is important to have a strong mathematical correlation and to determine whether the purported cause is necessary. Then we must investigate whether it is also sufficient or whether there are other things that need to be in place for the cause to be effective. In neuroscience, regions of the brain can be temporarily removed from the equation via special techniques like TMS or certain drugs that target specific regions of the brain for only a limited period of time. Then we can examine whether the effect still happens (for example, does the body part still move?). A possibility is that one event is not causing the other, but rather both are being caused by a third common cause. Once it has been established that there is a relationship of correlation and that the purported cause is both necessary and sufficient, then we can proceed to hypothesize a mechanism by which such effect takes place. In reality, scientists begin that process with some pre-existing suspicion of what regions in the brain are implicated in a given effect (i.e., the ROI). From the outset, scientists can aim the measuring instruments in that general area so that they can focus on their hypothesized connections. It is also becoming more common to use different techniques to test such hypotheses—for example, to combine fMRI with EEG. This meticulous process helps avoid wild speculations simply based on random associations observed in brain scans.

Despite these careful measures, scientists sometimes succumb to pressures that taint the results of their research. There is, for instance, the pressure to "publish or perish." There is also the tendency for confirmation bias, especially when neuroscientists seem to have discovered something that is too good to not be true. And then there is the unavoidable reality that brain research is very expensive, in part because it requires instruments that are very expensive and necessitates transdisciplinary collaboration with highly trained and skilled experts. Therefore, science often finds itself limited by the interests of those institutions, donors, grants, or other funders who have the money to support brain research. That defines the contours of the areas that will be investigated and those that will remain unexamined. Living in societies where the profit motive is sometimes a strong drive for scientific exploration and technological innovation means that the questions that are investigated will be shaped by economic interests at least as much as by scientific passion, often despite the best intentions of the scientists themselves. That which has the potential to be translated into a drug or a profitable therapeutic device has more chance of receiving funding than investigations into more abstract or philosophical questions, such as the mechanisms by which faith (in the sense of the trust of the heart) can contribute to healing—this is related to the miscalled placebo effect (I say "miscalled" because it is not the placebo that is producing the effect but rather the subject's faith in the placebo; the placebo is merely an opportunity for faith to do its work).[23]

The Abuses of Science

Again, remember the fact that science is done by humans who themselves carry prejudices and predilections that have profound effects in the science they pursue and produce. One example among many is phrenology, which we discussed in chapter 2. Phrenology was one of the "sciences" that was used to confirm the racist theories that justified slavery, racism, and coloniality, positing that peoples with brains less developed than Europeans' would benefit from being under the benevolent tutelage of the white man and his civilization. Science played a central role in the creation of worldviews and practices that subjected many to terrible abuses because they did not fit within the frame of what

23. Mario Beauregard, "Mind Does Really Matter: Evidence from Neuroimaging Studies of Emotional Self-Regulation, Psychotherapy, and Placebo Effect," *Progress in Neurobiology* 81, no. 4 (March 2007): 218–36, https://pubmed.ncbi.nlm.nih.gov/17349730/.

science considered normal, healthy, or well adapted. Thus, many peoples were, and continue to be, subjected to cruel treatments to supposedly "heal" or cleanse them of that which made them different from the norm established by the centers of power. This was all "scientific" and often motivated by (pseudo)benevolent intentions. That is an important lesson that we must never forget.

Consequently, a lot of science was at the service of the brutal project of coloniality, of white supremacy, of the patriarchal domination of women and of sexual and gendered minorities, and of the exploitation of nature, even to the point of genocide. Further, thanks to those power dynamics listed above, scientists had unfettered access to Black, brown, Indigenous, semitic, female, and LGBTQ bodies to probe and experiment on and wide swaths of newly "conquered/colonized" nature to investigate, not to mention the unacknowledged plagiarism of the traditional knowledges of other peoples. For instance, when I was a chemistry student, I remember hearing the story of how chemical anthropologists would sometimes investigate claims of traditional medicines and then test them using Western techniques. If the traditional medicines proved to be effective, they would then be produced in laboratories and sold back to the same peoples from whence they came but in the guise of a scientific alternative to the traditional remedies of the people. Furthermore, the fact that Western science was capable of producing such effective medicines was used as proof of the superiority of Western civilization over Indigenous, African, Asian, or any other ancient alternatives. One wonders what science would be like if, instead of being seen as antiquated, the ancient wisdoms/knowledges from other traditions had been appreciated, received, and incorporated into a process of respectful dialogue and mutual curiosity. Perhaps we would have developed an ethos of reverence for all nature rather than seen everything merely as raw material for the satisfaction of our desires, needs, vices, or curiosities. It is not too late. And, in fact, there are hopeful signs of such types of dialogue.[24] For the sake of our survival as a species, and for the sake of the survival of many of our fellow creatures on this planet, we are in urgent need of such a paradigm shift, away from the colonial matrix of power and toward the life-giving matrix of collaboration and wholeness.

---

24. See, for example, Harding, *The Postcolonial Science and Technology Studies Reader*, especially section IV, "Moving Forward: Possible Pathways," 365–458.

The Implicit Metaphysics and Ontology of Science

The scientific gaze is also strongly determined by the assumptions it makes about the nature of reality. Philosophers refer to this realm as metaphysics—namely, that which lies beyond physics—and ontology, which refers to the study of beings and being as such. Science always operates with a metaphysics and an ontology, whether it is made explicit or not. That metaphysics and ontology is the "hidden curriculum" taught in most science courses in colleges and universities. One of the first assignments I received when I was a freshman studying chemistry was given to us by my organic chemistry professor. She handed the class stickers that read "I am made of matter." She invited us to use the stickers and also challenged us to find anything in the world that was not made of matter or energy. Underlying that innocent game was a staunch materialism that already frames a lens excluding anything that is not matter or energy from the equation of the real.

Any attempt to challenge such limits is often met with ridicule, disbelief, and even censorship. Fortunately, sometimes reality is stronger, and the preponderance of evidence provokes what the historian of science Thomas Kuhn called a paradigm shift.[25] I believe we are currently witnessing a paradigm shift in the way medical science understands sickness and healing and the human person in general. There is much more attention being given to extrabiological factors (not instead of but in addition to) factors such as histories of trauma, belief systems, lifestyle, quality of relationships, and even religious practices such as meditation and prayer. A wonderful example is the work of the Canadian physician Gabor Maté on the ways in which our physical (and not just mental) illnesses are also symptoms of our toxic culture.[26]

This is not to dismiss the biological dynamics underlying disease, nor is it about blaming the victim, but it is about taking a realistic look at the ways our preconceived notions of where the body ends and culture begins are significantly limiting the impact of the healing arts. In a similar vein, the work of neuroscientists like Nazareth Castellanos, whom we met in chapter 2, regarding the intricate ways in which our bodies and brains are connected have tremendous implications for how

---

25. Thomas S. Kuhn, *The Structure of Scientific Revolutions*, 3rd ed. (University of Chicago Press, [1962] 1994), 10.

26. Maté, *The Myth of Normal*.

we view the relationship between mental health and gut health, just to give one example. It also reveals, as Castellanos insists, the need to pay attention to alternative sources of embodied and spiritual wisdom like yoga, meditation, and contemplative prayer.[27]

Fortunately, we are beginning to see more pop culture awareness of the importance of things like diet, exercise, and community on many aspects of our physical and mental health. Likewise, there are innovative physicians; for example, Jon Kabat-Zinn and colleagues have introduced meditation and mindfulness into the treatment of chronic and terminal diseases. By expanding the implicit ontology of biology to include the influences of things like meditation and faith in our scientific understanding of what a body is, we can help expand the scope of science and make possible the development of new forms of healing and improving people's health and general well-being.

The Captivity of the Symbolic in Science

Ironically, one of the problems with science is that it is indeed a powerful lens through which to view reality, and the pictures of reality that it allows us to see are breathtaking. But sometimes the picture has the effect of replacing rather than revealing reality. The French psychoanalyst Jacques Lacan has offered a provocative, if highly complicated, explanation of this phenomenon that I find very helpful.[28] He explains that as the human person matures from childhood and youth into adulthood, we develop different modes to represent reality to ourselves, including the reality of who we are. The first stage, which he calls the mirror stage, is where we see reality and ourselves reflected in others, especially those others who are important to us, like our parents, caregivers, and teachers. From the mirror image we pass to the imaginary, where through the imagination we image reality in ways that allow us to navigate our desires and fears. Then there is the symbolic stage, where through the use of symbols like language we represent reality (or aspects of reality) in ways that we can comprehend and manipulate.

---

27. Castellanos, *Neurociencia del cuerpo*, 66–68.

28. The following description of Lacan's concepts is based on Slavoj Žižek, *How to Read Lacan* (Granta Books, 2006).

The problem is that the symbolic inevitably replaces reality, occluding it like an eclipse rather than revealing it. The result is that the symbolic representation of reality that we have developed or inherited substitutes for reality, perhaps as a way to protect us from the elements of reality that scare us because they defy the control of our concepts, machinations, and desires. Reflecting on the implications of Lacan's analysis for liberation theology, Joerg Rieger explains that "'reality' or 'realism' is usually constructed on the grounds of some dominant symbolic order. What counts as reality in this sense is what is commonly accepted as true, the product of the social mechanisms of the text that determine the collective consciousness of society or the church."[29] Notice that his use of *text* here is similar to Westhelle's use of *representation* above. Rieger suggests that it is through encounters with the truly real that the captivity of the symbolic (whose frames are hidden) is loosened. He explains that "the symbolic order is challenged most constructively where it intersects with the real. In other words, in an encounter with the real other, the power of the text can be reconstructed."[30] In a similar vein, Westhelle speaks of the power that lies in the margins, where one encounters the other and from where one can gaze back at (the symbolic representation of) one's reality:

> Margins are a strange window to the world; they offer to sight a perspective into the everyday even while luring the gaze to a different world that defies visualization. And precisely because of these reasons they are dangerous: they bring to sight what should not be revealed and entertain visions unsettling to the order of things. Thus societies live with the compulsive behavior of hiding their margins. They hide them because, as Mary Douglas observed, margins reveal the fragility of the entire social fabric and threaten its center. Therefore, margins have a disturbing revelatory potential, the potential of disclosure and the power of exposure.[31]

---

29. Joerg Rieger, *Remember the Poor: The Challenge to Theology in the Twenty-First Century* (Trinity Press International, 1998), 76.

30. Rieger, *Remember the Poor*, 77.

31. Vítor Westhelle, "Knowledges Ajar," in *After Heresy: Colonial Practices and Post-Colonial Theologies* (Cascade Books, 2010), 122.

For that very reason, as we shall see toward the end of this book, it is from the margins that salvation comes.

I think that science is tempted to confuse its (*symbolic*, in the above sense) representations of reality through scientific formulae and mechanisms that come to replace reality to the point that it regulates what counts as real. And because, in a certain way, science can study only what it can control and manipulate, reality becomes only that which is subjected to the control of science—which, as we saw above, is indirectly subjected to the control of nonscientific influences such as the drive for profit or ideologies. Then science risks becoming dogma and a tool to bolster a reality rooted in injustice and oppression.

None of this is meant as a detraction from the marvel that science is or from its usefulness. It serves as a reminder that science, too, is in need of constant critique and dialogue from within and from outside itself, from other ways of knowing.

Conclusion

The Need for Many Lenses

We have seen that science is like a lens used to take a photograph of reality and that as such, it is framed by certain limits that reality overflows. Another aspect of this metaphor is that not all lenses are equal. Some lenses, like those used in microscopes, allow us to see aspects of reality that are very small; other lenses, like those of telescopes, allow us to see that which is very far away (both in space and time!). There are lenses besides science that allow us to perceive other aspects of the same realities that science studies. Is it not true, for instance, that there are aspects of the human experience that a good poem amplifies and allows us to explore in ways that the scientific lens does not? Similarly, religious literature and theology and sacred rituals allow us to touch regions of the human experience and of reality that escape the scope and resolution of the scientific lens. But this should not be surprising. There is an analogy to this in the way we experience reality through our senses. The same object is perceived differently through our eyes than through our ears or our sense of touch. And then there is the richness that memory and affect contribute to the experience, which are not just external things added to the object being perceived but actually constitute important revelations of otherwise unknown aspects of the objects. One way to understand this is to realize how much we are trained to think of things in terms of essences. But when we begin to follow the lead of other forms of knowledge and wisdom, which for example, conceive of objects as nodes of infinite relationships, then feelings and memories become true perceptions of important aspects of the reality we are perceiving.[32] And disciplines like poetry and theology become much more than what some would dismiss as imaginative elucubrations about nothing.

Therefore, just as the senses complement each other in our perception of reality, together with reason, memory, imagination, and the affects, science can be understood as one of our collective senses for understanding reality side by side with other ways of knowing that are very different but not unimportant. As we have seen, there is also the need for a critical attitude toward the nonscientific influences on science. The fact that science is such a powerful means to know and transform reality means that there will always be strong incentives to recruit science for nonscientific purposes and even for evil. Being in intentional relationship with other ways of knowing and other institutions that support those alternative knowledges could also provide science with an external perspective that can call it back to its life-giving purposes when it loses its way—and vice versa, because those other ways of knowing are not to be taken at face value. They are not beyond criticism or even scientific exploration. However, they ought to be taken with the seriousness that they deserve. Otherwise, our experience and understanding of reality will be the poorer for it, as would be the quality of our lives, individually and collectively.

How has science—its theories, assumptions, and worldview—been shaped (distorted) by its colonial and patriarchal past? And how has it shaped (distorted) the understanding of the human mind/brain/person that it presents to the world today as normal and therefore as normative? Is it possible to envision the universe, and the universe of the human and our fellow creatures, in ways that are congruous with the best science available while also escaping the ideological grip of dehumanizing

---

32. See, for example, Nhât Hanh, *Understanding Our Mind*, and B. Allan Wallace, *Contemplative Science: Where Buddhism and Neuroscience Converge* (Columbia University Press, 2007).

assumptions and views of nature that encourage its exploitation and neglect? A liberation theology of the brain is necessarily also a project of liberation of science for the sake of a more transparent view of reality and for the sake of practices that contribute to a more wholesome way of being human together, with other humans and with our nonhuman fellow creatures.

CHAPTER FIVE

Mystery

The Summons of the Beyond Within

> Now there was a great wind, so strong that it was splitting mountains and breaking rocks in pieces before the Lord, but the Lord was not in the wind, and after the wind an earthquake, but the Lord was not in the earthquake, and after the earthquake a fire, but the Lord was not in the fire, and after the fire a sound of sheer silence. When Elijah heard it, he wrapped his face in his mantle and went out and stood at the entrance of the cave. Then there came a voice to him.
>
> —1 Kings 19:11b–13a

Introduction

Self Transcendence Toward the Other

SELF-TRANSCENDENCE IS ONE of the abilities that we have because of the way our embodied brains and minds have been created. This is something that both science and theology have been able to elucidate. We have the capacity to reach beyond ourselves toward a beyond that is nonetheless available to us only from within us by way of our mental and affective embodied representations of that beyond. What lies beyond?

What lies beyond is the other: the other person; the other creature; the other reality; the other me/us that is possible; the holy Other to whom we owe our existence, our minds, our brains, our nervous systems, our entire world; the holy Other who calls us (from deep within the dark silence pregnant with promise—that is, the place beyond the reach of our minds, of our mental representations, of our distortions and manipulations) to step outside the caves of our solipsistic worlds and open up to new realities and new possibilities.[1]

1. Writing about this type of deeply embodied transcendence, in a similar vein as Rieger and Westhelle (see the previous chapter) but from the context and lived

People who have had the courage—the faith—to heed the summons have not only been transformed by what they experienced but have also become powerful agents of transformation for their communities, for society, for the world. These figures include Moses, Elijah, Mary of Nazareth, Harriet Tubman, Martin Luther King Jr., Óscar Romero, Mohandas Gandhi, Dorothy Day, Cesar Chavez, and so many more whose transformative actions happen not in the public arena but in the anonymity of their homes and their secular vocations.

This summons from beyond has the power to destabilize unjust social structures, which as we saw in the previous chapter, are an expression of sin and result in the exclusion, oppression, and exploitation of many, including the rest of nature, God's sacred creation. It even distorts the representations of reality made available through science. The summons from beyond the horizons of our frames/margins has the potential to liberate, expand, and fix our notions (representations) of what is real, what is possible, and what is desirable, loosening the grip that the colonial illusions have over our imaginations and emotions, allowing us to dream and enact different possibilities. It also has the potential to bring wider breadth and greater depth to our scientific explanations of reality, including the realities of our embodied brains and minds.

What is the summons? That is the subject of this chapter. What are the various expressions of that spiritual tug or transcendental lure that seems to be an important, even constitutive, part of the human experience and that has been called by many names, most famously, God? What is that silent but creative word (*logos* in Greek, i.e., *theologia*) that summons us beyond within?

Transcendence in Science

In the previous chapter, we saw that the vastness, depths, and dynamism of reality cannot be reduced to the limits of our theoretical frameworks,

---

experience of Latinas in the US, postcolonial theologian Mayra Rivera articulates what I also see as the goal I, too, try to pursue in this book—namely "that which exceeds representation and yet gives impulse to speaking and writing: the body's unruly materiality, its mysterious spirituality . . . I seek to allow Christian discourses to be affected, to be disturbed yet again, by accounts of the movements of the spirit found through the bodies of those it has often ignored" ("Thinking Bodies," in Isasi-Díaz and Mendieta, *Decolonizing Epistemologies*, 220).

whether those are science, philosophy, religion, or anything else. The vastness of reality overflows our systems. Human experience attests to a richness of reality that cannot be comprehended or constrained by the carefully drawn parameters of even our most exact sciences.[2]

Studying the World from Within

One of the challenges in drawing an all-encompassing picture of the universe is that the one doing the viewing and the drawing is also a part of the totality being described. We often forget what, for example, the early architects of quantum mechanics knew—namely, that the observer is interconnected with the observed. How much truer this is in the sphere of the study of human experience, particularly in the study of the spiritual dimension of the human experience!

When dealing with the dimension of spirit in human experience, we are dealing with a reality that, as theologian Paul Tillich puts it, is prior to the division of reality into subject and object.[3] It is also prior to the operations of our cognitive devices dividing the world into categories such as the mental versus the physical, the temporal versus the eternal, the finite versus the infinite, the religious versus the secular, and the sacred versus the profane.

Voices from the Margins

All these elements are part of the human experience. However, some elements are often dismissed and even derided, because they don't fit into the (colonial, patriarchal, and racist) schemas that have allowed us to get a sense of mastery and dominance over reality. To borrow an image from Harvard decolonial theologian Mayra Rivera, those experiences "haunt" the boundaries of our epistemic empires.[4] Furthermore, as Vítor Westhelle would say, they destabilize those epistemic systems

2. For a discussion of this surplus of meaning in the human experience of reality, see Paul Ricoeur, *Interpretation Theory: Discourse and the Surplus of Meaning* (Christian University Press, 1976).

3. See Tillich's elaborate explanation in his chapter on "The Reality of Revelation," in his *Systematic Theology*, vol. 1 (University of Chicago Press, 1951), 106–59.

4. Rivera, "Ghostly Encounters," 118–35.

from the very margins (*eschata*) or fissures (*xora*) that give them their defining contours and shape. (*La différance*, as a certain French philosopher might have said). Again, Rivera's use of the image of spectral haunting to describe the power of the margins is helpful here:

> The spectral elements, disconcerting as they may be, are not opposed to the body: they represent the fluent, fluid, dispersive aspects of flesh, of subjects that defy objectification. Ancestral memories haunt our present experiences, yet these do not exhaust the spectral elements of embodiment. A kind of ghostliness haunts even the most concrete characterizations, pointing beyond the represented to that which eludes representation, that for which we don't have concepts or words, that which unsettles established rationality and resists closure.[5]

One of the things I wish to examine in this book, from a transdisciplinary perspective, are those eschatological margins of society and of human experience that are spectrally dense and thus open up to dimensions of depth, transcendence, immanence, and intimacy that are not only part of the human experience but are also constitutive of it. I am including here both the experiences of those belonging to populations pushed to and kept in the margins of society and those personal experiences that push us individually to the margins of our reality and beyond. Those liminal cognitive-affective-spiritual spaces are charged with revelatory and liberatory potential, especially when viewed from the perspective of faith and analyzed theologically, because there, God meets us.[6] Those experiences are not marginal to normal human experience, but we become more aware or sensitive to them when we go through situations that push us close to the edge of our own limits.

I am not arguing here for a "god of the gaps" approach, whereby experiences and phenomena that science cannot explain are then

5. Rivera, "Thinking Bodies," 225.

6. The idea that God abides in marginal spaces is a fundamental insight of the liberation of theology (God makes an option for the poor) as well as of the theology of the cross (God reveals God's self-hidden in its opposite, in suffering and death). We will explore this idea further in the last part of the book; note that to say that God abides in marginal spaces does not mean that other spaces are deprived of God's presence.

attributed to divine intervention. There are, as I argued in the previous chapter and will continue to argue in this one, experiences and phenomena that lie beyond the scope of science. Nonetheless, religious experience and divine action are not limited to those instances. If theology affirms God as the creator of all that is, and the Spirit of God as interpenetrating all creation, then there is no experience, no place, no phenomenon that is alien to the presence of God or that cannot become transparent to that presence.

We look at the margins and fissures (the eschata and the xora) because it is there where the frames of the pictures or representations of reality that we tend to confuse for reality itself reveal themselves to us, and the contradictions between those representations and reality itself become hard to ignore. We will come back to that aspect of human (religious?) experience in the chapter on hope, where we will examine how certain experiences allow us to dislodge, or *delink*, affectively from social, political, economic, and cultural systems that are unjust and produce misery, exploitation, and death, not only for people but also for the entire creation. That is the decolonization of the emotions.

In the present chapter, we will focus on the way certain experiences point to a dimension of depth or transcendence in human experience and in reality itself, which since ancient times and in widely different contexts, humanity has come to know by that most misunderstood, misused, and abused name: God.

Gathering Testimonies

Rather than offering a dogmatic definition of God and a formal description of religious experience, we will proceed inductively, as we did in chapter 3 when dealing with religious experience, acknowledging that while we don't begin from scratch, we do start out with an initial idea of what the divine is and what experiences of the divine are like. Those initial ideas give impetus and direction to the search, but ideally, they are only provisional and acquire more definitive substance based on what is found in the evidence from the inductive search. In the case of this book, evidence means the testimonies from the tradition bequeathed to us plus the neuroscientific data, theories, and hypotheses relevant to those testimonies. Let's look at a sample of the evidence.

Finitude and Mortality

Perhaps one of the most common experiences that opens us up to the dimensions of depth and transcendence, and to the mystery of God, is experience of our finitude or of the finitude of those whom we love. Faced with our death or the death of our loved one(s), we become aware of the abyss of nothingness that surrounds life, that surrounds us and those whom we love and care about. A protest is born out of that encounter, a protest against death being the end.[7] This is the question of Ezekiel (37:3), standing before a valley of the dry bones of his people, of his beloved, of his hopes and dreams and aspirations, with the following question echoing in his heart, mind, and gut: "Can these bones live?"

Can the bones of my father, of your mother, of our beloved, of the children dead too soon live? What about the bones lying at the bottom of the Atlantic, silent witnesses of centuries of slavery; the bones of the Indigenous, Caribbean, and Pacific Islander peoples consumed by the hard labor and cruel abuses of five centuries of colonialism; the dry bones of myriad female victims of the sexual violence of patriarchy; or the bones of God's countless LGBTQ and transgender children, abused, deformed, killed, and humiliated, often even in the name of God? Can their bones live? The protest grows within, as rage, as pain, as hope against hope, as a summons for justice, a silent scream that another world must be possible.

But even just at the level of individual loss, the pressure created by the void of death is generative. The summons is generative. It generates a question, a possibility, born with the protest, whether there might be something rather than nothing on the other side of death, hidden within the void. That hope is as old as humanity itself. There are signs that since prehistoric times, we have buried our dead in ways that signal belief in an afterlife. This belief transcends geography, culture, and even religion.[8]

---

7. For a beautifully poignant examination of that dimension of the human experience, see Miguel de Unamuno, *Tragic Sense of Life*, trans. J. E. Crawford Flitch (Dover Publications, 1954).

8. For a provocative account of how the protest against death drives modern technology, see Yuval Noah Harari discussing "The Last Days of Death" in *Homo Deus: A Brief History of Tomorrow* (Harper Perennial, 2017), 21–29.

Of course, protest and desire do not prove anything, but they provide the existential and intellectual drive to posit the question and explore it passionately. Ancient examples include Plato's *Timeus* in ancient Greece, *The Book of the Dead* from Egypt and Tibet, African Bantu rituals for inquiring wisdom from the dead, Native American vision quests and sweat lodge ceremonies to enter the Spirit world, Santería and Candomblé rituals to seek access to the spirits of the deceased, and of course, the idea of the resurrection and eternal life in Islam, Christianity, and Judaism.

An interesting aspect about the biblical hope in the resurrection is that it seems to have emerged not so much as a protest against finitude and death but rather as a protest against injustice. The hope of the resurrection emerged as the answer to the question, Whence justice? The answer was that there will be a day when the living and the dead will have to come before the throne of God and give an account of their lives. Those who lived lives of injustice and evil will then have to confront the consequences of their choices and receive the just punishment for their sins. Those who were the victims of injustices, and those who lived lives marked by loving kindness, devotion, and righteousness, will receive their reward in the form of eternal life in abundance of bliss and happiness. This is illustrated by the words of the prophet Daniel, spoken from within the agonic experience of exile, after the destruction of what was most sacred to his people, the temple, and the murder of myriad peoples by the colonial violence of the rising Babylonian Empire:

> At that time your people shall be delivered, everyone who is found written in the book. Many of those who sleep in the dust of the earth shall awake, some to everlasting life and some to shame and everlasting contempt. Those who are wise shall shine like the brightness of the sky, and those who lead the many to righteousness, like the stars forever and ever. (Dan 12:1c–3)

This dual belief in resurrection and judgment became distorted and abused over the years. In fact, it ended up being used for the exact opposite of its original purposes, becoming a tool of empire to justify suffering and injustice in this life and postponing justice to a place beyond the clouds and outside time, "pie, pie in the sky." Likewise, God's passion for justice symbolized in the idea of a last judgment and a place for a reckoning (the Gehenna) became distorted by poets and religious leaders into a masochistic spectacle where a demonic God delighted in the suffering of his creatures, and what was meant to be a message of hope and a call to conversion became a religion of fear and a punitive God of retribution.[9] But beneath those distortions lies a potent theological intuition that continues to radiate with tremendous liberation and decolonizing power.

Near-Death Experiences

Hope in an afterlife, or in the power of life vis-à-vis death, is not founded solely on the protest of the human spirit in the face of death. It is also nurtured by the testimonies of those who have had extraordinary experiences at the gates of death. There are many testimonies of people who were declared clinically dead for a brief period (meaning that their hearts stopped beating—flatlined—and in some cases, their brain function stopped).

They tell stories of being surrounded by light, of having a sense of deep peace, and of feeling profoundly loved. They talk about being greeted by a loved one who had already passed or by a spiritual being of resplendent countenance. They speak of reliving or re-viewing their lives as in the scenes of a movie, but rather than feeling shame or guilt for their past trespasses, experiencing an all-encompassing sense of acceptance and understanding. And they often relate how when they are told that their time has not yet come, they feel so blissful and at ease in that place that exists in boundaries between life and death that they do not want to come back! Many speak of getting a renewed sense of purpose and meaning in their lives and of no longer being afraid of death.[10] Other kinds of near-death experiences include elements of being

9. Perhaps the most famous case is the otherwise beautiful work of Dante Alighieri (1265–1321), *The Divine Comedy: Inferno, Purgatory, Paradise* (Union Library Association, [1321] 1935).

10. For a first-person account of a near-death-experience, recounted by a neurosurgeon, see Eben Alexander, *Proof of Heaven: A Neurosurgeon's Journey into the Afterlife* (Piatkus, 2012); for other case studies, interviews, and analyses of near-death experiences, see Hagerty, "Are We Dead Yet?," in *Fingerprints of God*, 216–42; for a scholarly assessment of these kinds of experiences, see Jeffrey Long, "Near-Death Experiences Evidence for Their Reality," *Missouri Medicine* 111, no. 5 (September–October 2014): 372–80, https://www.ncbi.nlm.nih.gov/pmc/articles/PMC6172100/.

outside of one's own body, looking down on one's self, or having the ability to recall aspects of the operating room that should be impossible for them to remember because their brains were not functioning when they happened.[11]

From a scientific perspective, those stories need to be taken with a grain of salt because they cannot be verified (that is, reproduced) under the carefully controlled conditions that science demands. The experiences themselves are accepted by mainstream science, but the explanations of both the causes and the object of the experiences are hotly debated and contested. However, as I argued in chapter 4, science does not get to be the sole arbiter of what constitutes reality and what experiences are real or point to something real. Science has an important role in verifying as much as possible the claims made that fall within its purview and in generating plausible explanations for the biological and psychological substrates of those experiences. Other perspectives, however, should also be taken into consideration, especially, from a decolonial perspective, the wisdom of those cultures with centuries of experience guiding people through similar experiences and helping them make sense of them.[12]

From a liberation and decolonial theological perspective, these experiences are important because they can crack open the ironclad grip of the fear of death that is a powerful tool in the colonial strategy of control and domination. A common tactic of colonial powers has always been to use public executions as a means of inflicting terror on anyone contemplating the idea of resisting their dominion. That was, for instance, why the Roman Empire's powers and its proxies in biblical Palestine employed crucifixion as punishment for rebellion. It was no coincidence that Jesus of Nazareth was crucified right outside the city gates, where everyone coming in and out of Jerusalem had no choice but to see him, especially during those days of high holidays, and read the sign affixed to his cross declaring the juridical cause of his execution: "Jesus of Nazareth, the King of the Jews" (John 19:19). It was a

11. For an intriguing case, see Allan J. Hamilton, "Soul Survivor," in *The Scalpel and the Soul: Encounters with Surgery, the Supernatural, and the Healing Power of Hope* (Tarcher/Penguin, 2008), 188–212.

12. See, for example, Vine Deloria Jr., *The World We Used to Live In: Remembering the Powers of the Medicine Men* (Fulcrum, 2006), especially "Visions in Transitions, 39–42.

clear message to the Roman Jewish colonial subjects from the Roman imperial powers: this is what happens to anyone who dares to resist the power of Rome and its ruler, Caesar, who incidentally, was also known by the following titles: Lord, Savior, Son of God, and even *Pantokrator* (the Almighty).

"The fear of death is death itself," preached Luther.[13] To have evidence that death is not the end of life but that from death we are summoned to new life, even eternal life, is to tap into a source of untamable power and resilience. The testimony of Jesus's resurrection (especially while still bearing in his body the wounds of colonial violence, the sins of the empire) became an inexhaustible source of inspiration and courage for all those who, like him, dared to speak truth to power and bear testimony to the fact that another world is possible—and, furthermore, that God's desire is for that other world where colonial violence, injustice, and even death have no place.[14]

The many different voices from a wide range of experiences, religions, and traditions testifying to the fact that beyond death, life summons us should not be dismissed, whether by science, by theology, or by decolonial studies. They are not pie in the sky (even if they are often co-opted to that end); rather, they are an opening to new possibilities.

Mystical Experiences

We already discussed mystical experiences at some length in chapter 3. Only a few things need to be added. The word *mystical* comes from a word that means "to have your eyes closed." Mystical experiences are experiences that allow people to experience that which is present but invisible to the eyes. As the fox taught the little prince in Antoine de Saint-Exupéry's wonderful book: "It is only with the heart that one can see rightly; what is essential is invisible to the eye."[15] As we shall see below, this relates to God, whose reality overflows and overwhelms the limits of our senses and cognitive-affective apparatus.

---

13. See Martin Luther, "A Sermon on Preparing to Die," in *Luther's Works*, vol. 42, *Devotional Writings I*, ed. Martin O. Dietrich (Fortress Press, [1519] 1999), 95–115.

14. Joerg Riegel, *Christ and Empire: From Paul to Postcolonial Times* (Fortress Press, 2007), 4–5, 45–54.

15. Antoine de Saint-Exupéry, *The Little Prince*, trans. Katherine Woods (Harcourt Brace, 1943), 87.

What is it that we can perceive only with our eyes closed? If the world or "reality" as we perceive it is mediated by our cognitive-neural apparatus, and if that perception of reality (which, remember, is always an interpretation/representation) has been profoundly distorted by the hegemonic influences of racism, sexism, heterosexism, classism, ableism, white supremacy, patriarchy, and so on, then an indispensable step toward "seeing" past those illusions is to look at them with our eyes closed. Otherwise, we never see the other, we never really meet the other; we see reflected back to us only a representation of whom we have been taught to believe the other is.[16] (The same applies to ourselves. When we look at our own reflection in our mind's eye, what we see is the representation/illusion that has been given us). What happens when we close our eyes?

When we close our eyes, we must listen. Recently, I attended the retirement celebration of a long-time leader of my denomination. At the party, one of the women who worked under his leadership stood up and said: "I want to thank you for listening to me and to my ideas, because by listening to me you helped me find my own voice." By paying attention to reality with our eyes closed, we invite reality to define itself, to speak to us, rather than to conform to our preestablished ideas of what it is or what is supposed to be. This is not alien to the religious dimension of mysticism because mystics, including Muslim Sufis, Jewish prophets, Christian saints, Hindu gurus, Buddhist Zen masters, and Indigenous shamans emphasize the importance of seeing past the illusions of the way things appear to be in order to gain deeper, spiritual understanding of how things actually are.

Thus, through mystical experiences, not only are people able to listen to that sacred voice summoning them from deep within the sacred depths of reality, but they are also able to listen to dismantle the lies with which coloniality, white supremacy, heterosexism, and other ills have covered reality. Mystical experiences have the potential to allow us to listen to the voice of the other as the other and to find our own voice apart from the mask of the cognitive-affective schemas and scripts imposed on us, whether by societal collective structures or by events from our individual biography, like trauma, abuse, or addiction.[17] As a

16. Westhelle, "On Encountering the Other," in *After Heresy*, 15–32.

17. See, for example, Amy Hollywood, *Sensible Ecstasy: Mysticism, Sexual Difference, and the Demands of History* (University of Chicago Press, 2002).

pastor, I tried to remind people again and again that they are not what happened to them, they are not the terrible things that were done to them, and they are not the terrible things they might have done; they are much more than those things, and their future is open because it belongs to God alone. Therefore, the future is not a prisoner of the past.

Mysterium tremendum et fascinans

In terms of mystical experiences that open us up to the mystery of God, the German philosopher of religion Rudolf Otto offers a helpful clue about the nature of those types of experiences. In his now classic book *The Idea of the Holy*,[18] he examines primary testimonies from various religious traditions on experiences of what he refers to as "the sacred." He employs a method of analysis called phenomenology to investigate the suprarational aspects of those kinds of experiences where the numinous is encountered. He finds that there is one thing that many such experiences have in common. In addition to sensing a numinous presence reminiscent of the kind triggered by Persinger's God-helmet, discussed in chapter 3, the experience is also accompanied by the paradoxical feeling of fear and fascination—at the same time! Otto coined the Latin expression *mysterium tremendum et fascinans* (that is, the experience of a great mystery that produces fascination and dread at the same time) to describe that aspect of religious experiences. This brings to mind the occasion when Jesus's disciples were caught at sea in the middle of a storm that Jesus then proceeded to calm, prompting the disciples to fall on their knees, trembling in fear and asking themselves: "What sort of man is this, that even the winds and the sea obey him?" (Matt 23:27), and the other occasion when Peter exclaimed: "Go away from me, Lord, for I am a sinful man!" (Luke 5:8). When people have visions of messengers from heaven in the biblical texts, the messenger usually begins by saying "Fear not" (e.g., Luke 2:10; Rev 1:17).

The simultaneous experience of the *fascinans* and the *tremendum* calls to mind the neurophysiological model of religious experiences proposed by Newberg and d'Aquili, explored in chapter 3, and specifically how certain intense experiences can simultaneously trigger the sympathetic (arousal) and the parasympathetic (quiescent) responses

18. Rudolf Otto, *The Idea of the Holy: An Inquiry into the Non-Rational Factor in the Idea of the Divine and Its Relation to the Rational* (Oxford University Press, [1923] 1958).

in the autonomic nervous system, resulting in the experience of being hyperalert and profoundly relaxed at the same time. Recall that it is that embodied quality of the experience that emblazons it in memory and endows it with its feeling of sacredness and of it being more real than normal reality.

Therefore, from a decolonial theological perspective, we could speculate that these dynamics of embodied valuation of the experience endows people with a gut feeling of what is right and what is wrong.[19] This is particularly relevant in a society where moral values have been inverted by the pressures of the colonial matrix of power so that things that are abominable, such as lynchings, slavery, and burning of supposed witches and heretics, are perceived as normal and good, and things like tolerance, equity, and the celebration of difference are seen as reprehensible.[20] So, to have a *mysterium tremendum et fascinans* experience of the crucified and risen Christ is to have, at the same time, an embodied, affective confirmation of the truth of his message of love, forgiveness, justice, and abundant (eternal) life, for which he gave up his own life.

Unfortunately, I suspect that it is by similar neural-affective mechanisms that fear and hatred of those who are different from us becomes written into our embodied affective valuation apparatus. By painting the other in emotionally rousing narratives and depictions where the other is seen as vile, dangerous, or monstrously different, the other becomes encoded as one to be instinctively feared, mistrusted, and hated. Consequently, we must be mindful of what information we consume or, more accurately, what propaganda is fed to us.

Mystical Union

Another type of mystical experience, explored by William James in his groundbreaking work, *The Varieties of Religious Experience*,[21] is the

19. See the discussion on Damasio's SMH and Spezio and Adophs's cognitive-affective integrative model in chapter 2.

20. See the poignant analysis of James H. Cone, *The Cross and the Lynching Tree* (Orbis, 2012).

21. William James, *The Varieties of Religious Experience: A Study in Human Nature, Being the Gifford Lectures on Natural Religion Delivered at Edinburgh in 1901–1902* (Modern Library, 1994); see also Evelyn Underhill, *Mysticism: The Preeminent Study in the Nature and Development of Spiritual Consciousness* (Image Books, [1911] 1990).

experience of being absorbed into the totality of reality, beyond the limits of time and space. We examined these types of experiences in chapter 3 when discussing the neurotheological proposal of Andrew Newberg and Eugene d'Aquili, and Patrick McNamara's neuroscience of religious experience. Recall that these are experiences where the self initially becomes absorbed into another, greater self and later becomes one with the universe as a whole.

A metaphor often used to describe this experience is that of a drop of water dissolving in the sea. Interestingly, as I hinted at previously, some mystics have drawn heavily from the language of eroticism, including homoeroticism, to describe the experience of mystical union. For instance, Latinx theologian Miguel Díaz has written movingly on the homoerotic element in the mystical poetry of St. John of the Cross.[22] What is interesting about the use of sexual imagery to describe religious experience is that, as we saw in chapter 3, the neural systems that make religious experiences possible are the same as those that make the experience of orgasm and of intimate closeness to our mate possible. That means that the erotic images are not extraneous or forced but accurate descriptions, at the affective level, of what is taking place when the love between the believer and the *Holy One* is consummated.

But the experience of mystical union goes beyond the experience of union of the self with the self of a religious figure, such as Christ or the Buddha. From a neurological perspective, as we saw when discussing the neuroscience of religious experience, the brain (the hippocampus) eventually becomes tired of selectively filtering out neural information irrelevant to the intended focus of contemplation and ends up filtering everything out, leading to the experience of the self dissolving into a scared nothingness dense with everything. Halfway through the process, the experience leads to the death or extinguishing of the self so that only the greater self of the religious figure into which one has been absorbed remains. And then even that self disappears, giving way to a boundless totality that lovingly embraces everything—every creature, every space, every time—in a mantle of infinity and love that escapes verbal articulation or conceptual characterization. Silence! Nothingness/Everything![23]

22. Miguel H. Díaz, *Queer Dios de Amor* (New York: Fordham University Press, 2022).

23. For a fascinating testimony from a neuroscientist who had this type of experience triggered by a brain stroke, see Jill Bolte Taylor's TED Talk "Stroke of Insight,"

This experience is important because it not only intimates the reality of a divine Other who transcends everything and yet embraces it all, but it also reveals the deep interconnectivity of all reality and our dependence on each other. Thus, religious experiences do not pertain alone to the realm of the privacy of one's individuality; on the contrary, they drive us out of ourselves and into loving relationship with the rest of creation.[24]

Visions

A final type of religious experience, or summons of the transcendent within, are visions. Even though they are called visions, they are not exclusively visual phenomena because they often also involve other senses, like hearing, feeling, and even smelling. In the Hebrew, Christian, and Muslim traditions, the prophets are believed to have had such experiences given by God. The visions were meant to be messages for the people, not experiences for their individual spiritual edification. In a sense, they were public events. Those visions/messages were eventually put in writing and elaborated on by future generations, attempting to clarify what the message was, how to interpret it, and how it could be applied to new situations and novel challenges faced by the community.

Sometimes those visions involved self-disclosures of the divine being, but more often they had to do with revelations of God's will for the community or God's call for those in power who were misusing their authority to oppress others and enrich themselves at the expense of the misery of the most vulnerable members of their communities to repent and convert. The prophet Isaiah, for example, conveys God's disgust with the powerful members of society using religious rituals while neglecting the practice of justice:

> When you come to appear before me,
> who asked this from your hand?
> Trample my courts no more!
> Bringing offerings is futile;

available at https://youtu.be/mYD7Y9CXeUw?si=j_ZBsSsja-8AVZwB. I am grateful to Dr. José Irizarry, now president of Austin Presbyterian Theological Seminary, for pointing out this video to me during a presentation I gave on this topic at the Lutheran Center of the Seminario Evangélico de Puerto Rico.

24. See Rivera, *The Touch of Transcendence*, 88–97.

incense is an abomination to me.
New moon and Sabbath and calling of convocation—
I cannot endure solemn assemblies with iniquity.
Your new moons and your appointed festivals
my soul hates;
they have become a burden to me;
I am weary of bearing them.
When you stretch out your hands,
I will hide my eyes from you;
even though you make many prayers,
I will not listen;
your hands are full of blood.
Wash yourselves; make yourselves clean;
remove your evil deeds
from before my eyes;
cease to do evil;
learn to do good;
seek justice;
rescue the oppressed;
defend the orphan;
plead for the widow.
(Isa 1:12–17, italics added)

God's revelations through the prophets and the Scriptures were not meant for the philosophical, scientific, or theological curiosity of people like me. No. They were (and are) meant as instruction (*Torah* in the Hebrew Bible), practical wisdom (*Phronesis* in the Greek New Testament) for faithful living that would result in the flourishing of the community, so that the community or nation could be a blessing to other communities or nations and to the earth and its creatures.[25]

The word of God—that is, the agent of God's revelations—is an active and creative word (*Dabar* in Hebrew). It does not just communicate information but brings about new circumstances, a new reality.[26] Sometimes the revelation came in the form of an auditory experience, but most often it seems to have been multimodal, involving all the senses, including the sense of taste, as when prophets are given the

25. See, for example, Gen 12:2.

26. See Gen 1:3–26 and Isa 55:10–11.

Word to eat. All those revelations are highly symbolic and in need of careful discernment, interpretation, and application by the community, as is beautifully illustrated in the narratives of Joseph, the interpreter of dreams,[27]and in the book of the prophet Daniel, a seer and an unlikely model of nonviolent protest against the colonial hegemonic authority of empire (in his case, Babylonian), which tries to claim power even over people's religious conscience.[28]

From the perspective of a decolonial liberation theology of the brain, revelatory visions encoded and elaborated in the sacred writings of our religious traditions are important because they provide a counterweight to the authoritarian claims of governments and even of religious authorities. In my own tradition, the Lutheran-Protestant Reformation was rooted in the divine authority of the revealed Scriptures vis-à-vis (hegemonic) ecclesial and political institutions of human invention. And in modern times, social reformers have found inspiration and a rock-solid foundation in those traditions for their struggles for social justice, such as the Anglican Archbishop Desmond Tutu with the Truth and Reconciliation Commission in South Africa, the Baptist preacher Martin Luther King Jr. with the civil rights movement in the US, and the Lutheran laywoman Leymah Gbowee with the Christian-Muslim women's prayer movement to end Liberia's civil war. Even though those same Scriptures were usurped and used as weapons in the process of colonization, and used to justify slavery, patriarchy, and the oppression of sexual and racial minorities, there is something about the Scriptures that refuses to be domesticated and continues to pose a threat to authoritarian regimes and dictatorial leaders. In the provocative words of Margaret Atwood's *Handmaid's Tale*: "The Bible . . . is an incendiary device: who knows what we'd make of it, if we ever got our hands on it."[29]

Miracles

Yet another type of religious experience important to a decolonial liberation theology of the brain is that of miracles. This type of experience does not necessarily require the activation of the religious neural

27. Gen 41:15–36.

28. See Dan 3 and 6.

29. Quoted in Luis N. Rivera-Pagán, "God the Liberator: Theology, History, and Politics," in *Essays from the Margins* (Cascade, 2014), 63.

circuit posited by McNamara, but it simply involves witnessing something extraordinary and meaningful. This can happen at the level of individual, private experience, but more likely, it is an experience with communal and historical dimensions.[30] The fourth gospel calls such events "signs." That means that they are not simply favors granted by God to individuals or groups of peoples. Rather, they are coded messages that need to be understood as such. They need to be "read" (that is, decoded, interpreted, and applied).

The Holy Scriptures bears witness to many such events. The way they are reported in the Scriptures seeks to heighten that aspect of the event even if that means departing from absolute historical objectivity. This is akin to the way artists draw caricatures. You can recognize the person they drew, but you can also tell certain features have been exaggerated either for comedic effect or to highlight a point. This is what happens in the Scriptures. An event captured the imagination of the people because of its transparency to God's action or because of its powerful effects on the life of the people. Or on the contrary, an event was so catastrophic and contrary to the people's worldview that it demanded explanation, and not just any explanation but theological explanation.[31] These are events like the Babylonian captivity, the destruction of the temple, or the crucifixion of the Messiah.

The point is that the events themselves were charged with emotional significance and semiotic richness. It is important to note, however, as Paul Tillich indicates in his explanation of miracles in his *Systematic Theology*, that the event and the observer need each other.[32] For a miracle to be a miracle, it needs both something that has objectively happened and the perspective of faith that recognizes it, or interprets it, as miraculous. That is not that different from stating that writing only functions as writing if you have the objective set of signs printed on a surface, such as paper or a screen, plus a person who recognizes it as more than just random marks on a surface. Then comes the next step, which is applying the appropriate

---

30. See Tillich's brilliant discussion of miracles in his *Systematic Theology*, vol. 1, 115–118, 126–31.

31. Walter Brueggemann and Tod Linafelt, "Imaginative Remembering: The Theological Witness of the Old Testament," in *An Introduction to the Old Testament: The Canon and Christian Imagination*, 2nd ed. (Westminster John Knox Press, 2012), 3–15.

32. Tillich, *Systematic Theology*, vol. 1, 115–17.

grammar to read the message.[33] I will argue in the following chapter that it is through the process of acquiring something like what George Lindbeck has called grammar of faith[34] that one becomes able to recognize, and properly interpret the meaning of, religiously significant events such as miracles.

Among some of the many important miraculous events in the Christian grammar of faith, in the same grain as the Jewish faith, are the following:

- the exodus, when God heard the plight of an enslaved people and rescued them with mighty acts through the hands of Moses, Miriam, and Aaron
- the ensuing exodus, which turned out to be a journey of learning to trust fully in God and not in the strength and works of one's own hands or in false gods
- the sagas of the premonarchic judges of the tribes of Israel, faithful and flawed human beings stirred by the Holy Spirit of God, like Deborah and Gideon, willing to lead the people in acts of military self-defense against the abuses of the local proxies of the empires of their day
- the establishment of the Davidic monarchy, again as a symbol of God's power vis-à-vis the overwhelming bullish power of the surrounding nations (as extensions of colonial power), symbolized in the famous battle between the young David and the gigantic Goliath[35]
- the Babylonian captivity and the "prophetic imagination"[36]
- the messianic hope that was furnished in the fires of national catastrophes of biblical proportions[37]

---

33. I am borrowing this image from the discussion on "layered explanations" in John F. Haught, *Making Sense of Evolution: Darwin, God, and the Drama of Life* (Westminster John Knox Press, 2010), 23–27.

34. Linbeck, *The Nature of Doctrine*.

35. But see Brueggemann's critique of the monarchy as a betrayal of the prophetic, revolutionary consciousness embodied by Moses's leadership in "Royal Consciousness: Countering the Counterculture," *The Prophetic Imagination*, 40th anniv. ed. (Fortress Press, 2018), 21–37.

36. Bruggemann, 3.

37. See Walter Benjamin's intriguing reflections on the messianic in his "Theses on the Philosophy of History," in *Illuminations: Essays and Reflections*, ed. and intro. Hannah

In Christianity, there are two key foci around which the grammar of the Christian faith developed.[38] Those are the crucifixion of Jesus, so traumatic to his followers, and the witnesses of the resurrection.[39] It is from this standpoint that the rest of the life, teachings, and ministry of Jesus of Nazareth is remembered, with the backdrop of the messianic expectations born during the Babylonian captivity and the Maccabean Revolt (remembered every year by the Jewish community during Hanukkah) on the one hand and the horrendous destruction of Jerusalem and the temple by the Romans about thirty years after the crucifixion of Jesus on the other hand. From that vantage point, the "dangerous memory" of Jesus's life was retrieved and woven into the powerful message that is referred to as the gospel, the good news, or *evangelion* (a term originally used by the imperial powers that crucified Jesus to refer to the official, public proclamation of the victory of the Roman legions over its enemies).[40] Jesus himself was viewed as an event, a word-event that was the fulfillment of ancient prophecies and primordial yearnings.

Those events together weave a tapestry of meanings that become hermeneutically generative, allowing believers to perceive, recognize, and interpret other events from the perspective of the faith. That process of interpretation is a communal process not that different from science; it requires submitting one's "hypotheses" (i.e., proposed interpretations) for testing and for the consideration of the community of faith (akin to peer review in the academic world).[41]

Arendt, trans. Harry Zohn (Schocken Books, 1968), 262–64, and its discussion in Westhelle, *Eschatology and Space*, 125–29.

38. On the idea of doctrine functioning in a grammar-like way, see Lindbeck, *The Nature of Doctrine*, 16–19.

39. Westhelle, *The Scandalous God: The Use and Abuse of the Cross* (Fortress Press, 2006), 16–29.

40. The concept of the memory of the oppressed as a dangerous memory was articulated by the Catholic political theologian, Johan Baptist Metz; see his book *A Passion for God: The Mystical-Political Dimension of Christianity* (Paulist Press, 1998). From a US Hispanic and Latin American perspective, see Alejandro R. García-Rivera, *A Wounded Innocence* (Liturgical Press, 2003).

41. See, for example, J. Wentzel van Huyssteen, *The Shaping of Rationality: Toward Interdisciplinarity in Theology and Science* (William B. Eerdmans, 1999); and David

What is at stake in that process is not just abstract theories of how God is at work in the world, but ethical-hermeneutical frameworks to help guide how those who seek to be faithful to God's vision of abundant life for the world can live in synchrony with God's creative, redeeming, and life-giving work. Ethics and theology belong to each other, and together they depend on the ability to "read the signs of the times" (Matt 16:3) through the gaze of faith acquired from the great sign-events related in the sacred tradition.[42]

An important aspect of miracles for a decolonial liberational theology is that miracles destabilize the appearance of inevitability of the status quo regardless of its detrimental effects to the environment, to our siblings who belong to vulnerable communities, and even to ourselves. Miracles attest to the possibility of what decolonial activists/thinkers call "an otherwise." Miracles remind us that maybe, even if it is a long shot, things can be different; maybe things can be better. This is the beginning of liberation and delinking:

> Delinking means conceiving of and creating institutional organizations that are at the service of life and do not—as in the current state of affairs—put people at the service of institutions. Putting life at the service of institutions is the basic principle of modernity/coloniality, of Eurocentrism, and of the colonial matrix of power. Decolonial being, thinking, and doing begin from disrupting these assumptions and the naturalization of death.[43]

Faith

Most of the types of experiences examined so far could be seen as involving extraordinary circumstances, such as miracles or altered states of consciousness. Those are not, however, the majority of religious

---

Tracy, *Plurality and Ambiguity: Hermeneutics, Religion, Hope* (University of Chicago Press, 1987).

42. For this way of doing theology, see, for example, Robyn Henderson-Espinoza (now Roberto Che Espinoza), *Activist Theology* (Fortress Press, 2019).

43. Walter Mignolo, "What Does It Mean to Decolonize?," in Mignolo and Walsh, *On Decoloniality*, 127.

experiences. Most actual religious experiences are too mundane to inspire scientific investigation. I have put these experiences under the heading of faith because they are nothing other than expressions of that spiritual disposition that allows people to live with a sense of trust in God's invisible support and providence in their lives. It is the experience of knowing that our lives unfold in the field of grace, love, and awareness of the divine.

In his *On Religion: Speeches to Its Cultured Despisers* and later in his *The Christian Faith*, theologian Friedrich Schleiermacher explores this dimension of religious experience, which he considers to be the foundation of faith. He describes this foundation as "the feeling of absolute dependence," *Gefühl der schlechthinnigen Abhängigkeit* in his native German.[44]

Connecting faith with personal feeling (*Gefühl*, which in Schleiermacher's theology, is more than mere sentimentality) or, more accurately, "experience" opened the door, at least in the world of Protestant theology, for a way of doing theology that views people's lived experience as an important source for theology alongside the interpretation of the authorized Scriptures, dogmas, and doctrines of the religious institutions. That insight prepared the ground for a way of doing theology that takes the experiences of marginalized communities seriously. In India, reflecting about the experience of faith from a context of caste exclusion gave birth to Dalit theology. In the United States, the experiences of being Hispanic, Latinx, or Chicanx gave rise to various Hispanic/Latinx theologies; the experiences of the descendants of enslaved black Africans and of the Black church inspired Black liberation theology; the experiences of women in the context of faith became feminist theology; and the reflections of faith from within the particular experiences of Black women led to womanist theologies. Now we have a wide array of rich theologies, including queer theologies, Native American theologies, Caribbean theologies, minjung theologies, and so on. This was also, of course, a consequence of the simultaneous but independent development of liberation theology in Latin America in the 1960s and 1970s with Black liberation theology in the US.

44. F. Schleiermacher, *On Religion: Speeches to Its Cultured Despisers* (Harper, 1958); and Terrence N. Tice and Catherine L. Kelsey, eds., *The Christian Faith*, vols. 1 and 2, new trans. and critical ed. (Westminster John Knox Press, 2016).

If for Schleiermacher faith was the feeling of absolute dependence, for these emergent theologies, faith was the experience of the irruption of God as the source of resiliency, hope, inalienable dignity, and new possibilities. It was faith that allowed people to "make a way out of no way"[45] or that empowered them to hold on to their dignity amidst the indignities of oppression because they knew that God recognized what was happening and God is good and just. Faith is the proof of religion in that it is by the experience of living by faith alone ("walking by faith and not by sight", 2 Cor 5:7) that one is able to ascertain to the fundamental truth of religion—namely, that God is good and faithful.

As Kierkegaard observed, it is by leaping into the water first that one eventually learns how to swim.[46] It is by leaping into an attitude of trust in God's promises against all odds that one learns the power of faith. This is risky business: if one has placed one's faith in the wrong object, then rather than swimming, one will sink and might drown in the waters of a turbulent existence. Martin Luther famously stated that it is faith that makes both the idol and the true God. Only the true God can hold the weight of our existence. Wealth, success, status, party, race, ethnicity, country, tribe, leader, knowledge, relationships, and experiences can all become gods when we place our hope in any of them, as if any of those things, apart from God, could provide us with a solid foundation to build our lives.

Faith does not happen in a vacuum, nor is it created *ex nihilo* (out of nothing). Even though faith is purely a gift from God and is experienced in the solitude of one's spirit, it is cultivated in the bosom of a community. It is nourished with the stories of the faith of the spiritual ancestors in the Scriptures, which have been handed down throughout the centuries by the community of faith that are the churches, by the testimonies of others walking by faith, and by the witnessing of the power of faith to sustain, sooth, stir, and empower others in their own life journeys and struggles.

It is faith that sustains us and inspires us on the long journey of working for a decolonial, wholesome future that we will most likely never experience but that we help build nonetheless for those who

---

45. Delores S. Williams, *Sisters in the Wilderness: The Challenge of Womanist God-Talk* (Orbis, 2002), 158–61.

46. Niels Jørgen Cappelørn, *Kierkegaard's Journals and Notebooks*, vol. 4, journals NB-NB5 (Princeton University Press, 2011), 152.

will come after us. In the beautiful words of Rubem Alves, one of the founders of liberation theology:

> Let us plant dates, even though those who plant them will never eat them.
>
> . . .
>
> We must live by the love of what we will never see. This is the secret discipline. It is a refusal to let the creative act be dissolved away in immediate sense experience, and a stubborn commitment to the future of our grandchildren. Such disciplined love is what has given the prophets, revolutionaries, and saints the courage to die for the future they envisaged. They made their own bodies the seed of their highest hope, because they knew that "a grain of wheat remains a solitary grain unless it falls into the ground and dies" (John 12:24).[47]

Suffering

Suffering, as I have already mentioned above and in the previous chapter, can be a place of revelation and transformation where we are touched deeply by the summons of the sacred. In Buddhism, it was the witnessing of the suffering of his people that sent Prince Siddhartha on the journey to Buddhahood. In El Salvador, it was seeing the terrible suffering inflicted on the innocent by the powerful that led to the conversion of Monsignor Óscar Arnulfo Romero, Saint Romero de America. Even the controversial Ché Guevara, viewed as a secular saint by some and as a terrorist by others, was transformed by his experience of the suffering of impoverished workers in the southern hemisphere.

Suffering should not be romanticized or glorified. At the heart of the work of most, if not all, of the world's religions is a commitment to alleviate the suffering of others and address its root causes. But there are different kinds of suffering. Some suffering is simply a necessary part of life's processes and required for growth and maturation. Other kinds of

47. Rubem Alves, *Tomorrow's Child: Imagination, Creativity, and the Rebirth of Culture* (Harper and Row, 1972), 204.

suffering are the result of bad choices on our part or simply accidents of circumstances. Yet another kind of suffering is the suffering that is born from injustice, oppression, and exploitation. This is a kind of suffering that must be resisted. The suffering of martyrs like Monsignor Romero, the Jesuit priests assassinated in El Salvador, Dietrich Bonhoeffer, and countless others is suffering that came as a result of their speaking out against those unjust conditions that wrecked the lives of millions of beautiful children of God.

From a decolonial liberation theology perspective, as emphasized by Westhelle, Rivera, Rieger, and many others, the suffering of the innocent in situations of injustice is a locus of revelation because their suffering unveils the lies of systems that claim to be just, necessary, and ultimately, for the benefit of social order and stability. Order and stability for whom, and at whose expense? It was the genius of the civil rights leaders in the US, for instance, to force white people to witness with their own eyes the ways Black and brown folk were indecently abused by those who were supposed to be the paragons of decency. By bringing to millions of TV spectators, radio listeners, and newspaper readers across the US and the world the senseless, horrendous beatings that white police officers regularly inflicted on Black and brown people just for sitting on the "wrong side" of a bus or of a restaurant or for peacefully demanding to exercise their right to vote, they did something revolutionary. They allowed the power of the suffering of the innocent to remove the veil of convenient ignorance from the eyes of those who benefitted tremendously from that violence without having to sully their hands or even be bothered to know at whose expense their privilege was obtained.

Likewise, by bringing to general audiences, including classrooms, the historically accurate stories of the unjust suffering of Indigenous peoples, enslaved black Africans, migrants, ethnic and sexual minorities, white indentured servants, and colonial territories upon which the wealth and power of many of our countries have been built , peoples' consciences began to awake and things began to change.[48] Many began

48. See, for example, María Pilar Aquino, *Our Cry for Life: Feminist Theology from Latin America* (Wipf and Stock, 1993); the Spanish original is *Nuestro clamor por la vida: teología latinoamericana desde la perspectiva de la mujer* (San José, CR: Departamento Ecuménico de Investigaciones, 1992). See also Williams, *Sisters in the Wilderness*; and James H. Cone, *God of the Oppressed* (HarperSanFrancisco, 1975).

to understand the historical roots of their suffering, and others became aware of the historical roots of their privilege and their responsibility toward those on whose back their privilege had been built. Movements were launched; many people were shaken to their core, awakened. When we let the suffering of the innocent speak, the foundations of injustice are shaken.[49] But many also resisted and continue to resist. And they resist by trying to muffle the voice of the suffering of the innocent, by banning their testimonies, by forbidding stories that would make those in privilege uncomfortable, and by once again trying to tarnish the reputation of the victims, inverting reality so that the innocent might be seen as guilty and as responsible for their own suffering.

The apocalyptic tradition in Christianity is an example of the revelatory power of the suffering of the innocent.[50] At the heart of the vision of John of Patmos in Revelation is a throne in heaven. It is, in fact, the throne of God, with a splendor and glory that would have left the Roman emperor and all his colonial proxy rulers envious. Then John tells us the following: "Then I saw a Lamb, looking as if it had been slain, standing at the center of the throne." Later, he continues:

> Then I looked and heard the voice of many angels, numbering thousands upon thousands, and ten thousand times ten thousand. They encircled the throne and the living creatures and the elders. In a loud voice they were saying:
>
> "Worthy is the Lamb, who was slain,
> to receive power and wealth and wisdom and strength
> and honor and glory and praise!"
>
> Then I heard every creature in heaven and on earth and under the earth and on the sea, and all that is in them, saying:
>
> "To him who sits on the throne and to the Lamb
> be praise and honor and glory and power,
> for ever and ever!"

---

49. See James H. Cone, *The Cross and the Lynching Tree* (Orbis, 2012).

50. Pablo Richard, *Apocalypse: A People's Commentary on the Book of Revelation* (Orbis, 1995).

> The four living creatures said, "Amen," and the elders fell down and worshiped. (Rev 5:11–14)

Jesus, the innocent one who was slaughtered by the ruthless colonial power of the empire, now sits on the right hand of God and is the only one in the entire world who is found to be worthy. The resurrection and heavenly enthronement of the innocent lamb who was slain by the power of those who claimed to be the keepers of peace and order (*pax romana*), the models of the artistic and political achievement, is an indictment against the lies upon which such a system was built. This is reinforced later on when John recalls how he saw "a great multitude that no one could count, from every nation, from all tribes and peoples and languages, standing before the throne and before the Lamb, robed in white, with palm branches in their hands" (Rev 7:9) and is told by the angel that they are those who had been massacred, who had, so to speak, received the same baptism that Jesus had received.

The suffering of the innocent reveals the injustices of the system, whether colonialism, white supremacy, patriarchy, heterosexism, transphobia, classism, ableism, or any other ill. And through the revelation of Christ as the Lamb of God who was slain, the gospel makes clear on whose side God, the ultimate source and arbiter of what is good, true, beautiful and just, is.

Awe

We began this exploration of experiences that open up the human spirit to the summons of the transcendent within by reflecting on the existential protest that is born within when one has to confront the finitude and mortality of one's own self and, especially, of those whom we love. Now we end this exploration with the opposite experience, that of the opening up of reality into indescribable expansiveness, depth, infinity, and beauty, potentially present in every moment: the experience of awe.

Awe was the experience that brought me from science to theology. Training in the natural sciences and mathematics gave me a lens through which I could witness the astonishing beauty of God's creation at work even at the cellular, molecular, and subatomic levels. And what I saw through that lens was (is) indescribably beautiful! In chapter 2, I tried to share some of that beauty in my descriptions of how the brain and the nervous system works. In my doctoral dissertation, "Symptoms of God's Spirit? A Dialog Between Pneumatology and the Cognitive Sciences of Religion," I proposed that the Spirit of God is at work precisely through those natural processes that involve brains, bodies, and cognitive algorithms.[51] How else would the Spirit operate if not through the creation that, from the beginning, has been made possible, and continues to be possible, because the spirit/breath/wind/presence of God (*ruah elohim*) hovers over the primordial depths of creation (Gen 1:2) like a mother hen brooding over her eggs or covering her chicks under her wings (Ps 91:4, Ruth 2:12, and Matt 23:37)? Thus, it is also from within the depths of creation (which includes our brains, bodies, and minds) that a voice summons us:

> The heavens are telling the glory of God,
> and the firmament proclaims his handiwork.
> Day to day pours forth speech,
> and night to night declares knowledge.
> There is no speech, nor are there words;
> their voice is not heard;
> yet their voice goes out through all the earth
> and their words to the end of the world.
> (Ps 19:1–4)

Such experiences give rise not only to religious or spiritual feelings but also to important philosophical and theological questions:

- Why is there something rather than nothing?
- Why is the universe so finely tuned for life?
- How come the human mind is capable of unlocking the mysteries of nature and of the cosmos?
- Where does consciousness come from, or how does it happen?
- Why is there suffering and evil?
- How can we get justice and life?

From the perspective of the dialogue between science and religion, the experience of awe is an important meeting place. But awe is also important from a decolonial liberationist perspective. That is because

51. Carmelo Santos-Rolón, "Symptoms of God's Spirit? A Dialog Between Pneumatology and the Cognitive Sciences" (PhD diss., Lutheran School of Theology at Chicago, 2010).

the experience of awe resists the commodification of nature. The awe, or sense of wonder, that comes from the scientific study and religious contemplation of nature allows us to perceive the sacredness and inherent value of even the simplest members of the family of creation, from the minerals on the ground to the bacteria in our gut. Furthermore, Western science is now discovering what ancient wisdom has known for a long time—namely, the delicate interconnectivity and deep mutuality of all creation. Awe also keeps the inquiry open, resists the closure of great philosophical or scientific systems, and nurtures the dimension of mystery so important for the human soul. It protects creation from the transubstantiating powers of bottomless colonial-capitalistic greed, which like a modern Midas, transforms everything that it touches into a thing to be exploited, monetized, and instrumentalized and, in so doing, destroys it.

Conclusion

Finitude, mortality, near-death experiences, mystical experiences, miracles, faith, suffering, and awe: in this chapter, we have stepped outside the epistemic frame of science and have tried to listen to the voices there summoning us from within. What we have encountered there can be life-changing, even liberating and decolonizing if we don't resist it but rather let it work on us. A spirit of promise hovers in those spaces, loci where we can experience each other.

Reality resists enclosures, scientific, theological, colonial, epistemic, or otherwise. Reality summons us. From within its wounds we are called. By whom?

CHAPTER SIX

Excursus

On Naming the Mystery

> The LORD is a stronghold for the oppressed, a stronghold in times of trouble. And those who know your name put their trust in you, for you, O LORD, have not forsaken those who seek you.
>
> —Psalms 9:9–10

Introduction

EXPERIENCES SUCH AS those outlined in the previous chapter, and many others like them, point to "a surplus of meaning" in human experience.[1] They orient our gaze after that which lies beyond the horizons of the known and the knowable. They can be understood as "symptoms," in the positive sense of the word, of the spiritual depths of reality. Throughout the history of humanity there have been many attempts at naming the mystery that is the object, if we can use that word in this instance, or the referent of those experiences.

Delusions, Illusions, and Manipulations

Before delving into the positive ways of naming God, a word of caution is in order. Not all religious experiences are revelations of the divine or openings into the sacred depths of reality. Some experiences deemed religious might be greatly harmful. They can come as a result of neurological or psychological pathology, where people lose their grip on reality, no longer able to tell fantasy from reality. These experiences are not life-giving; rather than nurturing the soul of those undergoing them and bringing wholeness to their communities, they tear them both asunder. In biblical Greek the verb used to describe those types of experiences is

---

1. I am borrowing the concept from Paul Ricoeur, *Interpretation Theory*; see also Jean-Luc Marion, "The Saturated Phenomenon."

dia-bolein, from where we get *diabolos* and *diabolic*. They are diabolic experiences not because a demon, or the devil, or any other supernatural being is causing them, but simply because they are experienced as a tremendous force that has invaded the mind of the individual, overpowering them and inhibiting their ability for full agency.[2] Authentic religious experiences are meant to be life-giving, for the individual and for the community, even when they involve negative aspects and painful processes. In the end, they are part of the creative, redemptive, and healing activity of the divine Spirit and are meant to strengthen the community and the individual who undergoes them. Hence, many mystics include in their writings warnings against accepting any extraordinary experience as being from God without first undergoing a process of strict discernment. The community is also responsible for "discerning the spirits" (1 John 4:1) and not just accepting any claims of religious experiences, visions, or revelations at their face value.[3]

It is not only physiological or psychological pathology that can lead to religious delusions. There are also social and cognitive dynamics that can lead to beliefs and experiences that are considered religious at first but that upon careful examination turn out to be harmful to the individual and to the community. Sometimes there is manipulation involved, as when the sincere beliefs of some are distorted to make them commit acts that actually betray the fundamental tenets of the teachings of the founders of their religions. Sadly, this can be seen in all religions: the nauseating abuse of the cross by white supremacists in the US to terrorize people whom they deem not to be real Americans, and perhaps not even fully human; militant Buddhist groups in the Pacific; extremist Muslim movements throughout the world; the crusades of European Christendom; and even the violent repressions of supposedly secular movements such as communism or socialism that in reality functioned as secular, absolutist religions that demanded human sacrifices as much as actual "religions." And there are, of course, the horrific historical realities of slavery; of the brutal colonization of entire continents and nations of Indigenous peoples under the sign of the cross; of the burning of women accused of witchcraft; the mass extermination of Jews, Roma people, people with disabilities, gay and lesbian people, and others by

2. Westhelle, "Idols and Demons," 11–13.

3. Westhelle, "Idols and Demons," 13.

the Nazi regime; the forced displacement, collective punishment, and massive killing of the Palestinian people; and, sadly, so much more, often done in the name of God.

That long history of past and present abuses reminds us of the need for discernment, both at the individual level and at the level of the communities of faith (both intra- and inter-). Even within the Bible, as we will see in chapters 8 and 9, there is a constant struggle between the prophets and those who would distort religious claims and experiences for their own purposes at the expense of the community's well-being. To be truly liberative, a decolonial liberation theology of the brain must include a healthy dose of suspicion regarding claims of religious experiences and the truths derived from those experiences, as well as a strong dose of critical analysis even of those religious truths and claims deemed authentic. We shall see later on in this book, in chapter 9, how liberation theologies, as well as feminist, queer, postcolonial, and decolonial theologies, have embraced hermeneutics of suspicion that look at religious claims and practices through the lenses of critical thought in an attempt to constantly correct the way religion is used. In that sense, a liberation theology of the brain welcomes the critical analysis of religion carried out by other disciplines such as sociology, critical race theory, feminist theory, and psychology. However, it also warns against the often simplistic and distorted characterization of religion into which those analyses often fall, failing to properly distinguish among different expressions of faith and religion.

God

Perhaps the oldest name for the referent of the experiences outlined previously is God. In his book *The Experience of God*, the Jesuit, Hindu, and Buddhist theologian Raimon Panikkar explains that "the origin of the word *God* is Sanskrit: *Dyau*, day, suggests brilliance, the light, divinity (like *theos* in Greek). Light makes it possible to see and light gives life."[4] God is not what we see but what allows us to see. God is not a being among other beings but the life of all beings, the source of all that is. As Spirit, God is breath and air, which infuses creatures with life and dynamism. To think of God as anthropomorphic projection is

4. Panikkar, *The Experience of God*, 11.

too simplistic and inaccurate. Panikkar explains that "the experience of humanity, expressed in innumerable traditions, both oral and written, has called God by numerous names. Almost unanimously, it has named and understood God as name or as symbol, not as concept."[5] God is that cosmic life-giving, life-sustaining, and life-renewing love in whose all-encompassing presence we "live and move and have our being."[6] God is not a concept, but we need concepts, and symbols, to relate to God, even as we must be constantly reminded that our concepts, symbols, and images of God are not God, even when God might reveal something of God's self through them.

Thus, God is addressed as a person, but God is infinitely more than a person; God is perceived as a force, but God is much more than a force; God is understood to have authority the way that rulers, kings, queens, and emperors have authority, but God's authority is of an unfathomable kind; God is referred to by gendered nouns, such as *Father* and *Lord*, yet it is understood that such categories of gender or sex are inadequate when applied to God. When the symbolic nature of God-talk is forgotten, we risk distorting the reality such language is meant to point to. Furthermore, as feminist theologians have taught us, whenever we lift up a human category to name the mystery of God, such as Father, King, Warrior, and others like those, we are at the same time lifting up those human categories as more sacred than others and subjecting others to them. As theologian Elizabeth Johnson explains, "religious symbols are double-edged, directing attention both toward the infinite which they symbolize and toward the finite through which they symbolize it. Whenever a segment of reality is used as a symbol for God, the realm of reality from which it is taken is elevated into the realm of the holy."[7] Hence, Mary Daly's insight that "if God is male, then the male is God."[8] Similarly, when the images of God and, in the case of Christianity, of Jesus, are taken predominantly from the dominant culture, ethnic group, or race, soon two things happen: people forget

5. Panikkar, *The Experience of God*, 11.

6. Acts 17:28.

7. Elizabeth A. Johnson, *She Who Is: The Mystery of God in Feminist Theological Discourse* (Herder & Herder, 2002), 37.

8. Mary Daly, "Feminist Post-Christian Introduction," in *The Church and the Second Sex* (Harper & Row, 1975), 38, cited in Johnson, *She Who Is*, 37.

the symbolic nature of the representation and begin to believe that God and Jesus are in fact white, blond, Caucasian men, and, though in a more subtle way, they begin to sense that people who look like Jesus and God look are superior than others.

In order to avoid confusions that lead to idolatry, many of the world's religions have safeguards. For instance, the Torah has a prohibition against creating any image to resemble God, and some interpreters take that to include conceptual, intellectual, theoretical, and even theological images. In Islam, any kind of image of God is strictly forbidden, and in Buddhism, there is the koanic phrase "If you come across the Buddha, kill him." The Buddha is not believed to be God in Buddhism, but the phrase still conveys the same impulse for protecting the mystery of the sacred from the distortions of the human mind.

Perhaps that is why there has always been a close association between silence, nothingness, and God in the mystical traditions. And rather than "knowing God," one is invited to "unknow" in order to be able to experience. Panikkar's description here might be helpful:

> The experience of God thus consists in touching the totality of Being with the totality of our own being: to feel in our body, our intellect, and our spirit the whole of reality both *within* and *outside* us . . . The experience of God is the experience of the Mystery that governs our lives from both within and without.[9]

Deities

While in some traditions the absolute unity of the divine is emphasized (God is One), in others the inexhaustible vastness of the divine requires a plethora of deities, angelic beings, orishas, or jinns to adequately convey divinity. These avatars of the divine reality can represent different aspects of God's character and work. Some are irenic and benevolent, others are fierce warriors, and even others are closer to the demonic than to the holy, but together they all are meant to represent important aspects of that divine mystery to which humanity intuits that it owes its existence and well-being. I wonder if having divinities corresponding to the vast range of the human experience of reality, including

9. Panikkar, *The Experience of God*, 141. Italics in the original.

the tragic, the evil, and even the mischievous (a trickster character), makes it easier for people to be more in touch with aspects of the depths of their mental and emotional life that might otherwise be repressed or ignored. It is also interesting to note that there seems to be a connection between those traditions that celebrate the plurality of the divine and the veneration of one's ancestors. Unfortunately, those traditions, so prevalent in the African and Asian continents and exported from there throughout the world, were distorted by the Eurocentric colonial and racist gaze. Rather than expressions of the divinity, they were seen as satanic or idol worship. Much was lost because of that prejudice. That is not to say that everything in every tradition ought to be celebrated. An honest dialogue that treats the other with respect also involves a moment of mutual criticism, but it is done with respect and humility.

The Designer (Deism)

Another name that has been used to designate the mysterious source of all that exists is clockmaker. Obviously, this is more an analogy than a name. It emerged as a response to scientific discoveries of the delicate complexity of organisms, which consist of complexity within complexity within complexity, all the way to the cellular level and deeper.[10] Theologians employed the metaphor of a person stranded on an island coming across a watch on the ground. Given the complexity of the mechanism in the watch and its obvious signs of design, it would be more reasonable to assume that someone designed and built that object than that it came about by the work of random forces in nature. Similarly, if one contemplates even a simple eye, its rich complexity and delicate functioning drive the human intellect to the rational conclusion that there must have been a designer, a divine "clockmaker." Likewise, when one comes to understand the way the universe appears to be fine-tuned to bring about and sustain life, many can't help but agree with the psalmist:[11]

---

10. Barbour, *Religion and Science*, 21–23, 36–38.

11. One among many examples is Stephen Hawking's comment: "If the rate of expansion one second after the Big Bang had been smaller by even one part in a hundred thousand million million it would have recollapsed before it reached its present size." See Hawking, *A Brief History of Time* (New York: Ballantine Books, 1988), 121, quoted in Barbour, *Religion and Science*, 204.

When I look at your heavens, the work of your fingers,
the moon and the stars that you have established;
what are humans that you are mindful of them,
mortals that you care for them? (Ps 8:3–4)

Thus, the great scientist Isaac Newton described his quest to understand the fundamental physical laws governing the universe as an attempt at reading the mind of the Creator. And no less than Albert Einstein had in mind the idea of God as a clockmaker (or perhaps a maker of fine Swiss watches) when he protested against the randomness introduced into physics by quantum mechanics. He famously quipped: "God does not play dice with the universe."[12] On the other side of the equation, of seeing the universe as a fine-tuned mechanism, would be the perspective of the famous mathematician Pierre-Simon LaPlace. According to Barbour, "when Napoleon said to him: 'M. Laplace, they tell me you have written this large book on the system of the universe, and have never even mentioned its Creator,' Laplace [gave] his famous reply, 'I had no need of that hypothesis.'"[13]

This name for the mystery—namely, the designer—is often the name of an intelligence who created the initial conditions of possibility for the world to come into being and then set it in motion, letting it run its course without much intervention, with rare exceptions to make sure that it is back on its intended course.

An older version of this way of thinking about the mysterious source of all was articulated by the Greek philosopher Aristotle. He believed there was a first cause of all other causes in the world, a first cause that was by definition immovable, firmly grounded in itself, and needing nothing other than itself and therefore perfect in its being, omnipotent and omniscient. Different from the God of the deists, this version of the divine does not create directly but simply by virtue of its luring perfection, which makes all things reach toward their own perfection or fulfillment—an expression of the perfection of the divine. Despite its strong influence in different religious systems, neither the classical God of Aristotelean philosophy nor the clockmaker of classic deism should be confused with the personal, loving, prayer-answering

12. For Einstein's view on God, see Barbour, *Religion and Science*, 210–11.

13. Barbour, *Religion and Science*, 35.

God of the Abrahamic faiths and other similar religious traditions. Nonetheless, this way of naming God does highlight an important aspect of the mystery of God, the close correlation between the nature of the creation and the mind of the Creator.

Being Itself (Pantheism)

Another way of naming the divine source of reality that has been very influential across various cultures and religions is to think of creation itself not as the handiwork of a creator external to nature but rather as the modes by which the divine mystery exists. It is in that sense that the term *pantheism* is to be properly understood. It does not mean that trees, rocks, seas, and other elements of nature are worshipped as if they were God. It means that God is the ultimate substance of all reality, similar to the way the water is the substrate of waves, waterfalls, and rain. The universe, nature, humans, time, space, and other elements in nature are all aspects ("accidents") of the divine substance. That divine substance underlying everything that is has been called "being itself" or "the power of being," because it is what makes it possible for anything to exist. In Western thought, this way of naming the divine mystery was articulated most influentially by the excommunicated European Jewish philosopher Benedict Spinoza,[14] but it finds resonances in other traditions, especially in Eastern religion.[15] Explaining this conceptualization of the mystery of being as the power of being or being itself, Paul Tillich writes: "If God is identified with nature (*deus sive natura*), it is not the totality of natural objects which is called God but rather the creative power and unity of nature, the absolute substance which is present in everything . . . it is the structure of being, the essence of all essences, which is called God. Pantheism is the doctrine that God is the substance or essence of all things."[16]

One implication of this way of thinking about God is that we have access to the divine reality by reflecting on our own experience because everything that we are and that we experience is an expression of the divine power. To find God is to find the substance, power, and ground

---

14. Barbour, *Religion and Science*, 16.

15. Barbour, *Religion and Science*, 122.

16. Tillich, *Systematic Theology*, vol. 1, 233–34.

of our own being, and to find the ground of our own being is also to find that which connects us to every other being and to the sacred itself. A risk implicit in this way of naming the mystery of God is that it lends itself to easy distortions and the idolatry of the worst aspects of our own egocentric self (either individual or communal, as in race, blood, nation, or religion) projected onto an infinite screen where the frames have been hidden from view.

Nature (Naturalism)

An alternative to saying that nature and the rest of reality as such are expressions of the divine nature is to say that nature is enough and that there is no need to posit a divine being, mystery, ground, or substrate.[17] Naturalism is the philosophical stance that nature is sacred in its own right and is more than enough to satisfy the religious yearnings of humanity once one has come to fully understand it through the guiding tutelage of the natural sciences. In her book *The Scared Depths of Nature*, biologist Ursula Goodenough puts it thus:

> Humans need stories—grand, compelling stories—that help to orient us in our lives and in the cosmos. The Epic of Evolution is such a story, beautifully suited to anchor our search for planetary consensus, telling us of our nature, our place, our context. Moreover, responses to this story—what we are calling religious naturalism—can yield deep and abiding spiritual experiences. And then, after that, we need other stories as well, human centered stories, a mythos that embodies our ideals and our passions. This mythos comes to us, often in experiences called revelation, from the sages and the artists of past and present times.[18]

Naturalism, as can be seen in Goodenough's quote, still appeals to the religious sentiments of humanity, recognizing the importance

17. Willem B. Dress, *Religion, Science, and Naturalism* (Cambridge University Press, 1996).

18. See the beautiful book by Ursula Goodenough, *The Sacred Depths of Nature* (Oxford University Press, 1998).

of myth and ritual and the truths that religions claim to convey, but it believes that traditional religious doctrinal systems are no longer necessary or adequate to communicate those truths to a modern audience. Moreover, by highlighting the status of nature as sacred in itself, apart from any divine or religious being, it seeks to elevate the moral status of nature. That has been one of the great contributions of naturalism, to deinstrumentalize nature.

Nature is not there as a resource to satisfy human needs, as a domain for humans to dominate it according to a divine mandate, or as a trust to be stewarded by benevolent human beings as vicars of the divine to whom it ultimately belongs. Rather, nature is our home, our flesh, the only source of life, of nourishment, of healing, of wholesomeness. How humans collectively treat nature, of which we are part, will translate into how nature will then treat us.

Spirit (Panentheism)

An approach that seeks to open common ground among naturalism, theism, and pantheism is panentheism. This way of naming the divine mystery strives to maintain the integrity (the alterity or Otherness) of God and of creation while affirming their intricate, intimate, interactive relationship. Many Christian theologians from liberation and feminist perspectives have found panentheism to be a useful approach to thinking about the divine. One of the models that has been favored by these thinkers is the one first developed by the mathematician and philosopher Alfred North Whitehead and called process philosophy or process theology.[19]

According to this model, the world unfolds or happens within God, and as the world unfolds and happens, God is within the world, feeling it, knowing it intimately, and receiving into the divine self every new development that happens in and to the world. The world adds richness to the divine life, not that different from the way a parent's life is enriched by seeing the life of their beloved child unfold. But there is also pain involved, such as when our children suffer or when they make decisions that we know will threaten their well-being. Yet we accept them as they are and try to adapt to those decisions and provide

19. Alfred North Whitehead, *Process and Reality* (Free Press, [1929] 1978).

adequate guidance and advice, which our children (nieces and nephews, godchildren or grandchildren, adopted kids, sons and daughters, students, and so on) can accept and adopt, reject, or partially adopt. Thus is the relationship between the divine Spirit and her creatures and, in fact, all creation.[20]

The strength of this approach is that it allows for both the autopoiesis of natural phenomena and the possibility, in fact the necessity, of divine interaction. But it does so in a way that the world is not turned into a mere puppet of the divine, and God is not portrayed as a tyrant nor as a mere abstraction of what otherwise is nothing but natural processes. God is the creator of the world, not *ex nihilo* but in a never-ending process of *creatio continua* (continual creation) where the world and God exist together from eternity to eternity. Every moment, and every aspect of reality, is always an opportunity for divine creativity, healing, and redemption. The weakness of this approach, in my estimation, is that it is highly speculative in terms of the mechanism by which the divine interacts with the physical in a way that trespasses the boundaries of competencies of each discipline (theology on the one hand and physics on the other). To make such claims about the dynamics of the physical processes of the universe calls for some form of experimental corroboration or at least predictive confirmation. It also risks the hubris of wanting to know more about the divine than what the divine wishes to disclose about the divine self. Notwithstanding those criticisms, the panentheistic approach to naming God and the process theology variant of that perspective are powerful resources for an understanding of God and the world that respects the integrity and otherness of God and the world while allowing for rich interaction and a depth of intimacy that most other models of the divine lack.[21] Therefore some liberation theologians have found it to be a helpful interpretative tool.[22]

---

20. For an introduction to process theology, see John B. Cobb Jr. and David Ray Griffin, *Process Theology: An Introductory Exposition* (Westminster John Knox Press, 1976); Catherine Keller, *On the Mystery: Discerning God in Process* (Fortress Press, 2008); and Marjorie Hewitt Suchocki, *God, Christ, Church: A Practical Guide to Process Theology* (Crossroad, 2001).

21. For a very creative synthesis of process theology and science, see Ian G. Barbour, *Nature, Human Nature, and God* (Fortress Press, 2002).

22. See, for example, Jorge Pixley, *El Dios Liberador en la Biblia: Ensayos de Teología Bíblica que Aprovechan la Filosofía del Proceso* (Quito: Ediciones Abya-Yala, 2009).

Spirit (*Geist*)

Another name for the mystery is the German *Geist*, which encompasses the dimensions of mind, spirit, and power, especially at the collective, historical, and even universal levels.[23] I will follow here the convention of translating *Geist* as Spirit. Spirit, however, does not refer to a ghost in the way ghosts are often portrayed in popular culture. Rather, Spirit is a kind of intention or purpose that orients and drives processes in a certain direction, aiming at a certain goal. The implication of this view is that historical and natural processes are not really random or accidental, even if they include moments of randomness and fortuitous accidents within them. They are actually being guided by forces that transcend individual members and events but that operate by influencing the processes from within. We have history because we have Spirit; similarly, we have evolution because we have Spirit. Therefore, to analyze the forces driving historical developments and natural emergence is to inquire about the mind that is the Spirit driving them. Similar to the view of divine action in process thought, Spirit does not manipulate reality—it does not cancel the agency and free will of the main actors—but operates by means of the free agency of those actors. In a sense, it aligns or orients their agency in the direction of a certain general goal.

One of the main architects of this way of naming the mystery was the German philosopher Georg Wilhelm Friedrich Hegel. In his lectures on the philosophy of history, he explains this idea in the following way:

> It is the concrete spirit of a people which we have distinctly to recognize, and since it is Spirit it can only be comprehended spiritually, that is, by thought. It is this alone which takes the lead in all the deeds and tendencies of that people, and which is occupied in realizing itself—in satisfying its ideal and becoming self-conscious—for its great business is self-production.[24]

23. Paul Tillich defines Spirit as "the actualization of power and meaning in unity." See *Systematic Theology*, vol. 3 (University of Chicago Press, 1963), 111.

24. Hegel, *The Philosophy of History* (Dover, [1837] 1956), 71.

Hero figures play an important role in this process. Hegel uses Napoleon Bonaparte as a paradigmatic example. There are individuals who become aware of their historical vocation and, inspired by the movement of the Spirit, guide the people in the direction of the fulfillment of history's goal, which is the self-actualization of the Spirit. The process includes negative moments, but these are taken up by the Spirit-led movement of history and sublated into a greater whole that in the end, contributes to the fulfillment of history.

This perspective was very influential in the development of disciplines such as history, sociology, economics, biblical interpretation, theology, and even science. If historical and natural processes have a direction—guided by a rational if invisible force accessible to thought—then it is possible to scrutinize those processes to identify what that logic is guiding them toward and to what end (*telos*). In Biblical interpretation and theology, this reinforced the idea that reality is a drama that is unfolding and leading the world to a conclusion guided by the Spirit of God. Marxist thought emerged as an inversion of the Hegelian idea of Spirit. It is not that a Spirit is guiding history and we can read its mind by studying the way it has influenced the concrete structures of a civilization and its culture, art, philosophy, and religion. Instead, it is that the historical process is driven by the influence of concrete variables within the society itself, such as economic relations (and struggles among the classes), which exert pressure on the way that society will evolve over time. Spirit, in that view, is the result, not the cause, of the process, and therefore the expressions of Spirit found in a society are really a function (and at the service) of those concrete relations. In other words, the religion of a people (and the ways they name the mystery) will be a reflection of the dominant economic structures in which they are organized and will serve as a force to reproduce and perpetuate those structures. That is why Karl Marx, commenting on Hegel's philosophy, states that the beginning of criticism (and of a revolutionary process) is the criticism of religion.[25] He states: "Thus the criticism of heaven turns into the criticism of the earth, the criticism of religion into the criticism of right and the criticism of theology into the criticism of politics."[26]

---

25. Karl Marx, "Contribution to the Critique of Hegel's Philosophy of Right," in Karl Marx and Friedrich Engels, *On Religion* (Scholars Press, [1844] 1964), 41.

26. Marx, "Contribution to the Critique," 42.

Liberation theology was deeply influenced by the idea of Spirit articulated by Hegel, as well as its revisions and applications in Marx's works. For the early generation of liberation theologians, steeped in and inspired by the revolutions and national movements of liberation of their times, the biblical history of God's intervention to liberate an oppressed people from the tyrannical bondage of the Egyptian hegemony and their journey toward a promised land of liberty and human flourishing was a sort of blueprint of how the divine Spirit is at work in history even today. God's Spirit is the divine force that listens to the cries of the oppressed, sides with them in their struggle against injustice, and leads them to freedom.[27] However, liberation theologians also learned, especially from Marx's analysis of religion combined with Freud's and Friedrich Nietzsche's analyses of the hidden drives of human actions and thoughts and in line with the biblical prophetic tradition, to develop a hermeneutics of suspicion about their own religious symbols and theological traditions.[28]

Decolonial activists/thinkers have applied a similar hermeneutics of suspicion to Hegel and Marx themselves, uncovering the ways in which their insights and analyses were corrupted by the racist Eurocentrism prevalent in their times, the heyday of the European global colonial project.[29] In reading Hegel and those influenced by his thought, it becomes clear that what they saw as the self-realization of Spirit in history was none other than their own culture. This became decisive in the consolidation of the colonial project and its supportive columns of racism and sexism, because it allowed them to place peoples from different cultures, ethnic backgrounds, phenotypes, epistemes, and so on along an imaginary line of historical development or underdevelopment of Spirit. It also confirmed the European self-appointed vocation of civilizing the rest of the world—that is, of bringing them closer to a Eurocentric understanding of the self-fulfillment of Spirit in history and

---

27. Hugo Assmann, "The Christian Contribution to Liberation in Latin America," in *Theology for a Nomad Church* (Orbis Books, 1976),129–45.

28. María Pilar Aquino, "The Hermeneutics of Suspicion and Daring," in *Our Cry for Life*, 121–30.

29. See, for example, Enrique Dussel, *1492: El encubrimiento del Otro. Hacia el orígen del mito de la moderníndad* (Madrid: Nueva Utopía, 1993), available in English as *The Invention of the Americas* (Continuum Publishing Group, 1995).

of destroying and deriding elements of local culture, religion, science, and wisdom traditions that contradicted the European ones.[30] As we will see in the next chapter, through a process involving affective valuations and linguistic interpretation, those categories and ways of organizing the world evolutionarily acquired a heavy ontological weight, making them seem as if they were actual natural categories and even ordained by God or by whatever name was given to the mystery.

Trinity (Father-Son-Holy Spirit)

The name by which most Christian traditions know the divine mystery is the Trinitarian name.[31] This name is understood to be the result of divine self-revelation, not an invention of the church. This revelation, however, does not refer to God speaking to the church in the same way that the angel spoke to Moses from the flaming bush, answering his question, What is your name? with the unfathomable: *I am who I am*.[32] The revelation of the Trinitarian name corresponds to the revelation of God in the person of Jesus Christ and in the power of the Holy Spirit through the historical events of his life, ministry, teachings, passion, death, and resurrection; the pouring of the Holy Spirit upon the community of believers; and the theological reflections that followed them to make sense of such events. The Trinitarian name appears already in the earliest writings of the New Testament, a mere twenty to thirty years after the events of Jesus's crucifixion and resurrection and the outpouring of the Holy Spirit. However, it took the church centuries of praxis and theological reflection to be able to fully articulate the significance of God's holy name pointing to a relationship of three persons so

---

30. See Westhelle, "The Inverted World: From the Colonial to the Postcolonial" and "Shaking the Foundations of the Colonial Project," in *After Heresy*, 33–62.

31. For an analysis of the theological origins and justification of naming God, Father, Son, and Holy Spirit, see Robert W. Jenson, *The Triune Identity* (Fortress Press, 1982). I am not convinced by his argument that despite their gendered nature, the names Father and Son are irreplaceable, but I do agree with him that in their theological context, those names are not meant to be a statement on God's gender (nonetheless, see Elizabeth Johnson's and Mary Daly's concern above that if God is male, then male is implicitly equated with God).

32. Exod 3:14.

intimately united that they are one, or of one divine reality that exists as three distinct persons.[33]

It is easy to get lost in the "mathematics" of the Trinity. How can a being be one and be three at the same time? But that is not the point of the Trinitarian name of God. Ultimately, the point of the Trinitarian name of God is, as theologian Catherine Mowry LaCugna puts it, to claim the promise that the divine mystery is *for us*.[34] The Trinitarian name given to the divine mystery by the Christian tradition is intimately connected to the divine purposes revealed in the Scriptures of the Old and New Testaments, read through the lens of faith. The divine purpose, from the very beginning of creation, is for full communion between Creator and creature.[35] That is achieved, though, only proleptically, through the incarnation of the second person of the Trinity, in the womb of Mary of Nazareth, as Jesus, the son of the carpenter Joseph and the preacher from Galilee. God became incarnate in one human being of one culture, nation, language, gender, and religion for the sake of all peoples of all nations, cultures, genders, and even religions, and eventually, for the ultimate fulfillment of all creation. It was through the action of the Spirit of God that the incarnation was possible, just as it was (and still is) through the hovering of the Spirit over the primordial waters that creation and life become possible. It was that same Spirit that was apparent in the life and ministry of Jesus, and after his death, resurrection, and ascension, it was through the experience of the Spirit that the followers of Jesus were able to discern the presence of the risen Christ in their midst.

It is that experience of God as transcendent mystery to whom the entirety of creation owes its existence: as Spirit that hovers over creation and within believers, giving life, hope, faith, courage, and love; as the one anointed by Mary with precious perfume and crucified by the powers of the Roman Empire in cahoots with a small group of the religious leaders of his day; the one who even from the agonizing death of the cross overflowed with love for all, including for those crucifying

---

33. For an exposition and theological elaboration of the doctrine of the Trinity, see Catherine Mowry LaCugna, *God for Us: The Trinity in Christian Life* (HarperSanFrancisco, 1991).

34. LaCugna, *God for Us*, 15–17.

35. Leonardo Boff, *Holy Trinity: Perfect Community* (Orbis Books, 2000).

him; and the one whose body escaped from the tomb and Sheol itself and appeared mysteriously to his followers, with whom he even dined. That is what the Trinitarian name conveys, that each one of those instances is fully God, yet none of them exhausts the reality of God because the reality of God is ultimately relational. God exists in such perfect relationality that the three are indivisible in one and the one exists, from eternity and to eternity, in the loving relationship of the three. This love overflows over creation and into our hearts, inviting us all into the divine life for which creation is intended from its origins.

LaCugna summarizes the significance of the Trinitarian name of the mystery for the Christian community by stating that in it we can contemplate

> the life of God revealed . . . in the incarnateness of God in Christ and in the power and presence of God as Spirit. Revealed there is the unfathomable mystery that the life and communion of the divine persons is not "intradivine": God is not self-contained, egotistically and self-absorbed but overflowing love, outreaching desire for union with all that God has made. The communion of divine life is God's communion *with us* in Christ and as Spirit.[36]

A limitation of the Trinitarian name of the divine mystery is that to make sense of it, one must be immersed in the symbolic grammar of the Christian tradition, and even then, it requires careful teaching. Additionally, the classic formulation of the doctrine of the Trinity made heavy use of the conceptual categories of Greek philosophy and mysticism, especially Platonic, Neoplatonic, and Aristotelean categories, which in some ways changed the original meanings intrinsic to the semitic worldview from which the Trinitarian experience of God emerged.[37] It has also led to accusations of polytheism or even idolatry against the Christian tradition. An advantage of the Trinitarian

36. LaCugna, *God for Us*, 15.

37. See the analysis of the difference between the Hellenistic and Semitic ways of understanding reality and the human person in Enrique Dussel, *El humanismo semita: estructuras intencionales radicales del pueblo de Israel y otros semitas* (Buenos Aires: Editorial Eudeba, 1969).

name of God is that it helps to dislodge the emphasis on oneness-at-the-expense-of-diversity, inherited from imperial contexts, where the ruler dreams of the oneness of the world, unified by their rule.[38] The Trinitarian name of God highlights relationality and community as essential to divinity and therefore to humanity, which has been created in the likeness and image of the divine, and it therefore places love at the very essence of being rather than as something external.[39]

Conclusion

Why Name the Mystery?

Names make relationships possible. There are many more names of the divine mystery than those named in this chapter. Some ancient traditions speak of 99 names, others of 1001, and others of 3,000, some known only by angels and others by prophets. Be that as it may, the point is that the list offered above is not comprehensive or even representative. It only represents some of the most prominent attempts at naming the divine mystery in the traditions to which I belong and that are relevant to the work at hand.

Each name given to the mystery points to an important feature of that mystery, yet none exhaust it. Each way of naming the mystery is true in so far as it highlights an aspect of the way humans have encountered or experienced that mystery throughout history. Yet they can also be misleading, especially when taken on their own, because then they might give the impression of a closure and completeness of knowledge where none is possible. Such names or models of naming correspond to the particular, historically conditioned ways in which different communities, under different circumstances, have come to know and name the mystery of our origins, of our existence, of our being, of our becoming, of our redemption, of our healing, of our future, of the future of the world, and of the creative and sustaining grounds of everything that is. To lift up the name that has emerged from a particular tradition as the exclusive name is to betray the name itself, the unfathomable vastness to which it points. Even within one tradition, there are often several names,

38. See the arguments and counterarguments for this in Jeorg Rieger, *Christ and Empire* (Fortress Press, 2007).

39. Jürgen Moltmann, *The Trinity and the Kingdom* (Fortress Press,1993).

images, and metaphors used in relation to the divine. In her book *She Who Is*, theologian Elizabeth Johnson uses a metaphor to describe the proper use of names in relation to the mystery. Borrowing the image from Henri de Lubac, she explains that

> persons who seek to know God by compiling the names of God do not resemble misers amassing a heap of gold, a summa of truths. . . . Rather, such persons are better compared to swimmers who can only keep afloat by moving, by cleaving a new wave at each stroke. They are forever brushing aside the *representations* that are continually reforming, knowing full well that these support them, but that if they were to rest for a single moment they would sink. If you have understood, then what you have understood is not God.[40]

Then, why use names for the mystery at all? Why not just let the mystery be? Again, names make relationships possible. Sometimes those relationships can be possessive, as when we name what we own, or hierarchical, as when someone with power over another can decide what their name will be and in doing so further cements their authority over the one being named. But names can also be a way to establish agency and mutuality, to each other and sometimes also to one's own self. The Jewish philosopher Martin Buber wrote about the difference between naming objects and naming subjects: "I-it relationships versus I-thou."[41] Inspired by Buber, I believe that the moment we treat another human being as an "it" and forget their "thou-ness," we are no longer able to perceive the actual person in front of us as they actually are. Now when we look at them or think about them or remember them, we only see their distorted representation, which is a synthesis of caricaturized elements of them with elements of our selves projected onto them. We are looking at a sort of mirror (like those mirrors from funhouses that distort what they reflect) that blends into representation of the other elements of our own fantasies, fears, and desires.

---

40. Johnson, *She Who Is*, 120, italics added; the reference to de Lubac is from *The Discovery of God*, trans. Alexander Dru (P.J. Kennedy, 1960), 120–21.

41. Martin Buber, *I and Thou*, trans. Ronald Gregor Smith (Martino Publishing, [1923] 2010).

Something similar happens when dealing with the divine mystery. If we use the names of the divine mystery to try and gain control over it, to dissect it, or to comprehend it (trap it in a nicely delineated concept or image), have we not at that very moment lost the mystery? But if we use the name(s) as a way to open ourselves up to a relationship with the mystery, then we might find ourselves being summoned from beyond the frames of our reality to an I-thou relationship with . . . With what? Or whom?

Is that not also the case when we are willing to listen directly from the other, the human other, of flesh and blood like us, and use their names (the names that they speak of themselves), not to protect ourselves from their otherness but precisely to open ourselves up to the possibility of an I-thou relationship with them? And, likewise, how can anyone know you or me if they are not willing to call us by the names that we have told them are our names and then be willing to "close their eyes" to the distorted mental representations they might have of us and simply listen directly from us who we are? Thus, the mystery of each other opens us up to new possibilities, to new relationships that are life-giving and capable of renewing not only our minds but also the reality that we share in common, that reality gifted to us by that Other mystery.

Part III

The Power of God's Otherwise

CHAPTER SEVEN

Bodies

Made of Words

> "In the beginning was the Word, and the Word was with God, and the Word was God."
>
> —John 1:1

Introduction

Words Give Form to Experience

WORDS MATTER, JUST like names matter. The words we use to make sense of our experiences are not independent from those experiences and vice versa. Language and experience belong together. Jacques Derrida's dictum comes to mind—namely, that "there is nothing outside the text" or, alternatively, that "there is no 'outside the text'".[1] That does not have to mean that without language we cannot have any kind of experience. It simply means that once we have acquired language, it becomes an intricate part of the generative matrix where our experiences are produced. Language structures our experiences, and our experiences give flesh to our language. And this is a communal and transgenerational process.

Language Is Not Neutral

We are born into a language and culture that others have created, a language that has been shaped by their experiences, memories, bodies, desires, and material, social, and historical contingencies. A language and culture that, in turn, has played a role in shaping those same experiences, memories, bodies, desires, and material realities. But language

1. Jacques Derrida, *Of Grammatology* (Johns Hopkins University Press, 1998), 158.

is not merely accidental or innocent, for language has been used for millennia as a key weapon to subjugate peoples at the service of colonial, imperial, patriarchal, and other similar projects of domination. No wonder that it was by confusing their language that God chose to stop that first attempt of colonial formation, the building of the Tower of Babel (who was doing the labor?). The letter of dedication of the first grammar of the Spanish language for the queen of Spain is telling in that regard:

> Now, Your Majesty, let me come to the last advantage that you shall gain from my grammar. For the purpose, recall the time when I presented you with a draft of this book earlier this year in Salamanca. At this time, you asked me what end such a grammar could possibly serve. Upon this, the Bishop of Avila interrupted to answer in my stead. What he said was this: "Soon Your Majesty will have placed her yoke upon many barbarians who speak outlandish tongues. By this, your victory, these people shall stand in a new need; the need for the laws the victor owes to the vanquished, and the need for the language we shall bring with us." My grammar shall serve to impart them the Castillian tongue [Spanish], as we have used grammar to teach Latin to our young.[2]

Language is not innocent! Language can serve to open up new aspects of reality, or it can serve to eclipse other things from our awareness. That is why attention to words and language is so important for liberation theologies and for projects of decolonialization.

Language, Like the Brain, Is a Maker of Worlds

Moreover, the power of language is not merely external. The language we have received from our families, communities, education, and culture has a profound influence on how we experience the world in itself and

2. This letter was authored by the Spanish writer and humanist Antonio de Nebrija, sent to Queen Isabella of Castile (Spain) shortly after the miscalled "discovery" of the Americas by Christopher Columbus. For the quote and a thorough analysis of the use of language in the project of colonization, see Walter D. Mignolo, *The Darker Side of the Renaissance*, 38.

our place in it and even the reality of the divine. What I argue in this book is that the language that emerges from the experiences that take place in the margins (eschata) and the fissures or cracks (xora), spaces that are social, spiritual, psychological, and physical (see chapter five), have the potential to destabilize structures of oppression that are an expression of sin. This language can provide inspiration for new possibilities of social organization that are more wholesome and just, inspired by the divine Spirit.

Earlier I described how learning the language of science and mathematics alongside the language of theology allowed me to appreciate the immense beauty of God's creation and of the natural dynamics of creation. Those languages served as lenses that allowed me to "see" not just trees, for example, but leaves receiving photons from the sun plus carbon dioxide from the air and nutrients from the soil, weaving them into a magnificent cornucopia of leaves, flowers, fruits, bark, sap, wood, and the miraculous oxygen, feeding life, cleansing the environment, cooling the temperature, and making it possible for us to breathe. Without the language of science, all that would still be happening, but we would not be able to perceive it.

Likewise, the language of faith allows us to perceive the ways in which the divine mystery is present in, with, and under the elements of nature in a way that would not be possible without that language. Sometimes language also makes it impossible for us to perceive or experience certain things because the language we have received deems them unreal or simply because those types of realities and experiences were not part of the process whereby that language emerged. Could there be such a thing as "word-blindness," the inability to perceive that which you don't have the linguistic categories for? The languages of liberation theology and decoloniality allow us to perceive (conceive!) yet other dimensions of reality.

In this chapter, we will explore the role of language in shaping experience. For this we need to review what we learned about emotions in the first chapters of this book. Then we will explore a proposal by the neuroscientist Lisa Barrett Feldman of the possible mechanisms by which emotions, which shape our perception of reality, are born of words. It seems that from the perspective of our affective neurodynamics, it is also true that "in the beginning was the word."[3]

3. John 1:1.

E/motions, a Review

As we discussed in chapter two, emotions are physiological states that arise in the body (e.g., the gut, heart, lungs, kidneys, skin, eyes, and, of course, the nervous system) in response to the environment and circumstances—real, remembered, and/or imagined—that require us to act. Emotions prepare the body for action, hence the play of words in e/motion: E + motion = Emotion. When our senses perceive something, but before our conscious mind becomes aware of it, our emotions and non-reflective cognitive templates have already evaluated whether it is a threat that requires us to fight it, flee from it, or freeze to make it think we are dead or if it is an opportunity for us to pursue, maybe to feed on it or to mate with it. In order to accomplish this, the sense organs send signals directly to the structures in the brain that mediate emotions, especially the amygdala and the hypothalamus, which work closely together. The amygdala plays a special role in detecting salient aspects of the environment, so it is not a surprise that it receives signals from the sense organs. What is fascinating is that it also sends signals back to such organs. In addition to setting in motion a series of neurophysiological responses (emotions) and their corresponding actions, it also shapes perception.

Emotional Hijack of Memory

We learned from Damasio, Spezio and Adolphs, Jeeves and Brown, and McNamara in chapters 2 and 3 that emotions and cognition work in tandem to allow for the smooth perception of reality, including "the feeling of what happens" and the value assessments necessary to decide how to act. But sometimes the process gets out of whack, in extreme cases resulting in bizarre illusions like the certainty that my own leg is not mine, that an amputated limb is still there, or that my mother or my cat are impostors. A more common way in which the process sometimes backfires is during what is called an "amygdala" hijack. That is, when we are in the midst of a highly emotive situation, everything that is not directly connected to that situation becomes filtered out, including memories and perceptions. That leads to the dangerous situation where the only information allowed into our conscious mind is information that confirms and reinforces the reason why we are upset, scared, or angry or our biases and prejudices. That is why reasoning with someone who is having an amygdala hijack moment is futile. It is better to wait until the moment has passed.

This is also something to keep in mind when preparing to have difficult conversations, such as in mediating conflict or, in the case of religious leaders, preaching about a necessary but controversial topic. How can we set up the environment and design the conversation or worship experience in a way that will avoid situations leading to the amygdala hijack? This is also helpful as a tool for self-assessment and regulation.

Learning to detect when I am in the grip of an amygdala hijack allows me to decide when to engage, when to retreat, and how to interpret my visceral reactions to what others are saying or even to their mere presence or appearance. Perhaps this has some connections with the emphasis of many religious traditions on discerning illusions from reality. That doesn't mean, however, that the amygdala and our emotional responses are mere illusions. There is a reason why such processes are so strong and have become solidified throughout millennia in the evolutionary history of our species and our ancestors. In most cases, it works; it helps to keep us safe or to be able to seize opportunities that are ephemeral. Emotion, discernment, reason, and action are all needed for wisdom and wholesome living, both individually and in community.

Emotions as a Compass to Navigate Reality

Emotions are like the compass that guides our actions and our decision-making processes. We saw, when discussing Newberg and d'Aquili's research on neurotheology and McNamara's work on the neuroscience of religious experiences, that emotions, by way of the interactions of the sympathetic and parasympathetic nervous systems with the hypothalamus and the amygdala plus streams of hormones and neurotransmitters, endow the experiences with a feeling of indubitable factuality and a sense of sacredness. Hence, those experiences are felt to be more real than reality itself. A common image used to describe these experiences is that of the comparison between dreaming and being awake. Those experiences can make us feel normal consciousness is but a mere dream and religious experience is what is really real, what being awake feels like.

From a neuroscientific perspective, they feel that way because of the triggering of the autonomic nervous system with such force that both the sympathetic and parasympathetic systems spill over into each other and are active together, endowing the experience with a sense of eeriness and what Otto called the simultaneity of the *tremendum* and the *fascinans*.

We also saw, from our discussion of Damasio's somatic marker hypothesis and Spezio and Adolphs's integrative model, that experiences can become tagged in our bodies by means of what Damasio called somatic markers. Thus, experiences of the mystical type, but also other kinds of experiences that are highly emotive, like some of those described throughout this book, can become marked somatically in our bodies as sacred, holy, or transcendental. That is why they feel real and sacred. But are they in fact real, or are they invented? Yes.

Emotion as Perception/Interpretation

In chapters 1 and 2, we learned that our perceptions of reality are in fact interpretations, which sometimes result in bizarre illusions. We learned that it is through the cognitive devices of the embodied mind and the creative work of circuits in the brain that the world emerges as we experience it in all its multisensorial, three-dimensional, and temporal richness. Each sense adds nuance to our perceptual interpretation of reality. The same is true about the emotional or affective dimension of our experience of reality.

In an embodied and communal space, (interbodied?) affect opens for us important aspects of reality that would not be accessible to us otherwise.[4] Those aspects of reality that our emotional experience makes possible have to do with meaning, with values, with purpose, and with relationships, including our relationship to ourselves, to each other, and to God. Emotions help us know who loves us and whom we love. Who hates us, who might want to harm us? Who deserves our loyalty, our admiration, even our reverence? For whom would we sacrifice? In whom can we trust? It is through our emotional processing that we are able to perceive, in the language of classical philosophy, the good, the true, and the beautiful.

4. I am using the term *affect* to include all the dimensions of human emotional experience, from the physiological substrates of such experiences, instantiated as emotions, to their conscious interpretation as feelings to their more long-term expressions as moods and, as we explain below, the cognitive concepts (mediated by words) that give them their final shape.

Perceptions, including affective perceptions, have a certain ontological weight to them. That is, what is perceived is experienced as real, as an actual thing (*ontos* in Greek; *ens* in Latin, from where we get *entity*), as opposed to as a mere side effect of our sensorial apparatus. We say, "That tree is green." Is color an intrinsic feature of reality in itself? Affective interpretations/perceptions of different aspects of reality are experienced not as one's personal opinion but as an objective reality. This is also true about elements of reality that are the product of social convention. Many of them have a sense of naturalness and inevitability. Is race an intrinsic feature of human nature? What is the essence of "racialness"? The bumps on the head mapped by phrenologists? A certain amount of melanin in the skin? How much?

I remember how confused I felt when my biology professor asked the class to provide a precise scientific definition of sex (the identity, not the act). Is it defined by genitalia? What do we do with cases where the genitals of the newborn are ambiguous? Is it determined by the presence or absence of a Y chromosome? There are exceptions there as well, as there are female bodies with XY chromosomes, even supermodels, said the professor. What about hormones: is sex established by the presence or absence of testosterone or estrogen? But both hormones are present in men and women, even if in different proportions. Is sex, then, determined by how one behaves or acts? The point is that there is a strong element of social convention for what words like *sex*, *race*, and many others mean. They are not simple facts objectively found in nature.

In her book *How Emotions Are Made: The Secret Life of the Brain*, neuroscientist of emotions Lisa Feldman Barrett uses the term *affective realism* to refer to that socially constructed dimension of our perceptual experience of reality. She offers an example of how affective realism can sometimes go terribly wrong:

> The U.S. Department of Justice analyzed shootings by police officers between 2007 and 2013 and found that 15 percent of the victims were unarmed. In half of these cases, an officer reportedly misidentified "a nonthreatening object" (e.g., a cell phone) or movement (e.g., tugging at the waistband)" as a weapon. Many factors may contribute to these tragedies, ranging from carelessness to racial bias, but it is also possible that some of the shooters actually perceive a weapon when none is present due to affective realism in a high-pressure and

> dangerous context. The human brain is wired for this sort of delusion, in part because moment-to-moment interoception infuses us with affect, which we then use as evidence about the world.[5]

A decolonial liberation theological question would be, If the brain is wired for this sort of delusion, who wired it thus? In other words, why is the delusion that the person is armed created by affective realism, if not because the brain had previously categorized the person as belonging to a category that is instinctively believed to be fearsome and inherently dangerous? We discussed this in chapter 1. When affective realism plus the cognitive processes for categorizing reality and assigning intuitive beliefs to it combine within the formative cultural matrix created by coloniality, racism, and xenophobia, the tragic results are predictable. And even when after-the-fact investigations determine that the shootings were unjustified, they are perceived by many within the dominant groups in society as an understandable mistake, creating a cycle that further strengthens that cognitive-neural-affective wiring. It is easier to blame it on the victims, especially when they are not the perfect victim. As I have already said, these distortions are so pervasive and prevalent that they also affect the self-image and consciousness, even those of members of victimized and minoritized groups.

But it is important to remember that it is through those same processes, as prone as they may be to distortions and abuses, that we perceive all of reality. It is thanks to affective realism and the cognitive templates discussed in chapter 1 that we can have a world in common. Barrett reminds us that even such a concrete thing as money exists only because it has been socially invented and sustained by our embodied affective processes.[6] Let us take a closer look at how those processes take place and the role of the word in them.

Emotions Are Born in the Body

Like we learned in chapter 2, Barrett, too, emphasizes that what gives rise to the particular forms of our emotional and mental life is the need

---

5. Lisa Feldman Barrett, *How Emotions Are Made: The Secret Life of the Brain* (Mariner Books, 2018), 76.

6. Barrett, *How Emotions Are Made*, 133–34.

of our organisms to act (that is, to engage the world). This is necessary for the sake of seeking food, avoiding threats, fighting dangers, finding a mate to reproduce, and so on. All those things have one thing in common. They require energy. The first thing that happens when the organism needs to engage in action is that it will generate and allocate energy for action. Thus, the process begins not at the top (where the "executives" live in the mind's cortex) but in the "bottom," where our viscera extract energy from food and distribute it to where it is needed. And, as we saw in chapter 1's coda on the body, those organs are constantly sending and receiving signals to and from the brain.

The organism prepares to act because of what it has perceived, but how does it perceive it? We have already discussed in some length how the brain translates sensorial information into the perceptual images that are represented in our mind's eye (what philosophers call *qualia*). But there is one element we have not yet explained. What the senses are receiving is a flood of sensorial input: How do they know what to extract in meaningful patterns out of that flood? The division of labor among the sense organs themselves does some of that, so that electromagnetic waves are picked up by the retina's receptors; soundwaves by the ear's cochlea; temperature by the skin; sugars, acids, and salts by the taste buds, and so on. These go to primary areas that hyperspecialize in minute aspects of the sensorial information and then that information is sent to other brain circuits where it is combined with the information from other systems, such as memory, and woven together until it finally becomes a meaningful whole. But what drives the weaving? To borrow an analogy from language, what is the grammar guiding the formation of perceptions?

According to Barrett's proposal, the grammar that guides the process is precisely that: grammar, words, and language. She explains that "spoken words give the infant brain access to information that can't be found by observing the world and resides only in the minds of other people, namely *mental similarities*: goals, intentions, preferences. Words allow infants to begin growing goal-based concepts, including emotion concepts."[7]

She continues:

> A little human brain, bathed in the words of others around it, accumulates simple concepts. Some concepts are learned

7. Barrett, *How Emotions Are Made*, 98. Italics in the original.

> without words, but words confer distinct advantages to a developing conceptual system. A word might begin as a mere stream of sounds to the infant, just one part of the whole statistical language package, but it quickly becomes more than that. It becomes an invitation for the infant to *create* similarities among diverse instances. A word tells the infant, "Do you see all these objects that look different physically? They have an equivalence that is mental." That equivalence is the basis for a goal-based concept.[8]

The end result is that "infants thereby learn to categorize the world in ways that are consistent, meaningful, and predictable to us (the speakers), and eventually to themselves. Their mental model of the world becomes similar to ours, so we can communicate, share experiences, and perceive the same world."[9]

That process is most intense during infancy but does not end there. As we live through novel experiences, we grope for language to conceptualize them, and the more expansive our linguistic resources become, the more aspects of reality we can experience in concrete, differentiated ways. This is one of the reasons I said at the outset of this book that brains cannot be understood in isolation from other brains. Even in their process of being formed, brains depend on other brains to acquire the concepts and categories that will help them weave into being the mind's world. And, as we have already argued ad nauseam, brains and bodies belong together. As we are about to see, bodies and words also belong together.

As our senses are flooded by sensorial information that is then organized into conceptually meaningful perceptual categories thanks to language, our body's interior organs also are affected by that flood of sensorial input and the perceptual categories into which they are now intuitively organized. That is so because, as we saw above, the organism needs to generate and allocate the necessary energy to engage in action vis-à-vis what it is perceiving and what its goals are. This generates activity in the intestines (the enteric nervous system), the lungs, the heart, the kidneys, and so on as the organism prepares for action. Given the innervation of

8. Barrett, *How Emotions Are Made*, 98. Italics in the original.

9. Barrett, *How Emotions Are Made*, 99.

those organs by the peripheral nervous system, their activity generates sensations that neuroscientists call interoception—that is, the feeling of what is happening inside our organism. Neuroscientist Nazareth Castellanos quips that this is our real sixth sense (together with proprioception, which is the feeling of how the body is oriented in space—very important for athletes like gymnasts).[10]

Those interoceptive sensations are, according to Barrett (in agreement with Damasio), the raw material or substrate from which emotions are made.[11] It is again through the intervention of the word that those sensations will be transubstantiated into emotions. The infant's caregivers notice the baby's body movements, their facial expression, their sounds, and the circumstances and tell the child things like Oh, you are so happy! Or are you scared? Or yes, that is disgusting! Before even being able to comprehend the semantic meaning of those words, the child is able, nonetheless, to pair the sound with the interoceptive sensations plus the sensorial input that led to it. Thus emotions are born in the body.

Again, this process does not only take place during our infant years. It lasts a lifetime. And so, as our language expands—say, through poetry, through scientific training, or through the study of philosophical concepts or theological texts and religious mantras or by opening ourselves up to the language of the experiences of those living in circumstances very different from our own—our affective resources grow wider and our experience of reality becomes richer. And the future becomes pregnant with new possibilities.

There is one more piece that we need to add to the puzzle. One of the things that Barrett and her lab team have worked on is the mapping of the interoceptive receptors in the brain. They found that the brain circuits involved in this process are also part of what is called the default mode network.[12] When I attended the neuroscience boot camp, we were taught that this network was discovered by accident. Researchers noticed that when people were inside brain scanners, like fMRIs, but in between tasks, their minds wandered and the scanner

---

10. Castellanos, *Neurociencia del cuerpo*, 57–58.

11. Barrett, *How Emotions Are Made*, 57–64.

12. Barrett, *How Emotions Are Made*, 67–72.

detected "noise" being generated in different regions of the brain. For a while, researchers took that to be simply noise. But science is driven by curiosity, and so it didn't take too long before someone decided to pay attention to the "noise." It turns out that the noise is where "eureka" moments of new sudden insight come from. Have you ever had the experience of being intensely focused on a problem for a long time and then deciding to take a break and maybe "sleep on it," and when you are no longer thinking about it or thinking about anything (maybe while you are taking a warm shower or a relaxing walk), all of a sudden a solution comes to you like a lightning bolt of revelation from within the brain? The "noise" really is the different regions of the brain communicating with each other, consolidating the neural information from each region and integrating it in new ways.

It is not just perceptual information that becomes consolidated through that process. It is also our sense of self. We have already learned that the self is a story that our embodied brains and cognitive devices tell our self about itself and that it includes memories, goals, expectations, and feelings. All that leads Barrett to conclude that

> deconstructing the self offers a new inspiration for how to become the master of your emotions. By tweaking your conceptual system and changing your predictions, you not only change your future experiences; you can actually change your "Self."[13]

That means that by changing our affective grammars, we can begin to decolonize our emotions and transform our minds as part of a communal praxis of liberation. And we learned previously, thanks to McNamara, Newberg, d'Aquili, and others, that religious experience and practices have the potential to facilitate that process.

Rewriting the Body's Affective Grammar

I would like to propose that one way to think about what we have learned so far in this book is that our perceptions of reality, of others, and of ourselves are generated by grammar-like systems operating on

13. Barrett, *How Emotions Are Made*, 192.

our embodied emotional and cognitive systems. Even though we all have more or less the same neural and cognitive systems in our bodies, minds, and brains, our grammars differ. Different grammars will produce different expressions of language. Similarly, different affective grammars will produce different perceptions of reality, of others, of ourselves, and even of religious phenomena or phenomena deemed religious.

Some affective grammars are harmful and oppressive. Other grammars can be healing and liberating, allowing us to perceive the sacredness of each other within our differences and the sacred bonds that connect us.

Healing the wounds inflicted on all of us by centuries or even millennia of systems of oppression, exploitation, and marginalization requires a deep examination of the grammars that have been written in our flesh and intentional processes for dismantling those grammars and replacing them with new ones. That process will require the combination of embodied practices, cognitive work, and emotional mending. It will require individual work and communal work. And it will require intergenerational labor, even reaching back to touch the wounds of those who came before us and reaching forward to plant seeds of promise in the hearts of the new generations to come. They live in us, and we live in them; our healing and their healing, our liberation and their liberation are bound together. That includes perpetrators and victims, those who benefitted from oppressions and the exploitation of others and those whose oppression and exploitation benefitted others. Though in different ways, we all have been wounded. We all need the deconstruction of our selves, dying to our old selves (individual and collective), and the rebirth of our souls—that is, of our integrated, embodied sense of self—with new generative affective grammars.

A place to begin the journey of decolonizing our emotions and liberating our collective imaginary is by examining the affective grammars scripted in our own individual bodies, our embodied selves. As we mentioned in chapter 1, there are many possible approaches to doing so, from introspection to psychoanalysis to cognitive behavioral therapy, each approach with its strengths and weaknesses.[14] It is best to

14. At the time of writing, a new resource has come to my attention that I have not yet had the chance to review but looks very promising: Lillian Comas-Díaz et al., eds., *Decolonial Psychology: Toward Anticolonial Theories, Research, Training, and Practice* (American Psychological Association, 2024).

undertake this psychological-spiritual decolonial journey with proper guidance and support. Confronting the illusions generated by the colonial, racist, heterosexist, or other damaging affective grammars within us can be challenging and painful. Even recognizing aspects of reality itself, of others, of ourselves, and especially of that which we consider most holy (like God) as illusions can be daunting and disorienting. But that is the path to liberation, a journey that, even though we are using new language to describe it, is as ancient as the human spirit itself, as attested by the copious sacred testimonies from many different religions and cultures.

Self-examination is the first step, but on its own, it is not enough. We have seen how deeply rooted in the body our self is. Therefore, if we want to transform ourselves, then the body must be involved as well. Many of us need practices to help us learn how to feel our bodies again. We have been trained to ignore our bodies, their pains or their desires; the more disconnected we were from the body, the more sublime and spiritual and praiseworthy we were, according to the colonial model of humanity. The skin is the largest organ in the body; it needs to be touched, to be caressed, even tickled (with consent, of course). Even the most sublime and spiritual of all experiences, that of becoming one with the divinity, as we saw in chapter 3, is rooted in the same bodily neural systems as our sexual urges and orgasmic pleasures. You cannot have one without the other. Spirit, body, and soul are but different dimensions of the same reality.

Practices to get in touch with our own bodies include dance, yoga, and some martial arts, such as tai chi and aikido, that emphasize awareness of the energy flowing through our own bodies and the bodies of our training partners. Some religions and denominations include practices that touch the body deeply, such as fasting, using incense, collective chanting and singing, embracing each other during the passing of the peace, dancing in the Spirit in Pentecostal churches, Sufis whirling, and intense dancing to the rhythm of drums in Brazilian Candomblé and Caribbean Santería, just to name a few. But embodied practices need to be coupled with appropriate conceptual schemas in order to be liberating rather than alienating, as we saw in the discussion of McNamara's proposal of decentering.

Social worker Resmaa Menakem has authored a handbook for decolonial healing, even if he does not call it that, titled *My Grandmother's Hands: Racialized Trauma and the Pathway to Mending Our Hearts and*

Bodies.[15] He focuses on the ways that racial trauma becomes inscribed in the bodies of all members of society, especially in the US, regardless of where they stand in the continuum of racialized identities and whether they are members of the police or abolish-the-police activists. His sensitivity to the ways trauma touches us all, and his focus on healing practices that combine mind and body approaches, makes his book a powerful resource for the project of rewriting the oppressive affective grammars written in our bodies by centuries of coloniality, slavery, and patriarchy.[16]

Just as brains and bodies cannot exist in isolation from each other, so healing and decolonization and the rewriting of our effective grammars cannot take place in isolation from each other. Whatever our practices are, they must incorporate opportunities to enter into each other's reality and be transformed by them. The best way to correct the distortions of implicit bias and systemic racism, transphobia, xenophobia, and other ills is by personal encounters where people are willing to be vulnerable to each other and actually "close their eyes" (see chapter 5) and listen to the voice of the other. We also need opportunities to listen to the voices of the members of our own group—and to our own voice—without the colonial veils that distort the ways we see even ourselves and members of our own group. We need spaces and opportunities to be together frequently, in settings that are safe and feel safe and that are conducive to deep listening with a spirituality of curiosity (see the discussion on amygdala hijack above).

Finally, we need what historian Justo González calls a "non-innocent reading of history."[17] One of the reasons why it is so difficult to change social systems is that we do not understand their historical origins. We mentioned earlier, in reference to the work of decolonial theologian Jeorg Rieger, that the very idea of what is real is an area of contestation. Whoever controls our perception of what is real, possible, and necessary has the power to control us. We might not even be able to conceive

15. Resmaa Menakem, *My Grandmother's Hands: Racialized Trauma and the Pathway to Mending Our Hearts and Bodies* (Central Recovery Press, 2017).

16. Another resource for embodied approaches to self-transformation that I have found helpful is Richard Strozzi's trainings and retreats for embodied transformation: https://strozziinstitute.com/embodying-equity/.

17. Justo L. González, *Mañana: Christian Theology from a Hispanic Perspective* (Abingdon Press, 1990), 38–41.

that things could be otherwise since, after all, it is what it is. Therefore, investigating the actual events that led to the way things are now is an important step in the process of decolonial affective liberation.

To illustrate this, I often quip about how when I was born, I was just a baby, but once my parents took me to live in the continental US I became Puerto Rican. Later on, after having returned to Puerto Rico and lived there for most of my childhood and college years, I moved to Chicago to go to seminary, where I discovered that I was Hispanic. OK, sure. Not too long after that, I found out that I had been recategorized; now I was Hispanic/Latin@. More recently, that has morphed to Latinx and sometimes to Latiné. Meanwhile, I have also become aware of my significant African roots and native (Taino) heritage. What is at stake here is not only the fluidity of some identities but also the historical processes that led to those namings, the political struggles involved, and the affective grammars that come attached (as viruses) to some of those names/identities.

I was not born a Latinx, nor is anyone born white, Black, brown, Native, American, Canadian, etc.[18] Sure, we are born into those categories, and they become so deeply inscribed in our minds and bodies through affective grammars that they feel more real than real. But precisely for that reason, it is important to take a step back and ask ourselves, How did it get to be this way? We must know our history, and in many cases, we must recover it ourselves, because the history that we have been told about who we are and how we got here is not innocent.

Now, there is a tension here. There are no generic human beings. We are all born into a community, with a specific language, a unique culture, and a history that shapes us into who we are. I am not arguing against embracing that communal, relational aspect of being human. But we need to ask ourselves, How did it come to be the way it is? We need noninnocent readings of our history and of the history of our institutions and social practices and, especially, a noninnocent history of how we came to be who we are. Where did our names/labels come from, and what affective grammars are hidden within them?

---

18. On the invention of categories like "Oriental," and "Latino," see Eduard W. Said, *Orientalism*, 25th anniv. edn. (Vintage Books, 1994), and Laura E. Gómez, *Inventing Latinos*.

Conclusion

In this chapter, we have finished our explorations of how the embodied brain and mind create reality as we perceive it, although we have only scratched the surface of such complex neurophysiological and cognitive processes. We learned that emotions play an important part in how we experience the world and even in how we experience our own embodied selves. We learned that our embodied self is actually a construction of our emotions. But we also learned that our emotions are not premade in nature. We learned that emotions are the child of the pairing of interoceptive sensations vis-à-vis the body's need to engage with the world in action and the words we receive from our caregivers, our teachers, and our cultural milieu in general to name those sensations and experiences. Thus, our embodied selves are constructed from moment to moment.

We used that understanding to investigate possible pathways to healing the wounds inflicted on all of us by the systems of oppression, exploitation, exclusion, and marginalization in which we find ourselves embedded. We discussed that an analogy to understand the way those systems colonize our minds and bodies (our collective imagination and feelings) is by encoding a sort of generative affective grammar in the neural systems that undergird our perception of the world and the formation of our very selves. We surmised that a process of healing and holistic liberation must include a process of dismantling and rewriting those affective grammars.

We lifted up four necessary elements for such processes of decolonial healing and liberation. First, we discussed a process of reading the grammars inscribed in our affective systems. Second, we examined embodied practices capable of touching our beings, from our skins to our inner organs, from where we feel the world into being. Third, we invoked the inherently communal nature of our embodied selves and, consequently, the need for intentional opportunities to be together so that our lives can gently touch each other in ways that would foster mutual understanding through deep listening and a spirituality of curiosity. Fourth, we called for a noninnocent reading of the history of our present institutions, social practices, and ways of naming/categorizing each other and ourselves.

There is much more that can be done. For instance, it is important to recover and lift up the alternative stories of historically significant events as experienced from the perspectives of the victims, not just of the victors. And, of course, all that needs to be part of a larger project of social transformation that includes organized social action; political participation; the development of economic strategies for equity and justice; the creation, defense, and bolstering of institutions dedicated to the care of those in need; and public accountability for those who have been entrusted with power on behalf of the people. All that is in the background of the analysis and reflections in this book.

Now we turn, in our last chapters, to explore the particular contribution that theology can make to this project.

CHAPTER EIGHT

The Word

Generative Affective Grammars of Liberation

> Indeed, the word of God is living and active and sharper than any two-edged sword, piercing until it divides soul from spirit, joints from marrow; it is able to judge the thoughts and intentions of the heart.
>
> —Hebrews 4:12

> For as the rain and the snow come down from heaven
> and do not return there until they have watered the earth,
> making it bring forth and sprout,
> giving seed to the sower and bread to the eater,
> so shall my word be that goes out from my mouth;
> it shall not return to me empty,
> but it shall accomplish that which I purpose
> and succeed in the thing for which I sent it.
>
> For you shall go out in joy
> and be led back in peace;
> the mountains and the hills before you
> shall burst into song,
> and all the trees of the field shall clap their hands.
>
> —Isaiah 55:10–12

Introduction

Words That Heal the Past and the Future

THE BRAIN, WE have seen, is no passive mirror. The brain is a creator of worlds. And religions, with their sacred words, rituals, and practices, have the potential to be matrices where memories, percepts, emotions, and imagination can be woven together (*religare*) into a new creation. "In

Christ, a new creation!"[1] We have proposed that these religious matrices operate by producing a sort of generative affective-perceptual-cognitive grammar written into our bodies, from our viscera (in concert with our microbiome and neurochemicals) to our brain's systems, especially those involved in the default mode network and the formation of the sense of the self. We saw, in the previous chapter, that such process is shaped through a mechanism that involves a delicate dance among language, experience, and body practices. Emotions shape our perception of reality, and language shapes and gives granularity to our emotions. This process is beautifully illustrated by a classic of Latin American literature.

Eva Luna was a storyteller. She could be found in the city square, where people would pay her a few cents for a story. One day a soldier came to see her. He was clearly sad, his soul heavy with who knows what losses, what broken dreams, what shame. That is a scene from a novel written by the marvelous Chilean storyteller Isabel Allende. That scene, and what happens next, is lifted up by theologian Cecilio Arrastía to illustrate the power of the word. The story continues:

> He came tired, with a gun in his arm covered in the dust of far-away places. When he stopped she detected in him a scent of sadness and knew right away that this man was coming from the war. Loneliness and violence had stuck splinters of iron in his soul, and had deprived him of the faculty to love himself.
>
> Are you the one who tells stories?, asked the foreigner. At your service, she replied. The man got out a few gold coins and placed them on her hand. In that case, sell me a past because mine is filled with laments and does not work to transit through life, I have been in so many battles and somewhere along the way I lost even my mother's name, he said. She couldn't say no, because she was afraid that the foreigner would crumble in the plaza and turn into a handful of dust, as it finally happens to those who lack good memories.

1. "So if anyone is in Christ, there is a new creation: everything old has passed away; look, new things have come into being!" (2 Cor 5:17).

> She began to speak. All evening and all night she spent building a good past for this warrior . . . and she had to invent it all, from his birth to the present day . . . and even the geography and the history of his motherland. Finally a new day dawned and with the first light she noticed that the scent of sadness had faded away. She took a deep breath, closed her eyes, and upon feeling her spirit empty like that of a newborn, she understood that in her eagerness to please him, she had given him her own memory, she no longer knew what was hers and what was his, their pasts had become intertwined in one single braid.[2]

What if the storyteller is God? That mystery of life whose contours we tried to trace in chapter 5 and whose names we pondered in chapter 6? And the foreigner is us, all of us, lost in different ways in this centuries-old, never-ending colonial, racist, heterosexist labyrinth of lost memories, enfleshed trauma, and unspeakable historical shame. What if the past can be healed and the future can now be expected with hope and even eagerness? The eagerness and giddiness of a child the day before their birthday; the night before Christmas, Eid, Hanukkah, Diwali; or whenever else they might expect a nice surprise waiting for them on that new day?

What if the task of theology is more than just constructing a rational and coherent articulation of the faith but also a *poiesis*, a midwifery of the soul, or better yet, of embodied selves and worlds made of flesh and word?

We have learned from the sciences of the brain and the mind about axons and dendrites, neurotransmitters and action potentials, nervous systems and autonomic responses, cognitive devices and executive functions, amygdalae, hippocampi, hypothalami, interoception, and maps of the body in the brain; we've studied God-helmets, prayer scans, decentering processes, and the common roots of sex and religious experience. But we have also learned about the power of words to guide those neural processes, to shape emotions, and to give form to our reality and to our embodied selves from moment to moment!

---

2. Quoted in Cecilio Arrastía, *Teoría y práctica de la predicación* (Nashville: Editorial Caribe, A Division of Thomas Nelson, 1993), 24–25; for the original, see Isabel Allende, *Eva Luna* (Bogotá: editorial La Oveja Negra, 1987), 221. My translation.

What if theology and science could be at the service of God, the storyteller (*poietes* is what the Creed calls God in Greek, the cosmic poet!) in the sacred task of healing the open wounds of history and weaving new possibilities, a new future of hope?

Commenting on Eva Luna's story as a model of the preacher's (and, I would add, theologian's) task, Cecilio Arrastía concludes:

> If this is a description of the task of those who preach—to give back the memory that has been lost—the element with which we count is superior and different. We don't have to invent a tale, because we have a history; it is not necessary to design a new map, because we have been given a geography that still preserves the footprints of the Galilean walker. We do not preach [or do theology] *ex nihilo*, but with the "matter" that God has given us.[3]

In this chapter, we explore how that "'matter' that God has given us"—namely, the living word understood in its most expansive sense—not only brings salvation in the sense of forgiveness of sins and eternal life but also has the power to decolonize our emotions and liberate our brains and embodied minds from their colonial, racist, patriarchal, and heterosexist affective-cognitive illusions. We will see that for that purpose, the theological task demands two moments or (iterative) steps: a moment of destroying (or deconstructing) and wounding and a moment of constructing and healing. Theology is, after all, *theo* + *logos* = God + word, and God's word, the author of Hebrews claims, is "sharper than any two-edged sword" (Heb 4:12). Perhaps instead of a sword, we can think of it as a surgeon's scalpel, one that can cut deep within our souls to scrape off the old toxic affective grammar we have inherited from our colonial past and replace it with a new decolonizing, life-giving grammar.

A Transforming Word

In the Christian tradition to which I belong, the word of God is understood as a living word, inseparable from the divine Spirit through which

3. Arrastía, *Teoría y práctica*, 26. Italics in the original. My translation.

God is at work in the world, because both Word and Spirit are God, as we saw in chapter 6. It is through that living word, and the Spirit, that God brings the world into being, sustains it, and constantly renews it. It is also through the Word, and the Spirit, that humans are summoned by God from within those experiential places that we explored in chapter 5. It is that same word and Spirit that operates in, with, and on our embodied minds, our nervous systems, and our cognitive devices to free us (decolonize us) from the many ways in which sin imprisons us individually and collectively in habits and compulsions of beliefs, feelings, and behaviors that miss the mark of what we are meant to be—namely, communities of mutual care and human flourishing where each person can find plenitude and creation can thrive.

Like Iron Glowing in Fire

Pondering how it might be that the word of God transforms human minds and hearts, Martin Luther, the sixteenth-century reformer, found inspiration in the ironsmith's workshop and in the union of newlyweds. In his little but powerful book *The Freedom of a Christian*, he explains how when an iron rod is placed on fire, the iron rod is eventually transformed by the fire; it absorbs into itself the heat of the fire and glows with the same light as the fire. Analogously, when a person dwells in the word of God, that person begins to absorb into their soul the virtues of the Word until, eventually, their soul begins to glow with the very light of God's word.[4] What does that mean?

Not too long ago, I had the opportunity to have a conversation with the former presiding bishop of the Episcopal Church in the US, the Most Rev. Michael Curry. He spoke of a time when he went on sabbatical and spent his time studying the sermons of abolitionists and of those defending slavery. He said he was startled by the stark contrast between the two. Those who defended slavery never quoted the Jesus of the gospels, and those who opposed slavery were often quoting Jesus and the gospels. It is impossible, he said, to stay close to Jesus and defend something like slavery, racism, or patriarchy. By dwelling in the Word, the spirit of Jesus is absorbed into our souls, so to speak, and we begin

4. Martin Luther, *The Freedom of a Christian: Luther Study Edition*, trans. and intro. Mark D. Tranvik (Fortress Press, [1520] 2008), 59–60.

to shine with the light of Christ; that is, the loving kindness, his faith, and his hope begin to take form in us and to form us.

Like Loving Spouses Giving Their Entire Selves to Each Other

Luther's second image to illustrate how the Word achieves that transformation comes from marriage. He reflects on how when a couple gets married, regardless of the difference between their social status, wealth, or reputation, something happens: a happy exchange. All that once belonged to the one now also belongs to their beloved and vice versa. Luther explains that Christ is the groom in this betrothal, and humans are the beloved that Christ is marrying. In this happy exchange, made possible by faith, Christ takes upon his divine embodied self all that we bring with us: not only those things that we feel proud about, but also (and especially) those things that we hide, such as our sin, our shame, our hurts, and our broken pasts. At the same time, Christ gives us everything that is his, things like grace, love, peace, beauty, and justice.[5] Those are things that, for now, we only have imperfectly and partially, mostly as promise and hope, but they do have an effect on us.

Being Called Home

Like the foreigner in Isabel Allende's story above, those who come to believe in the promise are given a new past and a new future; their story becomes woven into God's own story, their life grafted into God's life. The result is a new identity or, as Lisa Feldman Barrett or Patrick McNamara might call it, a new Self, a self that is now understood in the light of God's grace, love, and forgiveness embodied in Jesus Christ and the history that came before him and after him. Their affective generative grammar is rewritten. The invisible bonds of centuries (or perhaps millennia) of coloniality, racism, and sexism begin to loosen their grip, and new possibilities appear on the future's horizon. No wonder slave owners didn't want the humans they were enslaving to know how to read the Bible for themselves, and no wonder they were very careful

5. See Kathryn A. Kleinhans, "Christ as Bride/Groom: A Lutheran Feminist Relational Christology," in *Transformative Lutheran Theologies: Feminist, Womanist, and Mujerista Perspectives*, ed. Mary Streufert (Fortress Press, 2010), 123–34.

about who preached to them and what was preached. Even with all those precautions, however, the living word of God kept finding ways to get to them and fill them with that sense of dignity, self-respect, self-love, and power that comes from recognizing our own image reflected back to us in the glowing face of our beloved divine, in whose image we have been made.[6]

In her book *Language for God: A Lutheran Perspective*, my colleague and friend, Lutheran theologian Mary J. Streufert, quotes Luther as saying that "when a preacher preaches in such a way that the word is not frustrated in producing fruit but is efficacious in the hearers—that is, when faith, love, patience, etc., follow—then God supplies the Spirit and performs powerful deeds in the hearers."[7] For that reason, she explains: "If we are going to proclaim the gospel of Jesus Christ in order to reach actual people so that their hearts are truly transformed by the power of the Holy Spirit, we need to use evangelical language—language that actually proclaims the gospel of God's grace to real people. We will use language or images that proclaim who God is and what God has done for us."[8] By using the word *evangelical* here, Streufert is trying to rescue it from its distortions whereby it has come to signify a very particular kind of Christianity sometimes associated with fundamentalism and intolerance. Instead, the word originally meant "gospel" or "good news." In fact, during the Reformation movement, when the Reformers began to be called "Lutherans," Luther expressly refused that name for the movement. He proposed instead that if a name other than Christian or Catholic was needed, then it should be "evangelical," to remember that we ought to be rooted in the gospel of God's grace made available to all through Jesus Christ, the living word of God made flesh. The Word is God's embrace of humanity and all creation, in the embrace of the beloved (see chapter 5), an embrace that reminds us how loved we are, all of us. An embrace that, when we believe it, when we trust in God's promises by faith, kindles in our hearts the same love with which we are loved. Luther puts it beautifully:

6. See Dwight N. Hopkins, *Being Human: Race, Culture, and Religion* (Fortress Press, 2005).

7. Mary J. Streufert, *Language for God: A Lutheran Perspective* (Fortress Press, 2022), 88.

8. Streufert, *Language for God*, 88.

> From faith there flows a love and joy in the Lord. From love there proceeds a joyful, willing, and free mind that serves the neighbor and takes no account of gratitude or ingratitude, praise or blame, gain or loss. We do not serve others with an eye toward making them obligated to us. Nor do we distinguish between friends and enemies or anticipate their thankfulness or ingratitude. Rather, we freely and willingly spend ourselves and all that we have, whether we squander it on the ungrateful or give it to the deserving. This is just as our Father does, who gives all things to all people richly and freely, making "his sun to rise on the evil and on the good" (Matt 5:45).[9]

Clearly, as Bishop Curry concluded, this is not the gospel that those enforcing slavery (and, I add, coloniality, racism, sexism, etc.) were dwelling in. Even the word of God can become a victim of the distorting forces of human sin and be put at the service of nefarious purposes. For that reason, because of how often the human heart becomes hardened by ideology, by hate, by fear, by life experiences, the Word, in the power of the Spirit, must first wound us—that is, break open our hearts of stone so that it can then pour on us the soothing, healing, renewing, and empowering balm of the gospel. But how does the Word accomplish that or, to be more theologically precise, how might the Spirit, through the Word, accomplish that work?

The Destructive and Constructive Functions of the Word

Luther's ideas here, once again, might be helpful. He believed that the word of God operates on the human being in two main ways, which he identified as law on the one hand and gospel on the other. The law refers to the expectations that the word of God places on us. As Tillich explains, since the law is the law of our Creator, it is not a law alien to our being, even if it feels that way because of our own self-alienation due to the effects of sin:

---

9. Luther, *The Freedom of a Christian*, 83.

> The law is, first of all, a divine gift; it shows to man[10] his essential nature, his true relationship to God, other men, and himself. Within existential estrangement it makes man's true nature manifest. But it does so in terms of commandments, just because man is estranged from what he ought to be.[11]

The law is merely a reflection of how we are meant to relate to each other, to God, and to ourselves in order to flourish individually and communally. However, due to the self-alienation of our sinful condition, this law that ought to feel natural and intuitive to our reason is instead experienced as strange and oppressive. Why shouldn't I covet my neighbor's possessions if I want them and think that I deserve them?

In order to make sure that the most vulnerable members of society are protected from abuse, Luther says that the law is accompanied by consequences for breaking it. This is what Lutheran theologians refer to as the first use of the law. It relates to the role entrusted by God to governments to use "the sword"—that is, to punish transgressions against the law, though such punishments should always be proportional to the harm done and should include means to repair that damage whenever possible.[12]

The second use of the law, in Luther's theology, can be understood as a kind of spiritual therapeutic use or, to use the metaphor introduced above, the surgical use. The Lutheran tradition refers to it as the theological use of the law. Its purpose is to make spiritual healing possible by leading people to a deep, existential awareness of their sin and, consequently, to a state of contrition and repentance. Only then are people capable of receiving fruitfully the good news of God's grace and love and the action of the Spirit to renew their minds and hearts—I would add, to rewrite their generative affective grammars.

The word of God, in this tradition, is often compared to a mirror where we get to see ourselves and understand how much we have missed the mark, how much our self has become distorted from the beautiful,

---

10. Tillich's use of the word *man* here is meant to be inclusive of all humanity.

11. Tillich, *Systematic Theology*, vol. 2, 81.

12. Rom 13:14

loving, peaceful, compassionate persons that we were created to be. The living and life-giving word of God calls us to return to our true self, as explained above, by confronting us with the lies we have come to believe about others and about ourselves and the ways in which we have been responsible for the suffering and pain of others and of our own selves. This step cannot be skipped. Otherwise, the result is that we end up misusing the gospel of God's grace and forgiveness, not to liberate us from the sin that harms others and ourselves but to actually justify it and protect ourselves from the difficult and painful process that is part of true healing.[13] We may refer to this moment in the work of theology as the destructive, or deconstructive, moment.

Notice the parallel between this theological, surgical, spiritually therapeutic function of the law and what McNamara refers to as "decentering" (discussed in chapter 3) and Lisa Feldman Barrett as "the deconstruction of the self" (discussed in chapter 7). This destruction or decentering of the self is necessary for spiritual transformation to take place. Many religions refer to this as dying to one's self. The letters of Paul in the New Testament speak of the death of the old Adam in us,[14] and Luther, in his ninety-five theses, wrote of the need to daily drown the old Adam through repentance.[15] This is so that the new Adam, Christ, can rise in us (that is, take form in us).[16] Despite the androcentrism of this image, the word *Adam* refers here to all humankind, and that encompasses all gender identities and sexualities.

Notice also how this destructive-constructive dynamic corresponds to the way we saw that the brain's mind operates in chapters 1 through 3. The brain, as we saw in chapters 1 and 2, is constantly issuing predictions, in the form of mental, neural, and affective representations,

---

13. See the discussion on "cheap grace" in *Discipleship*, trans. Barbara Green and Reinhard Krauss, Dietrich Bonhoeffers Works, vol. 4 (Fortress Press, [1937] 2003), 43–56.

14. Rom 6:3–11.

15. "When our Lord . . . said, 'Repent' [Matt 4:17], he willed the entire life of believers to be one of repentance," Martin Luther, "Ninety-Five Theses, 1517," trans. C.M. Jacobs and rev. Harold J. Grimm, Luther's Works, vol. 31, *Career of the Reformer*, ed. Harold J. Grimm (Fortress Press, 1957), 25.

16. Paul writes: "Therefore we were buried with him by baptism into death, so that, just as Christ was raised from the dead by the glory of the Father, so we also might walk in newness of life" (Rom 6:4).

of how things will be from moment to moment and then, based on the information made available by the senses, comparing those predictions with what seems to actually be the case. We also saw that intentions, desires, goals, memories, and emotions played an important role in that process by which the embodied mind and brain perceives reality, including the reality of our own selves. The Word, in its destructive function, as we will see below, operates by lifting up a representation of the current state of affairs (at the level of the community, of the world, and of the individual self) and contrasting it with representations of how things ought to be based on God's revealed intentions and purposes. This is often done with the use of dramatic imagery that brings shock to the intended recipient of the Word, a shock that is meant to open them up to the work of the Spirit, a shock that, as we have learned in previous chapters, happens in deeply embodied ways, beginning with the gut and impacting the entire body, cutting deep into the soul. Only then are people ready, like Eva Luna's soldier above, to receive from the Word and the Spirit a new memory, a new history, a new future, a new purpose, and a new way of experiencing and living reality.

The Prophets

The destructive-constructive dynamic of the Word is perhaps most clearly expressed in the prophets. Prophets are not fortune tellers, nor are they seers of a future that has already been irrevocably decided. The role of the prophets in the Hebrew and Christian Scriptures is to call the people, and especially their leaders, to repentance and conversion. They did this by sharing with the people God-given revelations and visions, often in graphic and sometimes gruesome detail, of the impending consequences that their actions, stubbornly unjust and unfaithful to God's way of shalom-peace-wholesomeness, would bring upon them, upon their community, and upon the larger world.[17]

The vision (or representation) lifted by the prophets of what God, the Creator, expects reality to be is simple. In the book of the prophet Micah, the expectation is set out succinctly and beautifully:

> He has told you, O mortal, what is good,
> and what does the Lord require of you

17. Brueggemann and Linafelt, *An Introduction to the Old Testament*, 129–37.

> but to do justice and to love kindness
> and to walk humbly with your God?" (Mic 6:8)

Unfortunately, that is not what the prophets observe happening in their society, especially among the ruling class and the well-to-do. Through the words of the prophets, God dismantles the facades of piety and righteousness used by the people to hide, even from themselves, the cruelty of their self-centeredness and greed. For example, through Isaiah, God thunders:

> Your new moons and your appointed festivals
> my soul hates;
> they have become a burden to me;
> I am weary of bearing them.
> When you stretch out your hands,
> I will hide my eyes from you;
> even though you make many prayers,
> I will not listen;
> your hands are full of blood.
> Wash yourselves; make yourselves clean;
> remove your evil deeds
> from before my eyes;
> cease to do evil;
> learn to do good;
> seek justice;
> rescue the oppressed;
> defend the orphan;
> plead for the widow. (Isa 1:14–17)

Similarly, speaking to the heads and rulers of the nation, the prophet Micah conveys this message from God:

> Should you not know justice?—
> you who hate the good and love the evil,
> who tear the skin off my people
> and the flesh off their bones,
> who eat the flesh of my people,
> flay their skin off them,
> break their bones in pieces,

and chop them up like meat in a kettle,
like flesh in a caldron.

Then they will cry to the Lord,
but he will not answer them;
he will hide his face from them at that time
because they have acted wickedly. (Mic 3:1b–4)

The prophetic message was ahead of its time by even calling attention to the impact that injustice has on the rest of creation:

Swearing, lying, and murder,
and stealing and adultery break out;
bloodshed follows bloodshed.
Therefore the land mourns,
and all who live in it languish;
together with the wild animals
and the birds of the air,
even the fish of the sea are perishing. (Hos 4:2–3)

The images used in the prophetic literature to convey God's wrath against the injustices of the rulers and the powerful but merciless wealthy elites are ruthless and often shocking, especially to modern sensibilities. However, they could be understood as dramatic (maybe hyperbolic) expressions of God's passion for justice—that is, for the well-being of all members of God's creation but especially those most vulnerable and oppressed, such as orphans, widows, foreigners, and the poor or, more accurately, the impoverished. Nonetheless, God's passionate love is also for those whose hearts have hardened so much that they have turned their backs to God and seek in other things and places what only God can provide, becoming callous to the needs of others and eventually behaving in ways that result in the suffering and oppression of others. Even when they are "abandoned" by God and turned over to their own desires and to the consequences of their injustices, it is with the hope that their hearts of stone will break and turn again into hearts of flesh (Ezek 36:26–27). Thus, the prophet Ezekiel (33:11) proclaims: "As I live, says the Lord God, I have no pleasure in the death of the wicked but that the wicked turn from their ways and live."

Not surprisingly, the leaders and the people often didn't like what the prophets had to say or the passion with which they said it. They would try to find alternative prophets, who wearing the prophetic mantle, would tell them what they wanted to hear rather than what God demanded of them. They would usurp the sacred words, rituals, and practices and twist them to fit other purposes than those intended by the Creator. Through the prophet Jeremiah, God challenges them to prove that rather than calling them to repentance, their words, covering injustice and soothing the guilty conscience of the unjust, were actually sent by God and not fashioned from the dreamy fantasies of the powerful:

> Is not my word like fire, says the Lord, and like a hammer that breaks a rock in pieces? See, therefore, I am against the prophets, says the Lord, who steal my words from one another. See, I am against the prophets, says the Lord, who use their own tongues and say, "Says the Lord." See, I am against those who prophesy lying dreams, says the Lord, and who tell them and who lead my people astray by their lies and their recklessness, when I did not send them or command them, so they do not profit this people at all, says the Lord. (Jer 23:29–32)

Through that prophetic word that is "like a hammer that breaks a rock," the divine Spirit brings about the death of the old self through contrition, confession, and repentance, opening up a space of possibility for the new self to be born or, perhaps more accurately, for the real God-shape self to be set free, both in the individual and in the community or nation. And just as the destruction of the old self was accomplished by the prophetic word, so the creation of the new self and of the new communal reality is brought about by the prophetic word in its creative function. Similarly, the poor, the oppressed, the marginalized, and all of creation is given the promise of a new future where justice shall triumph, and they shall thrive and flourish together with the rest of God's creation.

Thus, Isaiah (66:14) proclaims: "You shall see, and your heart shall rejoice; your bodies shall flourish like the grass." And Micah says:

> they shall beat their swords into plowshares
> and their spears into pruning hooks;
> nation shall not lift up sword against nation;

neither shall they learn war any more;
but they shall all sit under their own vines and under their own fig trees,
and no one shall make them afraid,
for the mouth of the Lord of hosts has spoken. (4:3b–4)

The destructive moment in the prophetic word is always ultimately at the service of God's mercy. The final goal of the destructive-constructive functions of God's prophetic word is the liberation of the people and the flourishing of creation. So the Psalmist sings:

Your steadfast love, O Lord, extends to the heavens,
your faithfulness to the clouds.
Your righteousness is like the mighty mountains;
your judgments are like the great deep;
you save humans and animals alike, O Lord.

How precious is your steadfast love, O God!
All people may take refuge in the shadow of your wings.
They feast on the abundance of your house,
and you give them drink from the river of your delights.
For with you is the fountain of life;
in your light we see light. (Ps 36:5–9)

Biblical scholar Walter Brueggemann sheds light on this iterative dynamic movement of the prophetic word between deconstructing and constructing. He proposes that "*the task of prophetic ministry is to nurture, nourish, and evoke a consciousness and perception alternative to the consciousness and perception of the dominant culture around us.*"[18] He draws a sharp contrast between the royal consciousness that benefits greatly from the status quo at the expense of the exploitation and oppression of vast segments of society and the prophetic imagination that awakens an alternative consciousness in the people: "The alternative consciousness to be nurtured, on the one hand, serves to *criticize* in dismantling the dominant consciousness. . . . On the other hand, that

18. Brueggemann, *The Prophetic Imagination*, 3. Italics in the original.

alternative consciousness to be nurtured serves to *energize* persons and communities by its promise of another time and situation toward which the community of faith may move."[19] In order to do that, Brueggemann explains, the prophet "*offers symbols* [recovered out of the people's historical past] that are adequate to confront the horror and massiveness of the experience that evokes numbness and requires denial."[20]

In line with Brueggemann's argument, I propose in this book that in addition to its other functions, the prophetic word works by making visible the invisible—that is, the false representations (illusions and delusions about others, about ourselves, about reality, and about God) that have been formed in our minds and affects through the influence that cultural, economic, and societal forces, like the colonial matrix of power, have on our cognitive devices and affective grammars through which we experience, know, and interact with reality. The prophetic word pushes us outside the frame that marks the horizons of our reality (see chapter 4), thus revealing the illusions and delusions for what they are, allowing us to see both the frame and the possibility of what decolonial activist/thinkers call "an otherwise."[21] This function of the prophetic word was carried forward in the New Testament.[22] It is essential to understanding the gospel.

The Gospel

In the gospels, the critical-destructive moment of theology can be seen throughout Jesus's ministry. In fact, Jesus aligned himself with the prophetic tradition from the beginning of his ministry when he read the text of the prophet Isaiah:

> The Spirit of the Lord is upon me,
> because he has anointed me

19. Brueggemann, *The Prophetic Imagination*, 3. Italics in the original.

20. Brueggemann, *The Prophetic Imagination*, 45.

21. Mignolo and Walsh, *On Decoloniality*, 34.

22. The epistle of James, for instance, states: "Religion that is pure and undefiled before God the Father is this: to care for orphans and widows in their distress and to keep oneself unstained by the world" (1:27). In context, the "world" here refers precisely to the illusion of false representations of reality that normalize poverty and the neglect of vulnerable members of society, such as widows, in James's biblical times.

> to bring good news to the poor.
> He has sent me to proclaim release to the captives
> and recovery of sight to the blind,
> to set free those who are oppressed,
> to proclaim the year of the Lord's favor.
>
> And he rolled up the scroll, gave it back to the attendant, and sat down. The eyes of all in the synagogue were fixed on him. Then he began to say to them, "Today this scripture has been fulfilled in your hearing." (Luke 4:18–21)

One of the moments in Jesus's ministry where the critical-destructive moment of the Word is most vivid is when he entered the temple, turned the tables of the money changers, and ran out the animals sold for the sacrifices (see Mark 11:15–18). His critical confrontations with the religious leaders of his day were also about the ways the words, rituals, and practices of the faith, given by God for life-giving purposes, had been transformed into unjust burdens for many people, especially the poor and marginalized, thus becoming more an obstacle than a channel of God's grace for the people.

It must be added that Jesus's criticisms were internal criticisms, presented in the biblical texts in hyperbolic form to emphasize their meaning, but they were tragically misused, contrary to Jesus's intentions, to justify anti-Semitism and anti-Jewish violence. Once again, it must be repeated that the purpose of the prophetic word, including in Jesus's ministry, was to call people to repentance and conversion (to God by faith and to the neighbor by love), so that sinners could find forgiveness, the oppressed justice, and that all could have the life-abundant that God intends for all.

Jesus did not only challenge sinners, evildoers, and structures of injustice and oppression. He also challenged those victimized by such structures and oppressors to see themselves in a new light apart from how they were framed by the status quo. In a world where illness and social destitution were interpreted as divine punishment for one's secret sins or as evidence of the inferiority of some people vis-à-vis others,[23] Jesus identified himself, God, and God's kingdom with those whom

23. For instance, the gospel according to John relates the following incident: "As he walked along, he saw a man blind from birth. His disciples asked him, 'Rabbi, who

his world deemed inferior and condemned: the poor, the handicapped, the marginalized, the beggars, and those forced into prostitution by the patriarchal structures of their time. In other words, despite the theological amnesia of much of Western Christianity, Jesus's message was not just one of forgiveness for sinners but also one of restitution to the destitute victims of sin and of the sinful structures of all times. This is clear in his inaugural sermon:

> [Jesus] came down with them and stood on a level place with a great crowd of his disciples and a great multitude of people from all Judea, Jerusalem, and the coast of Tyre and Sidon. They had come to hear him and to be healed of their diseases, and those who were troubled with unclean spirits were cured. And everyone in the crowd was trying to touch him, for power came out from him and healed all of them.
>
> Then he looked up at his disciples and said:
>
> "Blessed are you who are poor,
> for yours is the kingdom of God.
> "Blessed are you who are hungry now,
> for you will be filled.
> "Blessed are you who weep now,
> for you will laugh.
>
> "Blessed are you when people hate you and when they exclude you, revile you, and defame you on account of the Son of Man. Rejoice on that day and leap for joy, for surely your reward is great in heaven, for that is how their ancestors treated the prophets." (Luke 6:17–22)

And then he continued, again in line with the ancient prophetic tradition in which he stood, hoping for the repentance and conversion of those who had turned their backs on God's way of justice and mercy:

---

sinned, this man or his parents, that he was born blind?' Jesus answered, 'Neither this man nor his parents sinned'" (9:1).

> But woe to you who are rich,
> for you have received your consolation.
> "Woe to you who are full now,
> for you will be hungry.
> "Woe to you who are laughing now,
> for you will mourn and weep.
> "Woe to you when all speak well of you, for that is how their ancestors treated the false prophets." (Luke 6:24–26)

Jesus's word, like its prophetic antecedent, worked through an iterative dynamic process of deconstruction-construction that opened up a space of belonging that included everybody: oppressed and oppressor, poor and rich, Jewish and Gentile, citizen and foreigner, tax collector and zealot, priest and prostitute, friend and enemy. He even prayed for those who crucified him. Such a radical openness and profound love is something we are still trying to comprehend and catch up with. Through simple but powerful parables; through miracles and healings; through his life full of holiness, mercy, and compassion; and through his death and mysterious resurrection, he did not just communicate God's creative-constructive words but he was (and is) that Word. And from the perspective of the Christian faith, he continues to be that living word through which God's Spirit is at work in the world, dismantling oppressive systems and building up an alternative world, a reality of abundant life where all creation can flourish and, in the beautiful words of Psalms 85 (10), "Steadfast love and faithfulness will meet; righteousness and peace will kiss each other."

The Word as Matrix for an Otherwise

The power of empires, colonial systems, patriarchal arrangements, racial hierarchies, and other forms of systematic oppression and exploitation cannot depend, as we have seen, on blunt force alone to prevail. These powers need the people to internalize those social orderings as if they were inevitable and natural, either preordained by God or determined by nature and biology, and believe that to resist them is futile because there are no feasible alternatives. For that purpose, religion, theology, science, philosophy, statistics, and any other form of generating knowledge can be co-opted to solidify the system in such a way that its manufactured nature is rendered invisible, and the human and ecological costs that are paid to sustain it are seen as necessary and acceptable. As I write this, I see on the TV news that one country in the Middle East has bombed another country. The commentator immediately mentions the impact this action has had on the global markets, alleviating the concerns of the viewers; so far, no mention has been made of whether there were any deaths. In a world alienated by individual and structural sin, "casualties" seem normal, even natural.

To offer an "otherwise" capable of awakening the imagination of the people and stirring them into action, the way the prophets' words and Jesus's very life did, is already to destabilize the reigning systems of domination and exploitation. This is why the prophets' lives rarely had happy endings. They were often killed, tortured, exiled, and maligned, sometimes by the very people they so dearly loved and were trying to help. Even Jesus ended up being tortured, humiliated, and killed in the name of God! From biblical times, doing theology (that is, proclaiming the prophetic theos-logos) in a liberative and decolonial key can be dangerous business.

The Apocalyptic

Apocalyptic literature is another example of the intertwining of the critical-destructive with the creative-constructive moments in biblical theology. Despite the way these texts are used in contemporary culture (namely, as if they provided disguised clues of future events for people to decipher), they truly function otherwise. As Biblical scholars such as Barbara Rossing[24] in the global north and Pablo Richards[25] in the global south have observed, apocalyptic literature served as a devastating critic not only of the injustices committed by the empires of the day but also as a critique that went to the very heart of the legitimacy of the empires themselves. Employing mythical images, like dragons, sea monsters, and creatures that are half beast and half man, and images of terrible devastation, they were able to put into words (or, more accurately, word images) what the oppressed people were experiencing and feeling.

24. Barbara R. Rossing, *The Rapture Exposed: The Message of Hope in the Book of Revelation* (Basic Books, 2004).

25. Richard, *Apocalypse.*

Under the inspiration of the divine Spirit, the apocalyptic seers gathered the pains, sufferings, tragedies, indignities, and frustrations of the people and wove them together with the raw material of common religious symbols and narratives. In doing so, they were able to produce in the minds of their listeners and readers a double effect. On the one hand, they effected what the Brazilian popular educator Paulo Freire called *conscientização*[26]—that is, a deep understanding of the root causes of their oppression and a new sense of their power of agency, as limited as it may be. And on the other hand, it allowed the people to endure the unbearable by helping them keep their eyes on the future that had been promised by God, which not even death itself would be able to keep them from achieving (see Rev 7:9–17).

The Messianic

The messianic is yet another motif of the sacred Scriptures where we can see the critical-destructive and the creative-constructive moments of theology at work. Let us remember that the word *messiah* is a title in Hebrew that means "anointed." The expected messiah was the one anointed by God's mighty Spirit, who would bring salvation to an oppressed, colonized, and dispersed people. It did not pertain only to an individual who would come to rescue the people with the strength of God's own arm but also to the inauguration of a new era, a time/realm marked by true peace, justice, and the flourishing of all people.[27] In fact, all nations would be blessed by the arrival of the messianic era, including animals and nature:

> The wolf shall live with the lamb;
>   the leopard shall lie down with the kid;
> the calf and the lion will feed together,
>   and a little child shall lead them.
> The cow and the bear shall graze;
>   their young shall lie down together;
>   and the lion shall eat straw like the ox.

26. Paulo Freire, *Pedagogy of the Oppressed*, 50th anniv. ed., trans. Myra Bergman Ramos, with a new introduction by Donaldo Macedo and an afterword by Ira Shor (Bloomsburry, 2018).

27. Westhelle, *Eschatology and Space*, 122–29.

The nursing child shall play over the hole of the asp,
and the weaned child shall put its hand on the adder's den.
They will not hurt or destroy
on all my holy mountain,
for the earth will be full of the knowledge of the Lord
as the waters cover the sea. (Isa 11:6–9)

It is not just the prophetic, apocalyptic, and messianic texts of the Scriptures that function in this way. The entire biblical corpus, with its plurality of literary styles, historical contexts, and even theological nuances, functions in this dynamic fashion. Even the stories of creation, on the opening pages of the Bible as we have it today, were forged in the heat of the suffering of a people that had seen their most sacred institutions destroyed, their holy temple trampled by their enemies, their leaders executed, and their nobility sent into forced exile.[28] It is from within the Babylonian exile, according to the consensus of biblical historical scholarship, that the author (or community of authors) wove together (re/membered) the strands and fragments of the sacred stories of how God had created the sun, the stars, the waters, the land, and all the creatures (entities deemed as deities by their captors); of how God had patiently and benevolently parented humanity from its beginnings; of how their ancestors had been summoned by God into a future pregnant with promises of which they, too, were inheritors; of how God had heard the prayers and groanings of their ancestors, enslaved by the Egyptians (not just a country but a regional imperial power), and had commissioned a man, rescued from the genocidal wrath of the pharaoh by the wits and courage of his sister and mother; and of how God had delivered them, again and again, from situations of death into a broad place full of life and promise.[29]

Those stories inspired courage, enabled resilience, and knit them into a people united not by blood alone but also by story and ritual and belonging—belonging to God, belonging to each other, belonging to their ancestors, and belonging to those who were yet to come. It is through story that our embodied brains, as discussed in chapters 1–3

28. Brueggemann, *An Introduction to the Old Testament*, 35–60.

29. Brueggemann, *An Introduction to the Old Testament*, 3–32.

and 7, connect the fragments of a person's existence into the coherent sense of self that they experience themselves as. Similarly, the anointed authors in the Scriptures (and beyond) carefully gathered the fragments of the lives of the people—the good, the bad, the beautiful, and the ugly—and through a Spirit-led process wove them into a people capable of withstanding centuries of terrible persecutions, oppressions, and dispersion.[30]

A similar process was followed by the authors of the New Testament. Through the power of the Word, through the inspiration of the Holy Spirit, they wove the budding communities of the Jesus movement into a transhistorical, transpersonal, transcultural, polyphonic, universal body, self-identified as the living, breathing, communal mystical body of Christ alive in the midst of the community as the community.[31] That connection to each other and to the one who had been condemned as a criminal—humiliated, tortured, and executed mockingly but whom God had raised and vindicated in the power of the Holy Spirit—inspired them.[32] It gave them the courage to endure their own tortures and humiliations and to embody an alternative way of being in the world, of being human, an "otherwise," but an otherwise of universal, all-encompassing reach incorporating all aspects of human life and all "corners" and inhabitants of that magnificent opus of the divine mystery (the *poietes*—poet/maker—of heaven and earth)[33] who, looking at the creation, sighed from deep within the divine heart saying "It is good" or "It is so beautiful!"[34]

Thus, the words of the sacred Scriptures are powerful words, beautiful words. They are also coveted words, often usurped, distorted,

---

30. For a beautiful example of this task of theology, see S. D. Giere, *Freedom & Imagination: Trusting Christ in an Age of Bad Faith* (Fortress Press, 2023), especially chapter 4, "The Imagination of Faith," 73–98.

31. See Bonhoeffer's dissertation on "Christ existing as church-community" in *Sanctorum Communio: A Theological Study of the Sociology of the Church*, trans. Reinhard Krauss and Nancy Lukens, Dietrich Bonhoeffer's Works, vol. 1 (Fortress Press, 1998).

32. Matthew (27:37) tells us that when the Romans crucified Jesus, "over his head they put the charge against him, which read, 'This is Jesus, the King of the Jews.'"

33. Westhelle, *Eschatology and Space*, 51.

34. Brueggemann, *An Introduction to the Old Testament*, 56.

misused, and abused. Hence, the need for constant self-criticism, what I have called in this chapter the critical-destructive moment of theology. The words can be used for purposes alien to the Spirit that breathes through them, or they can become stifled and opaque, no longer being able to communicate the living word and the Spirit through them but actually eclipsing them, blocking them, replacing them.[35]

There is an important lesson there, in the history of intrabiblical hermeneutics, that even that which is most sacred, most precious, even the holiest of holies can be manipulated, used to justify that which betrays its very essence. Even God in the second person of the Trinity was tortured and killed, in the name of God and his Word, prodded, of course, by no small amount of cunning from the occupying Roman powers and their proxies. This is an important lesson to learn and to remember; not only are all our theologies and theories about reality representations never to be confused with that which they intend to represent, but even our best representations, and even that which is considered sacred and holy, can also be distorted for nefarious purposes. That is why we need to apply the critical-destructive function of the Word even to theology itself. Therein lies the insistence in Latin American and feminist liberation theologies for a robust hermeneutics of suspicion as an integral part of the theological task.

Conclusion

I have argued that the vision of God's promised future offered by the prophets, the apocalyptic literature, the messianic expectation, and the ways in which Jesus embodies those promises and expectations in the gospels serves as that matrix where the new self, as described by McNamara and Lisa Feldman Barrett, can begin to take form. From a decolonial perspective, that process also corresponds with a "delinking" not only from our old self but also from the old unjust systems inherited from our colonial past.[36] This process of delinking involves cognitive and affective aspects, in line with what we have discussed in this book

35. See, for example, the powerful work on dismantling of "gaslighting" in biblical interpretation in Angela N. Parker, *If God Still Breathes, Why Can't I?: Black Lives Matter & Biblical Authority* (Eerdmans, 2021), especially chapter 4, "Moving from Stifled Breath to Full-Throated Faith," 63–89.

36. Mignolo and Walsh, *On Decoloniality*, 125–30.

about the neuroscience of affective valuations and decision-making. In addition to delinking, that process also involves the insurgency of an otherwise. Decolonial activist/thinker Catherine E. Walsh summarizes that process in the following way: "It is in the *for* [and not only in the against], in the postures, processes, and practices that disrupt, transgress, intervene and in-surge in, and that mobilize, propose, provoke, activate, and construct and otherwise, that decoloniality is signified and given substance, meaning, and form."[37]

The Word, through the power of the Spirit, has the power to delink us from the distorted representation of reality that we have inherited from our colonial, racist, and sexist past. It has the power to liberate our minds, brains, bodies, imagination, emotions, and communities from the distortions of those illusions that perpetuate structures of oppression and marginalization that result in the death and suffering of too many of God's beloved children and creatures. The Word, in the power of the Spirit, destroys those illusions and instead inspires us with new possibilities. It also gives us the courage to work together for the insurgence of the otherwise promised by God, symbolized in the Jewish and Christian tradition as the coming of God's realm where all life thrives and justice and peace have their home.

37. Mignolo and Walsh, *On Decoloniality*, 34. Italics in the original.

CHAPTER NINE

Liberation

Lessons from Liberation Theology for Decolonizing the Brain

They have treated the wound of my people carelessly,
saying, "Peace, peace,"
when there is no peace.
They acted shamefully; they committed abomination,
yet they were not ashamed;
they did not know how to blush.
—Jeremiah 6:14–15a

Introduction

LET US PAUSE for a moment of confession. . . .

We need confession because the word of God has not always been used for its intended life-giving purposes described in the previous chapter. Too many people have been hurt by the church and by misappropriations and misinterpretations of the Word that constitute a form of theological malpractice. Therefore, before being able to say anything liberating and decolonizing, the first word that the church and its theology must utter is a word of confession, of contrition, of repentance, of true remorse, and of conversion. As part of the theological conversation, there needs to be a time for deep listening to the testimonies of those who have been hurt by such abuses of the word. One particular branch of theology that took that task seriously is what has come to be known as liberation theology or, more accurately, liberation theologies. In this chapter, we explore the genesis of such theologies, after which this book is named, and try to gather methodological insights about how to engage in the theological task without being usurped by interests contrary to God's life-giving will.

Origins

To understand the origins of Latin American liberation theology, we must first remember that Christian theology was at the heart of the European project of the occupation, violent conquest, and supposed evangelization of the lands called Turtle Island and Abya Yala by their original inhabitants and later known as the Americas.[1] A similar story, tragically, took place on the African and Asian continents. The theological nature of that project was made explicit by the juridical justification used by the European colonial powers—namely, the doctrine of discovery.[2] That doctrine invoked the right of the pope, as the representative of God (the Creator of heaven and earth) and vicar of Christ on earth, over any lands and territories that were not already ruled by "legitimate" governments.

Through that putative divine right, the pope gave the European rulers legal power over any new lands that might be discovered through the voyages of Columbus and those who would come after him. The original inhabitants of these lands were not viewed as having a legitimate claim over them because they did not fit the Europeans' expectations of what it meant to be civilized or even human. That is to say, they did not fit within the theological anthropology and sociopolitical expectations of the European gaze. For instance, the peoples and nations encountered by the Iberian explorers in their first trips were not seen to have a concept of private ownership of property or of sexual mores (they did not seem to be as bothered by nudity and sexual freedom as the Europeans were), and they showed more reverence for the forces of nature, such as the sun, the wind (storms), and the seas, then they did of the God the Father presented to them by the European invaders.

---

1. For an analysis of the theological roots of the conquest of what is now known as the Americas, see Luis N. Rivera-Pagán, *A Violent Evangelism: The Political and Religious Conquest of the Americas* (Westminster John Knox Press, 1992); in Spanish, Luis N. Rivera-Pagán, *Historia de la conquista de América: Evangelización y Violencia* (Barcelona: Editorial CLIE, 2021).

2. For an explanation of the doctrine of discovery, see Tink Tinker, "The Doctrine of Christian Discovery: Lutherans and the Language of Empire" *Journal of Lutheran Ethics* Doctrine of Discovery 17, no. 2 (March 2017),https://learn.elca.org/jle/the-doctrine-of-christian-discovery-lutherans-and-the-language-of-empire/.

Their systems of political organizations were odd, as it turns out they were more democratic than the Europeans, with their long traditions of monarchies and nobilities often vying for power and control, were used to. All those differences gave Europeans a sense of superiority and right of power over their newly found neighbors.

The colonial enterprise, as we explained in the introduction to this book, required more than just the justification for taking the ancestral lands of the original inhabitants. It also required immense amounts of human labor, especially to mine the minerals and natural resources in which these lands were rich. Thus, the Native communities were violently forced to work for the European colonists, desecrating the earth that they considered to be their sacred mother, for the enrichment of kingdoms on the other side of the ocean (incidentally, those kingdoms were in debt to the banks, so the colonial enterprise was a means for both church and crown to pay off their debt to the rising banking corporations of their day).[3] The inhuman treatment of the Native peoples by the overwhelming majority of the European colonists did not go unchallenged. Famously, Fray Bartolomé de las Casas, who started out as just another overseer (*encomendero*) of the Spanish colonial project, had a conversion experience when listening to a sermon featuring this text from the Scriptures:

> If one sacrifices ill-gotten goods, the offering is blemished;
> the gifts of the lawless are not acceptable.
> The Most High is not pleased with the offerings of the ungodly,
> nor for a multitude of sacrifices does he forgive sins.
> Like one who kills a son before his father's eyes
> is the person who offers a sacrifice from the property of the poor.
> The bread of the needy is the life of the poor;
> whoever deprives them of it is a murderer.
> To take away a neighbor's living is to commit murder;
> to deprive an employee of wages is to shed blood.
> (Sir 34:21–27)

3. Enrique Dussel, "The Real Motives for the Conquest," *Concilium* (1990): 33; see also Carlos Fuentes, "The Age of Empire," in *The Buried Mirror*, 151–69.

Those words pierced las Casas's soul deeply and brought him to a conversion that was to last for the rest of his life, which he dedicated to the defense of the Native peoples of the Americas. Thus, according to one of the founders of liberation theology, the Peruvian priest and theologian Gustavo Gutiérrez, las Casas became the forerunner of what later became known as Latin American liberation theology.[4] Important for this book is a legal debate that he forced in the Spanish city of Valladolid in the 1540s.

The debate of Valladolid was an official court proceeding of theological-juridical-anthropological character, meant to address the question of what kind of beings the Native peoples of the Americas were. Were they merely quasi-rational animals, were they actually fully human, or were they more like homunculi but not quite fully human? The consequences of the debate were not trivial; they were about what inherent rights they therefore had. If they were more like animals than like humans, then, according to the laws, theology, and mores of the time, it would be acceptable to submit them to forced labor even if they had not been captured as prisoners in a just war, because they could then be considered just like another brute animal. If they were determined to be homunculi but not quite fully human, then it would justify subjecting them to some kind of colonial tutelage, like children under the guidance of a legal mentor, until they would "grow up" and become as fully human as they could, given the inherent limits of their nature.

Bartolomé de las Casas defended the position that they were fully human even if they were so radically different from the types of humanity known until then to Europeans. Las Casas's position won the debate. Interestingly, as more legal decisions in the European continent began to establish fundamental rights for the Native populations, three things began to happen. First, the census lists began to show fewer people categorized as "indigenous" and more as mixed, or "mestizo."[5] Second, the colonists and their descendants grew distant from the continental legal institutions and initiated, ironically, movements of decolonizing and of establishing freestanding countries,

---

4. Gustavo Gutiérrez, *Las Casas: In Search of the Poor of Jesus Christ*, trans. Robert R. Barr (Wipf and Stock, 2003); the original Spanish is *En busca de los pobres de Jesucristo* (Lima: Instituto Bartolomé de las Casas y Centro de Estudios y Publicaciones, 1992).

5. Tony Castanha, *The Myth of Indigenous Caribbean Extinction: Continuity and Reclamation in Borikén (Puerto Rico)* (Palgrave Macmillan, 2011), 63–66.

liberated from the transatlantic control of the European powers. And third, black Africans were forcefully removed from their homelands and shipped to the "new world" to replace the Indigenous labor force lost to death (due to the genocidal violence of the colonial project, diseases for which the Indigenous peoples' immune system was not prepared) or to increasing protections given to the Native peoples by the European continental powers or some of the local religious orders (like the Jesuits, who ended up being expelled for their commitment to the protection of the Native people under their care). This pattern repeated itself with the Spanish colonists first, but then also with the Portuguese, the English, the French, and all the way to the founding of the colonies that later became the United States of America.[6]

Throughout the Americas and the Caribbean, most of the original movements of colonial independence were about the new ruling and landed classes, descended from the original colonists or newly arrived, freeing themselves from the burden of taxation from the European colonial metropolises and their imposition of laws that curtailed the economic interests of these new landed classes. A new identity was forged as, for example, "criollos" for the direct descendants of the Europeans and as "mestizos" for those of mixed Indigenous and European descent vis-á-vis the continental identity (the exact nomenclature varied from region to region). This new identity, however, was still deeply rooted in European culture, values, religion, and aesthetics. It became symbolized as "white" overagainst the ways of being of people of "Black" descent or "Indio" (that is, "Indian"), which was used with heavy pejorative connotations. Thus, the birth of the new American nations was implicated in the birth of the supremacy of whiteness, of which white supremacy is but an extreme form. A part of that supremacy of whiteness was the institutional, legal, political, theological, and scientific (because it was around this same time that, not coincidentally, modern science was born) scaffolding necessary to maintain the power of the ruling (white European or their descendents) and landed elites over and against what was seen as the potentially rebellious and "ungrateful" Natives, Blacks, mulattos, etc., who resisted their "right" to these lands, to their riches,

6. See, for example, Nikole Hannah-Jones et al., *The 1619 Project*; Gómez, *Inventing Latinos*; an older but still helpful account, from a Hispanic perspective, can be found in Justo L. González, "Who Are We?," in *Mañana*, 31–42; and from a Native American perspective, Deloria, *Custer Died for Your Sins*.

and the forced labor that allowed them to exploit them. That is the foundation upon which the economic, political, and cultural success and hegemony of those nations is built on to this day.

The Catholic and Protestant Churches (including the churches of my own Lutheran tradition), with some important exceptions, played an important role in the process of stabilizing those structures, though some did so more directly than others. One of the ways in which the church did that was theologically, by blending (through the alchemy of idolatrous biblical eisegesis) white European values, aesthetics, and prejudices into what was ordained by God, or "natural," and therefore closest to what is good and holy. (What was *contra natura*,—that is, against nature—was sin). Alternatively, that which was part of the cultures of the Indigenous, Black, and brown peoples was deeply demonized without any real attempt to understand it, especially from their perspectives and according to their own worldviews.

Thus, many generations of brown, Black, and Indigenous people unknowingly learned to hate parts of themselves and of their ancestral traditions because they had been deemed sinful, diabolic, or at least backward. They (we) were taught to experience and even feel European ways of being as more sublime, beautiful, good, and worthy of imitating and aspiring to than our own traditional, Indigenous, brown, and Black ways. Even as I write "Black ways," I wonder if its meaning will be confused to imply "bad ways" as opposed to the wise ways of thinking, being, feeling, and worshipping coming from Africa and people of African descent. In other words, to use the framework we have lifted up in this book regarding how the brain works, "whiteness" became the cognitive-affective mental representation against which everything else is measured. It became the model self used to calibrate our generative cognitive-affective grammars. As a young friend from Zambia told me once, "In the past Europeans colonized us; now we colonize ourselves!"

Nonetheless, movements of resistance and for liberation were always part of the story, even if they are not mentioned in many historical accounts, making it seem as if Native and enslaved people simply acquiesced to colonial exploitation.[7] Some of those movements for

7. See, for example, in Spanish, Jalil Sued Badillo, *Agüeybaná el Bravo: La recuperación de un símbolo* (San Juan: Ediciones Puerto, 2008), where he argues that when the native peoples of the Caribbean and especially of Puerto Rico were submissive to the Spaniards, they were referred to by names like Taínos or Naborias, but when they rose in rebellion, they were referred to as man-eating and war-loving Caribes, even though

liberation in Latin America and the Caribbean resulted in imperfect but important advances in securing new rights and justice for people who had so far been excluded, exploited, or marginalized, such as the agrarian reforms that came after Uruguayan independence led by General José Gervasio Artigas, the inter-American liberation movement of Simón Bolivar, and the Caribbean movements of liberation inspired by José Martí.

In many other cases, however, the result of decades of terrible bloodshed that pitted sibling against sibling were opportunistic dictatorships that had no qualms in employing violence against whomever might oppose them or dare to speak against them. It was from that historical background, and from within those turbulent and dangerous times, that liberation theology was born.

Liberation theology was born from a community that, like Jacob, stubbornly wrestled with God and wouldn't let go of God, Christ, or the Scriptures, claiming the promises of peace, true justice, liberation, and life-abundant inherent in the Christian faith even as they lived in a daily hell of death, unjust imprisonments, tortures, and never-ending injustices and indignities.[8] It is not possible to understand liberation theology without first understanding the bloodied soil and the suffering of the people from where it emerged.

Method

Liberation theology was not born in academic classrooms or university conference halls, even if it later found a place there and even if some of

---

careful analysis of the lists of names reveal that they were most likely the same people. Thus, the story of the submissiveness of the peace-loving Taínos is an invention; the reality was more complicated, involving political negotiations, alliances, and armed rebellion in coalitions with other peoples from neighboring islands.

8. For a powerful depiction of the background from which liberation theology emerged, see the 1989 film *Romero*, produced by Paulist Pictures, which tells the story of the now Saint Monsignor Óscar Arnulfo Romero, the archbishop of El Salvador who was assassinated for his stance against the constant abuses, murders, and tortures of innocent people in his country by local soldiers, trained by the then US military's School of the Americas; the movie is specific to El Salvador, but its depiction of the violence endured by the people and the dilemmas faced by their pastors is representative of the general situation at the time in other Latin American countries; see "Controversial 'School of the Americas' Closes," *ABC News* (December 14, 2000), https://abcnews.go.com/International/story?id=81917&page=1.

the original founders of that theology were trained there.[9] Liberation theology, like the Christian faith before it, was born at the foot of the cross and of the crosses and anonymous mass graves of the millions of innocent martyrs sacrificed on the altars of wealth, coloniality, national and transnational greed, political ideologies, and hateful prejudices. Liberation theology is an attempt (or, actually, many attempts) to answer the question of how to speak of the God of life in a context of death, how to proclaim the God of justice in the midst of blatant injustice and impunity.[10] How do we speak of the God of peace when there is no peace in sight?[11]

Even though many left Christianity altogether because of its obvious complicity in centuries of oppression and exploitation, others found in its Scriptures and traditions a powerful message that resonated with the experiences of the suffering people and provided them with the power to resist and the inspiration to work for the transformation of their societies. Reading the Scriptures and the tradition anew from the perspective of the suffering people, with their questions and insights, transformed theology.

Read from the perspective of the poor, the oppressed, and the marginalized, it became apparent that the God of the Scriptures was never neutral or passive in the face of injustice. In the biblical texts, God takes sides! The story of the liberation of the Hebrew people from the terrible bondage in Egypt makes clear that God had made an option for the oppressed and against the oppressors. Read from the perspective of the maid rather than of the lady, the Magnificat of Mary had a different tone. Mary did not seem like a submissive, obedient girl, the model of virtue for Christendom and, especially, Victorian femininity. Rather, Mary spoke with the fire of a prophet, feisty and

9. My understanding of the development of Latin American liberation theology is indebted to the work of my first professor of the sociology of religion, Samuel Silva Gotay, *El pensamiento cristiano revolucionario en América Latina y el Caribe: Implicaciones de la teología de la liberación para la sociología de la religión* (Salamanca, España: Sígueme, 1981).

10. For a brief introduction to liberation theology, see Leonardo Boff and Clodovis Boff, *Introducing Liberation Theology*, trans. Paul Burns (Orbis, 1990); the original version in Portugese is *Como fazer Teologia de Libertação* (Petrópolis, Brazil: Editora Vozes, 1986).

11. See, for example, María Pilar Aquino, *Our Cry for Life*.

uncompromising in her critique of injustices and the modus operandi of God: to lower the haughty and to raise the lowly (that is, the oppressed and marginalized). Read from that perspective, biblical text after biblical text makes it obvious that the official Christianity brought and taught by the colonizing church to support the colonial project (including Protestants, Lutherans, Catholics, and, more recently, Evangelicals) did not accurately represent the heart of the Christian faith. In fact, it had betrayed it because it had lost the unmistakable divine option for the poor so prevalent in the Scriptures, from the prophets and the Torah to the gospels and the epistles.[12]

Liberation theologians paid a hefty price for their commitment to the oppressed and to reading the sacred texts and the tradition from the perspective of the oppressed. Many were arrested, tortured, and murdered. Others were excommunicated, defrocked, or seen as persona non grata by the official authorities of their ecclesial bodies, and many others were reprimanded, maligned, or belittled by the world of professional theology as not being well versed enough in "real" (read: Eurocentric) theology. But they persevered, and today liberation theologies have emerged around the planet, giving voice to the laments, prayers, wisdom, hopes, and Spirit-inspired resilience of people of faith from different cultures and traditions. Today, in addition to the original Latin American liberation theology and Black liberation theology, there are many others, such as minjung liberation theology in South Korea, Dalit liberation theology in India, Palestinian liberation theology, womanist (Black feminist) liberation theology in the US, mujerista (Latina feminist) liberation theology in the Americas, queer liberation theology, and even ecological or planetary liberation theology.

The original scope of liberation theology has broadened. Initially, liberation theologies in Latin America were mostly (though never exclusively) concerned with the economic and political dimensions of pastoral work and theological reflection. The reason for that emphasis was both biblical and contextual: contextual because the violence that the people were facing in those contexts had clearly economic and political causes and biblical because, as we saw above, a careful reading of

12. Elsa Támez, *Bible of the Oppressed*, trans. Matthew J. O'Connell (Wipf and Stock, 2006); the original Spanish version from which this one was adapted is *Bíblia de los oprimidos: La opresión en la teología bíblica* (San José, Costa Rica: Departamento Ecuménico de Investigaciones, 1979).

the prophetic tradition in the Scriptures and of Jesus's ministry makes obvious that the Scriptures are concerned not merely with the salvation of individual souls but rather with matters of economic justice and communal well-being.

In order to articulate a prophetic critique of the economic, political, and social structures that were responsible for the exploitation and pauperization of the vast majorities of the peoples of Latin America, liberation theologians found it necessary to employ scientific tools of social analysis, including those developed by thinkers like Karl Marx, Louis Althusser, Max Weber, and Émile Durkheim. Even though it is true that some of the early liberation theologians considered themselves to be Christian and Marxist, they were very critical of the actual ways in which Marx's ideas had been distorted in the socialist countries of their day. What mattered to them in Marx's analysis was his penetrating critique of the dehumanizing effects of capitalism on the human person, especially on the poor.[13]

Liberation theologians appropriated the tools of economic and social analysis from secular scholars, but they did so critically and from within their own Christian theological traditions. They were convinced that such secular criticism was inspired by the same spirit as the criticism of the biblical prophets. Using the Scriptures, read through the lenses of its own internal prophetic tradition, combined with sophisticated analyses from sociology and economics, they laid bare the injustices of the societal structures and systems in the Latin America of their day, demonstrating that not only were they unjust, but that they were also against God's will revealed in the Scriptures and incarnated in Christ. That combination of social scientific analysis and biblical theological critique was powerful, shaking the foundations of many dictatorships across Latin America and abroad. That is why priests, pastors, theologians, and lay workers standing in the tradition of liberation theology were viciously targeted by many regimes, disappearing them, torturing

13. For example, Enrique Dussel, an Argentinian theologian, historian, and political philosopher considered one of the founders of "la filosofía de la liberación" (liberation philosophy), wrote a powerful analysis on the religious-prophetic roots of Marx's original writings: *Towards an Unknown Marx: A Commentary on the Manuscripts of 1861–63*, trans. Yolanda Angulo and ed. with an intro. by Fred Mosley (Routledge, 2001). Many of Dussel's books in Spanish are available at https://enriquedussel.com/novedades/libros/.

them, killing them, and tarnishing their reputations as "communists" or "terrorists" rather than real Christians.

A powerful contribution of liberation theologians was to help people realize that inequality and injustice were not a reflection of the will of God but a result of a long history of strategic exploitation and marginalization. They also helped people come to understand that the realm of political struggle is not excluded from the realm of God's work of salvation and that salvation did not only mean going to heaven after we die but also a holistic state of well-being including individuals, communities, and the planet.

In addition to economic and social analyses, liberation theologians also engaged in deep historical research, uncovering the processes by which the present structures of injustice were set up and recovering voices and wisdoms that had been silenced or pushed to the margins. Those voices were also the voices of the ancestors of the colonized, whom the colonial project had tried to convince that their ancestral traditions were backward, ignorant, and in desperate need of help from the supposedly more advanced European rescuers.

In that process of analyzing the socioeconomic-political-historical circumstances of the people in light of scientific and biblical analysis, a new perspective also began to emerge about the Scriptures. As mentioned above, it became apparent that the Scriptures, as well as the Christian tradition, needed to be reexamined in light of its own contexts of composition and interpretation. In other words, why had certain biblical texts and readings been privileged while others, equally valid, were ignored or dismissed? Highly spiritualized interpretations of Scriptures began to be questioned in light of both the biblical texts and the results that such readings had had on the community of believers. An example close to my own Lutheran tradition is the frequent distortion of the good news that we are justified by grace through faith. For those who have come to experience the weight of guilt, shame, and responsibility in their lives, that message can bring about a radical transformation and liberation in their lives, as we saw in the previous chapter. But when the message is turned into the cheap grace of "how you live doesn't matter because God loves you anyway," the message no longer serves its function. In fact, it does the opposite; instead of justifying the sinner, it justifies the sin, allowing the sinner to continue to live immersed in the false illusions of the representations of reality that perpetuate injustice and oppression. Thus, it is important to understand the context in which specific doctrines emerged and the circumstances that they were trying to address.[14] If we keep a word intact but change its context, the meaning of the word can change radically. I remember walking back home from seminary with a classmate from El Salvador. He invited me over to his apartment for coffee. I said, "Voy horita," which in Puerto Rico, means "I will go later, in a little while." I kept walking. He stared at me and asked me again: "Are you coming?" I said, "Sí, horita." Then he asked me, "When you say 'horita,' what do you mean?" I told him, "In a little while." He laughed and said: "Where I come from, that word means 'right away.'" Context and circumstances matter![15]

Liberation theology emerged as a mutually transformative conversation between the sacred texts of divine revelation, the contexts from where they emerged, and the circumstances of those studying them.[16] Juan Luis Segundo, one of the original architects of liberation theology, describes its interpretative strategy as a hermeneutical circle.[17] Some background here might be helpful. In a different context, the German biblical scholar Rudolf Bultmann had written about the need to

14. For an analysis of the doctrine of justification in Paul that takes the social and economic context of both the author and the reader seriously, see Elsa Támez, *The Amnesty of Grace: Justification by Faith from a Latin American Perspective*, trans. Sharon H. Ringe (Abindgon Press, 1993); the original Spanish version is *Contra toda condena: La justificación por la fe desde los excluidos* (San José, Costa Rica: Departamento Ecuménico de Investigaciones y Seminario Bíblico Latinoamericano, 1991).

15. There were always exceptions to this distortion of the words of God. Two notable examples in Lutheranism were Dietrich Bonhoeffer's sharp critique against cheap grace and Søren Kierkegaard's relentless critique against the hypocrisy of the Danish church of his day. See Eliseo Pérez Álvarez, *A Vexing Gadfly: The Late Kierkegaard on Economic Matters* (Wipf and Stock, 2009), and Dietrich Bonhoeffer, *Discipleship*, Dietrich Bonhoeffer's Works, vol. 4 (Fortress Press, [1937] 2003).

16. Three classic original texts of liberation theology, illustrative of the interpretive movement described above, are Gustavo Gutiérrez, *A Theology of Liberation: History, Politics, and Salvation*, 50th anniv. ed., trans. and ed. Sister Caridad Inda and John Eagleson, intro. Michael Lee (Orbis, 1973, rev. 1978] 2023; Rubem Alves, *A Theology of Human Hope* (New York: Corpus, 1971); and, from the context of the Black experience in the US, James Cone, *God of the Oppressed*.

17. Juan Luis Segundo, *Liberación de la teología* (Mexico City: Carlos Lohle, 1974), available in English as *Liberation of Theology*, trans. John Drury (Orbis, 1976).

demythologize the biblical narratives—that is, to distill their core teachings from their mythological husks in order to apply the message to the contemporary existential situation of human beings. He referred to this as a hermeneutical circle between the existential questions raised by the interpreter and the answers implicit in the message of the Scriptures.[18] Later, another German theologian, Paul Tillich, whose work we have already referenced throughout the book, developed that insight further into what he called the "method of correlation," whereby the biblical symbols offer answers to people's existential questions (namely, questions of ultimate concern).[19] Liberation theology, according to Segundo, offers a more complete process of interpretation. Not only do the Scriptures offer answers to the questions posited by the community of interpreters, but the message of the Scriptures is also enriched by the questions and circumstances of those raising the questions and interpreting the Scriptures.

Liberation theology's hermeneutical circle begins with praxis rather than theory. It begins from the concrete commitment of a discipleship that is committed to the liberation of the oppressed from the oppressive situation. Thus, Gustavo Gutiérrez speaks of theology as a second act, a reflection on the first act that is the attempt to act in faithfulness to the living word of God. From the praxical commitment to the liberation of the poor, questions emerge. Those questions can be succinctly described by the lapidary words of Brazilian bishop and liberation theologian Dom Hélder Câmara on being nominated for a Nobel Peace Prize: "When I fed the poor, they called me a saint. When I asked, how come they are poor? They called me a communist."[20] The second step in liberation theology's hermeneutical circle is a questioning and critical analysis of the structural—economic, social, political, historical, etc.—foundations of the injustices faced by the people. This second step is in line with the prophetic critique we saw above that contrasted the reality of the people, especially of the oppressed, with the vision of God's purpose for the entire community.

---

18. Rudolf Bultmann, "New Testament and Mythology," in *Kerygma and Myth*, ed. H. W. Bartsch (SPCK, 1953), 1–16.

19. Tillich, *Systematic Theology*, vol. 1, 8–15.

20. See the reflection "Dom Hélder Câmara" in Center for Action and Contemplation, October 20, 2015, https://cac.org/daily-meditations/dom-helder-camara-2015-10-20/.

The third step consists of studying the revelation of God in the Scriptures intentionally from the particular location of the community and its concrete circumstances. Just as what people can see is a function of where they are seeing it from, the meanings that can be found in the word of Scripture will depend on the place (that is, the social location) from where it is studied. Studying the Bible with and from the perspective of the oppressed, liberation theologians arrived at the conclusion that the oppressed (or "the poor" in the original nomenclature of liberation theologians) have a hermeneutical advantage over the well-to-do and powerful because most of the texts of the Scriptures were composed from the perspective of the oppressed.[21] Another insight gained from reading the Bible from that locus is that throughout the Bible, again and again, as we saw above when briefly studying the prophets, God makes an option for the oppressed and against the oppressors. This is transparently clear in the second part of Jesus's inaugural sermon, also quoted above:

> "But woe to you who are rich,
> for you have received your consolation.
> "Woe to you who are full now,
> for you will be hungry.
> "Woe to you who are laughing now,
> for you will mourn and weep.
> Woe to you when all speak well of you, for that is how their ancestors treated the false prophets. (Luke 6:24–26)

Furthermore, when studied from the perspective of the oppressed and utilizing the critical tools developed from disciplines such as historical criticism, social analysis, and linguistics, it also becomes clear that the texts of the Scriptures have suffered distortions due to ideological pressures. Those distortions happen at the level of the received official interpretations of the texts but also at the level of the translation and reconstruction of the texts. Moreover, as the prophets made clear, not all that claims to be the word of God is indeed from God. Therefore, liberation theology, in tandem with feminist theology, lifts up the need

---

21. See, for example, the centrality of the lived experience of Latinas in Ada María Isasí-Díaz, *En la Lucha: Elaborating a Mujerista Theology* (Fortress Press, 2004), 182–87.

to develop a hermeneutics of suspicion, or to paraphrase Justo González, a nonnaive (or noninnocent) reading of the biblical texts.[22] For that purpose, tools from economics, psychoanalysis, sociology, and criticism were borrowed.

The fourth step in the hermeneutical circle of liberation theology is to listen to the word of God that addresses the community from within Scripture in this new light. Thus, the word of God is a living word, always contemporary to the people. Interpretation, then, is conversation between God and the people, and in that conversation, new insights are received about the people's reality; about their personal and collective lives; about the church; about the government and the economic, political, and social systems that shape their lives; and about God, faith, and the Scriptures.

The hermeneutical circle never stops. The community begins with praxis and commitment and ends with praxis and commitment. And informing that praxis and commitment is a serious engagement with the word of God, from the perspective of the oppressed and through the application of the most relevant tools of analysis available to the community. Each one of those steps is flexible and needs and feeds the others.

Beyond Liberation Theology

The following generations of liberation theologians both in Latin America and abroad soon realized that economic and political analysis alone was not enough. The issue of gender (in)justice, for example, risks being hidden if the focus is on only economics and politics generically and if the interpretive process is more often than not led by male clergy or leaders. Similarly, issues of the distinct realities of Indigenous populations within the Americas and beyond became an important question, particularly given their deep ancestral religious and wisdom traditions that are very different from the worldviews of Christianity, whether Protestant, Catholic, or Orthodox.

In the United States, Hispanic[23] theologians trained in the Latin American liberation tradition realized that issues of culture and

22. González, *Mañana*, 75–87.

23. There have been many names used to designate this community. Throughout this book, I have chosen to use the name that was most accepted at the time of the

minoritization had to be at the center of theologizing in their contexts because those were some of the key issues that their communities were facing.[24] New methodological approaches began to emerge, focusing on the people's lived experiences, paying particular attention to how they expressed their faith through popular religiosity (like the devotion to the saints or to the Virgin of Guadalupe, the singing of devotional songs called *coritos*, and other ways in which people brought the contents of the faith to their daily struggles). The tools of cultural anthropology and sociology became an important aspect of this new way of doing theology, which became known at the time as Hispanic/Latin@ Theology. Similar developments took place in other minoritized communities in the US context and beyond. Furthermore, given the complexities of intersectionalities or imbrications[25]—that is, the ways people inhabit different social locations depending on characteristics including race, gender, socioeconomic status, or physical ability—and because of long histories of minoritized communities having to compete against each other for meager resources and the attention of those in power, the process of proliferation of liberation theologies sometimes included sharp mutual criticism, divisions, and internal struggles. The result in many cases, however, has been an awakening to the life-giving, healing, and empowering possibilities of the gospel, a living word capable of speaking

---

work being referred to: in the late 1980s and 1990s, the term most frequently used among theologians to name themselves was *Hispanic* and later, *Hispanic/Latin@*; later, the more favored term was *Latinx*, used to avoid strict binary exclusions; and more recently, the term *Latiné* has been used.

24. I use the term *minoritization* instead of *minority* to highlight the fact that being a minority is not a fact of nature or an ontological essence; it is, as I argue throughout this book, an artificially constructed social, political, and economic representation, which through the mechanisms of affective valuations, has acquired an ontological weight that makes it seem normal or a simple fact of nature.

25. Patricia Hill Collins, *Intersectionality as Critical Social Theory* (Duke University Press, 2019), 128. In the Latin American context intersectionality is theorized differently as imbrication; see, for example, Ochy Curiel Pichardo, "Construyendo metodologías feministas desde el feminism decolonial," in *Reflexiones, herramientas y aplicaciones desde la investigación feminista*, ed. Irantzu Mendia Azkue et al. (Biblao, España: Universidad del País Vasco y Seminario Interdisciplinar de Metodología de Recerca Feminista, 2014), 45–60, https://publicaciones.hegoa.ehu.eus/uploads/pdfs/269/Otras_formas_de_reconocer.pdf?1488539836.

a relevant word to each context without needing to make claims of exclusivity or dogmatism.

Decolonial theology emerged in Latin America and the global south as parallel, but not identical to, liberation theology.[26] Decolonial thought goes beyond liberation theology in that it tries to recover epistemologies and methodologies from outside the Christian and Euro-American intellectual cannon. One critique decolonialists make of liberation theologians is that despite their stringent criticism of systems of oppression, including epistemic systems of oppression, they nonetheless fall into the trap of operating with tools developed within the same system they are trying to criticize.[27] The alternative pathway opened by decolonial thinkers is to engage traditions and voices from outside modernity.[28] Those voices and traditions are the ones of the Indigenous peoples whose ancestors thrived in these lands now called the Americas (known as Abya Yala and Turtle Island by their original inhabitants). Similarly, decolonial thought has sought to recover the ancestral living wisdom brought to these lands and cultivated by enslaved Africans and their descendants across the American continents. This is done in solidarity with other similar movements around the planet, incorporating local Indigenous wisdom traditions as alternatives to the Eurocentric, white-centered, male, heteronormative logos imposed by the colonial project.

The present project of tracing the contours of a possible decolonial liberation theology of the brain agrees with the charge against Christian theology for its aiding and abetting in the colonial, patriarchal, white supremacist, ecocidal project. But it also sees that such uses of the Christian faith and of the prophetic Jewish traditions from which it emerged are distortions of a religious tradition that was born precisely as an alternative to imperial domination and demonic systems incarnated in social structures and psychological patterns that dehumanized people. Christian theology has a contribution to make to

26. Juan José Tamayo, *Teologías del Sur: El giro descolonizador* (Madrid: Editorial Trotta, 2017).

27. Mignolo, "Decolonizing Western Epistemologies/Building Decolonial Epistemologies," in Isasi-Díaz and Mendieta, *Decolonizing Epistemologies*, 23.

28. Mignolo, "Decolonizing Western Epistemologies," 36–43.

decolonial and liberation struggles. After all, the Christianities of the colonial project were not the only Christianities. Moreover, Christian symbols and beliefs have been at the heart of important movements of liberation around the world. The Mexican Revolution was fought under the banner of the Virgin of Guadalupe, as was the farmers' rights movement led by Dolores Huerta and César Chávez in California. Both Desmond Tutu and Nelson Mandela found inspiration in Christian sources to lead the process of liberation and peace building in South Africa. Gandhi, while firmly rejecting Christianity as an institution, found inspiration in Jesus, particularly in his teachings from the Sermon on the Mount. The civil rights movement in the US was led in part by preachers (both lay and ordained), women leaders of the church, and Christian student movements and with strong references to the symbols of the Black Christian tradition. Interestingly, those movements were also interreligious to some degree. If it is true that religion and theology have often been used to manipulate people, then it is also true that it is because the symbols of religion (not only of Christianity) are very powerful and have the potential to ignite social change and to birth new social, political, economic, and cultural worlds.

Decolonial Liberation Theology and Neuroscience

A Hermeneutics of Suspicion for Neuroscience

We have learned that knowledge is not innocent, and that includes both theological knowledge and scientific knowledge. Scientific knowledge, we saw in chapter 4, is the result of the questions that scientists ask, and the questions that scientists ask are circumscribed by their own epistemic prejudgments, by the resources available to them, and by the institutional pressures supporting and restricting their research The first contribution that liberation theology can make to brain science is its hard-earned tendency for a hermeneutics of suspicion.

How has brain science been shaped by and shaped notions of being human that serve the purpose of solidifying the power of certain kinds of humans over others, not to mention over other, nonhuman, creatures? We need a noninnocent history of brain science and of cognitive science.[29]

29. See, for example, Donna J. Haraway, *Simians, Cyborgs, and Women: The Reinvention of Nature* (Routledge, 1991).

The shameful uses of scientific and pseudoscientific approaches, like phrenology, to prove the superiority (and inferiority) of certain races to others, and the abuses of lobotomies to pacify populations deemed aberrant, calls for careful analyses of the knowledge we have received and that is taken for granted in psychology and brain science. The fact that the vast majority of psychology, neuroscience, and cognitive science experiments are performed on mostly white subjects, usually college students, is often recognized by researchers, but the methods to "correct" for that sample disparity do not seem adequate because they continue to view a particular segment of humanity (white eurodescendants) as the standard of normality, and then others are adjusted vis-à-vis that standard.

The human brain is a contested site, a place of social struggle. Neuroscience has a lot of power in society. Criminal sentences can be reduced or even reversed because of evidence from neurology; defense lawyers can argue that the criminal behavior was caused by a sick brain and therefore their client should not be held accountable.[30] Alternatively, policymakers can decide that there is a particular type of brain configuration that is more prone to criminality and therefore impose draconian laws against that community. Neuroscience can be used to investigate the best approaches to teaching and learning and then use that information to improve a community's schools. And it can also be used to profile certain kinds of neurodiversity as deviant and therefore as in need of correction or disciplining measures. It can be misused to add weight to stereotypes attached to the artificial categories our society uses to divide us into immutable classes of humans along lines of race, ethnicity, tribe, nation, gender, sexual orientation, disability, socioeconomic status, migration status, and so on. There is nothing like invoking the power of brain scans and of neuroscience as evidence of our false representations of reality, the illusions we have been trying to dismantle throughout this book.

It is not only the uses of neuroscience that can be problematic. It is also the view of humanity that it paints, a view that, as mentioned above, does not flow from the objective data alone but includes heavy elements of the cultural assumptions embedded in the scientists' gaze and in the institutions that support and guide scientific research. We have seen throughout this book that the human mind and brain does not have

---

30. David Eagleman, "Why Blameworthiness Is the Wrong Question," in *Incognito*, 151–92.

direct access to the way things are in themselves, but rather it is always in a process of constructing representations of how things are, despite its painstaking procedures for testing hypotheses and probing the feasibility and accuracy of theories through processes of falsification.[31]

Science is not exempt from those limitations to our cognitive access to reality, including the reality of the human mind/brain.[32] It is necessary, then, for science to be done in open conversation with other disciplines, especially those that can provide it with the lenses of a hermeneutics of suspicion. Not doing so risks confusing unexamined assumptions for conclusions. The metaphors used to describe the operations of the brain can be telling in that respect. For example, the brain has an executive with executive functions, there is division of labor across the brain, and there is competition among neural systems.[33] Biology (i.e., that which is manipulable, that which can be handled and controlled and put under careful experimental conditions in a laboratory) is considered more fundamental and real than mental, psychological, affective, and spiritual experience. We have learned from thinkers such as Donna Haraway to become suspicious when objective scientific descriptions come curiously close to resembling our economic, social, political, and military structures.[34] Thus, historically contingent social arrangements become baptized by science as more natural than other possibilities, granting them an aura of inevitability and even of desirability without regard for their human and ecological costs. Other possibilities, other ways of understanding ourselves, and other ways of being human individually and communally are therefore disregarded as naive or unscientific.

Science, neuroscience, and cognitive science have important contributions to make to our understanding of what it means to be human and how we can thrive as individuals, as communities, as species, and as a planet. But in order to be able to do this effectively and not serve as an ideological weapon in the colonial matrix of power and other unjust

---

31. Karl Popper, *The Logic of Scientific Discovery* (Routledge, [1935] 1992).

32. Paul Thagard, *The Cognitive Science of Science: Explanation, Discovery, and Conceptual Change* (MIT Press, 2012).

33. See Eagleman, "The Brain is a Team of Rivals" and "Life After the Monarchy," in *Incognito*, 101–50, 193–224.

34. Haraway, *Simians, Cyborgs, and Women*, 185.

systems, science must be constantly self-critical and in ongoing conversation with other disciplines and communities of inquiry.

A Neuroscientific Theopoetics of Hope?

There is also a positive role for neuroscience and the sciences of the mind/brain in general to play in the work of liberation and decolonial theologizing/praxis/spirituality. For instance, neuroscience can provide liberation and decolonial theologies with empirical ways to assess the effects of certain words, symbols, practices, and theologies on people's brains and nervous systems in general.[35] Is a certain theology truly healing? Is a religious practice conducive to a person's well-being? Are rituals truly having the effect of creating in people a sense of unity and common humanity with others? How do people's bodies and brains respond to sacred narratives and texts? Are there ways of reading sacred texts, of proclaiming the good news, or of embodying ritual that are more effective than their alternatives?

Furthermore, neuroscientific research, in collaboration with psychology and cognitive science, can help assess the ways by which individual and communal bodies have been inscribed with affective responses and valuations that perpetuate the condition of oppression, marginalization, and minoritization of a community. With the help of epigenetics, it is also possible to examine how those neuralgenetic "viruses" get passed across generations. It can be a powerful tool in helping diagnose the effects of systemic oppression (which, as we have seen, is an expression of sin) on the body and brain. But diagnosis is not enough. There is also the possibility, with the new understanding of the neural dynamics of human cognition, affection, decision-making, and behavior, to refine communal spaces for transformation, not only for those victimized by systems of oppression but also for all who are caught up in its field of influence, which inevitably causes a distortion in the fundamental humanity of victim and victimizer, of passive participant and active enabler alike, even if in different forms and to different degrees.

The human brain and nervous system do not live on bread alone. It also needs a cultural and spiritual milieu. We have seen that the

---

35. See, for example, Andrew Newberg and Mark Robert Waldman, *How God Changes Your Brain* (New York: Ballantine, 2009).

environment and the embodied human mind/brain shape each other and that emotions and language play a significant role in how we perceive reality and engage with it. That points to the possibility of a sort of theopoetics of neuroscience. *Poetics* comes from the Greek *poietes*, which means "to construct, to build." It is the word used in the Christian creeds to describe God's work of creation. God is the poietes of the universe, the poet whose words weave a world into being. The world that God's words give life to is a world that is also capable of speaking poetry, of joining the Creator in speaking the poem that is the world: a poem that includes moments of joy and moments of sorrow, times for life and times for death, periods for destroying and times for creating. We creatures, living poems of the poietes of the cosmos, have been gifted with the power of continuing the poem that we are a part of and that other generations will one day join.[36]

The poem first comes to being in our affective imaginaries, deep in our guts, hearts, kidneys, wombs, and brains, connected through invisible strings of connectivity to other brains, hearts, guts, bodies, and ecosystems. It is from there that the holy breath of the divine and the sacred breath of the human summon each other, talk to each other, and sing to each other and, in the process, bring new worlds into being. Theology can give us the grammar to speak that silent poem out loud. Neuroscience helps us understand how the poem becomes flesh. Like the spider weaves a universe that is born from within them, so we have been given the means to weave or reweave worlds where the wounds of oppression are healed, the hard lessons have been learned, and God's dreams—spoken through the prophets, incarnated in the Messiah, and watered with the sacrifice of the martyrs (those dreamers who dared to wager it all to the cosmic dream, to the divine poem)—have been birthed in actual communities trying to make it real. This occurs even with the full awareness that it is always an ongoing task, and no actual human arrangement should be confused with the eschatological otherwise from where the Spirit of God, our future, summons us: that time/space where heaven and earth touch, where peace and justice kiss, where life overflows, and creation has found itself at home, in God and in itself.

36. This insight is inspired by the work of Vítor Westhelle. See, for example, "Labor: A Suggestion for Rethinking the Way of the Christian," *Word & World* 6, no. 2 (1986): 194–206, and "A 'Theory' of the Cross: The Human Arts: *Poiesis*, *Praxis*, and *Theoria*," in *The Scandalous God*, 125–43.

Conclusion

Our selves, our communities, our environments, and our worlds have been deeply wounded by millennia of accumulated injustices and systems of oppression. Through cognitive and affective processes explored throughout this book, we find ourselves living in a socially constructed world marked by profound inequalities and injustices. Just by virtue of the color of our skin, of the place where we were born, of the bodies and genes that we have been born with, of the language or dialect with which we communicate, of the sexual orientation or gender identities that we happen to have, and of the family into which we were born or adopted, some of us find ourselves in positions of privilege and complicity with power that we didn't even ask for and others in positions of subjugation and minoritization that erode our souls and wound our spirits. Most of us, through the dynamics of intersectionality or imbrication, find ourselves in both positions in different moments and spaces. Like Eva Luna's broken interlocutor, we, too, are in need of a new memory, of a new story, of a new future, of a new identity.

We have seen that through their effects on our embodied emotional systems, words have the power to deconstruct us and to make us anew. And we have seen that from ancient times, the divine word has been understood to have the power of a surgeon's scalpel to cut through the scars of false identities and open up spaces for our true self to emerge. We saw that the divine word does that through a dynamic iterative process of destruction and construction. Liberation theology and decolonial theologies allowed us to explore how that process goes beyond individuals and can actually transform entire communities, societies, and even nations.

Let us summarize some lessons drawn from liberation and decolonial theology:

- Thinking and acting belong together. Theologizing is done for the sake of the praxis of a faith that is liberating and faithful to the prophetic and life-giving spirit of the Scriptures, and praxis is informed by the critical, communal, and prayerful study of the faith tradition.
- Thinking and acting must include criticism. A hermeneutics of suspicion is necessary to avoid the idolatry of mistaking for divine revelation, or as God's will, what in reality is either a

manipulation of the Scriptures for unholy purposes or, perhaps, an innocent misinterpretation at odds with God's holistic life-giving purposes. Criticism cannot be only self-criticism; we need others to help us see our blind spots or to call us to repentance when we stubbornly hold on to that which is hurtful to others and not truly from God.

- Context matters. Ideas, beliefs, practices, institutions, and even affections have a context and a history. And it is that context and history that endow them with their meanings and with their power. This is something that liberation theology has learned from the structuralist and poststructuralists. It is important to investigate what is "outside the frame" (as we elaborated earlier in the book) and what is the history by which our beliefs became solidified in the ways in which we have received them.
- Location matters. What we can see is a function of where we are standing in relation to others within the social, economic, and intellectual structures of our world. And what we hear depends on whom we are standing with. The way reality seems to me (what feels like common sense) and even the meanings in Scripture that seem just obvious to me are strongly influenced by the social location from where I/we are seeing things. Hence the need for a diversity of perspectives.
- God cares about justice. When the Scriptures speak of sin and of the need to repent, these do not refer only to personal shortcomings in our individual morality. They refer mostly to our actions, decisions, attitudes, and passivity that cause undue suffering and even death to our neighbors and fellow creatures, whether we know it or not. The salvation that Christianity proclaims has to do with God's way of addressing that reality in a holistic way. Salvation is forgiveness of our sins, but it is also liberation of the victims of our sins. It must include a process whereby God brings about transformation, healing, justice, and true peace to individuals, communities, and creation in general. God's concern for justice is not an abstract concept; it is an expression of God's parental love for every human being and living creature. In situations of injustice and inequality, according to the Scriptures, God opts for the oppressed and

the poor, but God never ceases to love even the perpetrator of injustice.

- Liberating theology must include destruction/criticism and construction/creativity. Through the proclaimed word, God, like a skilled surgeon, wounds us in order to heal us. Theology and proclamation must shed light on the lies and injustices prevalent in our society, à la Jonah, to call people to repentance. Theology and proclamation must also invite the people to dream God's dreams of peace, fullness of life, true justice, and beauty, so as to mobilize peoples' imaginations and affections, thus becoming God's collaborators, "created co-creators" of God's future, a future that we cannot bring about on our own but for which we can plant seeds and water them.

CHAPTER TEN

Hope

The Neural Irruption of God's Otherwise

> [Jesus] answered: "The kingdom of God is not coming with things that can be observed, nor will they say, 'Look, here it is!' or 'There it is!' For, in fact, the kingdom of God is among you."
>
> —Luke 17:2

Introduction

Internalized Hopelessness

THROUGHOUT THIS BOOK, we have investigated how systems of oppression cannot be perpetuated only through external means of domination but also need the reinforcement of internalized cognitive and affective processes. The result is that those social, political, and economic arrangements, even though unjust, feel inevitable (even necessary), ordained by God, or just an expression of nature, the way things are. We have seen that feelings and emotions shape the way we experience reality, and that, in turn, those emotions and feelings are shaped by language, education, and culture. We have discussed, in light of the theories of emotional valuation and identity formation explored in this book, that all of us have a sort of generative affective grammar written in our bodies and brains, through which our perception of reality is organized and generated at the level of affect, cognition, and behavioral scripts.

The feelings, perceptions, and valuations written on us by what decolonial activist-thinkers call "the colonial matrix of power" are, however, an illusion.[1] They do not offer an accurate representation of reality, but they do contribute, through our mostly unconscious behavioral scripts, to the distortion of reality in the direction of those colonial illusions.

1. Mignolo and Walsh, *On Decoloniality*, 141–45.

They are the result of centuries of cultural, spiritual, and emotional programming, written in our collective affective imaginary through direct indoctrination but also by more subtle means such as a distorted version of Christian spirituality and theology; a highly selective presentation of history through monuments, museums, national holidays, and heroes; mis/representations in literature, film, music, and theater; and actual daily practices that reinforced the apparent naturalness of the inequalities upon which those systems of oppression were built.[2]

In other words, we have come to experience reality and to act as if those inequalities and the prejudices and unconscious biases that come with them are intrinsic to reality, just the way things are, or even ordained by God. Eventually, they just feel true, and through the neurological alchemy of emotional realism become real (see chapter 7). For that reason, we have argued that a process of liberation and decolonization requires that we pay as much attention to the internal dynamics whereby emotions and imagination become colonized as to the external political struggles for liberation from the institutions and systems that enforce oppression and inequality.

We have further argued that the prophetic Spirit, active through the Word, has the power to enter our bodies and go deep into our nervous systems, even into our guts, wombs, hearts, and kidneys, and all the way up to our brains, loosening up the colonizing grip of such idolatrous ideologies in the human imaginary and affective valuation systems.

Another World Is Possible!

The beginning of such a process of internal liberation involves recognizing the illusions for what they are and coming to the realization that such oppressive social systems are fabricated, historically contingent, and not inevitable. Therefore, they can be undone. Things don't have to be this way; things can be different! Or, as liberation ecotheologian Leonardo Boff expressed it: "Another world is possible."[3]

2. Néstor García Canclini, *Hybrid Cultures: Strategies for Entering and Leaving Modernity*, trans. Christopher L. Chiappari and Silvia L. López (University of Minnesota Press, 1995); the Spanish original is *Culturas Híbridas: Estrategias para entrar y salir de la modernidad* (MéxicoCity: Editorial Grijalbo, 1990).

3. Leonardo Boff, *Virtues: For Another Possible World*, trans. Alexandre Guilherme (Cascade, 2011).

Not only is another world possible, but the prophetic liberation tradition also emphasizes that the current order is against the will of God. In fact, as we saw in chapter 8, the terrible biblical symbols of the wrath of God serve as a hyperbolic highlighting of just how at odds the current world of injustice and oppression is against the intentions of the Creator.[4] Such symbols have been distorted and manipulated to promote a very particular kind of morality and spirituality with a heavy emphasis on sexual mores and the control of women's bodies and reproduction while neglecting the very heart of the symbol that is God's burning passion for the well-being of all creation, especially of the most vulnerable members of society who are often exploited, oppressed, marginalized, excluded, and ultimately, condemned to death, either directly or indirectly because of poverty. God cares deeply about justice because justice is life and injustice is death.

Now we are ready for the next step in the process of spiritual decolonization and liberation: hope!

Hope is not to be confused with optimism. Hope is a theological virtue, a gift of the Spirit. Optimism can be important, but hope is something else. Optimism is based on the possibilities made available to us by the circumstances in which we find ourselves. It's the silver lining in the stormy clouds. Hope is not something that is sought after or found in the actual circumstances out there. Hope is an active, creative, poietic force!

By the act of hoping, a spiritual space where a new reality can begin to emerge is opened up. Hope is an opening of the fabric of time and space in the here and now through which the Spirit of God's promised future can irrupt in the present and transform it. Since the future does not yet exist, its irruption in the here and now is the birth of freedom, the freedom to create something new that is not merely a repetition of what already was. By hope, our minds are renewed, our generative affective grammars are rewritten, purified from inherited colonial, racist, and sexist illusions, and a new world is conceived within us. From there, it overflows and connects with the worlds generated by the hope of

---

4. See the discussion on the "anti-kingdom" in Jon Sobrino, "Jesus and God (2): Jesus' Prophetic Praxis as Upholding the True God," in *Jesus the Liberator: A Historical-Theological View*, trans. Paul Burns and Francis McDonagh (Orbis, 1993), 160–79; the original version in Spanish is *Jesucristo liberador: Lectura histórica-teológica de Jesús de Nazareth* (San Salvador: UCA Editores, 1991).

other members of the community and, together, a new reality begins to gush forth like rivers of living waters. Thus begins the transformation of reality into a new creation. But where does that hope come from?

Sources of Hope

God

Just as much as faith and God are inextricably linked (see chapter 5's excursus on naming the mystery), so do hope and God belong together. God is the warrantor of hope. God, in the majestic mystery of the divine transcendence, which includes and overflows immanence, keeps the tyranny of the past over the present from closing up on us as a prison. To speak of God in this sense is also, at the same time, to speak of the openness of reality to the new rather than as the mere cyclical, never-ending, repetition of the same. It is also to speak of the possibility of good to emerge even from the depths of evil, of suffering, of despair, of guilt, and of death.

The Risen Crucified Messiah

In my own Christian tradition, God's power to create good even from within the depths of suffering, pain, and evil is expressed in the symbol of the cross or, more precisely, of the crucified Messiah.[5] The fact that the one hanging on the cross is the Messiah that had been long expected, the Savior, the very Son of God, according to the Christian faith, is also a statement about the cross, which was a tool of death devised by the Roman Empire for torturing dissidents and for terrorizing any opposition to its colonial hegemony.[6] The cross of Christ (re)presents all the crosses in the world or, more accurately, all the ones being "crucified," from the beginning of creation, all the suffering, evil, injustices, and deaths that have been and that shall be.[7] The wounds on the risen Christ are an indictment against the cross and all the crosses where

---

5. Yacob Tesfai, ed., *The Scandal of a Crucified World: Perspectives on the Cross and Suffering* (Orbis, 1994), 9.

6. Sobrino, *Jesus the Liberator*, 196–200.

7. Jon Sobrino, *Where Is God? Earthquake, Terrorism, Barbarity, and Hope*, trans. Margaret Wilde (Orbis, 2004), see especially chapter 4, "The Crucified People."

the innocent are crucified, oppressed, humiliated, excluded, exploited, intimidated, and silenced. But in the end, the cross didn't win; in the end, God's justice prevails, and those who were crushed are vindicated and their lives redeemed.

The cross is a statement of the power of God to be present in the depths of pain, suffering, and death, in a redemptive way even beyond our understanding and in ways that force us to rethink our understanding of what power is. The presence of God in the cross is the source of hope in the Christian tradition.[8] It is not meant to be a glorification of suffering or of the cross—the cross is not to be sought or glorified, but it is to be picked up and carried when we must, with the conviction that the cross, a symbol of death, evil, injustice, and suffering, does not have the last word.[9] That knowledge has the power to crack open a fissure through which hope breaks in, even within a hopeless situation. And that fissure, no matter how small, makes all the difference, first, within us, then, among us, and eventually, around us: "The kingdom of God is among you" (Luke 17:2).

Mystical union with the crucified and risen Messiah, of the kind described earlier in this book (see chapter 3), is at the same time union with all that the crucified Christ (re)presents. It is to find oneself in deep spiritual and affective solidarity with those who, like him, are also being crucified/crushed in life, whether by systems of injustice, oppression, and marginalization or simply by the circumstances of life like illness, untimely death, and other forms of loss.[10] And when someone is being crucified by injustice or the circumstances of life, they find themselves buoyed by the same invisible power that sustained Christ during his betrayal, sham trial, torture, humiliation, crucifixion, and descent to hell.[11]

---

8. Jürgen Moltmann, *Theology of Hope: On the Ground and Implications of a Christian Eschatology* (Fortress Press, 1993), especially part III, "The Resurrection and Future of Jesus Christ," 139–229.

9. Westhelle, *The Scandalous God*, 119–124.

10. Mary Solberg, writing from her experiences in Central America during the civil war, offers a penetrating analysis of the epistemological effects of witnessing in solidarity the suffering of the ones being crucified by injustice and violence; see Solberg, *Compelling Knowledge: A Feminist Proposal for an Epistemology of the Cross* (State University of New York Press, 1997).

11. According to the Apostle's Creed, Jesus "descended to Hell" before the resurrection and ascension. See Robert Kolb and Timothy Wengert, eds., "The Three Ecumenical Creeds," Robert Kolb and Timothy Wengert, eds., *The Book of Concord:*

The Spirit

To be united with the crucified and risen Christ is to find oneself filled with the same Spirit that breathed life anew into the dead body of the crucified Messiah, raising him into life beyond life; the same Spirit that came upon his mother, empowering her to bear God in herself (the tradition calls her *Theotokos,* the bearer of God); the same Spirit that Jesus said was upon him to proclaim liberation to the captives, sight to the blind, and good news to the oppressed; the same Spirit that hovered over the face of the deep transforming chaos into cosmos, nothingness into the vast panoply of beautiful forms that is our universe and all its marvelous creatures; and the same Spirit that spoke through the prophets of yesterday and today to denounce and dismantle systems of oppression and announce God's promise for a new world where justice and compassion are at home and where temples, and churches are no longer necessary because God, who is all goodness, truth, and beauty, is all in all (see Rev 21:22).

That new world that the cross and the resurrection point to is not a reality apart from this one but a transformation, a fulfillment of this world, so qualitatively different from the present one in terms of the presence of true justice, peace, and well-being for all that it feels like a different world altogether even though it is a coming to wholeness of this one.[12]

This is a process that does not represent a final point after which nothing happens, but rather it is a horizon of becoming that the world reaches toward and is forever in a process of constant transformation, a gushing well of living waters of never-ending hope.[13] To become united with the crucified Christ, then, is to become pregnant with hope, to become bearers of the future of God, to humbly but boldly accept our calling to be created co-creators of ourselves, of our communities, and of our world with the divine Creator. It is to be filled with the divine Spirit.

The Confessions of the Evangelical Lutheran Church (Fortress Press, 2000), 19–25; see also 1 Pet 3:19.

12. See Westhelle, "The Postcolonial Challenge: Quotidian *Eschata*, in *Eschatology and Space*, 91–102.

13. A theologian who has developed this way of understanding the rich interplay of the world's becoming and divine creativity, rooted in process theology, contemporary science, liberation theology, and feminist thinking, is Catherine Keller, *Face of the Deep.*

Scripture

That union with Christ is made possible by the Spirit through the mediation of the Word that speaks to us through the written Scriptures. We saw in chapter 7 how that word makes it possible for the believer to be absorbed into the reality of the risen crucified Messiah. Without the element of the written and proclaimed Word, Christ and the cross would not be available to us.[14] Or, even worse, without the word of the Scriptures, the cross is misunderstood and even usurped and abused. Then the cross can become like a screen upon which all sorts of ideas, desires, and fears are projected, as we saw in the previous chapter, and these ideas are often in direct contradiction with what the cross and the crucified Messiah stand for. In those cases, we risk using theology to actually protect ourselves from the cross and its transformative power rather than as a means to place ourselves at the foot of the cross, on the other side of the "frames"—discussed in chapter 4—of the epistemic horizons of our understanding and existence. There we are met by the piercing gaze of the crucified God and are absorbed by his words, the words uttered from the cross, but also the words and actions for which he was crucified, the words and actions of his radical commitment to love and mercy and to the vision of his coming realm. Those are the words that he preached and taught, the words that he incarnated in his life and flesh, words that he bequeathed to humanity, enfleshed in sacramental bread and wine, in baptismal water and sacred community.

Preparing for Hope

Dying to Our (False) Selves

We have seen in chapters 8 and 9 that the Word reveals the ways in which the social order that is an expression of systemic sin has also distorted our very identities and sense of self. The Word reveals our sin to

14. "But how are they to call on one in whom they have not believed? And how are they to believe in one of whom they have never heard? And how are they to hear without someone to proclaim him? And how are they to proclaim him unless they are sent? As it is written, 'How beautiful are the feet of those who bring good news!' But not all have obeyed the good news, for Isaiah says, 'Lord, who has believed our message?' So faith comes from what is heard, and what is heard comes through the word of Christ" (Rom 10:14–17).

us by making us realize the ways in which we have been complicit in the unjust and oppressive systems that cause the crucifixion of so many of our siblings on the crosses of prejudice, economic injustice, homophobia, sexism, white supremacy, xenophobia, ableism, and even exploitation of nature, as well as any other form of injustice that brings suffering and death to our human and nonhuman relations. That complicity can be direct commission of sins and evil acts, but it can also be passive quietism in front of injustices that we witness and that we knowingly or unknowingly benefit from.

We have seen that the Word, when properly proclaimed and taught, has the power to trigger a Spirit-led process of contrition and repentance leading to the death of the old self and the birth of a new, more authentic, self. Dying to the old self also means letting go of the sense that some of us are superior to others or more deserving than others simply because of our ancestry, our professional or economic success, the color of our skin, the place of our birth, our sexual orientation or gender identity, the particularities of our mental and physical condition, or even our religion.

There is, however, another kind of false self that the Word reveals and to which many of us are called to die. Many of us have been made to believe we are inferior to others or less developed or evolved than others or not as intrinsically competent as others or just not quite enough as we are. That false identity comes with deeply rooted feelings of inferiority vis-á-vis those whom our society lifts up as models of success, of beauty, of competence. That is the result of the internalization of the structures of oppression that we have been trying to trace in this book. To believe those lies about ourselves is to deny the fullness of the sacred image of God in us.

I have witnessed those mechanisms of internalized oppression many times. Once, at a congregation of immigrants from Central America, I heard how one girl got mad at another one and, as if it were an insult, shouted "India!" at her. The word simply means "Indian, or Native," and, incidentally, both girls were actually "Indias." Somehow, they both had been convinced that what they are is an insult. Likewise, in Puerto Rico, people who are from the mountains or who trace their roots back to the Taínos are called "jíbaros." Nowadays, it is beginning to be reclaimed as a term of pride, but when I was growing up, it was used as an insult, not too different from the way the word *hillbilly* is often used in the US. Somehow, we were taught that who we were—jíbaros—was offensive, an insult. Contrast that with the way the word *Americano* was used. It meant "of high quality," "done properly." If you wanted someone to show up on time, you would tell them "American time," and when I would hear my elders speak of US (white) Americans, they did so with a strange sense of reverence and respect. Rather than understanding that there are different ways of doing things and different ways of being human, we order differences hierarchically, driven by nonreflective cognitive processes such as those discussed in chapter 1.

Inadvertently, we have become the perpetrators of the very systems of racialization and minoritization by which we are oppressed. And then we use them to oppress others as well!

The Word, I have argued, destabilizes and dismantles those false identities and in doing so opens up a space for hope. It makes us aware of our complicity in our own oppression, the ways in which we have believed the lies that we were told about ourselves, and we have passed them on to others and to newer generations. Furthermore, even as I come to realize how I and my community have been victimized, oppressed, or marginalized, and how I/we have participated inadvertently in that process, the Word also makes us aware of the ways in which we might have also victimized other people's or communities, oppressed them, marginalized them, or benefitted from their exploitation.

We do not want to surrender those false identities, even after knowing how much they harm others or how much they harm us. Surrendering them is like dying.

Rebirth Through Forgiveness

The death of the self (of the false self) is only a preamble to the birth of our authentic selves. The transition from the death of the self to the birth of the new authentic self is mediated by the experience of forgiveness. If the Word leads us to the awareness of our guilt and complicity in sin and sinful structures that result in real death and suffering of our siblings and fellow creatures, it is not for the sake of making us feel ashamed and guilty.

Rather than speaking of guilt, perhaps it would be more helpful to speak of responsibility—that is, awakening to a sense of responsibility, which includes becoming aware of a sense of agency that guilt and shame might not help awaken. In any case, whether through the experience of guilt and shame or of responsibility, the purpose of the proclamation of the law function of the Word is for the sake of making forgiveness possible. From the overflowing grace of God made manifest on the cross, we are offered forgiveness and the ability to forgive. In what Paul refers to as the foolishness of the cross (1 Cor 1:18), God on the cross offers to take upon the divine self the guilt, sin, and shame that we carry so as to make us free from it (see Matt 8:17, 1 Pet 2:24, and 2 Cor 5:21). How?

Atonement

Most of us no longer live in a world where sacrifices must be made as propitiation for our sins. But we must remember that the symbol of the crucified Savior, the "Lamb of God that takes away the sin of the world," emerged from a world where justice demanded a balance between offense and reparation. Recall the discussion in the first chapter of how the human mind has cognitive devices that produce in us expectations for how things are and ought to be and how great tension emerges in our psyches when things don't match those expectations.

Our inherent sense of right and wrong demands that wrongdoing cannot just be ignored but must be somehow atoned for. In the biblical world, that was done symbolically through sacrifices that were very costly to people, including the best livestock that one had, the purest lambs, or the first fruits of one's crops. It is against the backdrop of that symbolic universe that the message of the cross proclaims that God has provided the perfect sacrifice to atone for our sins and the sins of all humanity, God has provided that which is of most value to God (namely, God's own only child). To our modern sensibilities, that sounds like cosmic child abuse, and in the contemporary symbolic world, such images can be dangerous and should probably be avoided. But in the symbolic world of the Scriptures (and we all live in different kinds of symbolic worlds), that image is an astounding expression of divine love. And the fact of the resurrection, of course, means that God's child was rescued from death and hell, so justice and goodness prevailed in the end.

Even if the traditional doctrines of atonement seem incomprehensible to modern ways of thinking, it is nonetheless possible for us to imagine what it is like for someone to risk their own life to rescue ours or even to lay down their life so that others can live. Thanks to the Trinitarian framework for thinking about God, it is then possible to think in terms of God, the second person of the Trinity, accepting to bear the weight of the sin of the world even to the point of laying down his own life so that the balance of justice can be fulfilled and we can be made free of the captivity of sin.

This is where faith comes into play. It is only when we are truly able to believe that the message of the cross is true and that it is for my sake, AND for the sake of all of humanity, that God has performed such an astounding fit of divine love that its transformative power can have its effects on us and transform us from inside out. Thus, the event of the cross has consequences not only for our relationship with God but also for our relationship with others and with ourselves.

As forgiven sinners, we live with an awareness of our sin and the responsibility that we bear for the suffering that our sin has caused, but we also live in the awareness that we have been forgiven, that we have died to our old (false) selves, and that a new reality is now possible.

Solidarity

But the Word is not only a word about sin and forgiveness. It is also a word of divine solidarity with the victims of oppression. The Word is a voice that whispers in the hearts of the oppressed and marginalized that they are not alone in their misery and in their suffering. It whispers to them that in the eyes of God, they are precious and of infinite value, made in the image of God and therefore deserving of great dignity, a dignity that many might deny but no one can strip away from them because it is rooted in the divine self.

The Word, more specifically, the message of the cross, is scandalous because it declares that God is not among the victorious but amongst the victims. God is with those crushed by the powerful; the Almighty is among those humiliated by the victorious. Even from the very beginning of the incarnation, the child God was born in a stable, to a family that had to seek asylum in a foreign country because of the political violence in their own country, violence directed against this child, just one more among the many who suffered under the murderous jealousy of Herod. And as we saw in the previous chapters, Jesus favored the poor, the oppressed, and the marginalized, those who were suffering.

From the cross, Jesus gathered the cries, laments, and despair of all humanity and creation and voiced them in his own prayer of despair, as Matthew tells us: "About three o'clock [from the cross] Jesus cried with a loud voice, 'Eli, Eli, lema sabachthani?' that is, 'My God, my God, why have you forsaken me?'" (Matt 27:46). Ever since then, no one has to pray that prayer alone again. Right there, next to them, God is with them and God prays along with them, not as a distant cosmic monarch observing his subjects from the distance of the heavenly throne, occasionally choosing to show benevolence to some, but rather as a divine companion who has pitched his tent among the victims, the ones abused, exploited, discarded, or simply ignored by the powerful of society, by the "gods" of this world.

The power of solidarity should not be underestimated. For two millennia, the dying have found deep consolation in the experience of the presence of Christ in their pain and suffering and often have been able to die with the name of Jesus on their lips and a "peace that surpasses all understanding" in their hearts (Phil 4:7). That has been my experience as a pastor and chaplain who has accompanied many people through the journey from this shore of life to the next. The image of Christ full of love and compassion, the deep trust of the heart that Christ is really present here and now, with them and within them, even in their time of suffering and dying, is a source of great peace and comfort.

In situations of great systemic injustice and in contexts of the struggle for justice, especially when the struggle feels like it is that of little David against the gigantic, unbeatable Goliath, the conviction of the solidarity of Christ in the struggle can make all the difference, just as David's profound faith in God's solidarity with him and his people (whose victimization by Goliath was a symbolic representation of their oppression at the hands of the proxy armies of the empires of the time) made all the difference in his struggle. The point is not that faith gave David and the Israelites the victory. The point is that faith allowed David, little David, on behalf of the people who were frozen by fear, to find the courage to face their oppression with the conviction that things didn't have to be the way they were and, furthermore, that it was God's will for things to be different.

Similarly, faith in the solidarity of Christ with the victims, the oppressed, and the marginalized allows them to not give in to despair or hopelessness. It provides them with a fountain of courage that allows them to endure and resist without losing their sense of dignity. And then, when the time is ripe, they can destabilize and eventually dismantle the systems of oppression in order to bring about a different order, one that is more just and life-giving. I wonder if that experience of an improbable gushing forth of courage and spiritual power due to faith in the divine presence amidst injustice corresponds to an increase in adrenaline (epinephrine) and a cognitive-affective dislodging, as argued above, of one's sense of self-identity imposed by the systems of injustice (the masks that Fanon diagnosed among the colonized) and the sudden realization of the experience of being who we are without depending on fitting or not fitting within the hegemonic frames of power. One of the best examples of that experience of spiritual power and courage is embodied in the life testimony of that amazing woman and US American hero, Harriet Tubman, known as Moses among slaveholders and enslaved Africans alike for her ministry of aiding enslaved people to escape from bondage and navigate the Underground Railroad on their way to freedom.

Love

Courage, endurance, and consolation are not the only things that people undergoing oppression get from the experience of Christ's solidarity. There is also a particular modus operandi that is inspired by the Spirit of the crucified and risen Christ. It is too easy, and very human, to fall into a Manichaeism where the victims are always good and right and the group identified as the oppressor is seen as evil and irredeemable. Such ways of perceiving each other, rooted in the cognitive templates of our nonreflective beliefs and affective realism, can be very harmful, as we saw in chapters 1 and 7. They also stand against Christ's way of dealing with evil and injustice. If one is not careful, it is easy to cross a line from justified defense to excessive aggression. Nietzsche's warning might be helpful here: "Whoever fights monsters should see to it that in the process he does not become a monster. And when you look into an abyss, the abyss also looks into you."[15] Love must always be the foundation of any Christ-inspired action even when (or maybe especially when) that action is an action of defense and of combating evil.

---

15. Friederich Nietzsche, *Beyond Good and Evil: Prelude to a Philosophy of the Future*, trans. Walter Kaufmann (Vintage Books, 1989), 89.

To experience the presence of Christ in our struggle is also to experience being guided by his Spirit of mercy and compassion, never demonizing the other, but rather seeing them as victims who are in the grip of ideologies or distorted views that lead them to hate and to behaviors that wound the image of God in themselves. That was the approach followed in the civil rights movement by leaders and activists such as Fannie Lou Hamer, Ida B. Wells, John Lewis, and, of course, Martin Luther King Jr. Theirs was a faith active in love-seeking justice; their struggle against the evils of lynching, segregation, and Jim Crow laws were done in such a way that they did not allow the hate to poison their soul but rather imbued their struggle with the love and faith that flows from the experience of the presence of Christ in and among the oppressed and suffering people and in their struggle. Theirs was a cruciform struggle, guided by the love of the crucified Christ and inspired by the hope of the resurrection, not just the resurrection of the flesh but also the resurrection of justice and peace.

Birthing Hope

In Our Bodies

Hope is not born of logic but of faith. It does not rise from the prefrontal, temporal, and parietal cortices of the brain but from deep within the viscera, the womb, and the heart, the same organs where the Scriptures tell us that God's compassion resides. As we saw in the first part of this book, there is a constant exchange of information between the brain and organs such as the heart, the lungs, the uterus, and the intestines. We learned that it is from the rhythms produced by the palpitations of the viscera and the heart, as it prepares the organism for action, that the brain takes its lead. The microbiome, those microorganisms that live mostly in our large intestine, plays a leading role in peoples' moods and emotional dispositions. It is in the gut that we first feel when things are amiss. We are moved to compassion and pity in our guts, as well as to anger and outrage. It is also in our guts that our bodies first register the arrival of good news, the imminence of joyful circumstances. Do you ever feel "butterflies" fluttering in your stomach? Of course, the rest of the brain, nervous system, and cognitive systems also play an important role in the process, but without the initiative of the gut and the heart, they would probably remain as abstract ideas, distant possibilities. It is, then, in the gut and heart that hope takes flesh.

It is through the proclamation of the good news that the gut and heart begin to resonate with hope (quite literally—see the discussion on brain waves in chapter 2). Therefore, the means used to proclaim that message need to be adequate to the message of hope it is trying to convey. That proclamation must be done in such a way that those receiving it feel themselves in the real presence of that which is being proclaimed. The Jewish mystic and philosopher Martin Buber makes a similar point in his book *Tales of the Hasidim* when he relates the story of how an older man who was no longer able to walk would tell stories of his teacher who loved to dance. In the midst of telling the story of how his teacher danced with such delight, the man himself would actually get up and, despite his disability, begin dancing![16] The Word must be proclaimed in such a way that we find ourselves right amid the world that the Word (or, more accurately, the Spirit through the Word) is opening up for us. "Were you there when they crucified my Lord?" asks the ancient spiritual song, but in the asking, with the tone and gravitas of the words, the listener is transported to the foot of the cross and is able to answer, Yes, of course, I am there right now, as we sing! Likewise, through the Word people journey with the band of Hebrews freed from bondage, can taste the manna with them, and can feel their despair as well as their joy. They can climb the tree with Zacchaeus, full of curiosity for who this Jesus is, and can stand next to the empty tomb in fear and trembling and awe at the appearance of the angels and the risen Lord.

But in addition to bringing the Scriptures alive or bringing us affectively into the world of the Scriptures, effective proclamation will also weave those stories with the tears, broken dreams, and laments of the people and invite them to an open, expansive space of hope. As the prophet Joel proclaims:

> Then afterward
>   I will pour out my spirit on all flesh;
> your sons and your daughters shall prophesy,
>   your old men shall dream dreams,
>   and your young men shall see visions. (2:28)

16. Martin Buber, *Tales of the Hasidim*, with a foreword by Chaim Potok (Schocken Books, 1947), xvii–xviii.

Through proclamation, we collect a harvest of those dreams and visions granted by the Spirit to the people and reflect them back to the people (to each other) in testimony, preaching, singing, poetry, and art. Together, we paint a picture or, better yet, open up a window into the possibility of a blessed otherwise, a Spirit-inspired future of healing, consolation, justice, peace, abundant life, and wholesomeness, from where God summons us—from within our guts and hearts!—through the Word.

Via Mystical Union with the Future

In chapter 3, we explored the neuroscientific processes by which experiences of mystical union might take place. We saw how, through contemplation, one can become absorbed into that which one contemplates, through the mediation of a cascade of neural events involving networks from our prefrontal cortex and limbic system to our autonomic nervous system and the neurotransmitters and brain waves that run through our brains and bodies. We saw that such experiences of mystical absorption can lead to a sense of union with a sacred figure, such as Christ, but also to a sense of union with the universe in its totality. We learned that one of the marks of those types of experiences is that it becomes tagged in the body and brain as so real that it feels even more real than normal reality.

Here I would like to propose that a similar experience is possible not only with a sacred figure, such as Christ, or with the universe as a whole but also with the future that is hoped for. Through the mediation of the proclamation of such future, one can not only visualize it but also taste it, smell it, hear it, and become absorbed into it, even with its openness and uncertainty. In a sense, to become absorbed into the reality of the living Christ is also, at the same time, to be caught up by the Spirit of the future that he announced and inaugurated proleptically. This experience of having the certainty of the imminence of another world, radically different from the one we are immersed in right now, with its injustices, untimely deaths, and meaningless pain and sufferings, has been a feature of Christianity since its beginnings.

However, because of the strong influence of platonic dualism, that other world was often projected into a heaven disconnected from the present world of bodies and matter. For some people, that has been a great source of consolation; for many others, it became an impetus for neglecting this world and for resigning themselves to injustice and suffering in this world because they had the hope that in the next world, all would be redeemed, all would be fine. This led to alienation from the historical dimension of the message and praxis of the cross with its prophetic antecedents. But it doesn't have to be that way.

An alternative way to think about the Christian hope in another world is to place it not only above us (in the heaven of heavens, detached from this reality) but also in front us, so to speak, within the realm of the adventure of the history of becoming of this world. Once upon a time, the earth and the universe in general were unhabitable for humans, and the possibility of a human creature arriving on the scene would have been far-fetched and laughable (that is, if there had been anyone to laugh). Yet thanks to a series of accidents of cosmic, planetary, and genetic mutations, here we are! Similarly, the future we dream and yearn for, represented in Christianity by the symbols of resurrection and eternal life, is a reality that encompasses all of creation, not as a creation of that which God created and saw that was good but rather as a fulfillment of that which God is in the process of creating and will shepherd to fulfillment. For now, our brains cannot fathom such future; for now, only our wombs, guts, and hearts can conceive it. But through proclamation, ritual, praxis, and a committed spirituality, we do our part to plant the seeds that will become that world and cultivate those planted by those who came before us. We keep the hope alive, and in doing so, we decolonize emotions and loosen the grip of the hegemony of injustice.

Through Tasting, Smelling, and Touching Hope

One important aspect of many religious traditions, especially the Catholic, Orthodox, Episcopalian, and Lutheran branches of Christianity, is the use of sacraments through which the transcendent mystery of the divine is made available to the community tangibly, incorporated (incarnated) "in, with, and under" material elements such as bread, wine, water, and oil and making the infinite divine available through the finite material (*finitum capax infinitum*) for people to receive via their senses and to consume into their bodies. In my own tradition, Lutheranism, great emphasis is placed on the sacramental meal of Holy Communion and the sacramental bath of new birth in baptism.

Through the waters of baptism and the unction with oil, under the light of the triune flames of the paschal candle, catechumens are bathed in the promises of God and soaked in the Holy Spirit. They begin the life-long process of dying to their old (false) selves and their compulsions and being born again to newness of life, into that future that does not yet exist but that has been promised to us all. From then on, water becomes a holy reminder of the divine promises received in baptism, promises of forgiveness, solidarity, and eternal life on the part of God, and of our own commitment to renounce evil in all its guises and empty promises, to plant seeds of loving kindness on all with whom we interact, and to boldly anticipate the future to which God is calling the world. By faith, water is felt on the skin as the gentle, loving fingers of God tenderly caressing our face and our head, washing off our sins but also our pain and suffering and drenching us in hope, courage, serenity, and patience, granting us the very presence of Christ and the Spirit in our lives here and now. All this happens in ways that our intellectual minds cannot grasp, but the wisdom of our skins, guts, and hearts know how to receive.

The second sacrament emphasized in my own Lutheran tradition is the eating of the bread and drinking from the cup that is a partaking in the body and blood of Christ (in his life, in his words, in his crucifixion, in his resurrection, and in his very body). Again, it is through the mediation of the Word, because of the divine intention, that in eating this piece of bread and in drinking from this cup we dare to believe that it is Christ himself whom we consume, and he consumes us, in anticipation of the consummation of the mystical union on the other side of eternity (see chapter 3). I wonder if one of the things that makes the sacrament so powerful, in addition of course to the theological mystery that it is, has to do with the strangeness of such a claim—namely, that it is an eating and drinking of blood and flesh—and how it activates the amygdala and hypothalamus when the worshipper hears and takes seriously the words "This is the body of Christ, given for you." "This is the blood of Christ, shed for you." Body! Blood! Of Christ, the Son of God! For Me!

When all that is contemplated deeply and taken with the seriousness that it deserves, that act of eating and drinking becomes another way by which we become absorbed into the divine, from our taste buds and mouths all the way to our stomachs and guts. In a way, as our bodies digest the bread and the "fruit of the vine," our bodies (our entire selves) are at the same time being "digested" into the mystical body of Christ. This absorption into the body of Christ is also, at the same time, a process of becoming incorporated into a community that transcends the boundaries of race, ethnicity, gender, and sexuality but also transcends the limits of time and space. This is the mystery of the "communion of saints." (*Saints* does not refer here, at least not in the Lutheran tradition, to "superhumans" but simply to forgiven sinners who have learned to dare to trust in the promises of God's grace and forgiveness more than fear their own shortcomings and sins.)

That eating and drinking of the sacramental meal, therefore, is never done in isolation. It is always done in the context of community, including that community of saints. The community of saints includes those alive and those who have gone ahead of us to the other shore of life. What is meaningful about this is that the experience of unity with Christ that is made possible by the sacrament, is at the same time an experience of unity with the community writ large. And depending on the theology underpinning the sacramental meal, that experience can come to encompass an experience of solidarity and union with ALL of humanity and even with the rest of God's creatures and creation. This aspect of taking part in Holy Communion is amplified in the liturgy by the ritual gesture of giving each other—whether you like them or not and whether you agree with their politics or not—the "kiss" of peace (in my church growing up, it was an actual kiss, but in other churches, the gesture is a hug or a shaking of hands).

Rehearsing Hope

The hope that is conceived by the Word and the Spirit deep within us, beginning in our guts and hearts, and that is nurtured by the very presence of the divine in the material elements of the sacraments, also needs to be practiced, rehearsed. Just as music doesn't become music until it is performed by an artist, sung by a voice, or played on an instrument, hope is only an abstract possibility until it is put into action. As we saw in the previous chapter, action (praxis of liberation) is the first and last step in the practice of liberation and decolonial theologies.

Ideally, the worship and spirituality of many religious traditions provides a format and rhythm for practicing the contents of the hope that is in us. Sometimes this includes highly ritualized, symbolic ceremonies, and at other times, it might include social practices and even civic engagement.

In worship, we lament with those who are grieving and suffering; we rejoice with those who are celebrating; we intercede for those who are sick or in trouble; we lift up our leaders and ask for them to be wise, compassionate, and just; we ask for forgiveness for the ways in which we have hurt others; and we ask for God's Spirit to guide us as we strive to live up to the model of who we have been called to be, individually and as a community. In worship, we can practice generosity through tithing or offering, making a tangible, monetary, investment in the world that we hope for. In worship, we also get a small foretaste of the experience of oneness: when we sing together, our hearts synchronize; when we embrace and kiss in the passing of the peace, our scents and sensations interpenetrate us with each other; and when we hold hands to pray, we are reminded that our lives are interlaced and in the Spirit we belong to each other.

We are then sent out into the world to continue our worship in the form of acts of loving kindness and compassion, seeking justice, truth, peace, and reconciliation in our relationships with others and glorifying God in our daily vocations, whether at home, in the field, at school, or at work. Thus, worship becomes a communal space for rehearsing the future that we eagerly hope for. When our churches and other places of worship are faithful to that vision, they become like oases in the here and now of God's future, God's promise of wholesomeness, justice, and peace in the present desert of indifference and injustices that many experience in contemporary society. Then we can understand what Jesus meant when he said that "in fact, the kingdom of God is among you" (Luke 17:21).

Conclusion and a Word of Caution

Thus, through word, sacrament, ritual, praxis, and spirituality, the divine Spirit is at work in us and through us (and despite us) to bring about the new creation, not in an ethereal place beyond the clouds but in this physical, embodied, world where we all live.

A word of caution is necessary. The same cognitive-affective processes investigated in this book that mediate union with the divine and with the future of healing, peace, justice, and wholesomeness to which the divine is calling are the same processes that can be manipulated to brainwash people into following cults or into surrendering their will and intellect into unscrupulous, manipulative leaders. That can happen in all realms of life, whether in religion, in politics, in romantic relationships, in social movements, or in businesses.

Therein lies the importance for an unswerving commitment to truth, wherever it may lead us, and to justice as an expression of the good, as well as to relationships of mutual accountability coupled with a strong internal habitus of a hermeneutics of suspicion, as outlined throughout this book. As Luther reminds us in the Large Catechism, faith makes both the true God and the idol, and as we saw in the chapter on liberation theologies, idols are not just religious phenomena but are also political, economic, and social forces. Idols are a theological way of naming the forces that, through the lure of the desirable and/or the fear of the terrible, lead us to orient our collective behaviors and to shape our institutions toward goals that on the surface, appear necessary but, in the end, are destructive, such as the accumulation of wealth for wealth's own sake (whether individually, corporately, or nationally), military dominance as a means for safety and security at the expense of the death and unjust suffering of millions around the world, plus the suicidal destruction of ecosystems all justified by the desirability of those goals. It is no exaggeration to say, like some liberation theologians, that it was not just the Aztec gods who demanded human sacrifices from their followers; the modern secular gods of national security, economic growth, and social order demand the same.[17]

The secular idols also have sacraments and rituals through which people become absorbed into the version of reality they represent. Things and occasions like national holidays, observances, monuments, and museums can function as quasi-religious rituals intended to forge in individuals and communities a particular sense of national identity and loyalty. Additionally, there are commercials and memes engineered

---

17. See, for example, Franz Hinkelammert, *The Ideological Weapons of Death: A Theological Critique of Capitalism*, trans. Phillip Berryman (Orbis, 1986); and Mark Lewis Taylor, *Religion, Politics, and the Christian Right: Post-9/11 Powers and American Empire* (Fortress Press, 2005).

to orient our affective imaginaries toward the erotic lures of material and economic success (wealth, power, fame, sex), even at the expense of neglecting our common humanity and the ecological costs of pursuing such mirages. The allure of such idols is so strong that even churches become trapped in their field of influence, paying generous amounts of money to consultants who will teach them to be successful like this or that famous corporation or to be able to market effectively the way that certain brands have been able to market successfully. Idols can be subtle and know how to slither their way even into the best-meaning organizations, luring them to trade the substance of their soul, the very reason for which they exist, in exchange for effectiveness and success. I am not exempt. I know the well-supported claims of how children labor in countries like Congo make it possible for me to have the convenience of certain electronic devices. But what can I do? I just need them. The idol laughs; the crucified Messiah groans.

It is because of those dynamics described above that a process of decolonization of the emotions is necessary. It is not only the colonized, the minoritized, the oppressed, and the marginalized who need a thorough affective decolonization. We all do. As I argued previously in this book, in the context of the prophetic Christian tradition, it is through the effect of the prophetic word on the listener, the receiver of that word, that the process of decolonization begins. But it also requires entering those eschatological, xoraic fissures and margins of the world, where we cannot avoid but contemplate the crosses of here and now, and receive on our bodies the transformative impact that, mediated through the word, such contemplation can have on us. In those spaces, the idols are immediately unmasked, unveiled for the demonic destructive powers that they are, feeding on the flesh of their human victims and ecological casualties. Contrast that with the crucified Messiah, who offers his own flesh and blood for the life of the world!

In those eschatological, xoraic spaces, we do not only contemplate suffering and death. We also encounter, or are encountered, with unlikely hope, with staunch faith. It is there that the parousia (a "being with") happens.[18] Perhaps the second coming of Christ will not be so much a returning of Christ but a revealing of how he had been among us all along, if we had but dared to pay attention to those spaces of crucifixion and resurrection. It is from those spaces that a harvest of

---

18. Westhelle, *Eschatology and Space*, 26–27.

divinely inspired visions and dreams is gathered. It is with those who have been pushed to the cracks and margins of life and society, with those who no longer have anything to lose; it is with them who are able to look at the idol in the face and to begin to imagine an otherwise. It is also from communities that have learned to survive and thrive on the margins, as we are reminded by decolonial theorists-activists, that we can access alternative knowledges, epistemes, and praxes that can offer an alternative to the ones sold to us by the secular idols.

From those xoraic/eschatological spaces that defying the strictures of time and space, coalesce at Golgotha, irrupt the new heavens and new earth announced by the prophets and inaugurated by the crucified and risen Messiah. In those spaces excreted by the idols of modern success, in the intestines of the world where people, communities, and ecosystems are excreted once their wealth and labor has been squeezed out of them, hope is born, because precisely there, among them, the promised Messiah, the divine incarnate, pitched his tent and made his throne: a cross, a cross of solidarity with the unjust suffering and pain of the world. It is also there, therefore, where the first glimmers of resurrection can be experienced, even if proleptically, as defiant hope against hope. But when this hope is experienced, we become absorbed into it and into the one who is the bearer of this hope, the risen crucified Messiah and the future that he (re)presents. Those glimmers and winds of proleptic hope become gusts of unstoppable change. Thus, the liberation of the brain and the decolonization of the emotions are effected, and a praxis and spirituality for a new creation, of a holistic otherwise, are made possible.

Conclusion

Decolonizing Emotions

I am still a chemist at heart. I like to mix things that others might think don't belong together: neuroscience and theology, decoloniality and sacramental theology, cognitive science and liberation theology. Did it work, or will it explode in my face? As my dear chemistry professor used to tell me, I will find out in the lab. In this case, we will find out in the realm of praxis, in the field where activists, deacons, teachers, pastors, social workers, everyday people, and so many others are doing the hard work of planting the seeds to liberate our brains and decolonize our emotions from centuries of distortions. In the lab, my hope was to synthesize new molecules that would be helpful to humanity. I was only an undergraduate student, so I didn't get very far in that area. As a pastor and theologian, my desire is to weave together words that will destabilize and dismantle systems of injustice and that will open spaces of hope, courage, love, and peace.

I have argued, like many others before me, that the present bears the marks of our colonial past. Our emotions, our embodied brains, and our imaginations carry the wounds inflicted on all of us, individually and collectively, by the legacy of hierarchical systems of cognitive and affective valuation that were necessary for the perpetuation of the inequalities that are fundamental for the colonial system to function without the constant use of overt violence. Deep within our bodies, in our viscera, through our nervous system and through the brain's emotional valuation networks, representations of reality (illusions) are created where some humans of different races, gender identities, ethnicities, socioeconomic class, immigration status, physical and mental abilities, and so on, are seen and felt as fundamentally inferior to others. Those "others" are experienced nonreflectively to be inherently suspicious, potentially dangerous, possibly incompetent, hypersexual, too naive, too emotional, too passive, too lazy. The privileged group, on the other hand, privileged by centuries of colonial, racist, and heteronormative hegemony, is perceived as inherently (and immediately) trustworthy, safe, competent, respectable, and worthy of emulation. Tragically, these cognitive illusions and affective distortions are internalized by the othered groups as well, even to the point that many even begin to play their given role and act the part, not unlike the infamous Stanford prison experiments.[1] In those experiments, some students were randomly given the role of prisoners and others were given the role of guards. The experiment had to be cut short because the student guards soon began to abuse their power and the student prisoners began to act as if they truly were prisoners. The artificial categories created by society acquire a certain ontological weight given to them by our affective and cognitive systems. In turn, they become programmed in our bodies and brains as behavioral scripts and as affective grammars that generate and organize the way we experience reality, especially the reality of others and of our relationship to them.

Which groups have been linked with what categories is not hard to assess; it suffices to do an inventory of what roles different kinds of people play in most movies, shows, and soap operas, to listen carefully to how language is used in everyday life (because, as we have seen, language, too, is haunted by the specters of our colonial past),[2] to examine what kinds of people are hired for what kinds of jobs, or to look at the statistics of what kinds of people are incarcerated for what types of crimes even when the same statistics show that the incarcerated group is not more prone toward crime than the other groups, just more likely to be prosecuted than others. Indeed, we carry the germ of injustice and inequality within our own bodies and brains. Based on the work of the neuroscientists and theologians explored throughout this book, I have proposed the idea of a generative affective grammar to describe how that germ operates. It reproduces inequalities in terms of race, gender identity, sexual orientation, ethnic origin, physical or mental disabilities, neural divergence, and other characteristics. The specifics vary from context to context, but the underlying cognitive-affective processes that power them seem to be the same.

I have also argued that the effects of our colonial past on our generative affective grammars are not an irrevocable destiny. Throughout

1. Philip Zimbardo, *The Lucifer Effect: Understanding How Good People Turn Evil* (Random House, 2007).

2. Rivera, "Thinking Bodies," 223–25, and *The Touch of Transcendence*, 119–22.

the chapters of this book, we have been harvesting insights about what is needed for the liberation of our brains and the decolonization of our emotions. I will distill those insights here into five movements necessary for rewriting our generative affective grammars in ways conducive to the divine vision of human flourishing and the well-being of creation.

Going Outside the Frame

When we step outside the horizons of our experience, our world opens up and begins to expand. Until we do so, we don't realize how small our world is, how immense actual reality is, and how much we are missing. There is also something liberating about being able to step outside our epistemic frame of reference and observe the frame from its outside. In doing so, we begin to realize all that was left out by the particular framing of our worldview. At once, we become aware of the paradoxical truth that it is only thanks to our epistemic-experiential frames that we can know reality and yet our frames never present to us the whole of reality. Our experiences, knowledge, and understanding are always partial, contextual, and provisional, yet coming to realize the limitations of our truth does not become less true but, in fact, more reliable.

How can we step outside the frames through which we know the world, especially if their boundaries are not visible to us? Sometimes life experiences will do that for us. We find ourselves tossed beyond the limits of what we thought was certain because of tragedy, illness, or death. In other cases, a constellation of coincidences can lead people to find themselves having experiences that make them challenge what they thought they knew: a meningioma just in the right spot on the temporal lobe ignites a neural storm, resulting in visions of light, love, and mystical union with the mystery of all; a special plant, mushroom, or chemical compound triggers a certain circuit in the brain, melting away the boundaries not only of our frames but also even of our very selves and then putting us back together as a new creation, with a renewed mind, more expansive, more integrated, more inclusive and appreciative of others, and more kind and loving. In yet other instances, it is a gift from God that wounds us, killing our old false selves, and, through the wound, lures us outside the frame of ourselves in search of the beloved Other/others.

But there are also other, less dramatic ways to transcend the boundaries of our frames. We can quite literally choose to step outside our world and enter the world of our neighbors, especially those whom we know very little about, those whom we have been taught (programmed) to fear, to be weary of, or simply to avoid because, for whatever reason, we feel uncomfortable in their presence. This is better done by invitation and with an appropriate guide. It is also helpful sometimes to "close our eyes," forcing us to actually listen to what the other has to say rather than be distracted by the false representations we have of them in our minds and emotions. Otherwise, we risk merely projecting onto their faces the caricatures that our colonized affective grammars, our unconscious bias and prejudices, generate of them. This includes entering into the world of the religious other,[3] of the cultural other, of the racial, the sexual, the gender other, of the ideological other, and of the socioeconomic other and doing so with a sincere attitude of curiosity and humility. We don't enter the world of the other to fix them. We don't enter the world of the other to seek self-affirmation, justification, or forgiveness. We enter the world of the other to be surprised. If we already know what we will find, then it wouldn't be a surprise.

Sometimes we can get a glimpse of the world of the other(s) via good literature, film, theater, art, or even comedy. But it is always better when we get to converse with actual human beings who can talk back, push back, challenge misunderstandings, or offer clarifications. We can also invite others into our worlds, giving them the opportunity to step outside their frames, even as in conversing with them, we also step outside of ours. I have found that once we get to know people personally, and communities intimately, it is very hard to accept the caricatures of them generated by our internalized prejudices.

There is something sacred that happens when we do step outside our frames and abide for a while in the worlds of each other with humility and honest curiosity. But there is something even more powerful when that stepping into the world of the other is a stepping into the margins of our society and cracks of our world. There we meet those crushed by the systems of coloniality, patriarchy, white supremacy, ableism, and ruthless capitalism. There we meet the cross (see the previous chapter)

3. By "other" I don't mean to "otherize" any group. Rather, I am assuming that all of us, regardless of our social location, have people whom we would perceive as others simply by virtue of our own social location and life experiences; similarly, at the same time, we are the "others" of some groups. In other words, I am not assuming here a standard vantage point or central social location in relation to which everyone else is an "other."

and are confronted by the divine word that has the power to deconstruct us, to kill our false selves, and remake us anew. The places of the cross are spaces we all instinctively avoid, yet it is there where the divine summons us for healing and transformation.

Words

It is through words, through language, that we make sense of our experiences of the world. That doesn't mean that we are able to put into words everything that we experience, nor does it mean that experiences that cannot be articulated verbally are vacuous. It simply means that language functions as a mold that gives concrete form to our experiences. We saw that even when it comes to our emotions, words play a significant role in shaping the precise form that those emotions assume. Language shapes emotions and emotions shape perception, experience, action, and decision-making.

We need the proper language to make sense of what is experienced on the other side of our frames. Not language that imprisons reality into preconceived categories but language that opens us up to novelty, that allows us to truly perceive the previously unknown, and language that evokes affective points of connection between the old known and the new unknown ("deep calls to deep," Ps 42:7). This is religious language, theological language—not in the sense of the rational articulation and systematization of the mysteries of the faith, but in the sense of *faith seeking understanding* as the beloved couple of the Song of Songs seek each other.

Preachers, teachers, theologians, writers, musicians, and poets but also scientists, anthropologists, sociologists, economists, and even politicians have the responsibility to provide that language. They are the spiritual spiders, the storytellers entrusted by the divine with the awesome responsibility of weaving a new memory and a new future for a people that have lost theirs. Their words must be anchored on the reality of the many worlds that are the lived experiences of people. They must be staunchly true and accurate, even when inconveniently so, but also inspired, imaginative, creative, and new.

We need words that weave bridges of relationality among disparate worlds and life experiences. Words that allow us to meet each other, to know each other, to feel the awe of being in the presence of the image of God in each other. Words can build castles in the air, words can be used to lie, deceive, and swindle, but words can also be used to comfort, to edify, and to plant seeds of future, of an *otherwise*, in the here and now. Nothing can happen without action and praxis, but without words, our actions are aimless and our praxis hollow. We need words that properly shape our emotions, providing us with adequate generative affective grammars, so that our perceptions, valuations, judgments, decisions, and actions can be effective and life-giving, aiming at human flourishing in all our rich diversity and the well-being of God's beautiful creation.

Practice

Even the most accomplished musicians practice their scales regularly, and even the best athletes need to practice constantly. Through practice, difficult skills become like second nature. The scales become written in the musician's fingers, so to speak, and the skills become programmed in the athlete's muscles. This is made possible through intentional, thoughtful, guided practice.

If we wish to dismantle the systems of oppression that perpetuate injustices in our world, we, too, must practice regularly, intentionally, and thoughtfully and under proper guidance. We saw in chapter 1 that underlying the operations of our minds are nonreflective beliefs (like unconscious bias) and a panoply of unconscious cognitive algorithms that determine our reality. And we saw in chapters 2, 3, and 7, in addition to those cognitive processes, there are also physiological, emotional, and linguistic processes that inscribe in our bodies valuations of reality in the form of feelings. These are the elements that make up what I have been referring to as our generative affective grammars. If we are to be successful in having that grammar rewritten, we need constant practice, repetition, and simulations.

I argued, in chapter 10, that religious liturgies and practices are ideal matrices for rewriting our generative affective grammars. But for them to carry out that function, which theologically speaking, is one of the ways through which the divine Spirit operates on us, they need to be properly interpreted, expounded, and taught to the people. For instance, from a Christian perspective, every time I make the sign of the cross over myself, I remember that I have been claimed by God as a child of God, that I have been promised forgiveness, eternal life, and the faithful presence of God's presence in my life, not because I deserve any of that but because God, who is rich in mercy and abounding in steadfast love, offered it to us all out of pure grace. This overrides the false identities that society tries to place on me, whether in terms of guilt and shame or in terms of things like race, gender, or socioeconomic status.

Every time I cross myself with that understanding in mind, I am destabilizing and eroding the grip of hierarchies of inequality in me. But only if I do it with the proper understanding. If I do it thinking that because I am a Christian, I am therefore somehow better than others or more loved by God than others, or because I am a particular kind of Christian, I am closer to God than others, then I am actually reinforcing the grammars of injustice in me and probably enacting them around me. Hence the need to pair proper practice with adequate interpretive language. That interpretive language, in my opinion, when sourced from the original founders, prophets, and teachers of the world religions and when interpreted in their proper context, is indeed conducive to dismantling systems of injustice and building up more just societies. But, as we saw previously, those words themselves have been usurped and distorted by other interests. Therefore, they need a healthy dose of a hermeneutics of suspicion as a purifying element so that they can once again carry the liberating message for which they were originally intended. This would then inform a quotidian spirituality of decolonial transformations.

Praxis

Beyond ceremonies and rituals, we must practice in our daily lives what it would be like to live in the otherwise we yearn for. At home, at work, at school, in the field, at the gym, in the market, in the voting booth, in person, in social media, in the public square, or in the internet square, we must rehearse how we would live if the hoped-for future was already here. From family systems theory, which I did not cover in this already too-thick book, I have learned to realize that I am a part of the system I wish to change. That means that how I show up influences the system of which I am a part. This is not about trying to manipulate others into conformity with how I think they should be, nor is it about hammering the world to the shape I think it should have. It is about showing up as the person I wish to be and witnessing (with an attitude of openness to being surprised by God) what happens then.

True change, from a faith perspective, can come only from God. When we open up to the influence of the Spirit of God in our lives, we become nodes of divine influence in the systems we are a part of. In this book, the focus is on the brain, and therefore I have emphasized individual practices, even those carried out in community, but alongside those individual-communal practices, there are also important movements of organized social, political, and economic transformation that are necessary to bring about effective systemic change, such as the civil rights movement, women's suffrage movement, and the immigrants' rights movements, just to mention a few. It is also important to bear in mind that political participation (whether as an elected official, a career civil servant, or a volunteer) as well as the realms of business and science, among many others, are also vocations that can be holy and the means for communal healing and divine social transformation when done with a genuine desire to contribute to the common good.

All movements of social change should be intentionally attentive to their real impact in the world, especially on the most vulnerable members of society. It is too easy to become so immersed in the ideology of the movement that one loses the ability to critically assess whether the actions of the movement are actually in line with the best values inspiring the movement and whether they are being effective. For that reason, I must emphasize once again the need to step outside our reality and into the world of the other. We must ask others how they perceive our movement, how they are being impacted by the movement, what they wish to say to us. This is especially helpful from those that disagree with us and with whom we disagree. We also need objective, scientific tools, as we learned from Latin American liberation theology, to assess the real conditions of the people, to analyze their root causes, and to measure the impact of the movement's efforts.

Prayer

At the time of this writing, it has become commonplace among many activists in the United States to mock people who as a response to tragic events share "thoughts and prayers." This dislike for "thoughts and prayers" is a reaction to people in power substituting their responsibility to fix the problem with a phrase that sounds hollow and even inane in the absence of real commitment to address the situation. However,

I wonder if the real problem stems from the fact that many who say "thoughts and prayers" are neither praying nor giving much thought to possible solutions to the crises at hand.

Prayer is everything. What air is to our lungs, and sunlight to plants, prayer is to the human spirit. Without prayer, we wither and fade. Prayer is the way life fills us up and the way we feel life filling us up. According to the Genesis story of human origins, it was by receiving God's own breath that humans went from being a mere pile of clay to being living, breathing, thinking, feeling creatures, with great responsibility for the rest of creation. Prayer is reconnecting to that originating breath that enlivens the dust-clay we are made of into the beings we are—capable of transcending the limits of our own frames, capable of entering empathically into the worlds of others, capable of understanding words and language that give shape to our reality and to our ideas—beings forging meaningful relationships with other humans beings (including those who are different from us and even those with whom we do not agree), with fellow creatures, and even with God. Prayer nurtures our spirits with the breath of life that softens our hearts of stone and replaces them with hearts of flesh.

True prayer is not transactional. True prayer is relational. Prayer is sitting with God as we sit with a dear friend, with a trusted parent or grandparent, or with a loving, gentle wisdom figure to pour out our soul and receive the healing touch of a listening ear and a loving presence. It is true that prayer comes with a promise of divine intervention, but that intervention cannot be manipulated or forced. Prayer is an act of trust whereby we entrust to God our concerns, trusting that God is faithful, and thus we let go of our own ideas of what the solutions should be and open ourselves up to be surprised by the unfathomable wisdom and mercy of God's ways.

When we truly pray, when we place ourselves intentionally in the presence of God, something happens to our bodies. The parasympathetic nervous system sets in motion a wave of neural events that results in our being able to relax. Anxiety loosens its grip on us. Even the boundaries of our self become softer, allowing us to feel the spiritual embrace of the divine, absorbing us into the divine self , full of peace, love, understanding, and compassion. The default mode network of the brain begins its gentle dance in our brains, information from across different sensorial, cognitive, and affective domains crossing over from their regions to their neighbors through the undulating magic of brain waves and the flow of electrochemistry. Whispers of the Spirit's wisdom reach our inner ear. Insights emerge. Hope irrupts. Paths of helpful action become clear. New, truer, and more wholesome understandings of reality, of others, and of ourselves emerge. Our emotions become charged with the joy of God's promised future, decolonizing our perceptions, our cognitions, and our affective valuations in a dynamic iterative process that continues until we find ourselves on the other side of eternity from where the Spirit of God's future calls us.

An Invitation

I said in the introduction that this book is an invitation to a conversation. I look forward to that conversation. The ideas I have shared in this book are intuitions, insights born from years of pastoral ministry, of theological reflections, of readings in various branches of science, of many hours of teaching undergraduate students from many different disciplines, of teaching clergy during retreats and continued education programs, of serving in various ecumenical spaces where theology is done collaboratively, of serving in the office of the presiding bishop with an amazing team of theologians discerning together how the biblical and theological witness speaks to particular situations of urgency here and now, and of serving alongside activists who dedicate their lives to defend the dignity of vulnerable members of society.

My debt for what I have learned from all of them and from all those spaces is immeasurable. The insights in this book owe a lot to them, but of course, they do not represent in any way the official positions of any of the institutions I have had the pleasure to serve. The opinions in this book are my own. But I offer them for conversation, for testing, for revisions and corrections. Above all, I hope they will be useful for the decolonializing, liberating praxis that I understand to be directly connected with the task of working for God's vision of human flourishing and the well-being of all creation.

BIBLIOGRAPHY

Alessandri, Mariana. *Night Vision: Seeing Ourselves Through Dark Mood*. Princeton University Press, 2023.

Alexander, Eben. *Proof of Heaven: A Neurosurgeon's Journey into the Afterlife*. Piatkus, 2012.

Alexander, Michelle. *The New Jim Crow: Mass Incarceration in the Age of Colorblindness*. New Press, 2012.

Alighieri, Dante. *The Divine Comedy: Inferno, Purgatory, Paradise*. Union Library Association, [1321] 1935.

Allende, Isabel. *Eva Luna*. Bogotá: Editorial La Oveja Negra, 1987.

Álvarez, Eliseo Pérez. *A Vexing Gadfly: The Late Kierkegaard on Economic Matters*. Wipf and Stock, 2009.

Álvarez, Marino Pérez. "El magnetismo de las neuroimágenes: Moda, mito e ideología." *Papeles del Psicólogo* 32, no. 2 (2011): 98–112. https://www.papelesdelpsicologo.es/pdf/1946.pdf.

———. "The Magnetism of Neuroimaging: Fashion, Myth and Ideology." *Papeles del Psicólogo* 32, no. 2 (2011): 98–112.

Alves, Rubem. *A Theology of Human Hope*. Corpus, 1971.

———. *Tomorrow's Child: Imagination, Creativity, and the Rebirth of Culture*. Harper and Row, 1972.

Anzaldúa, Gloria. *Borderlands/La Frontera: The New Mestiza*. Aunt Lute Books, [1987] 2007.

Aquino, María Pilar. *Nuestro clamor por la vida: teología latinoamericana desde la perspectiva de la mujer*. San José, Costa Rica: Departamento Ecuménico de Investigaciones, 1992.

———. *Our Cry for Life: Feminist Theology from Latin America*. Wipf and Stock, 1993.

Arrastía, Cecilio. *Teoría y práctica de la predicación*. Nashville, TN: Editorial Caribe, 1993.

Ashbrook, James B., and Carol Rausch Albright. *The Humanizing Brain: Where Religion and Neuroscience Meet*. Pilgrim Press, 1997.

Assmann, Hugo. *Theology for a Nomad Church*. Orbis Books, 1976.

Bandettini, Peter A. "Functional Magnetic Resonance Imaging." In *Methods in Mind*, edited by Carl Senior, Tamara Russell, and Michael S. Gazzaniga. MIT Press, 2006.

Barbour, Ian G. *Nature, Human Nature, and God*. Fortress Press, 2002.

———. *Religion and Science: Historical and Contemporary Issues*. A Revised and Expanded Edition of *Religion in an Age of Science*. HarperSanFrancisco, 1997.

Barrett, Justin L. *Cognitive Science, Religion, and Theology: From Human Minds to Divine Minds*. Templeton Science and Religion Series. Templeton Press, 2011.

———. *Why Would Anyone Believe in God?* Cognitive Science of Religion Series. Altamira Press, 2004.

Barrett, Lisa Feldman. *How Emotions Are Made: The Secret Life of the Brain*. Mariner Books, 2018.

Beatie, Geoffrey. *Our Racist Heart? An Exploration of Unconscious Prejudice in Our Everyday Life*. Routledge, 2013.

Beauregard, Mario. "Mind Does Really Matter: Evidence from Neuroimaging Studies of Emotional Self-Regulation, Psychotherapy, and Placebo Effect." *Progress in Neurobiology* 81, no. 4 (March 2007): 218–36. https://doi.org/10.1016/j.pneurobio.2007.01.005.

Beauregard, Mario, and Denyse O'Leary. *The Spiritual Brain: A Neuroscientist's Case for the Existence of the Soul*. HarperOne, 2007.

Benjamin, Walter. "Thesis on the Philosophy of History." In *Illuminations: Essays and Reflections*. Edited and with an introduction by Hannah Arendt. Translated by Harry Zohn. Schocken Books, 1968.

Berthoz, Alain. *Emotion & Reason: The Cognitive Neuroscience of Decision Making*. Translated by Giselle Weisse. Oxford University Press, 2003.

Bhabha, Homi. *The Location of Culture*. Routledge, 1994.

Blasdel, G. G., D. E. Mitchell, D. W. Muir, and J. D. Pettigrew. "A Physiological and Behavioural Study in Cats of the Effect of Early Visual Experience with Contours of a Single Orientation." *Journal of Physiology* 265, no. 3 (1977): 615–36.

Boff, Leonardo. *Holy Trinity: Perfect Community*. Translated by Phillip Berryman. Orbis Books, 2000.

———. *Virtues: For Another Possible World*. Translated by Alexandre Guilherme. Cascade, 2011.

Boff, Leonardo, and Clodovis Boff. *Introducing Liberation Theology*. Translated by Paul Burns. Orbis, 1990.

Bonhoeffer, Dietrich. *Discipleship*. Translated by Barbara Green and Reinhard Krauss. Dietrich Bonhoeffer's Works, vol. 4. Fortress Press, [1937] 2003.

———. *Sanctorum Communio: A Theological Study of the Sociology of the Church*. Translated by Reinhard Krauss and Nancy Lukens. Dietrich Bonhoeffer's Works, vol. 1. Fortress Press, 1998.

Boyer, Pascal. *Religion Explained: The Evolutionary Origins of Religious Thought*. Basic Books, 2001.

Branson, Susan. "Phrenology and the Science of Race in Antebellum America." *Early American Studies* 15, no. 1 (Winter 2017): 164–93.

Brueggemann, Walter. *The Prophetic Imagination*. 40th anniv. ed. Fortress Press, 2018.

Brueggemann, Walter, and Tod Linafelt. *The Old Testament: The Canon and Christian Imagination*. 2nd ed. Westminster John Knox Press, 2012.

Buber, Martin. *I and Thou*. Translated by Ronald Gregor Smith. Martino Publishing, [1923] 2010.

———. *Tales of the Hasidim*. With a foreword by Chaim Potok. Schocken Books, 1947.

Bulkeley, Kelly. *The Wondering Brain: Thinking About Religion with and Beyond Cognitive Neuroscience*. Routledge, 2005.

Bultmann, Rudolf. "New Testament and Mythology." In *Kerygma and Myth*, edited by H. W. Bartsch. SPCK, 1953.

Caldwell, H. K., and H. E. Albers. "Oxytocin, Vasopressin, and the Motivational Forces That Drive Social Behaviors." *Current Topics in Behavioral Neuroscience* 27 (2016): 51–103.

Campbell, Jan. *Arguing with the Phallus: Feminist, Queer, and Postcolonial Theory. A Psychoanalytic Contribution*. Zed Books, 2000.

Canclini, Néstor García. *Culturas Híbridas: Estrategias para entrar y salir de la modernidad*. México City: Editorial Grijalbo, 1990.

———. *Hybrid Cultures: Strategies for Entering and Leaving Modernity*. Translated by Christopher L. Chiappari and Silvia L. López. University of Minnesota Press, 1995.

Canobbio, Giacomo. *Sobre el alma: Más allá de mente y cerebro*. Translated by Luis Rubio Morán. Salamanca, Spain: Ediciones Sígueme, 2010.

Cappelørn, Niels Jørgen, K. Brian Söderquist, Vanessa Rumble, Bruce H. Kirmmse, and Joel Rasmussen, eds. *Kierkegaard's Journals and Notebooks*, vol. 4, journals NB-NB5. Princeton University Press, 2011.

Carter, Rita. *Mapping the Mind*. University of California Press, 1999.

Castanha, Tony. *The Myth of Indigenous Caribbean Extinction: Continuity and Reclamation in Borikén (Puerto Rico)*. Palgrave Macmillan, 2011.

Castellanos, Nazareth. *El espejo del cerebro*. 7th ed. Madrid: La Huerta Grande, 2021.

———. *Neurociencia del cuerpo: Cómo el organismo esculpe el cerebro*. Barcelona: Editorial Kairos, 2022.

Center for Action and Contemplation. "Dom Hélder Câmara." October 20, 2015. https://cac.org/daily-meditations/dom-helder-camara-2015-10-20/.

Chomsky, Noam. *Language and Mind*. 3rd ed. Cambridge University Press, 2006.

Cobb, John B., Jr., and David Ray Griffin. *Process Theology: An Introductory Exposition*. Westminster John Knox Press, 1976.

Collins, Patricia Hill. *Intersectionality as Critical Social Theory*. Duke University Press, 2019.

Cone, James H. *A Black Theology of Liberation*. 20th anniv. ed. Orbis Books, 2002.

———. *The Cross and the Lynching Tree*. Orbis, 2012.

———. *God of the Oppressed*. Fortress Press, [1975] 1997.

"Controversial 'School of the Americas' Closes." *ABC News*, December 14, 2000. https://abcnews.go.com/International/story?id=81917&page=1.

Cryan, John F., and Timothy G. Dinan. "Mind Altering Microorganisms: The Impact of the Gut Microbiota on Brain and Behavior." *Nature Review Neuroscience* 13, no. 10 (October 2012): 701–12.

Daly, Mary. "Feminist Post-Christian Introduction." In *The Church and the Second Sex*. Harper & Row, 1975.

Damasio, Antonio. *Descartes' Error: Emotion, Reason, and the Human Brain*. Quill, 2000.

———. *Feeling & Knowing: Making Minds Conscious*. Vintage, 2021.

———. *The Feeling of What Happens: Body and Emotion in the Making of Consciousness*. Harcourt, 2000.

———. *Looking for Spinoza: Joy, Sorrow, and the Feeling Brain*. Mariner Books, 2003.

Damour, Lisa. *Untangled: Guiding Teenage Girls Through the Seven Transitions into Adulthood*. Ballantine, 2017.

Danticat, Edwidge. *Breath, Eyes, Memory*. Vintage Contemporary, 1994.

d'Aquili, Eugene, and Andrew Newberg. *The Mystical Mind: Probing the Biology of Religious Experience*. Fortress Press, 1999.

———. "Religious and Mystical States: A Neuropsychological Model." *Zygon* 28, no. 2 (June 1993): 177–200.

Deane-Drummond, Celia. *Creation Through Wisdom: Theology & the New Biology*. T&T Clark, 2000.

Deloria, Vine Jr. *Custer Died for Your Sins: An Indian Manifesto*. University of Oklahoma Press, [1969] 1988.

———. *The World We Used to Live In: Remembering the Powers of the Medicine Men*. Fulcrum, 2006.

de Lubac, Henri. *The Discovery of God*. Translated by Alexander Dru. P.J. Kennedy, 1960.

De Mello, Anthony. "Searching in the Wrong Place." In *The Song of the Bird*. Image Books, 1984.

Derrida, Jacques. *Of Grammatology*. Johns Hopkins University Press, 1998.

Descartes, René. *Meditations on First Philosophy*. 3rd ed. Hackett, 1993.

Díaz, Miguel H. *Queer Dios de Amor*. Fordham University Press, 2022.

Donne, John. "Expostulation." In *Devotions upon Emergent Occasions*. University of Michigan Press, [1624] 1959.

Dress, Willem B. *Religion, Science, and Naturalism*. Cambridge University Press, 1996.

Du Bois, W. E. B. *The Souls of Black Folk*. Dover Publications, [1903] 1994.

Duigan, John, dir. *Romero*. 1989; Warner Bros. Pictures.

Dumit, Joseph. *Picturing Personhood: Brain Scans and Biomedical Identity*. Princeton University Press, 2004.

Dussel, Enrique. *1492: El encubrimiento del Otro. Hacia el orígen del mito de la modernidad*. Madrid: Nueva Utopía, 1993.

———. *El humanismo semita: Estructuras intencionales radicales del pueblo de Israel y otros semitas*. Buenos Aires: Editorial Eudeba, 1969.

———. *The Invention of the Americas*. Continuum Publishing Group, 1995.

———. "The Real Motives for the Conquest." *Concilium* (1990): 30–46.

———. *Towards an Unknown Marx: A Commentary on the Manuscripts of 1861–63*. Translated by Yolanda Angulo and edited with an introduction by Fred Mosley. Routledge, 2001.

Eagleman, David. *Incognito: The Secret Lives of the Brain*. Pantheon, 2011.

Fanon, Frantz. *Black Skins, White Masks*. Grove Press, [1952] 2008.

Fazio, R. H., J. R., Jackson, B. C. Dunton, and C. J. Williams. "Variability in Automatic Activation as an Unobtrusive Measure of Racial Attitudes: A Bona Fide Pipeline?" *Journal of Personality and Social Psychology* 69 (1995): 1013–27.

Frederickson, George M. *Racism: A Short History*. Princeton University Press, 2002.

Freire, Paulo. *Pedagogy of the Oppressed*. 50th anniv. ed. Translated by Myra Bergman Ramos, with a new introduction by Donaldo Macedo and an afterword by Ira Shor. Bloomsbury, 2018.

Fuentes, Carlos. *The Buried Mirror: Reflections on Spain and the New World*. Mariner Books, 1999.

García-Rivera, Alejandro R. *The Garden of God: A Theological Cosmology*. Theology and the Sciences. Fortress Press, 2009.

———. *A Wounded Innocence*. Liturgical Press, 2003.

Gazzaniga, Michael S., Richard B. Ivry, and George R. Mangun. *Cognitive Neuroscience: The Biology of the Mind*. 4th ed. W. W. Norton, 2014.

Giere, S. D. *Freedom & Imagination: Trusting Christ in an Age of Bad Faith*. Fortress Press, 2023.

Gilkey, Langdon. *Nature, Reality, and the Sacred: The Nexus of Science and Religion*. Theology and the Sciences. Fortress Press, 1993.

Gómez, Laura E. *Inventing Latinos: A New Story of American Racism*. New Press, 2020.

González, Justo L. *Mañana: Christian Theology from a Hispanic Perspective*. Abingdon, 1990.

Goodenough, Ursula. *The Sacred Depths of Nature.* Oxford University Press, 1998.

Gotay, Samuel Silva. *El pensamiento cristiano revolucionario en América Latina y el Caribe: Implicaciones de la teología de la liberación para la sociología de la religión*. Salamanca, España: Sígueme, 1981.

Gould, Stephen Jay. *The Mismeasure of Man*. W. W. Norton, 1996.

Granqvist, Pehr, Mats Fredrikson, Patrick Unge, Andrea Hagenfeldt, Sven Valind, Dan Larhammar, and Marcus Larsson. "Sensed Presence and Mystical Experiences Are Predicted by Suggestibility, Not by the Application of Transcranial Weak Complex Magnetic Fields." *Neuroscience Letters* 379, no. 1 (2005): 1–6. https://doi.org/10.1016/j.neulet.2004.10.057.

Green, Joel B., ed. *What About the Soul? Neuroscience and Christian Anthropology*. Abingdon Press, 2004.

Greenwald, Anthony G., Debbie E. McGhee, and Jordan L. Schwartz. "Measuring Individual Differences in Social Cognition: The Implicit Association Test." *Journal of Personality and Social Psychology* 74, no. 6 (1998): 1464–80. https://doi.org/10.1037/0022-3514.74.6.1464.

Greenwald, A. G., and B. A. Nosek. "Attitudinal Dissociation: What Does It Mean?" In *Attitudes: Insights from the New Implicit Measures*, edited by R. E. Petty, R. H. Fazio, and P. Briñol. Erlbaum, 2008.

Gutiérrez, Gustavo. *En busca de los pobres de Jesucristo*. Lima: Instituto Bartolomé de las Casas y Centro de Estudios y Publicaciones, 1992.

———. *Las Casas: In Search of the Poor of Jesus Christ*. Translated by Robert R. Barr. Wipf and Stock, 2003.

———. *A Theology of Liberation: History, Politics, and Salvation*. 50th anniv. ed. Translated and edited by Sister Caridad Inda and John Eagleson, with an introduction by Michael Lee. Orbis, [1973, rev. 1978] 2023.

Hagerty, Barbara Bradley. *Fingerprints of God: The Search for the Science of Spirituality*. Riverhead Books, 2009.

Hamer, Dean. *The God Gene: How Faith Is Hardwired into Our Genes*. Doubleday, 2004.

Hamilton, Allan J. "Soul Survivor." In *The Scalpel and the Soul: Encounters with Surgery, the Supernatural, and the Healing Power of Hope*. Tarcher/Penguin, 2008.

Hanh, Thích Nhât. *Teachings on Love*. Parallax Press, 2007.

———. *Understanding Our Mind*. Parallax, 2006.

Hannah-Jones, Nikole, Caitlin Roper, Ilena Silverman, and Jake Silverstein, eds. *The 1619 Project: A New Origin Story*. One World, 2021.

Harari, Yuval Noah. "The Last Days of Death." In *Homo Deus: A Brief History of Tomorrow*. Harper Perennial, 2017.

Haraway, Donna J. *Simians, Cyborgs, and Women: The Reinvention of Nature.* Routledge, 1991.

Harding, Sandra, ed. *The Postcolonial Science and Technology Studies Reader.* Duke University Press, 2011.

Haught, John F. *Making Sense of Evolution: Darwin, God, and the Drama of Life.* Westminster John Knox Press, 2010.

Hawking, Stephen. *A Brief History of Time.* Ballantine Books, 1988.

Hefner, Philip. *The Human Factor: Evolution, Culture, and Religion.* Fortress Press, 1993.

———. *Technology and Human Becoming.* Fortress Press, 2003.

Hegel, Georg Wilhelm Friedrich. *The Philosophy of History.* Translated by J. Sibree. Dover, [1837] 1956.

Heider, Fritz, and Marianne Simmel. "An Experimental Study of Apparent Behavior." *American Journal of Psychology* 57 (1944): 243–49.

Henderson-Espinoza, Robyn (now Roberto Che Espinoza). *Activist Theology.* Fortress Press, 2019.

Hickok, Gregory. *The Myth of Mirror Neurons.* W. W. Norton, 2014.

Hinkelammert, Franz. *The Ideological Weapons of Death: A Theological Critique of Capitalism.* Translated by Phillip Berryman. Orbis, 1986.

Hollywood, Amy. *Sensible Ecstasy: Mysticism, Sexual Difference, and the Demands of History.* University of Chicago Press, 2002.

Hopkins, Dwight N. *Being Human: Race, Culture, and Religion.* Fortress Press, 2005.

Isasí-Díaz, Ada María. *En la Lucha: Elaborating a Mujerista Theology.* Fortress Press, 2004.

Isasi-Díaz, Ada María, and Eduardo Mendieta, eds. *Decolonizing Epistemologies: Latina/o Theology and Philosophy.* Fordham University Press, 2012.

James, William. *The Varieties of Religious Experience: A Study in Human Nature.* Being the Gifford Lectures on Natural Religion Delivered at Edinburgh in 1901–1902. Modern Library, 1994.

Jeeves, Malcolm, and Warren S. Brown. *Neuroscience, Psychology, and Religion: Illusions, Delusions, and Realities about Human Nature.* Templeton Science and Religion Series. Templeton Press, 2009.

Jenson, Robert W. *The Triune Identity.* Fortress Press, 1982.

Johnson, Elizabeth A. *She Who Is: The Mystery of God in Feminist Theological Discourse.* Herder & Herder, 2002.

Joseph, Rawn. "The Limbic System and the Soul: Evolution and the Neuroanatomy of Religious Experience." *Zygon: Journal of Religion and Science* 36, no. 1 (March 2001): 105–36.

———. *The Transmitter to God: The Limbic System, the Soul, and Spirituality.* University Press of California, 2001.

Kable, Joseph W. "The Cognitive Neuroscience Toolkit for the Neuroeconomist: A Functional Overview." *Journal of Neuroscience, Psychology, and Economics* 4, no. 2 (2011): 63–84. https://doi.org/10.1037/a0023555.

Kahneman, Daniel. *Thinking, Fast and Slow*. Farrar, Straus and Giroux, 2011.

Keller, Catherine. *Face of the Deep: A Theology of Becoming*. Routledge, 2003.

———. *On the Mystery: Discerning God in Process*. Fortress Press, 2008.

Kendi, Ibram X., and Jason Reynolds. *Stamped: Racism, Antiracism, and You*. Little, Brown & Co., 2020.

Kierkegaard, Søren. "From the Papers of One Still Living." In *The Essential Kierkegaard*, edited by Howard V. Hong and Edna H. Hong. Princeton University Press, [1838] 2000.

———. *The Sickness unto Death: A Christian Psychological Exposition for Upbuilding and Awakening*. Translated and edited by Howard V. Hong and Edna H. Hong. Princeton University Press, [1849] 1980.

Kirste, Imke, Zeina Nicola, Golo Kronenberg, Tara L. Walker, Robert C. Liu, and Gerd Kempermann. "Is Silence Golden? Effects of Auditory Stimuli and Their Absence on Adult Hippocampal Neurogenesis." *Brain Structure and Function* 220, no. 2 (2015): 1221–28. https://doi.org/10.1007/s00429-013-0679-3.

Kleinhans, Kathryn A. "Christ as Bride/Groom: A Lutheran Feminist Relational Christology." In *Transformative Lutheran Theologies: Feminist, Womanist, and Mujerista Perspectives*, edited by Mary Streufert. Fortress Press, 2010.

Kolb, Robert, and Timothy J. Wengert, eds. *The Book of Concord: The Confessions of the Evangelical Lutheran Church*. Fortress Press, 2000.

Kuhn, Thomas S. *The Structure of Scientific Revolutions*. 3rd ed. University of Chicago Press, [1962] 1994.

LaCugna, Catherine Mowry. *God for Us: The Trinity in Christian Life*. HarperSanFrancisco, 1991.

Lawson, E. Thomas, and Robert N. McCauley. "The Cognitive Representation of Religious Ritual Form: A Theory of Participants' Competence with Religious Ritual Systems." In Ilkka Pyysiäinen and Veikko Anttonen, *Current Approaches in the Cognitive Science of Religion*. Continuum, 2002.

LeDoux, Joseph. *The Emotional Brain: The Mysterious Underpinnings of Emotional Life*. Simon & Schuster, 1996.

Lindbeck, George A. *The Nature of Doctrine: Religion and Theology in a Postliberal Age*. Westminster John Knox Press, 1984.

Long, Jeffrey. "Near-Death Experiences Evidence for Their Reality." *Missouri Medicine* 111, no. 5 (September–October 2014): 372–80. https://www.ncbi.nlm.nih.gov/pmc/articles/PMC6172100/.

Luther, Martin. *The Freedom of a Christian*. Luther Study ed. Translated and introduced by Mark D. Tranvik. Fortress Press, [1520] 2008.

———. "Ninety-Five Theses, 1517." Translated by C. M. Jacobs and revised by Harold J. Grimm. In *Luther's Works*, vol. 31, *Career of the Reformer*, edited by Harold J. Grimm. Fortress Press, 1957.

———. "A Sermon on Preparing to Die." In *Luther's Works*, vol. 42, *Devotional Writings*, edited by Martin O. Dietrich. Fortress Press, [1519] 1999.

Madrigal, Alexis. "Scanning Dead Salmon in fMRI Machine Highlights Risk of Red Herrings." *Wired*, September 18, 2009. https://www.wired.com/2009/09/fmrisalmon/.

Maduro, Otto. "An(other) Invitation to Epistemological Humility: Notes Toward a Self-Critical Approach to Counter-Knowledges." In *Decolonizing Epistemologies: Latina/o Theology and Philosophy*, edited by Ada María Isasi-Díaz and Eduardo Mendieta. Fordham University Press, 2012.

Marion, Jean-Luc. "The Saturated Phenomenon." In *The Visible and the Revealed*. Fordham University Press, 2008.

Marx, Karl. "Contribution to the Critique of Hegel's Philosophy of Right." In Karl Marx and Friedrich Engels, *On Religion*. Scholars Press, [1844] 1964.

Maté, Gabor. *The Myth of Normal: Trauma, Illness & Healing in a Toxic Culture*. Avery, 2022.

Maturana, Humberto R., and Francisco J. Varela. *El árbol del conocimiento: Las bases biológicas del entendimiento humano*. Santiago: Lumen, Editorial Universitaria, [1984] 2004.

———. *The Tree of Knowledge: The Biological Roots of Human Understanding*. Translated by Robert Paolucci. Shambhala Publications, 1992.

McKim, Donald K., ed. *Westminster Dictionary of Theological Terms*. Westminster John Knox Press, 1996.

McNamara, Patrick. *The Neuroscience of Religious Experience*. Cambridge University Press, 2009.

Menakem, Resmaa. *My Grandmother's Hands: Racialized Trauma and the Pathway to Mending Our Hearts and Bodies*. Central Recovery Press, 2017.

Metz, Johan Baptist. *A Passion for God: The Mystical-Political Dimension of Christianity*. Translated and edited by J. Matthew Ashley. Paulist Press, 1998.

Mignolo, Walter D. *The Darker Side of the Renaissance: Literacy, Territoriality, & Colonization*. University of Michigan Press, 1998.

———. "The Invention of the *Human* and the Three Pillars of the Colonial Matrix of Power: Racism, Sexism, Nature." In *On Decoloniality: Concepts,*

Analytics, Praxis, edited by Walter D. Mignolo and Catherine E. Walsh. Duke University Press, 2018.

———. "What Does It Mean to Decolonize?" In *On Decoloniality: Concepts, Analytics, Praxis*, edited by Walter D. Mignolo and Catherine E. Walsh. Duke University Press, 2018.

Mignolo, Walter D., and Catherine E. Walsh. *On Decoloniality: Concepts, Analytics, Praxis*. Duke University Press, 2018.

Miller, George A. "The Magical Number Seven, Plus Minus Two: Some Limits on Our Capacity for Processing Information." *Psychological Review* 63 (1956): 81–97.

Moltmann, Jürgen. *Theology of Hope: On the Ground and Implications of a Christian Eschatology*. Fortress Press, 1993.

———. *The Trinity and the Kingdom*. Fortress Press, 1993.

Morrison, Toni. *Beloved*. Vintage International, 1987.

Murphy, Nancey. *Bodies and Souls, or Spirited Bodies? Currents Issues in Theology*. Cambridge University Press, 2006.

Murray, Elisabeth A., and Mark G. Baxter. "Cognitive Neuroscience and Nonhuman Primates: Lesion Studies." In *Methods in Mind*, edited by Carl Senior, Tamara Russell, and Michael S. Gazzaniga. MIT Press, 2006.

———. "Lesion Studies." In *Methods in Mind*, edited by Carl Senior, Tamara Russell, and Michael S. Gazzaniga. MIT Press, 2006.

Myers, Allen C., ed. "Mind." In *The Eerdmans Bible Dictionary*. Eerdmans, 1987.

Ñapa, "Eugenics and Reproductive Coercion in Puerto Rico," Center for Latin American & Caribbean Studies, April 28, 2002. https://uwm.edu/clacs/eugenics-and-reproductive-coercion-in-puerto-rico/.

National Archives. "Treaty of Guadalupe Hidalgo (1848)." https://www.archives.gov/milestone-documents/treaty-of-guadalupe-hidalgo.

Newberg, Andrew B., A. Alivi, M. Baime, P. Mozley, and E. d'Aquili. "The Measurement of Cerebral Blood Flow During the Complex Cognitive Task of Meditation Using HMPAO-SPECT Imaging." *Journal of Nuclear Medicine* 38 (1997): 95.

Newberg, Andrew, A. Alavi, A. Bhatnagar, M. Baime, and E. d'Aquili. "The Neurophysiological Correlates of Meditation: Implications for Neuroimaging." *Journal of the Indian Academy of Clinical Medicine* 3 (1998): 13–18.

Newberg, Andrew, Eugene d'Aquili, and Vince Rause. *Why God Won't Go Away: Brain Science and the Biology of Belief*. Ballantine, 2001.

Newberg, Andrew, and Mark Robert Waldman. *How God Changes Your Brain*. Ballantine, 2009.

Nichols, Shaun, and Stephen Stitch. "A Cognitive Theory of Pretense." *Cognition* 74, no. 2 (2000): 115–47.

Nietzsche, Friedrich. *Beyond Good and Evil: Prelude to a Philosophy of the Future*. Translated, with commentary, by Walter Kaufmann. Vintage Books, 1989.

Nix, Elizabeth. "Tuskegee Experiment: The Infamous Syphilis Study." History, May 16, 2017. https://www.history.com/news/the-infamous-40-year-tuskegee-study.Otto, Rudolph. *The Idea of the Holy: An Inquiry into the Non-Rational Factor in the Idea of the Divine and Its Relation to the Rational*. Translated by John W. Harvey. Oxford University Press, [1923] 1958.

Panikkar, Raimon. *The Experience of God: Icons of the Mystery*. Fortress Press, 2006.

Parker, Angela N. *If God Still Breathes, Why Can't I? Black Lives Matter & Biblical Authority*. William B. Eerdmans, 2021.

Patterson, Sue. *Realist Christian Theology in a Postmodern Age*. Cambridge University Press, 1999.

Penfield, Wilder, and Edwin Boldrey. "Somatic Motor and Sensory Representation in the Cerebral Cortex of Man as Studied by Electrical Stimulation." *Brain: A Journal of Neurology* 60 (1937): 389–443.

Persinger, Michael A. "Religious and Mystical Experiences as Artifacts of Temporal Lobe Function: A General Hypothesis." *Perceptual and Motor Skills* 57, no. 3 (1991): 1255–62.

Persinger, Michael A., and Katherine Makarec. "The Feeling of a Presence and Verbal Meaningfulness in Context of Temporal Lobe Function: Factor Analytic Verification of the Muses?" *Brain and Cognition* 20, no. 2 (1992): 217–26. https://doi.org/10.1016/0278-2626(92)90016-F.

Peters, Karl E. *Dancing with the Sacred: Evolution, Ecology, and God*. Trinity Press International, 2002.

Peterson, Gregory R. *Minding God: Theology and the Cognitive Sciences*. Fortress Press, 2003.

Phelps, Steven, Zoe Donaldson, and Dev Manoli. "Monogamous Prairie Voles Reveal the Neurobiology of Love." *Scientific American* (February 1, 2023). https://www.scientificamerican.com/article/monogamous-prairie-voles-reveal-the-neurobiology-of-love/.

Pichardo, Ochy Curiel. "Construyendo metodologías feministas desde el feminismo decolonial." In *Reflexiones, herramientas y aplicaciones desde la investigación feminista*, edited by Irantzu Mendia Azkue, Marta Luxán, Matxalen Legarreta, Gloria Guzmán, Iker Zirion, and Jokin Azpiazu Carballo. Bilbao, España: Universidad del País Vasco y Seminario Interdisciplinar de Metodología de Recerca Feminista, 2014. https://

publicaciones.hegoa.ehu.eus/uploads/pdfs/269/Otras_formas_de_reconocer.pdf?1488539836.

Pixley, Jorge. *El Dios Liberador en la Biblia: Ensayos de Teología Bíblica que Aprovechan la Filosofía del Proceso*. Quito: diciones Abya-Yala, 2009.

Pyysiäinen, Ilkka, and Veikko Anttonen. *Current Approaches in the Cognitive Science of Religion*. Continuum, 2002.

Ramachandran, V. S. *A Brief Tour of Human Consciousness*. Pi Press, 2004.

Reep, R. L. "Comparative Neurobiology: History." *Encyclopedia of Neuroscience*. Academic Press, 2009. https://doi.org/10.1016/B978-008045046-9.00951-7.

Richard, Pablo. *Apocalypse: A People's Commentary on the Book of Revelation*. Orbis, 1995.

Ricoeur, Paul. *Interpretation Theory: Discourse and the Surplus of Meaning*. Christian University Press, 1976.

Rieger, Joerg. *Christ and Empire: From Paul to Postcolonial Times*. Fortress Press, 2007.

———. *Remember the Poor: The Challenge to Theology in the Twenty-First Century*. Trinity Press International, 1998.

Rippon, Gina. "Electroencephalography." in In *Methods in Mind*, edited by Carl Senior, Tamara Russell, and Michael S. Gazzaniga. MIT Press, 2006.

Rivera, Mayra. "Ghostly Encounters: Spirits, Memory, and the Holy Ghost." In *Planetary Loves: Spivak, Postcoloniality, and Theology*, edited by Stephen D. Moore and Mayra Rivera. Fordham University Press, 2011.

———. "Thinking Bodies: The Spirit of a Latina Incarnational Imagination." In *Decolonizing Epistemologies: Latina/o Theology and Philosophy*, edited by Ada María Isasi-Díaz and Eduardo Mendieta. Fordham University Press, 2012.

———. *The Touch of Transcendence: A Postcolonial Theology of God*. Westminster John Knox Press, 2007.

Rivera-Pagán, Luis N. "God the Liberator: Theology, History, and Politics." In *Essays from the Margins*. Cascade, 2014.

———. *Historia de la conquista de América: Evangelización y Violencia*. Barcelona: Editorial CLIE, 2021.

———. *A Violent Evangelism: The Political and Religious Conquest of the Americas*. Westminster John Knox Press, 1992.

Rossing, Barbara R. *The Rapture Exposed: The Message of Hope in the Book of Revelation*. Basic Books, 2004.

Runehov, Anne L. C. *Sacred or Neural? The Potential of Neuroscience to Explain Religious Experience*. Vandenhoeck & Ruprecht, 2007.

Sacks, Oliver. *The Man Who Mistook His Wife for a Hat and Other Clinical Tales*. Vintage, [1970] 2021.

Said, Eduard W. *Orientalism*, 25th anniv. ed. Vintage Books, 1994.

Saint-Exupéry, Antoine de. *The Little Prince*. Translated from the French by Katherine Woods. Harcourt Brace & Co., 1943.

Salzman, Mark. *Lying Awake*. Knopf, 2001.

Sandoval, Chela. "US Third World Feminism: The Theory and Method of Oppositional Consciousness in the Postmodern World." In *Feminist Postcolonial Theory: A Reader*. Edinburgh University Press, 2003.

Santos, Carmelo. *Estudiando la Biblia desde una perspectiva de neurociencia: cuatro estudios bíblicos*. http://www.esperanza.us/wp-content/uploads/2021/09/Estudiando-la-Biblia-desde-una-perspectiva-de-neurociencia-cuatro-estudios-bíblicos.pdf.

———. "Exploring the Role of Unconscious Bias in the Immigration Debate and the Transformative Power of the Church." *Journal of Lutheran Ethics* (December 13, 2013). https://www.elca.org/JLE/Articles/27.

Santos-Rolón, Carmelo. "Eutonia: The Cross (In)Between Science and Theology." In *Embracing the Ivory Tower and Stained Glass Window: A Festschrift in Honor of Archbishop Antje Jackelén*, edited by Jennifer Baldwin. Springer, 2016.

———. "Lutheran Theological Resources to Confront White Supremacy." In *Confronting Racism and White Supremacy in the US: Theological Perspectives for the Twenty-First Century*, edited by Michael R. Fisher Jr., Michael R. Trice, Whitney Wilkinson Arreche, and Don Thorsen. Friendship Press, 2024.

———. "Symptoms of God's Spirit? A Dialog Between Pneumatology and the Cognitive Sciences." PhD diss., Lutheran School of Theology at Chicago, 2010.

Schleiermacher, F. *The Christian Faith: A New Translation and Critical Edition*. Translated and edited by Terrence N. Tice and Catherine L. Kelsey. Westminster John Knox Press, 2016.

———. *On Religion: Speeches to Its Cultured Despisers*. Harper, [1799] 1958.

Schultz, Duane P., and Sydney Ellen Schultz. *A History of Modern Psychology*. 6th ed. Harcourt Brace, 1996.

Segundo, Juan Luis. *The Liberation of Theology*. Translated by John Drury. Orbis, 1976.

Senior, Carl, Tamara Russell, and Michael S. Gazzaniga, eds. *Methods in Mind*. MIT Press, 2006.

Sherwin, E., Seth R. Bordenstein, J. L. Quinn, T. G. Dinan, and J. F. Cryan. "Microbiota and the Social Brain." *Science* 366, no. 6465 (November 1, 2019): eaar2016. https://doi.org/10.1126/science.aar2016.

Silva Gotay, Samuel. *El pensamiento cristiano revolucionario en América Latina y el Caribe: Implicaciones de la teología de la liberación para la sociología de la religión*. Salamanca, España: Sígueme, 1981.

Sobrino, Jon. *Jesucristo liberador: Lectura histórica-teológica de Jesús de Nazareth*. El Salvador: UCA Editores, 1991.

———. *Jesus the Liberator: A Historical-Theological View*. Translated by Paul Burns and Francis McDonagh. Orbis, 1993.

———. *Where Is God? Earthquake, Terrorism, Barbarity, and Hope*. Translated by Margaret Wilde. Orbis, 2004.

Solberg, Mary. *Compelling Knowledge: A Feminist Proposal for an Epistemology of the Cross*. State University of New York Press, 1997.

Solomon, Robert C. *Continental Philosophy since 1750: The Rise and Fall of the Self*. History of Western Philosophy, vol. 7. Oxford University Press, 1988.

Sperber, Dan. "The Epidemiology of Beliefs." In *The Social Psychological Study of Widespread Beliefs*, edited by C. Fraser and G. Gaskell. Oxford Science Publications and Clarendon Press, 1990.

Sperber, Dan, and Lawrence Hirschfeld. "The Cognitive Foundations of Cultural Stability and Diversity." *Trends in Cognitive Sciences* 8, no. 1 (2004): 40–46.

Spezio, Michael L. "Engaging d'Aquili and Newberg's *The Mystical Mind*: Understanding Biology in Religious Experience: The Biogenetic Structuralist Approach of Eugene d'Aquili and Andrew Newberg." *Zygon* 36, no. 3 (September 2001): 477–84.

Spezio, Michael L., and Ralph Adolphs. "Emotional Processing and Political Judgment: Toward Integrating Political Psychology and Decision Neuroscience." In *The Affect Effect: Dynamics of Emotion in Political Thinking and Behavior*, edited by W. Russell Neuman, George Marcus, Ann N. Crigler, and Michael MacKuen. University of Chicago Press, 2007.

Stanton, Robert J., ed. *Contemporary Debates in Cognitive Science*. Blackwell, 2006.

Steffen, Patrick R., Dawson Hedges, and Rebekka Matheson. "The Brain Is Adaptive, Not Triune: How the Brain Responds to Threat, Challenge, and Change." *Frontiers in Psychiatry* (April 1, 2022). https://doi.org/10.3389/fpsyt.2022.802606.

Stewart, Lauren, and Vincent Walsh. "Transcranial Magnetic Stimulation in Human Cognition." In *Methods in Mind*, edited by Carl Senior, Tamara Russell, and Michael S. Gazzaniga. MIT Press, 2006.

Streufert, Mary, ed. *Transformative Lutheran Theologies: Feminist, Womanist, and Mujerista Perspectives*. Fortress Press, 2010.

Suchocki, Marjorie Hewitt. *God, Christ, Church: A Practical Guide to Process Theology*. Crossroad, 2001.

Sued Badillo, Jalil. *Agüeybaná el Bravo: La recuperación de un símbolo*. San Juan, Puerto Rico: Ediciones Puerto, 2008.

"Symposium 1: Cognitive Insights into Mechanisms of Belief," Washington, DC: Georgetown University, June 2, 2017.

Tamayo, Juan José. *Teologías del Sur: El giro descolonizador*. Madrid: Editorial Trotta, 2017.

Támez, Elsa. *The Amnesty of Grace: Justification by Faith from a Latin American Perspective*. Translated by Sharon H. Ringe. Abingdon Press, 1993.

———. *Bible of the Oppressed*. Translated by Matthew J. O'Conell. Wipf and Stock, 2006.

———. *Bíblia de los oprimidos: La opresión en la teología bíblica*. San José, Costa Rica: Departamento Ecuménico de Investigaciones, 1979.

———. *Contra toda condena: La justificacion por la fe desde los excluidos*. San José, Costa Rica: Departamento Ecuménico de Investigaciones y Seminario Bíblico Latinoamericano, 1991.

Tang, Yi-Yuan, Qilin Lu, Hongbo Feng, Rongxiang Tang, and Micahel I. Posner. "Short-Term Meditation Increases Blood Flow in Anterior Cingulate Cortex and Insula." *Frontiers in Psychology* 6 (February 25, 2015): 212. https://doi.org/10.3389/fpsyg.2015.00212.

Taves, Ann. *Religious Experience Reconsidered: A Building-Block Approach to the Study of Religion and Other Special Things*. Princeton University Press, 2009.

Taylor, Jill Bolte. "Stroke of Insight." TED Talk, November 14, 2012. 18 min., 41 sec. https://youtu.be/mYD7Y9CXeUw?si=j_ZBsSsja-8AVZwB.

Taylor, Mark Lewis. *Religion, Politics, and the Christian Right: Post-9/11 Powers and American Empire*. Fortress Press, 2005.

Teilhard de Chardin, Pierre. "The Heart of Matter." In *The Heart of Matter*. Harcourt, [1968] 1978.

Tesfai, Yacob, ed. *The Scandal of a Crucified World: Perspectives on the Cross and Suffering*. Orbis, 1994.

Thagard, Paul. *The Cognitive Science of Science: Explanation, Discovery, and Conceptual Change*. MIT Press, 2012.

———. *Mind: Introduction to Cognitive Science*. 2nd ed. MIT Press, 2005.

Tice, Terrence N., and Catherine L. Kelsey, eds. *The Christian Faith*. Vols. 1 and 2. A new translation and critical edition. Westminster John Knox Press, 2016.

Tillich, Paul. *Dynamics of Faith*. Perennial Classics, 1957.

———. *Systematic Theology*. Vol. 1. University of Chicago Press, 1951.

———. *Systematic Theology*. Vol. 2. University of Chicago Press, 1958.

———. *Systematic Theology*. Vol. 3. University of Chicago Press, 1963.

Tinker, Tink. "The Doctrine of Christian Discovery: Lutherans and the Language of Empire." *Journal of Lutheran Ethics*, 17, no. 2 (March 2017). https://learn.elca.org/jle/the-doctrine-of-christian-discovery-lutherans-and-the-language-of-empire/.

Tooby, John, and Leda Cosmides. "The Psychological Foundations of Culture." In *The Adapted Mind: Evolutionary Psychology and the Generation of Culture*, edited by John Tooby and Jerome H. Barkow. Oxford University Press, 1992.

Tracy, David. *Plurality and Ambiguity: Hermeneutics, Religion, Hope*. University of Chicago Press, 1987.

Tragán, Pius-Ramón, ed. *Neurociencias y espíritu: ¿Abiertos a una vida eterna?* Navarra, Spain: Verbo Divino, 2012.

Unamuno, Miguel de. *Tragic Sense of Life*. Translated by J. E. Crawford Flitch. Dover Publications, 1954.

Underhill, Evelyn. *Mysticism: The Preeminent Study in the Nature and Development of Spiritual Consciousness*. Image Books, [1911] 1990.

"The Untreated Syphilis Study at Tuskegee Timeline." U.S. Center for Disease Control and Prevention, n.d. https://www.cdc.gov/tuskegee/about/timeline.html?CDC_AAref_Val=https://www.cdc.gov/tuskegee/timeline.htm.

van Huyssteen, J. Wentzel. *The Shaping of Rationality: Toward Interdisciplinarity in Theology and Science*. William B. Eerdmans, 1999.

Van Slyke, James A. *The Cognitive Science of Religion*. Ashgate, 2011.

Varela, Francisco J., Evan Thompson, and Eleanor Rosch. *The Embodied Mind: Cognitive Science and Human Experience*. MIT Press, 1995.

Vuong, Ocean. *On Earth We're Briefly Gorgeous*. Penguin, 2019.

Wallace, B. Allan. *Contemplative Science: Where Buddhism and Neuroscience Converge*. Columbia University Press, 2007.

Wertheim, Margareth. *Pythagoras' Trousers: God, Physics, and the Gender Wars*. W. W. Norton, 1997.

Westhelle, Vítor. *After Heresy: Colonial Practices and Post-Colonial Theologies*. Cascade Books, 2010.

———. *Eschatology and Space: The Lost Dimension in Theology Past and Present*. Palgrave Macmillan, 2012.

———. "Idols and Demons: On Discerning the Spirits." *Dialog: A Journal of Theology* 41, no. 1 (Spring 2002): 9–15.

———. "Labor: A Suggestion for Rethinking the Way of the Christian." *Word & World* 6, no. 2 (1986): 194–206.

______. *The Scandalous God: The Use and Abuse of the Cross*. Fortress Press, 2006.

———. "Scientific Sight and Embodied Knowledges: Social Circumstances in Science and Theology." *Modern Theology* 11, no. 3 (July 1995): 341–61.

Whitehouse, Harvey. "Implicit and Explicit Knowledge in the Domain of Ritual." In Ilkka Pyysiäinen and Veikko Anttonen, *Current Approaches in the Cognitive Science of Religion*. Continuum, 2002.

Whitehead, Alfred North. *Process and Reality*. Free Press, [1929] 1978.
Williams, Delores S. *Sisters in the Wilderness: The Challenge of Womanist God-Talk*. Orbis, 2002.
Zimbardo, Philip. *The Lucifer Effect: Understanding How Good People Turn Evil*. Random House, 2007.
Žižek, Slavoj. *How to Read Lacan*. Granta Books, 2006.

INDEX

I